Lecture Notes in Comp

Founding Editors

Gerhard Goos
Juris Hartmanis

Editorial Board Members

Elisa Bertino, *Purdue University, West Lafayette, IN, USA*
Wen Gao, *Peking University, Beijing, China*
Bernhard Steffen, *TU Dortmund University, Dortmund, Germany*
Moti Yung, *Columbia University, New York, NY, USA*

The series Lecture Notes in Computer Science (LNCS), including its subseries Lecture Notes in Artificial Intelligence (LNAI) and Lecture Notes in Bioinformatics (LNBI), has established itself as a medium for the publication of new developments in computer science and information technology research, teaching, and education.

LNCS enjoys close cooperation with the computer science R & D community, the series counts many renowned academics among its volume editors and paper authors, and collaborates with prestigious societies. Its mission is to serve this international community by providing an invaluable service, mainly focused on the publication of conference and workshop proceedings and postproceedings. LNCS commenced publication in 1973.

Don Harris · Wen-Chin Li · Heidi Krömker
Editors

HCI International 2024 – Late Breaking Papers

26th International Conference on
Human-Computer Interaction, HCII 2024
Washington, DC, USA, June 29 – July 4, 2024
Proceedings, Part VIII

Springer

Editors
Don Harris
Coventry University
Coventry, UK

Wen-Chin Li
Cranfield University
Cranfield, UK

Heidi Krömker
Ilmenau University of Technology
Ilmenau, Germany

ISSN 0302-9743 ISSN 1611-3349 (electronic)
Lecture Notes in Computer Science
ISBN 978-3-031-76823-1 ISBN 978-3-031-76824-8 (eBook)
https://doi.org/10.1007/978-3-031-76824-8

© The Editor(s) (if applicable) and The Author(s), under exclusive license
to Springer Nature Switzerland AG 2025

This work is subject to copyright. All rights are solely and exclusively licensed by the Publisher, whether the whole or part of the material is concerned, specifically the rights of translation, reprinting, reuse of illustrations, recitation, broadcasting, reproduction on microfilms or in any other physical way, and transmission or information storage and retrieval, electronic adaptation, computer software, or by similar or dissimilar methodology now known or hereafter developed.
The use of general descriptive names, registered names, trademarks, service marks, etc. in this publication does not imply, even in the absence of a specific statement, that such names are exempt from the relevant protective laws and regulations and therefore free for general use.
The publisher, the authors and the editors are safe to assume that the advice and information in this book are believed to be true and accurate at the date of publication. Neither the publisher nor the authors or the editors give a warranty, expressed or implied, with respect to the material contained herein or for any errors or omissions that may have been made. The publisher remains neutral with regard to jurisdictional claims in published maps and institutional affiliations.

This Springer imprint is published by the registered company Springer Nature Switzerland AG
The registered company address is: Gewerbestrasse 11, 6330 Cham, Switzerland

If disposing of this product, please recycle the paper.

Foreword

This year we celebrate 40 years since the establishment of the HCI International (HCII) Conference, which has been a hub for presenting groundbreaking research and novel ideas and collaboration for people from all over the world.

The HCII conference was founded in 1984 by Prof. Gavriel Salvendy (Purdue University, USA, Tsinghua University, P.R. China, and University of Central Florida, USA) and the first event of the series, "1st USA-Japan Conference on Human-Computer Interaction", was held in Honolulu, Hawaii, USA, 18–20 August. Since then, HCI International is held jointly with several Thematic Areas and Affiliated Conferences, with each one under the auspices of a distinguished international Program Board and under one management and one registration. Twenty-six HCI International Conferences have been organized so far (every two years until 2013, and annually thereafter).

Over the years, this conference has served as a platform for scholars, researchers, industry experts and students to exchange ideas, connect, and address challenges in the ever-evolving HCI field. Throughout these 40 years, the conference has evolved itself, adapting to new technologies and emerging trends, while staying committed to its core mission of advancing knowledge and driving change.

As we celebrate this milestone anniversary, we reflect on the contributions of its founding members and appreciate the commitment of its current and past Affiliated Conference Program Board Chairs and members. We are also thankful to all past conference attendees who have shaped this community into what it is today.

The 26th International Conference on Human-Computer Interaction, HCI International 2024 (HCII 2024), was held as a 'hybrid' event at the Washington Hilton Hotel, Washington, DC, USA, during 29 June – 4 July 2024. It incorporated the 21 thematic areas and affiliated conferences listed below.

A total of 5108 individuals from academia, research institutes, industry, and government agencies from 85 countries submitted contributions, and 1271 papers and 309 posters were included in the volumes of the proceedings that were published just before the start of the conference. Additionally, 222 papers and 104 posters were included in the volumes of the proceedings published after the conference, as "Late Breaking Work". The contributions thoroughly cover the entire field of human-computer interaction, addressing major advances in knowledge and effective use of computers in a variety of application areas. These papers provide academics, researchers, engineers, scientists, practitioners and students with state-of-the-art information on the most recent advances in HCI. The volumes constituting the full set of the HCII 2024 conference proceedings are listed on the following pages.

I would like to thank the Program Board Chairs and the members of the Program Boards of all thematic areas and affiliated conferences for their contribution towards the high scientific quality and overall success of the HCI International 2024 conference. Their manifold support in terms of paper reviewing (single-blind review process, with a minimum of two reviews per submission), session organization and their willingness to act as goodwill ambassadors for the conference is most highly appreciated.

This conference would not have been possible without the continuous and unwavering support and advice of Gavriel Salvendy, founder, General Chair Emeritus, and Scientific Advisor. For his outstanding efforts, I would like to express my sincere appreciation to Abbas Moallem, Communications Chair and Editor of HCI International News.

September 2024   Constantine Stephanidis

HCI International 2024 Thematic Areas and Affiliated Conferences

- HCI: Human-Computer Interaction Thematic Area
- HIMI: Human Interface and the Management of Information Thematic Area
- EPCE: 21st International Conference on Engineering Psychology and Cognitive Ergonomics
- AC: 18th International Conference on Augmented Cognition
- UAHCI: 18th International Conference on Universal Access in Human-Computer Interaction
- CCD: 16th International Conference on Cross-Cultural Design
- SCSM: 16th International Conference on Social Computing and Social Media
- VAMR: 16th International Conference on Virtual, Augmented and Mixed Reality
- DHM: 15th International Conference on Digital Human Modeling & Applications in Health, Safety, Ergonomics & Risk Management
- DUXU: 13th International Conference on Design, User Experience and Usability
- C&C: 12th International Conference on Culture and Computing
- DAPI: 12th International Conference on Distributed, Ambient and Pervasive Interactions
- HCIBGO: 11th International Conference on HCI in Business, Government and Organizations
- LCT: 11th International Conference on Learning and Collaboration Technologies
- ITAP: 10th International Conference on Human Aspects of IT for the Aged Population
- AIS: 6th International Conference on Adaptive Instructional Systems
- HCI-CPT: 6th International Conference on HCI for Cybersecurity, Privacy and Trust
- HCI-Games: 6th International Conference on HCI in Games
- MobiTAS: 6th International Conference on HCI in Mobility, Transport and Automotive Systems
- AI-HCI: 5th International Conference on Artificial Intelligence in HCI
- MOBILE: 5th International Conference on Human-Centered Design, Operation and Evaluation of Mobile Communications

Conference Proceedings – Full List of Volumes

1. LNCS 14684, Human-Computer Interaction: Part I, edited by Masaaki Kurosu and Ayako Hashizume
2. LNCS 14685, Human-Computer Interaction: Part II, edited by Masaaki Kurosu and Ayako Hashizume
3. LNCS 14686, Human-Computer Interaction: Part III, edited by Masaaki Kurosu and Ayako Hashizume
4. LNCS 14687, Human-Computer Interaction: Part IV, edited by Masaaki Kurosu and Ayako Hashizume
5. LNCS 14688, Human-Computer Interaction: Part V, edited by Masaaki Kurosu and Ayako Hashizume
6. LNCS 14689, Human Interface and the Management of Information: Part I, edited by Hirohiko Mori and Yumi Asahi
7. LNCS 14690, Human Interface and the Management of Information: Part II, edited by Hirohiko Mori and Yumi Asahi
8. LNCS 14691, Human Interface and the Management of Information: Part III, edited by Hirohiko Mori and Yumi Asahi
9. LNAI 14692, Engineering Psychology and Cognitive Ergonomics: Part I, edited by Don Harris and Wen-Chin Li
10. LNAI 14693, Engineering Psychology and Cognitive Ergonomics: Part II, edited by Don Harris and Wen-Chin Li
11. LNAI 14694, Augmented Cognition: Part I, edited by Dylan D. Schmorrow and Cali M. Fidopiastis
12. LNAI 14695, Augmented Cognition: Part II, edited by Dylan D. Schmorrow and Cali M. Fidopiastis
13. LNCS 14696, Universal Access in Human-Computer Interaction: Part I, edited by Margherita Antona and Constantine Stephanidis
14. LNCS 14697, Universal Access in Human-Computer Interaction: Part II, edited by Margherita Antona and Constantine Stephanidis
15. LNCS 14698, Universal Access in Human-Computer Interaction: Part III, edited by Margherita Antona and Constantine Stephanidis
16. LNCS 14699, Cross-Cultural Design: Part I, edited by Pei-Luen Patrick Rau
17. LNCS 14700, Cross-Cultural Design: Part II, edited by Pei-Luen Patrick Rau
18. LNCS 14701, Cross-Cultural Design: Part III, edited by Pei-Luen Patrick Rau
19. LNCS 14702, Cross-Cultural Design: Part IV, edited by Pei-Luen Patrick Rau
20. LNCS 14703, Social Computing and Social Media: Part I, edited by Adela Coman and Simona Vasilache
21. LNCS 14704, Social Computing and Social Media: Part II, edited by Adela Coman and Simona Vasilache
22. LNCS 14705, Social Computing and Social Media: Part III, edited by Adela Coman and Simona Vasilache

23. LNCS 14706, Virtual, Augmented and Mixed Reality: Part I, edited by Jessie Y.C. Chen and Gino Fragomeni
24. LNCS 14707, Virtual, Augmented and Mixed Reality: Part II, edited by Jessie Y.C. Chen and Gino Fragomeni
25. LNCS 14708, Virtual, Augmented and Mixed Reality: Part III, edited by Jessie Y.C. Chen and Gino Fragomeni
26. LNCS 14709, Digital Human Modeling and Applications in Health, Safety, Ergonomics and Risk Management: Part I, edited by Vincent G. Duffy
27. LNCS 14710, Digital Human Modeling and Applications in Health, Safety, Ergonomics and Risk Management: Part II, edited by Vincent G. Duffy
28. LNCS 14711, Digital Human Modeling and Applications in Health, Safety, Ergonomics and Risk Management: Part III, edited by Vincent G. Duffy
29. LNCS 14712, Design, User Experience, and Usability: Part I, edited by Aaron Marcus, Elizabeth Rosenzweig and Marcelo M. Soares
30. LNCS 14713, Design, User Experience, and Usability: Part II, edited by Aaron Marcus, Elizabeth Rosenzweig and Marcelo M. Soares
31. LNCS 14714, Design, User Experience, and Usability: Part III, edited by Aaron Marcus, Elizabeth Rosenzweig and Marcelo M. Soares
32. LNCS 14715, Design, User Experience, and Usability: Part IV, edited by Aaron Marcus, Elizabeth Rosenzweig and Marcelo M. Soares
33. LNCS 14716, Design, User Experience, and Usability: Part V, edited by Aaron Marcus, Elizabeth Rosenzweig and Marcelo M. Soares
34. LNCS 14717, Culture and Computing, edited by Matthias Rauterberg
35. LNCS 14718, Distributed, Ambient and Pervasive Interactions: Part I, edited by Norbert A. Streitz and Shin'ichi Konomi
36. LNCS 14719, Distributed, Ambient and Pervasive Interactions: Part II, edited by Norbert A. Streitz and Shin'ichi Konomi
37. LNCS 14720, HCI in Business, Government and Organizations: Part I, edited by Fiona Fui-Hoon Nah and Keng Leng Siau
38. LNCS 14721, HCI in Business, Government and Organizations: Part II, edited by Fiona Fui-Hoon Nah and Keng Leng Siau
39. LNCS 14722, Learning and Collaboration Technologies: Part I, edited by Panayiotis Zaphiris and Andri Ioannou
40. LNCS 14723, Learning and Collaboration Technologies: Part II, edited by Panayiotis Zaphiris and Andri Ioannou
41. LNCS 14724, Learning and Collaboration Technologies: Part III, edited by Panayiotis Zaphiris and Andri Ioannou
42. LNCS 14725, Human Aspects of IT for the Aged Population: Part I, edited by Qin Gao and Jia Zhou
43. LNCS 14726, Human Aspects of IT for the Aged Population: Part II, edited by Qin Gao and Jia Zhou
44. LNCS 14727, Adaptive Instructional System, edited by Robert A. Sottilare and Jessica Schwarz
45. LNCS 14728, HCI for Cybersecurity, Privacy and Trust: Part I, edited by Abbas Moallem
46. LNCS 14729, HCI for Cybersecurity, Privacy and Trust: Part II, edited by Abbas Moallem

47. LNCS 14730, HCI in Games: Part I, edited by Xiaowen Fang
48. LNCS 14731, HCI in Games: Part II, edited by Xiaowen Fang
49. LNCS 14732, HCI in Mobility, Transport and Automotive Systems: Part I, edited by Heidi Krömker
50. LNCS 14733, HCI in Mobility, Transport and Automotive Systems: Part II, edited by Heidi Krömker
51. LNAI 14734, Artificial Intelligence in HCI: Part I, edited by Helmut Degen and Stavroula Ntoa
52. LNAI 14735, Artificial Intelligence in HCI: Part II, edited by Helmut Degen and Stavroula Ntoa
53. LNAI 14736, Artificial Intelligence in HCI: Part III, edited by Helmut Degen and Stavroula Ntoa
54. LNCS 14737, Human-Centered Design, Operation and Evaluation of Mobile Communications: Part I, edited by June Wei and George Margetis
55. LNCS 14738, Human-Centered Design, Operation and Evaluation of Mobile Communications: Part II, edited by June Wei and George Margetis
56. CCIS 2114, HCI International 2024 Posters: Part I, edited by Constantine Stephanidis, Margherita Antona, Stavroula Ntoa and Gavriel Salvendy
57. CCIS 2115, HCI International 2024 Posters: Part II, edited by Constantine Stephanidis, Margherita Antona, Stavroula Ntoa and Gavriel Salvendy
58. CCIS 2116, HCI International 2024 Posters: Part III, edited by Constantine Stephanidis, Margherita Antona, Stavroula Ntoa and Gavriel Salvendy
59. CCIS 2117, HCI International 2024 Posters: Part IV, edited by Constantine Stephanidis, Margherita Antona, Stavroula Ntoa and Gavriel Salvendy
60. CCIS 2118, HCI International 2024 Posters: Part V, edited by Constantine Stephanidis, Margherita Antona, Stavroula Ntoa and Gavriel Salvendy
61. CCIS 2119, HCI International 2024 Posters: Part VI, edited by Constantine Stephanidis, Margherita Antona, Stavroula Ntoa and Gavriel Salvendy
62. CCIS 2120, HCI International 2024 Posters: Part VII, edited by Constantine Stephanidis, Margherita Antona, Stavroula Ntoa and Gavriel Salvendy
63. LNCS 15374, HCI International 2024 - Late Breaking Papers: Part I, edited by Masaaki Kurosu, Ayako Hashizume, Hirohiko Mori, Yumi Asahi, Dylan D. Schmorrow and Cali M. Fidopiastis
64. LNCS 15375, HCI International 2024 - Late Breaking Papers: Part II, edited by Adela Coman, Simona Vasilache, Fiona Fui-Hoon Nah, Keng Leng Siau, June Wei and George Margetis
65. LNCS 15376, HCI International 2024 - Late Breaking Papers: Part III, edited by Vincent G. Duffy
66. LNCS 15377, HCI International 2024 - Late Breaking Papers: Part IV, edited by Jessie Y.C. Chen, Gino Fragomeni, Norbert A. Streitz, Shin'ichi Konomi and Xiaowen Fang
67. LNCS 15378, HCI International 2024 - Late Breaking Papers: Part V, edited by Panayiotis Zaphiris, Andri Ioannou, Robert A. Sottilare, Jessica Schwarz and Matthias Rauterberg
68. LNCS 15379, HCI International 2024 - Late Breaking Papers: Part VI, edited by Margherita Antona, Constantine Stephanidis, Qin Gao and Jia Zhou

69. LNCS 15380, HCI International 2024 - Late Breaking Papers: Part VII, edited by Aaron Marcus, Elizabeth Rosenzweig, Marcelo M. Soares, Pei-Luen Patrick Rau and Abbas Moallem
70. LNCS 15381, HCI International 2024 - Late Breaking Papers: Part VIII, edited by Don Harris, Wen-Chin Li and Heidi Krömker
71. LNCS 15382, HCI International 2024 - Late Breaking Papers: Part IX, edited by Helmut Degen and Stavroula Ntoa
72. CCIS 2319, HCI International 2024 - Late Breaking Posters: Part I, edited by Constantine Stephanidis, Margherita Antona, Stavroula Ntoa and Gavriel Salvendy
73. CCIS 2320, HCI International 2024 - Late Breaking Posters: Part II, edited by Constantine Stephanidis, Margherita Antona, Stavroula Ntoa and Gavriel Salvendy
74. CCIS 2321, HCI International 2024 - Late Breaking Posters: Part III, edited by Constantine Stephanidis, Margherita Antona, Stavroula Ntoa and Gavriel Salvendy

https://2024.hci.international/proceedings

26th International Conference on Human-Computer Interaction (HCII 2024)

The full list with the Program Board Chairs and the members of the Program Boards of all thematic areas and affiliated conferences of HCII2024 is available online at:

http://www.hci.international/board-members-2024.php

HCI International 2025 Conference

The 27th International Conference on Human-Computer Interaction, HCI International 2025, will be held jointly with the affiliated conferences at the Swedish Exhibition & Congress Centre and Gothia Towers Hotel, Gothenburg, Sweden, June 22–27, 2025. It will cover a broad spectrum of themes related to Human-Computer Interaction, including theoretical issues, methods, tools, processes, and case studies in HCI design, as well as novel interaction techniques, interfaces, and applications. The proceedings will be published by Springer. More information is available on the conference website: https://2025.hci.international/.

General Chair
Prof. Constantine Stephanidis
University of Crete and ICS-FORTH
Heraklion, Crete, Greece
Email: general_chair@2025.hci.international

https://2025.hci.international/

Contents – Part VIII

HCI in Automated Vehicles and Automotive

What Humans Should Be Thinking While Driving: Method for Integration
of Driver Cognitive Load Information with Map Data 3
   Arun Balakrishna and Tom Gross

The Role of UI/UX Designs for Enhancing Safety and Motorcycle Riders'
Experience 13
   *Gabriel Chilro, Pedro Oliveira, Ricardo Nunes, João Barroso,
and Tânia Rocha*

Challenges and Opportunities of Automotive HMI 23
   Zaiyan Gong

The History of Automotive Human-Machine Interaction: Seven Directions
of Evolution 36
   Zaiyan Gong

How Do Different HMIs of Autonomous Driving Monitoring Systems
Influence the Perceived Safety of Robotaxis Passengers? a Field Study 51
   Yaoqin Gu, Youyu Sheng, Yujia Duan, and Jingyu Zhang

Better Together: 3D Anthropomorphic Assistant Avatars and Empathetic
Voice Interventions on Emotion Regulation 61
   Bofei Huang, Xinyue Gui, Chia-Ming Chang, and Haoran Xie

Unlock Your Trust: Experiencing a Biophilic Autonomous Driving
Through Gamification 78
   Saeedeh Mosaferchi, Salvatore Cesarano, and Alessandro Naddeo

An Interactive Game for Improved Driving Behaviour Experience
and Decision Support 92
   *Gonçalo Penelas, Tiago Pinto, Arsénio Reis, Luís Barbosa,
and João Barroso*

Analyzing Usage Behavior and Preferences of Drivers Regarding Shared
Automated Vehicles: Insights from an Online Survey 103
   Verena Pongratz, Lorenz Steckhan, and Klaus Bengler

Research on Slow-Moving Transportation Scenarios in Large Suburban
Campuses from the Perspective of Autonomous Vehicle-Based Mobility
Service Design 122
   Jintian Shi

Exploring the Perceived Cognitive Workload: The Impact of Various
Scenarios and Emotions on a Driving Simulator 144
   *Buse Tezçi, Luca Tramarin, Edoardo Pagot, Marco Marchetti,
Giuliana Zennaro, Paolo Denti, Stefano Giannini, Maura Mengoni,
and Silvia Chiesa*

Design of Automotive Interior and Human-Computer Interaction
for Time-Sharing Rental: A Chinese Study 156
   Hao Yang, Na Chen, Quanxin Jin, and Ying Zhao

A Unified Framework for Hierarchical Pedestrian Behavior Generation
in Urban Scenario 172
   *Zhengming Zhang, Vincent G. Duffy, Mark R. Lehto,
Zhengming Ding, and Renran Tian*

HCI in Aviation, Transport and Safety

RPAS Over the Blue: Investigating Key Human Factors in Successful
UAV Operations 191
   Felix Adams and Maria Hagl

Piloting Continuous Neurophysiological Monitoring for Adapted Training
of Public Safety Officers 207
   *Danielle Benesch, Tanya S. Paul, Alexandre Marois, Simon Paré,
and Gregory P. Kratzig*

A Pilot Approach and Landing Workload Assessment Method for Flight
Crew Workload Airworthiness Certification 225
   Nongtian Chen, Ting Ma, Yiyang Han, and Kai Chen

Wings of Wisdom: Learning from Pilot Decision Data with Interpretable
AI Models 241
   Boris Djartov, Anne Papenfuß, and Matthias Wies

Enhancing Safety in Business and General Aviation Through Real-Time
Aircraft Telemetry 257
   Hannes S. Griebel, Simon Hewett, and Juliette O. Littlewood

Which Train Should Be Stopped First? The Impact of Working Memory
Capacity and Relative Risk Level on Priority Judgment of High-Speed
Railway Dispatchers During Emergency 269
   *Yan Jiang, Lei Shi, Jun Zhang, Jingyu Zhang, Zizheng Guo,
   Zhenqi Chen, Qiaofeng Guo, and Yan Zhang*

Field Trials of an AI-AR-Based System for Remote Bridge Inspection
by Drone 278
   Jean-François Lapointe, Mohand Saïd Allili, and Nadir Hammouche

Proactive Workload Estimation for Pilots 288
   Miwa Nakanishi and Riku Adachi

CRM for Providing Distress Assistance with Real-Time Aircraft
Telemetry – DART 298
   Daniel C. Smith and Hannes S. Griebel

The Devil Between the Details: Limitations of Probability-Based
Approaches to Human Error 308
   Lauren J. Thomas and Kathy H. Abbott

Detection of Arousal of Pilots in Event-Related Heart Rate Responses 326
   Karl Tschurtschenthaler and Axel Schulte

Emerging Technologies in Aviation Competency-Based Training
and Assessment Framework: The Simulated Air Traffic Control
Environment (SATCE) Influence on Communication Competency 337
   Dimitrios Ziakkas, Neil Waterman, and Konstantinos Pechlivanis

Author Index 349

HCI in Automated Vehicles and Automotive

What Humans Should Be Thinking While Driving: Method for Integration of Driver Cognitive Load Information with Map Data

Arun Balakrishna[1](✉) and Tom Gross[2]

[1] Professional Services, HERE Technologies, Frankfurt, Germany
arun.balakrishna@here.com
[2] Human Computer Interaction Group, University of Bamberg, Bamberg, Germany
tom.gross@uni-bamberg.de

Abstract. The current navigation map data does not contain information regarding the cognitive load associated with the navigation related entities on the road (i.e., road segments, junctions, manoeuvers, etc.). The associated root cause as well as the optimum guidance information to address the cognitive load is not a part of the current navigation map data. There is no mechanism to create and store this as a part of the current navigation map data. Cognitive load /stress levels on different parts of navigation have a significant impact on road safety, but the navigation map data does not integrate this information to support these cases related to cognitive load while navigating, to reduce the stress associated with navigation. Routing based on cognitive load associated with the route is currently not possible. This paper demonstrates an effective method of integration of cognitive load levels to navigation map data using HERE map as well as technologies offered by HERE Technologies as a reference for creating the necessary infrastructure for the integration of human cognitive load to navigation map data.

Keywords: BeaCON · Navigation System · HMS · Cognitive Load · OEM · Machine Learning

1 Introduction

A car Navigation System (NS) highlights the current location on the navigation map and provides guidance information for the user to reach the target location [1]. NS itself is supposed to create only minimal driver interruptions while providing guidance information [2]. Driver distraction contributes to 5–10% of the crashes in Europe [3]. Also, it is identified that drivers are engaged in activities other than driving for half of the driving time [3]. This indicates that proper guidance should be given to the driver so that the necessary use of cognitive resources is ensured when needed. The creation of cognitive load information and integration into the navigation map to use for relevant use cases is a current gap in the navigation map. The research framework BeaCON (Behaviour and Context-based Optimal Navigation) enables conducting research on optimum integration between human and navigation systems, but the results from this framework and another similar mechanism are not integrated into the navigation map as well and there is no efficient method for this integration. To conduct research in this area, collecting the input needed to calculate the cognitive load associated with the route from different sources as well as associating the cognitive load with the navigation map data by enhancing the current data model to incorporate cognitive load is necessary.

The conventional navigation system is not a human-in-the-loop system but is a standalone system which considers only some static or hard-coded rules as shown in Fig. 1. This paper proposes an optimal method for creating the Human-in-the-loop navigation system by incorporating the cognitive load scenarios as well as the resolution for high cognitive load scenarios as shown in Fig. 1.

This paper is organized into multiple sections. Section 3 describes the integration of the cognitive load information to the map data in detail. This section also covers the cognitive load data processing component, which is responsible for collecting the preprocessed cognitive load information to the map data. Section 4 covers the representation of the cognitive load data in the navigation map. Section 5 covers the integration of cognitive load root cause and optimum guidance information to address the root cause in the navigation map data.

2 Related Work

[4] introduces a research framework that facilitates efficient analysis for generating optimal guidance information. But [4] does not provide any method for the consumption of the created optimal guidance information. [5] demonstrates the essential role of detailed human behaviour analysis in the development of intelligent navigation systems, but [5] does not contain a navigation map or any other methods for the integration of human behaviour data to reduce cognitive load. Even though [6] considers the human cognitive state for navigation systems, [6] does not consider real-world navigation entities as well as not providing any methods for the consumption of guidance information. In [7] a detailed analysis of driving attention by considering the subprocess of monitoring, control and decision-making is conducted, but in [7], the driving scenarios considered are very limited, as well as it does not integrate the results into any driving simulator framework or navigation map. [8] focuses on the situation awareness of driving contexts but not directly related to the cognitive load reduction or representation. [9] provides a cognitive model for navigation but does not conduct research related to cognitive load reduction or representation.

3 Integration of Cognitive Load Information to the Navigation Map Data

A block diagram indicating the method for integration of driver cognitive load with map data is shown in Fig. 2. The cognitive load data creation identifies the cognitive load associated with each road segment as well as for other navigation-relevant entities like junction manoeuvers, construction sites, etc. The collected cognitive load is also associated with other attributes like time, weather, traffic, etc. The cognitive load data creation algorithm has the following main tasks.

What Humans Should Be Thinking While Driving 5

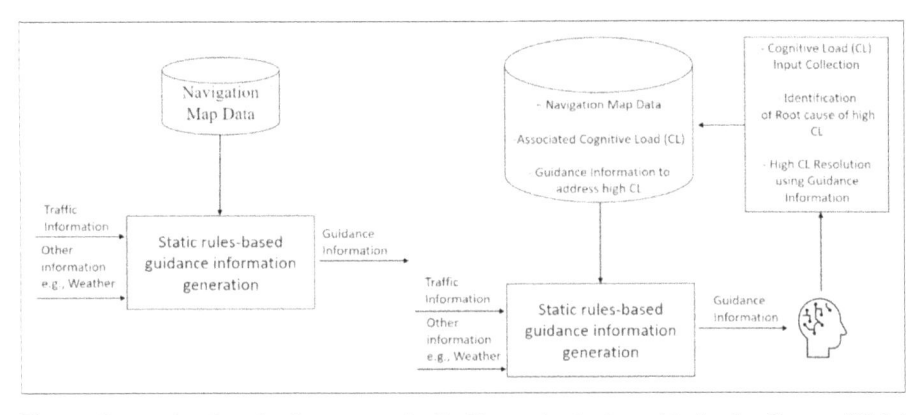

Fig. 1. Conventional navigation system (Left), Human-in-the-Loop Navigation System (Right)

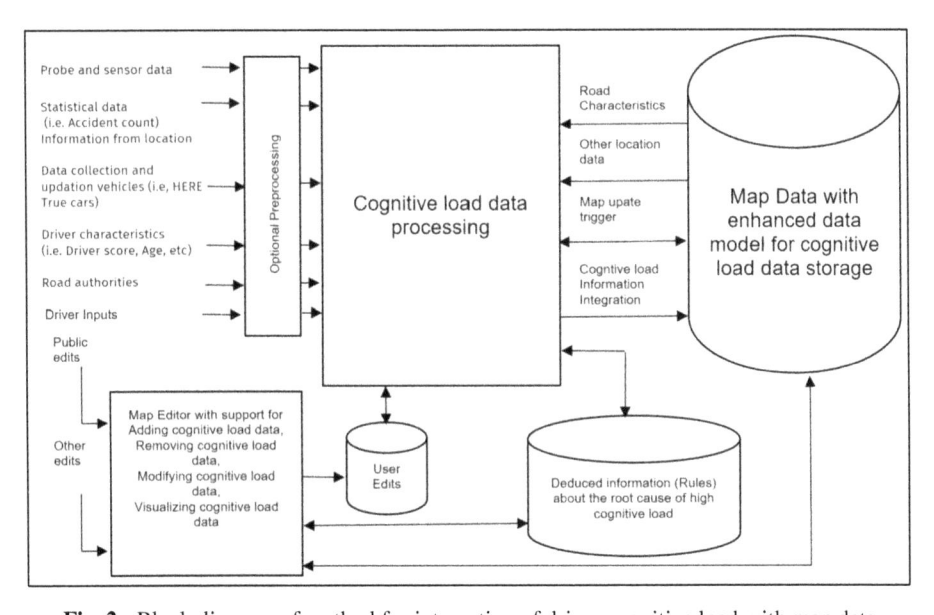

Fig. 2. Block diagram of method for integration of driver cognitive load with map data

- Collect the cognitive load at different locations from different sources.
- Perform initial validation.
- Map matches the data to road segments.
- Attach the cognitive load data with other necessary attributes to different road segments and other entities (i.e., deduced root cause).
- Deduce and publish information on the root cause as well as use these rules to provide cognitive load data for the road segments where direct information about the cognitive load data is not available from the sources.
- Storing the identified root cause.

Two of the main components of the system are.

- Input data collection and processing.
- Cognitive data processing.

During input data collection and processing, different input data is collected from different sources. The strategies applied for different input data are given in Table 1. Cognitive load data processing correlates the cognitive load with different location attributes as well and the correlation rules of this correlation can be stored in a database. These rules can be used to deduce the cognitive load of the locations where direct input about the cognitive load data is not available. The rules created by identifying the correlation can make use of machine learning algorithms. A brief overview of the data processing sequence is shown in Fig. 3.

Table 1. Strategies applied for different input data

SN	Input	Description
1	Probe and sensor data	Basic cleaning as well as standardization. This data shall be collected and provided by different OEMs (Original Equipment Manufacturers)
2	Statistical information	Information from statistical reports that identify or correlate the cognitive load associated with a route. The preprocessing of the statistical information can include standardization. Statistical data can also be contributed as deduced or assumed cognitive load data information. For example, if a particular road segment has a higher number of accidents, an assumption that this part of the road induces higher cognitive load to the user is possible
3	Data collecting and updating vehicles	Probe and sensor as well as other information from the test vehicles. Test vehicles can be used for map-making as well as for collecting other location-related information by driving along the route. The preprocessing can include standardization
4	Driver characteristics	Information related to correlating the driver characteristics with cognitive load information. The preprocessing of this can include standardization
5	Road authorities	Information or reports from the road authorities identify or correlate the cognitive load associated with a route. The preprocessing of the road authority data can include standardization

(*continued*)

Table 1. (*continued*)

SN	Input	Description
6	Driver inputs	The input from the driver correlates the road with cognitive load data. The preprocessing of this can include using a human language interpretation model to convert driver inputs to a standard format where a standard format correlates the cognitive load with location characteristics
7	Map edits	The user can add, modify, and delete the cognitive load values for road segments as well as other entities like junction, manoeuver, etc. The reason for the cognitive load can also be entered. The newly added data shall be integrated into the map after the necessary verification and validation steps

4 Representation of Cognitive Data in the Navigation Map

The data model for cognitive load integration shall enable the following.

- Calculate cognitive load for the road segments.
- Calculate cognitive load for point locations as well as for the road segments.
- Calculate cognitive load for entities like junctions, manoeuvers, etc.
- Enable calculation of total cognitive load by using the cognitive load associated with road and other entities.
- Identify the root cause of cognitive load associated with roads and other entities, which can be used for cognitive load reduction (For example by providing navigation information as per the root cause).
- Integration of the guidance information, which is needed as per the identified, calculated, and assumed cognitive load where the guidance information can contain the following.

– Necessary guidance information which is needed to reduce cognitive load.
– Guidance information in user-preferred language if necessary

- Time-dependent cognitive load information associated with road and other entities.
- Weather-dependent cognitive load associated with road and other entities.

Generally, standard attributes like the speed limit are uniformly spread across the navigation entities, for example, a road segment. Also, the reason why a specific speed limit is applied to a road segment is not of interest to the driver. But these characteristics are different when it comes to the cognitive load associated with road entities.

The way the driver cognitive load is represented in the navigation map data is driven by its purpose, which is reducing the cognitive load associated with road entities. Also, the representation shall be suitable to include different cognitive load analysis standards without significant changes in the data model. The HERE map data model for the Advanced Navigation Attributes layer [10] is taken as a reference data model. The geographic area is divided into multiple partitions. An example of partition data is shown in Fig. 4. The lines showing the topology segments in the partition as well as the properties corresponding to each topology segment are also shown in Fig. 4. The cognitive load analysis result can be attached to the road topology layer by using segment anchors [11] wherever needed, like the other attributes. The specific data model for cognitive load representation in a map data layer is shown in Fig. 5. The mechanism of the cognitive load measurement result representation varies depending on the specific method used [12]. The data model is not limited to the methods specified in the data model in Fig. 5. For example, the advanced steering entropy method used by BeaCON [4] is another efficient method which can be used to identify high cognitive load areas.

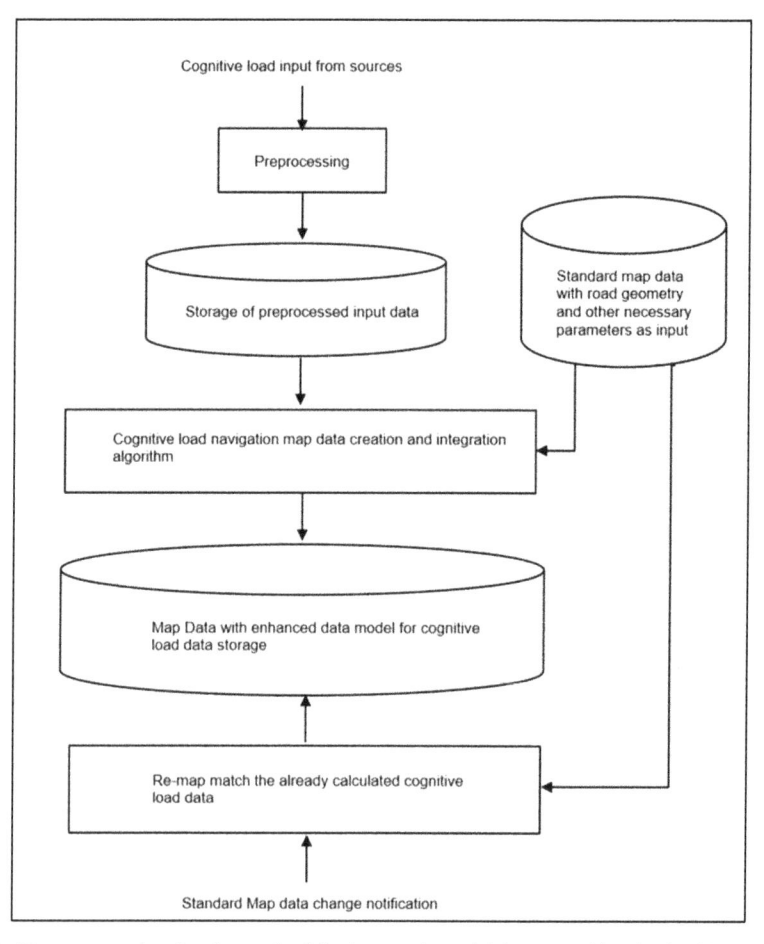

Fig. 3. Data processing for the method for integration of driver cognitive load with map data

Fig. 4. An example of partition data

5 Creation and Integration of Optimum Guidance Information

To create the optimum guidance information, not only the information about the cognitive load values but also the root cause of guidance information is necessary. The principles generated by the research framework BeaCON can be used to identify the optimum guidance information from the cognitive load data as well as from the context information. Currently, BeaCON supports the following.

1. Conduct tests on the selected test route in the virtual environment.
2. Create cognitive load information from the probe data.
3. Data mining uses the data analytics framework provided by BeaCON to generate insight into the cognitive load data as well as to generate principles to address the high cognitive load.
4. Create optimum guidance information.

After step 3 from above, BeaCON shall contain the identification of the root cause as well as the principles to address the root cause. The principles from the virtual test route in BeaCON can be applied to the navigation map data where the navigation context is similar to the corresponding test environment. From the principles identified from the BeaCON framework or by using other methods, static rules shall be deduced. These rules can be used to identify and address the navigation scenarios by integrating the cognitive load values, root cause and the guidance information into the navigation map. Creation and integration of optimum guidance information using BeaCON is shown in Fig. 6.

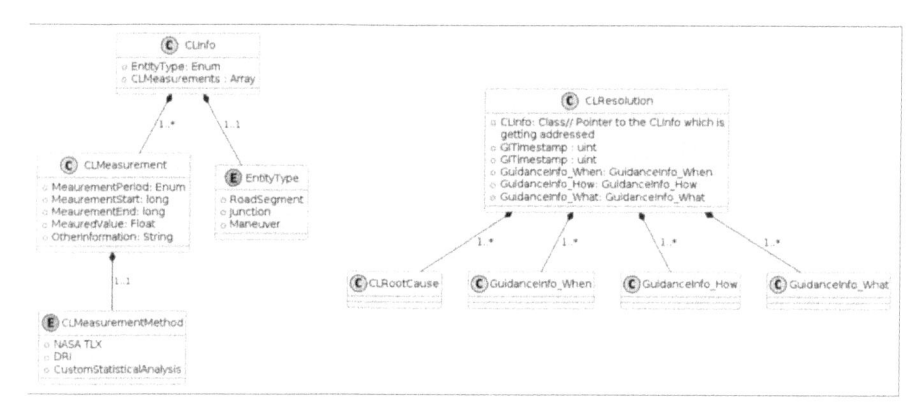

Fig. 5. Data model for cognitive load analysis and representation in a map data layer

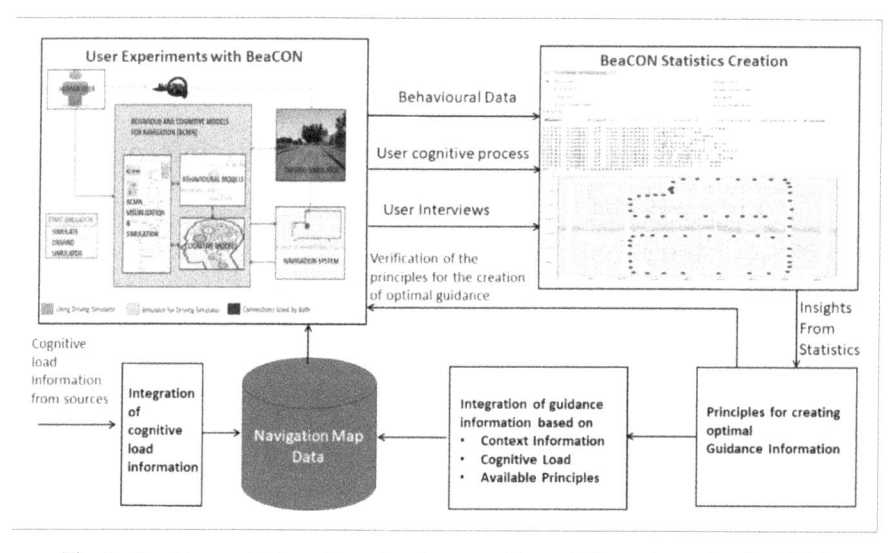

Fig. 6. Creation and integration of optimum guidance information using BeaCON

6   Representation of Cognitive Load Root Cause and Optimum Guidance Information into the Navigation Map

The BeaCON framework or any other methods (i.e., user interviews, information from road authority etc.) for cognitive load analysis shall provide the following for reducing the cognitive load associated with navigation.

- What guidance information shall be provided.
- When to provide the guidance information.
- How the guidance information shall be provided

Each of this information shall be represented as a part of navigation data, so the navigation system using this can act effectively to reduce the cognitive load. A class diagram shown in Fig. 5 can be used for this purpose. The segment anchors can be used in this case in order to attach information related to the reduction of cognitive load. In this case, the segment anchors may not be the same as those of the segment anchors used to store the measured cognitive load. The cognitive data layer can be a separate layer similar to the arrangement of topology geometry and road attributes as shown in Fig. 7. The cognitive load values associated with the road elements can be in a separate layer in order to provide the decoupling of the cognitive load root cause and solution. For example, if a user wants to retrieve only the measured cognitive values without the resolution, the data model shall support it accordingly.

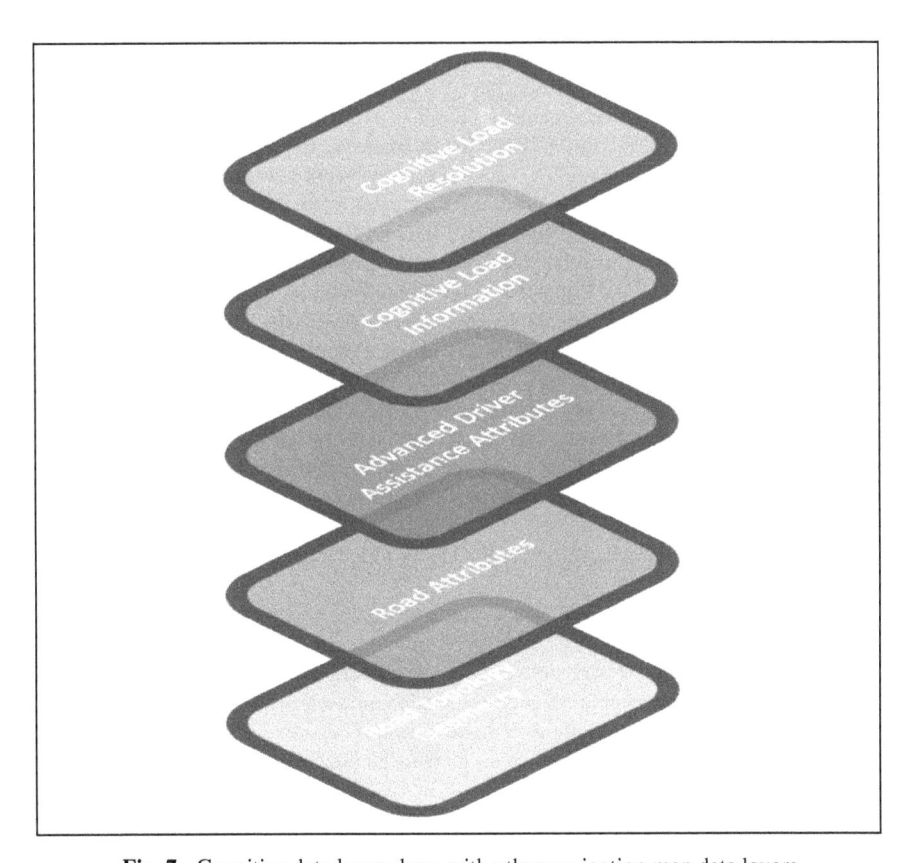

Fig. 7. Cognitive data layer along with other navigation map data layers

7 Conclusion and Future Work

The method for integration of the human cognitive load data is presented. Related works on the same topic are described. Comparison with the state of the art in this field is covered. Different categories of input data which is needed to enable the cognitive load calculation are briefly covered in a tabular form. Cognitive data processing as well as the representation of the cognitive data by using an optimum data model is described in detail. Integration of optimum guidance information to address the high cognitive load situations is also presented. Enhanced input data collection as well as the cognitive load data generation based on this enhanced data collection can be considered for the road map. More traffic situations can be integrated into the BeaCON framework so that the optimum guidance information to reduce cognitive load for a wide range of traffic situations can be identified.

References

1. Skog, I., Händel, P.: In-car positioning and navigation technologies. IEEE Trans. Intell. Transp. Syst. (2009)
2. European Commission: Driver Distraction Summary (2018)
3. European Road Safety Observatory: Road Safety Thematic Report-Driver Distraction (2022)
4. Balakrishna, A., Gross, T.: BeaCON – a research framework towards an optimal navigation. In: 22nd International Conference on Human Computer Interaction HCII 2020, Copenhagen, Denmark, pp. 556–574 (2020). (ISBN: 978-3-030-49064-5)
5. Brügger, A., Richter, K.F., Fabrikant, S.I.: How does navigation system behavior influence human behavior? Cogn. Res. Principles Impl. **4**(1) (2019)
6. Yoshida, Y., Ohwada, H., Mizoguchi, F., Iwasaki, H.: Classifying cognitive load and driving situation with machine learning. Int. J. Mach. Learn. Comput. **4**(3) (2014)
7. Haring, K.S., Ragni, M., Konieczny, L.: A cognitive model of drivers attention. In: Proceedings of the 11th International Conference on Cognitive Modeling (2012)
8. Krems, J.F., Baumann, M.R.K.: Driving and situation awareness: a cognitive model of memory-update processes. In: Kurosu, M. (eds.) Human Centered Design. HCD 2009. Lecture Notes in Computer Science, vol. 5619. Springer, Heidelberg (2009). https://doi.org/10.1007/978-3-642-02806-9_113
9. Daniel, K., Kühne, R., Wagner, P.: A car drivers cognition model. In: ITS Safety and Security Conference, vol. CD (2004)
10. HERE Navigation Attributes Schema. https://platform.here.com/data/hrn:here:data::olp-here:rib-2/navigation-attributes/schema
11. HERE Segment Anchor Description. https://www.here.com/docs/bundle/on-street-parking-api-developer-guide/page/topics/data-type-segment-anchor.html
12. Stojmenova, K., Sodnik, J.: Methods for assessment of cognitive workload in driving tasks. In: ICIST 5th International Conference on Information Society and Technology (2015)

The Role of UI/UX Designs for Enhancing Safety and Motorcycle Riders' Experience

Gabriel Chilro[1], Pedro Oliveira[1], Ricardo Nunes[1,2], João Barroso[1,2], and Tânia Rocha[1,2(✉)]

[1] Universidade de Trás-os-Montes e Alto Douro, Vila Real, Portugal
trocha@utad.pt
[2] INESC TEC, Vila Real, Portugal

Abstract. This study delves into the critical role of third-party applications in enhancing motorcycle interface design, particularly focusing on their potential to revolutionize the rider experience through innovative UI/UX designs. As motorcycles increasingly serve as primary modes of transportation in urban environments, safety concerns escalate, needing effective solutions. The research scrutinizes the main safety challenges faced by motorcycle riders, the influence of third-party applications on safety outcomes, and the advantages these applications offer over traditional dashboards. In this context, it is presented a Systematic Literature Review (SLR) methodology. Specifically, articles were selected based on predefined inclusion and exclusion criteria. Results indicate that third-party applications provide customizable solutions that not only offer real-time information about the motorcycle's condition but also mitigate safety risks by minimizing distractions. However, the literature reveals a lack of studies specifically addressing these applications, underscoring their potential as pioneering initiatives to reinforce motorcycle safety.

Keywords: Motorcycle interfaces · rider safety · Third-party applications · UI/UX design

1 Introduction

Motorcycles have emerged as indispensable modes of transportation in urban settings, offering a practical solution to traffic congestion and granting individuals flexibility in navigating through crowded streets. The growing popularity of motorcycles, particularly in densely populated cities like Istanbul, highlights their appeal as cost-effective alternatives to traditional automobiles [1]. However, this surge in motorcycle usage also brings forth significant safety concerns, as evidenced by the alarming rates of accidents and fatalities associated with their operation.

In regions such as the Philippines, where motorcycles serve as the primary means of transportation, the impact of traffic-related incidents is particularly pronounced. In 2017 alone, over 11,000 deaths were recorded due to accidents, with motorcycle riders comprising a significant portion of the casualties [2]. Factors contributing to these incidents range from adverse weather conditions and alcohol intoxication to inadequate vehicle maintenance, underscoring the multifaceted nature of motorcycle safety.

Another contributing factor is the struggle faced by road management authorities in implementing effective pavement repair approaches and allocating sufficient finances to maintain the existing road network at its optimal functionality [3]. In countries experiencing rapid urbanization and limited resources, inadequate road maintenance exacerbates safety hazards for motorcycle riders and other road users.

Addressing these challenges necessitates not only heightened awareness among riders but also a comprehensive approach to promoting regular vehicle maintenance. By enhancing safety standards and advocating for responsible motorcycle usage, we can strive towards creating safer road environments and reducing the incidence of accidents.

However, riding a motorcycle presents distinct difficulties for riders compared to other road travelers. These riders have less storage space, are more exposed to weather conditions and face increased safety risks. Additionally, they must keep their bikes in good condition to ensure performance and safety. Conventional ways of checking bike status and maintenance can be very inconvenient and time-consuming. These factors open the opportunity to develop a mobile application that can tackle all these problems at once.

2 Method

A Systematic Literature Review (SLR) serves as exploration, evaluation, and interpretation of existing research pertinent to a specific research question, thematic area, or broader phenomenon. Developed by Barbara Kitchenham, the "Systematic Literature Review" (SLR) approach offers a structured methodology to analyze the existing body of research in a particular domain comprehensively and rigorously. This systematic process entails various stages, including the formulation of research questions, establishment of inclusion and exclusion criteria, identification of information sources, selection of studies, evaluation of study quality, data extraction, and synthesis, and finally, interpretation and presentation of results. [4–6].

In the context of motorcycle safety and UI/UX applications, the objective of this SLR diverges from conventional explorations. We aim to unravel the intricate relationship between motorcycle safety and innovative UI/UX applications. Specifically, our focus lies in dissecting how cutting-edge user interface and user experience designs revolutionize motorcycle dashboards, fundamentally reshaping the landscape of rider safety. By delving into studies conducted in the last ten years, we seek to unearth pivotal insights into the synergistic amalgamation of technology and safety in the motorcycle domain.

2.1 Research Questions

To structure our investigation and guide our analysis, we have formulated the following research questions (RQ):

- RQ1: How does the lack of critical information on motorcycle dashboards contribute to rider safety risks and potential accidents?

This question is crucial for understanding the role of motorcycle dashboards in rider safety. The absence of critical information can lead to poor decisions by riders, increasing the risk of accidents. This could include information such as fuel levels, engine temperature or road conditions, which are essential for safe riding.

- RQ2: What is the impact of third-party applications on motorcycle rider safety?

This question aims to assess the impact of third-party applications on motorcycle devices on rider safety. With the advancement of technology, many riders are using apps to access additional information or specific features while riding. It is crucial to understand whether these apps enhance or compromise rider safety.

- RQ3: What are the advantages of third-party applications compared to traditional motorcycle dashboards?

This question seeks to compare the benefits of third-party applications against traditional motorcycle dashboards. As technology evolves, riders have access to a range of third-party apps that offer various features and functionalities. Understanding the advantages of these apps over traditional dashboards can provide insights into potential improvements in motorcycle technology and safety.

- RQ4: What are the problems and solutions found regarding safety in motorcycle UI development?

This question functions as a groundwork of our study. Understanding which problems exist regarding safety in motorcycle UI development is the first step and therefore very important to our study. Once we've pinpointed these problems, our next objective is to explore existing solutions. If none are found for a certain problem, we will then turn our attention to developing new solutions to address that problem. This approach allows us to thoroughly assess both existing solutions and the potential for creating new ones to improve safety in motorcycle UI design.

- RQ5: How do motorcycle manufacturers leverage mobile applications to enhance brand loyalty and engagement among their customers?

Brand loyalty and engagement among customers are a pivotal part of a company's business strategy. Ensuring customer satisfaction is important for retaining a loyal customer base, thereby positively impacting the company's profitability. When developing mobile applications, developers should consider how to use these apps to keep clients satisfied and loyal to the company. Therefore, understanding how to leverage mobile applications to enhance client engagement and loyalty is essential.

2.2 Search Strategy

As previously mentioned, a Systematic Literature Review (SLR) was conducted to gather academic literature from various databases, including Web of Science, Scopus, IEEE Xplore, and Google Scholar. The research used the PICOC (Population, Intervention, Comparison, Outcome, Context) framework to guide the search strategy.

The search strategy employed a systematic keyword-based approach, utilizing terms such as "motorcycle safety," "third-party applications," "urban traffic," "vehicle maintenance," "Motorcycle app UI/UX design," and "UI/UX." Advanced search options and filters, including publication date ranges, document types, and subject categories, were used to refine the results.

The first search string, SS1, consisted of "motorcycle safety" OR "third-party applications" OR "urban traffic" OR "vehicle maintenance" OR "Motorcycle app UI/UX design" OR "UI/UX". The second search string, SS2, was, ("Motorbike" OR "Bike" OR "Bike rider" OR "Motorbike rider" OR "Motorbikes" OR "Motorcycle" OR "Motorcycles" OR "Rider") AND ("Accessibility in motorbike apps" OR "App Development" OR "Front-end mobile development") AND ("Mobile apps" OR "Apps" OR "Mobile" OR "Mobile apps for bikers") AND ("Safety").

Additionally, the DOI of documents not fully accessible on these platforms was used to search for them on alternative databases. The search strategy aimed to identify relevant literature that addressed the research questions formulated in the PICOC framework, contributing to a comprehensive understanding of the topic.

3 Inclusion and Exclusion Criteria

To ensure the selection of studies that are directly relevant to the research topic and align with the research questions, clear inclusion and exclusion criteria were established. These criteria guided the screening process of articles retrieved from databases such as Web of Science, Scopus, IEEE Xplore, and Google Scholar.

For inclusion criteria, priority was given to articles that directly addressed the impact of third-party applications on motorcycle safety. The criteria included papers published within the last 10 years, scientific journals and conference papers, peer-reviewed scientific articles, systematic review articles, studies based on front-end mobile development, UI/UX features in mobile applications, and technology used for road security. Additionally, articles were required to focus on topics related to motorcycle safety, third-party applications, urban traffic, and vehicle maintenance.

Conversely, the exclusion criteria aimed to eliminate studies that did not meet the predefined standards of relevance or quality. Articles not written in English or Portuguese, those not directly addressing topics relevant to the research questions, and those focusing primarily on modes of transportation other than motorcycles were excluded. Duplicate articles were also removed.

4 Document Selection

During the document selection process, articles were selected based on the predefined inclusion and exclusion criteria, as well as their alignment with the research questions specified in the Data Extraction Strategy. The initial phase focused solely on the assessment of article titles and abstracts obtained from databases such as Web of Science, Scopus, Google Scholar, and other relevant academic sources. each article's abstract underwent a thorough examination to ascertain its relevance to the study's objectives and its adherence to the established criteria. This methodical approach tries to ensure the identification of studies that best addressed the research topic, ensuring both consistency and rigor in the article selection process (Fig. 1).

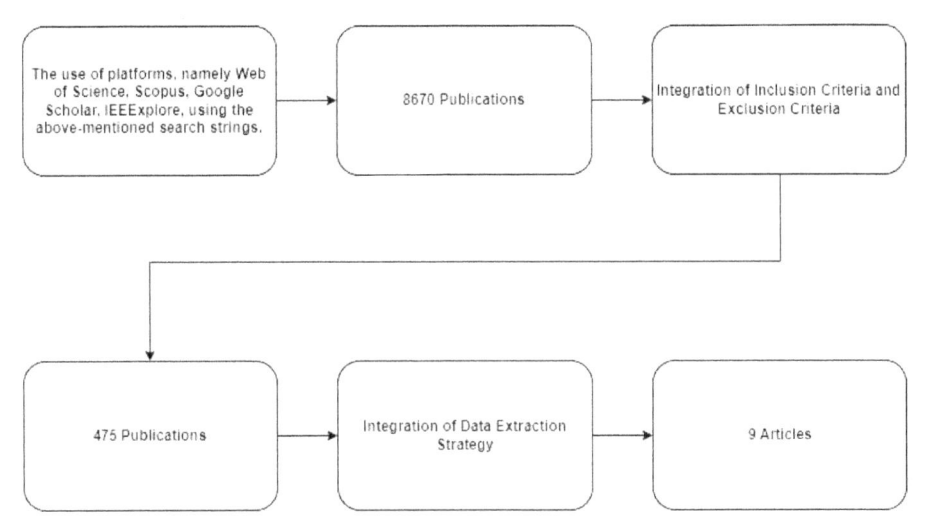

Fig. 1. Document Extraction Procedure

5 Quality Assessments

Quality assessment (QA) plays a pivotal role in a Systematic Literature Review (SLR), as it enables an investigation into potential variations in results across different studies [6]. In our review, QA of the selected studies was conducted using a scoring technique to evaluate relevance, those that fully meet the established criteria receive one point, while those that partially meet the criteria receive 0.5. Articles that do not meet any of the criteria receive a score of 0. This approach ensures a fair and accurate assessment of the articles selected for analysis.

To evaluate the quality of the studies, we developed seven quality questions. These questions included determining whether the study identified a specific population (Q1), if the identified population was the intended target (Q2), if any security improvements while riding a motorbike were mentioned (Q3), if features that an application for motorbike riders should have in terms of UI/UX were discussed (Q4), if the study's limitations were acknowledged by the authors (Q5), if the methodology and its results were clearly explained (Q6), and if the study had been cited by other authors (Q7).

The quality score for each study was determined by summing the scores for the responses to these quality questions. According to our research, studies scored at 7.0 included [7–10], those with a score of 6.0 were [2, 3, 11, 12] received a score of 5.5, and [1] was assigned a score of 5.0.

6 Data Extraction Strategy

In the systematic literature review (SLR) process, an organized and systematic approach to data extraction is essential to ensure consistency and accuracy in capturing relevant information from the selected studies. Our data extraction strategy was designed to extract key data points and insights pertinent to our research questions and objectives.

The extraction process involved identifying and recording crucial details from each selected study, such as study authors, publication year, research methodology, key findings, and conclusions. Additionally, specific data related to our research questions, including insights on motorcycle safety, third-party applications, urban traffic, and vehicle maintenance, were also extracted.

To maintain consistency across the data extraction process, a standardized data extraction form was developed. This form served as a guide, ensuring that all relevant information from each study was captured systematically. Each extracted data point was cross-checked to minimize errors and discrepancies, thereby enhancing the reliability and validity of the data collected.

By employing a structured data extraction strategy, we aimed to streamline the synthesis of information from diverse sources, facilitating a comprehensive analysis and interpretation of the findings in alignment with our research objectives.

7 Results

Regular maintenance of motorcycles is essential, and performing general maintenance is a must to always keep the motorcycle in good condition. The more regulated the maintenance, the safer it will be to ride the motorcycle.

As smartphones are ubiquitous nowadays, it's beneficial to have all the information about motorcycles for the user. This information can alert them to any potential danger that may occur in any of the motorcycle components.

8 RQ1: How Does the Lack of Critical Information on Motorcycle Dashboards Contribute to Rider Safety Risks and Potential Accidents?

Regarding RQ1, manufacturers already offer various technologies related to alerts and hazards, but only in high-end motorcycles, or they come at exorbitant prices as optional extras. Additionally, some of these manufacturer applications only provide basic functionalities, such as displaying maintenance history, upcoming service appointments, and real-time updates about available updates and campaigns. [13].

Furthermore, in several developing countries, motorcycles are more antiquated in terms of technology and safety features, hence the importance of regular maintenance at a more affordable price, leading to the increasing presence of these third-party apps.

The system described in [7] reflects this point well: "As most people own a smartphone, it would be perfect for riders to be able to watch their motorcycle's condition records on their phones. Since most Malaysian motorcycle riders own low-end motorcycles, low-cost sensors are used so that the notification system is affordable to most riders."

Therefore, it can be concluded that having information such as tire pressure visible to the rider is necessary. For example, in the case of tire pressure, besides causing poor performance and fuel economy, it can also pose safety issues." [11].

9 RQ2: What is the Impact of Third-Party Applications on Motorcycle Rider Safety?

An excess of information can lead to heightened driver distraction. In the current landscape, infotainment displays are increasingly expansive and assume control over a majority of the vehicle's functionalities, diverting the driver's attention away from pertinent matters. This phenomenon poses additional risks to road safety, as drivers may become preoccupied with non-essential features rather than focusing on the road ahead [12]. As such, striking a delicate balance between providing necessary information and mitigating distraction becomes imperative in ensuring optimal safety standards for motorcycle riders.

To address the issues, the implementation of user interface (UI) applications emerges as a viable solution. These applications are designed with a driver-centric approach, aiming to mitigate the problems outlined earlier. Unlike conventional dashboards provided by manufacturers, many of these applications offer users the ability to customize their interface according to their preferences before embarking on any journey. This customization allows riders to prioritize essential information such as tire pressure, range, GPS navigation, among others.

In the referenced article [7], the functionality of these applications is detailed. Figures 2 and 3 (corresponding to Figs. 15 and 17 in the original article) showcase the application interface, displaying the status of critical components such as tires, chain, oil filter, and temperature. If any of these components fall below the desired level, the application promptly sends a notification to the user's smartphone.

Fig. 2. Screen displaying the condition of mo-torcycle parts

Fig. 3. Notification alert for the engine temperature

10 RQ3: What Are the Advantages of Third-Party Applications Compared to Traditional Motorcycle Dashboards?

Regarding the advantages of these applications over conventional motorcycle dashboards, customization is key. While manufacturers may offer some degree of customization, particularly in certain aspects, the dashboard's customization remains relatively uniform for all customers. This can sometimes require riders to interact with the infotainment system while driving, potentially leading to distractions. [8].

In the contemporary digital era, many successful products heavily rely on user experience (UX) to determine their success. Consequently, the design assumes a pivotal role in the final product. These UI/UX applications are defined by their user interface and user experience, respectively encompassing how users interact with and experience the application.

It is feasible to develop an application that allows users to interact and tailor it to their preferences, rendering it distinct without the need for manipulation while driving. For instance, users can specify the quantity and type of information they wish to view on the main dashboard, such as tire pressure or weather updates. Another crucial aspect to mention is the option to adjust colors and brightness according to the user's preference and visual appeal. [9].

Overall, the ability to customize these applications offers a significant advantage over traditional dashboards, enhancing user experience, minimizing distractions, and ultimately improving safety on the road.

11 RQ4: What Are the Problems and Solutions Regarding Safety in UI Motorcycle Development?

After conducting this research, there is very limited information or previous studies addressing this topic specifically. While some articles discuss motorcycle safety from a mechanical perspective, they do not align with our focus. The closest relevant findings are smart helmets [10], which offer various safety features. However, our goal is to design a user interface (UI) directly integrated into the motorcycle to achieve similar safety goals.

By designing a UI directly integrated into the motorcycle, there is an opportunity to leverage the vehicle's existing systems and capabilities to provide a comprehensive safety solution. Some examples of this are intuitive dashboard displays, haptic feedback controls, advanced sensor networks, and real-time data analytics to provide timely warnings and assist riders in making informed decisions while on the road, thereby increasing their safety.

12 RQ5: How Do Motorcycle Manufacturers Leverage Mobile Applications to Enhance Brand Loyalty and Engagement Among Their Customers?

Motorcycle manufacturers need to leverage third-party applications to guarantee brand loyalty and engagement among their customers. These apps serve as centralized platforms for users to access detailed product information, including specifications, features, and pricing, while also receiving timely updates on new releases. Also, manufacturers can facilitate ongoing engagement by offering service and maintenance reminders, encouraging riders to stay on top of essential tasks for optimal performance and safety.

Furthermore, these apps can also play a huge part in providing a sense of community among the riders. The existence of forums for discussion, sharing experiences, and connecting with fellow enthusiasts can be very rewarding and fulfilling for customers. By enabling personalization options and delivering unique brand experiences, manufacturers can strengthen their connection with their clients, therefore guaranteeing long-term loyalty and advocacy within the motorcycle community.

With these considerations in mind, despite limited literature on this subject, there is potential to develop a creative and successful application that could not only enhance rider safety but also enrich their passion for riding.

13 Conclusion

In conclusion, this systematic research into the role of third-party applications in motorcycle safety has shed light on several crucial aspects. Firstly, motorcycles play a vital role in urban transportation, offering a convenient solution to traffic congestion and time-saving benefits. However, the increased use of motorcycles also brings about safety concerns, particularly in developing countries where maintenance practices may be inadequate. The lack of access to advanced safety features in motorcycles further exacerbates these risks.

The integration of third-party applications presents a promising solution to enhance motorcycle safety by providing riders with real-time information about their vehicle's condition and potential hazards. These applications offer customization options, allowing riders to tailor their experience according to their preferences. Moreover, they can serve as a cost-effective alternative to expensive built-in safety features, especially in regions where access to such technology is limited.

Through comprehensive research and evaluation, it has become evident that third-party applications have the potential to significantly improve motorcycle safety by promoting awareness, facilitating maintenance, and offering personalized safety features. However, further studies and advancements in technology are necessary to maximize their effectiveness and ensure widespread adoption among motorcycle riders worldwide.

Additionally, it is notable that there is a scarcity of articles addressing these specific situations, indicating that these applications may be pioneering initiatives to enhance motorcycle safety. By leveraging the insights gained from this research, manufacturers, and technology developers can collaborate to implement innovative solutions that prioritize rider safety and contribute to the overall improvement of road safety for all commuters.

Acknowledgements. The study was developed under the project A-MoVeR – "Mobilizing Agenda for the Development of Products & Systems towards an Intelligent and Green Mobility", operation n.º 02/C05-i01.01/2022.PC646908627-00000069, approved under the terms of the call n.º 02/C05-i01/2022 – Mobilizing Agendas for Business Innovation, financed by European funds provided to Portugal by the Recovery and Resilience Plan (RRP), in the scope of the European Recovery and Resilience Facility (RRF), framed in the Next Generation UE, for the period from 2021–2026."

References

1. Sarısoy, G., Üniversitesi, Y., Özgün, S., Sarisoy, G., Selçuk, K.: Investigation of the motorcycle usage in İstanbul (2017). https://www.researchgate.net/publication/333386249
2. Institute of Electrical and Electronics Engineers. In: 2020 IEEE 7th International Conference on Industrial Engineering and Applications: ICIEA 2020, Bangkok, Thailand, 16–21 April 2020
3. Khahro, S.H., Javed, Y., Memon, Z.A.: Low-cost road health monitoring system: a case of flexible pavements. Sustainability (Switzerland), **13**(18) (2021). https://doi.org/10.3390/su131810272
4. Kitchenham, B., Pearl Brereton, O., Budgen, D., Turner, M., Bailey, J., Linkman, S.: Systematic literature reviews in software engineering - a systematic literature review. Inform. Softw. Technol. **51**(1), 7–15, January 2009. https://doi.org/10.1016/j.infsof.2008.09.009
5. Kitchenham, B.: Procedures for performing systematic reviews. https://www.researchgate.net/publication/228756057
6. Kitchenham, B.: Guidelines for performing Systematic Literature Reviews in Software Engineering (2007). https://www.researchgate.net/publication/302924724
7. IEEE Control Systems Society: Chapter Malaysia and institute of electrical and electronics engineers. In: Proceedings, 2017 IEEE Conference on Systems, Process and Control (ICSPC 2017), 15–17 December 2017, Conference Venue, Hattan Hotel, Melaka, Hatten Square, Jalan Merdeka, Bandar Hilir, 75000 Malka, Malaysia (2017)
8. Marx, C., Kalayci, E.G., Moertl, P.: Temporal Dashboard Gaze Variance (TDGV) changes for measuring cognitive distraction while driving. Sensors **22**(23), December 2022. https://doi.org/10.3390/s22239556
9. Arezes, J.M.: Learning on Navigation Information Presentation for Motorcycle Head-Up Displays (2019). http://www.bike-hud.com/
10. 2019 4th International Conference on Information Systems and Computer Networks (ISCON). IEEE (2019)
11. Bansal, A., Jain, A., Srivastava, P., Tiwary, A.K., Dear, R.K.: Significance of tire pressure monitoring system in motorcycle. In: SAE Technical Papers, SAE International (2016). https://doi.org/10.4271/2016-01-1634
12. Infotainment Screens Actually Distract Drivers, Study Shows. Accessed 09 Apr 2024. https://www.autoweek.com/news/technology/a42384978/infotainment-screens-make-distracted-drivers-swedish-study-finds/
13. My Ducati: A Ducati a qualquer hora e em qualquer lugar - Ducati Portugal. Accessed 12 Apr 2024. https://ducati.pt/2022/05/16/my-ducati-a-ducati-a-qualquer-hora-e-em-qualquer-lugar/

Challenges and Opportunities of Automotive HMI

Zaiyan Gong(✉)

HVR Lab, Tongji University, Shanghai 201804, China
gongzaiyan@foxmail.com

Abstract. Automotive Human-Machine Interaction (HMI) has evolved over decades and has now become one of the most critical components in modern vehicles. This paper introduces the automotive HMI human factors model, designed to provide a deep analysis of the intricate automotive HMI system which encompasses numerous complexities and human factor challenges. The model details the interplay between driving-related and non-driving-related tasks, highlights the diversity of interaction tasks and modalities, and addresses the challenges of integrating software and hardware effectively within automotive systems. Additionally, the paper identifies three significant opportunities that are emerging as a result of rapid technological advancements. These include the development of Artificial Intelligence Generated Content (AIGC) technologies, enhancements in multimodal interaction capabilities, and the progress of autonomous driving technologies. Each of these areas offers potential to vastly improve the functionality and user experience of automotive HMI systems. By using the automotive HMI human factors model, the study not only outlines the existing challenges but also frames the potential for future advancements that could redefine the interaction between drivers and their vehicles.

Keywords: Automotive HMI · Human Factors · Secondary Tasks

1 Introduction

The automotive industry has undergone unprecedented transformations over the 130 years since the inception of the automobile. Electrification has fundamentally changed how automobiles work, placing batteries and electric motors at the heart of new technological developments, while the role of internal combustion engines and transmissions has diminished. Additionally, the rise of intelligent systems has changed how the value of a vehicle is assessed. In modern vehicles, software and user experience have become the core values, with the plethora of functions and configurations acting as supplementary benefits. The intertwined trends of electrification and intelligent technology are propelling the automotive industry's transformation. Within this landscape, automotive human-machine interaction (HMI) plays a crucial role, standing at the forefront of these evolutionary changes [1].

Human-machine interaction (HMI) is the study of the design, evaluation, implementation, and other related aspects of interactive machine systems intended for direct use by humans [2]. To make the definition more specific, automotive HMI is a system that enables the transmission of dynamic information and emotions between a human and a vehicle, except for the main driving task [3].

Over the past 100 years, automotive HMI functions have been gradually expanded and their popularity has progressively increased. In the past decade, starting from the 2010s, automotive HMI has experienced unprecedented rapid development and has become one of the most important modules in automotive product design.

Unlike other HMI systems like smart phones or household appliances, automotive HMI system is more complicated [1]. Thus, the analysis of automotive trend is not easy. This paper proposes a model of automotive HMI human factors to show the comprehensive process when human interact with HMI system while driving. This model indicates the difference between automotive HMI and other normal HMI systems, and we can find out special challenges and opportunities.

2 Method

To make in-depth analysis and find out challenges and opportunities of automotive HMI, a model is required to understand how driver think and do when using HMI system while driving.

An information processing model (IPM) of an HMI system is commonly used for normal HMI systems, as shown in Fig. 1 [3]. This model shows how user perceive, think and react when using an HMI system. However, this model regards user and machine as a closed system, ignoring the impact from driving and environment issues.

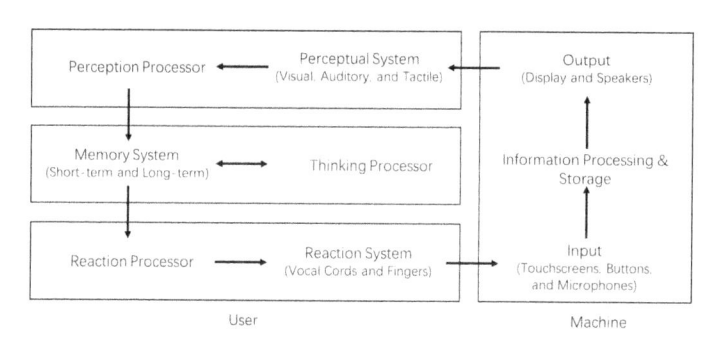

Fig. 1. Information processing model (IPM) of an HMI system.

Another Human-Machine System (HMS) is also widely used, especially for automotive ergonomics, see Fig. 2 [4]. This model considers environment impact for both human and machine. However, it is defined for easy and direct tasks, for example, turn the steering wheel to make the car turn. It does not consider the complex of HMI system, nor the secondary tasks while driving.

To combine the advantages of both models above and eliminate their limitations, we proposed a model of automotive HMI human factors, see Fig. 3. This model has many advantages for automotive HMI. First, primary tasks (driving related tasks) and

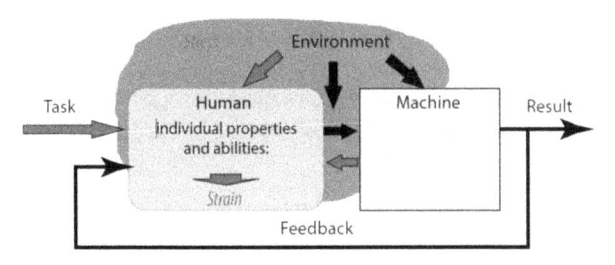

Fig. 2. General Structure Scheme of the Human-Machine System (HMS).

secondary tasks (non-driving related tasks) are considered parallelly. They happen at the same time and affect each other. Second, environment impact is fully considered for both primary tasks and secondary tasks, for human, human input and machine. Third, information processing model is included when analyze HMI tasks, and it is also affected by driving related tasks. However, the elements of human factors for driving related tasks are simplified, because this model is mainly for automotive HMI, rather than driving. Forth, a feature of stress and strain concept from HMS model is considered, as marked by blue arrows in Fig. 3. Under stress, all the influences that can influence the working process of a human being are summarized, which are the same for every person who is in this situation. Strain is the individual reaction to this stress [4].

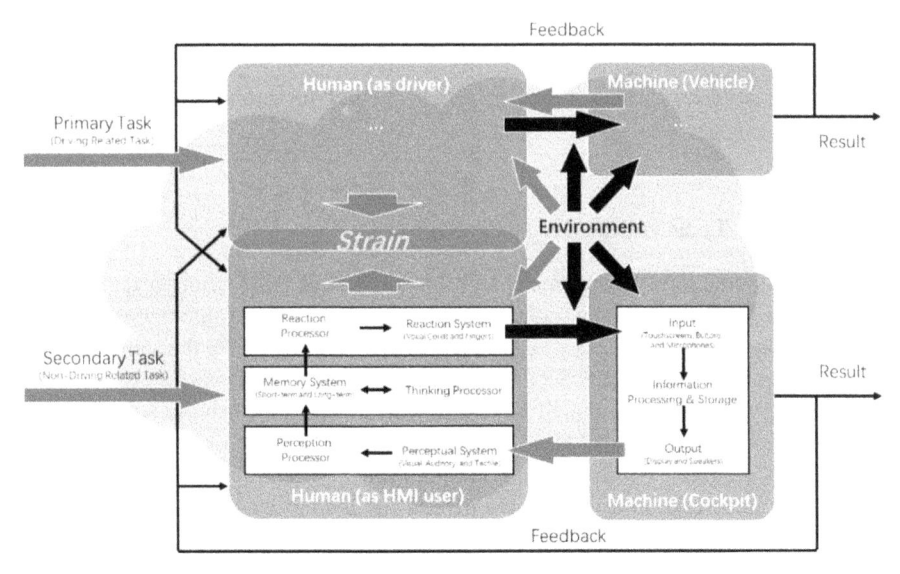

Fig. 3. The automotive HMI human factors model.

This model shows the difference between automotive HMI and other HMI systems. The differences are reasons why automotive HMI has special challenges, as well as why there are new opportunities for the next-generation intelligent cockpits.

3 Challenges of Automotive HMI

Based on the automotive HMI human factors model proposed above, we can find out 3 special challenges for automotive HMI, which are marked as C1, C2, and C3 in red circles in Fig. 4.

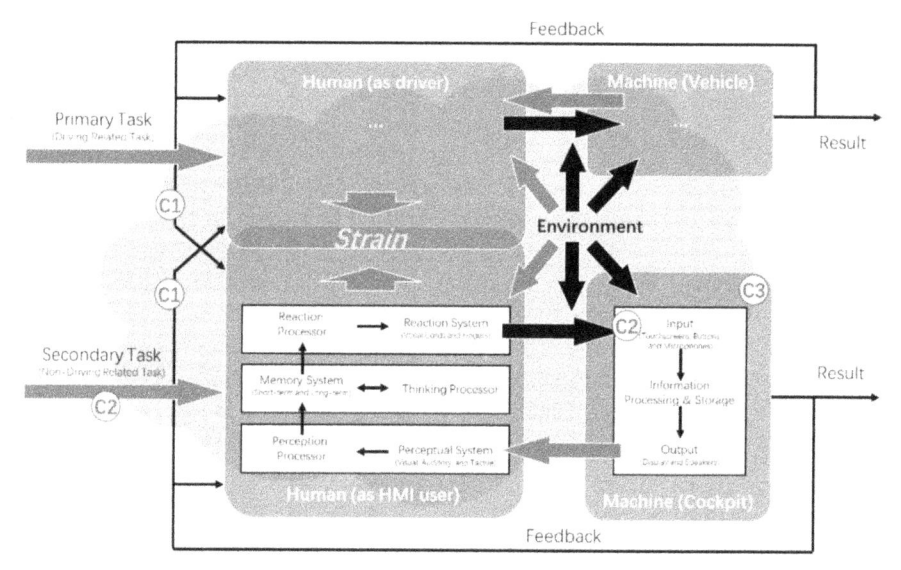

Fig. 4. Three challenges from the automotive HMI human factors model.

3.1 Secondary Tasks and Driver Distraction

Unlike most interaction systems, many tasks in automotive HMI require user operation while driving instead of concentration on the interaction. These interaction tasks are called secondary tasks. Secondary tasks and primary tasks happen at the same time, and one's results can affect the other. Secondary task execution should not carry considerable driver distraction, otherwise it will have a negative impact on driving safety, see C1 markers in Fig. 4.

A driver's attention is limited, and attempting to perform any secondary task can contribute to a decrease in driving performance due to distraction [5]. There are three types of driver distractions caused by secondary tasks: (1) visual distraction, where the driver diverts their gaze away from the road to interact with a device, leading to observation errors; (2) cognitive distraction, where the driver shifts their attention from driving to a secondary task, which can induce errors in information processing or memory retrieval; and (3) manual distraction, which occurs when the driver removes their hands from the steering wheel to operate other equipment, consequently leading to errors in physical actions [6, 7]. The causes and manifestations of these three types of distraction are summarized in Table 1.

Table 1. Causes and manifestations of the three main types of driver distraction

	Visual distraction	Cognitive distraction	Manual distraction
Causes	Gaze diversion from the road to observe the displays or buttons	Attention shift from driving to secondary tasks	Taking one hand off the steering wheel to operate other devices
Manifestations	Inability to observe the surrounding road environment	Slower processing and memory retrieval of driving-related information	Decreased control precision of the steering wheel
Major effects on driving	Reduced speed, lane departure, slower emergency response	Slower emergency response, increased following distance, going the wrong way	Lane departure

Automotive HMI tasks are the important part of secondary tasks [8]. There are some ways to decrease driver distraction: (1) less operation steps and shorter operation time; (2) easy-to-learn interaction logic; (3) better element visibility, understandability and memorability; (4) good interaction feedback; (5) interaction modalities with less gaze diversion, like voice control; (6) more intelligent recommendation and decision-making [1].

3.2 Numerous Interaction Tasks and Various Interaction Modalities

There are numerous interaction tasks and various interaction modalities in automotive HMI system, and some tasks should be done at the same time via various modality, as shown in C2 markers in Fig. 4. This results in challenging design and evaluation.

The central information display and the instrument cluster display in a vehicle typically showcase over 1000 different items and functions. Evaluating these based on only a subset of information and tasks might not accurately represent the full capabilities of the entire interactive system. For instance, a system optimized for music search may not perform as effectively when used to locate navigation destinations. Specifically, even if a system is designed for easy text input, it might still struggle to accurately locate a desired navigation destination.

During driving scenario, some HMI tasks are frequently done at the same time. Thus, in recent years, there has been a notable trend in the hierarchical design of automotive HMI, wherein the shortcut layer is used as the home screen instead of the root directory layer. The shortcut layer can be used as the home screen to arrange several widgets on the home screen, as shown in Fig. 5. These widgets consist of a map widget that displays routes and guidance information, alongside a music widget that shows the current song track and facilitates the transition to the next track.

There is a variety of operating modalities for automotive HMI. The same interaction task can frequently be accomplished through various interaction modalities, transforming the research focus from a simple linear catalog to a complex interlaced matrix. For

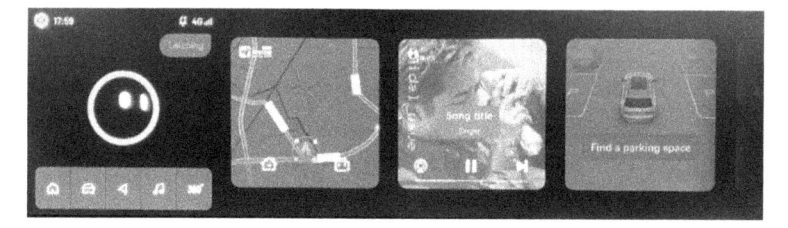

Fig. 5. Widgets on the central information display of Li Auto One, translated from Chinese.

instance, entering a navigation destination can be done using different modalities like keystroke typing, touchscreen handwriting, and voice control. A vehicle that excels in touchscreen handwriting recognition might not perform as well in speech recognition. Consequently, evaluating whether a vehicle's navigation input performance is effective or deficient necessitates the use of specifically tailored computational methods.

These are suggestions for interaction modality selection for different categories of interaction tasks, which can serve as a reference for automotive HMI design.

For simple tasks typically involving one or two steps using touchscreens or buttons (e.g., adjusting the music volume and answering phone calls), steering wheel buttons as the optimal interaction modality. Central console buttons should also be available, while touchscreens need not be involved in these tasks.

For intermediate tasks, typically involving 2–4 steps using touchscreens or buttons (e.g., calling a designated contact and switching audio sources), voice control is the optimal interaction modality. Although touchscreens and central console buttons can increase driver distraction, at least one of them should be retained for controlling intermediate tasks due to better learnability.

For complex open-input tasks (e.g., entering a destination and starting navigation, or inputting a phone number and making a call), voice control is the optimal interaction modality. While touchscreens should also include these task types.

3.3 System, Software, and Ecological Integration

Although automotive HMI systems are similar to smartphones in terms of function and logic, they have a larger research and design scope than smartphones.

In the case of smartphones, emphasis is placed on the operating system, such as page layout, shortcut menus, and on-screen gestures, rather than on individual applications like Apple Maps, Spotify, and WeChat. This is because these applications typically perform similarly across all major smartphones and do not necessitate a unique evaluation. In contrast, the HMI systems in vehicles differ not only in their operating systems but also in their interface design and interaction logic, particularly in functions related to navigation, music, and communication. As such, research of automotive HMI systems needs to specifically address these functions or the application software involved.

Moreover, as automotive HMI systems gain access to a growing array of online ecological resources, the diversity and richness of these resources must also be taken

Challenges and Opportunities of Automotive HMI 29

into account. For instance, even if a vehicle's music software is exceptionally well-designed in terms of interaction, it may not be frequently used if the online music library does not include the latest popular songs.

Traditional automotive companies typically do not excel in software and algorithms. When data becomes interconnected, robust software and algorithms are essential for analysis. In this aspect, the automotive industry often falls behind the internet industry, which restricts the development of intelligent user experiences. For instance, while the idea of suggesting two to three meal options based on user preferences might seem straightforward, there is currently no smartphone software capable of adequately performing this task. Consequently, most users end up spending significant time navigating through extensive menus.

In the realm of consumer electronics, it is quite clear whether hardware should serve content or content should serve hardware. Users primarily care about the content displayed on their smartphone screens, not the unique designs of the screens themselves, and they wouldn't compromise on content for the sake of a novel screen design. However, the situation is markedly different in automotive HMI design, where there is considerable disagreement over this question. Designers who believe that hardware should serve content typically use screens with a 16:9 aspect ratio, aligning with the majority of content available in most ecosystems. However, such screens can be challenging to integrate aesthetically with the rest of the car's interior and might lead to a homogenization among different car models. On the other hand, designers who advocate for content serving hardware prioritize creating unique and aesthetically pleasing screen designs first, and then adapt the content to fit these designs, although this approach often sacrifices some user experience, see Fig. 6. Both design philosophies are widely prevalent today, each with its own set of strengths and weaknesses. Whether one will continue to coexist with the other, or if one will dominate—or even overwhelmingly surpass—the other, remains uncertain.

Fig. 6. Left: Tesla Model S has a normal 16:9 screen which fit most games and videos; Right: Mini Cooper has a special round screen which should be adapted by various apps.

4   Opportunities of Automotive HMI

Nowadays, we see that voice interaction systems in automotive HMI have become very natural, navigation systems exceedingly powerful, and the expansion of screen sizes in many models has ceased. Does this mean automotive HMI has reached its developmental peak? Far from it. On one hand, automotive HMI is considered the ideal platform for future intelligent living. On the other hand, innovations in new technologies present numerous breakthrough opportunities for automotive HMI.

4.1 Automotive HMI as the Best Carrier of Intelligence

It is anticipated that automotive HMI will evolve into the most intelligent device accessible to consumers. Similarly, the automotive cockpit is expected to become the most advanced intelligent space available to them. Such predictions might seem ambitious, particularly since the current intelligence of automotive HMI systems does not match that of smartphones. Yet, if we deconstruct both automotive HMI systems and smartphones to their fundamental computational machinery and examine their architectures, the benefits of automotive HMI become evident.

All computational machines require input and output devices. In 1949, John von Neumann, "the Father of the Modern Computer," proposed a computer architecture that consists of five components: input devices, memory unit, arithmetic/logic unit, control unit, and output devices, as shown in Fig. 7 [9]. Input and output devices are not unique to electronic computers. As early as 1833, the British inventor Charles Babbage incorporated punched cards as input devices in his Analytical Engine (a purely mechanical calculator) and used a printer, plotter, and bell as output devices.

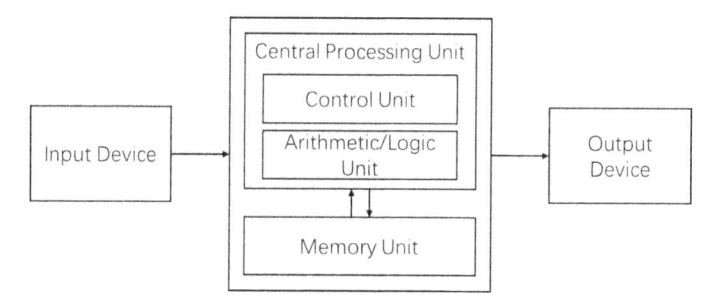

Fig. 7. Computer architecture proposed by John von Neumann

The intelligence level of a machine relies heavily on its input and output devices. According to David Wechsler's definition of intelligence, the machine should be able to adapt to specified environments, that is, it should receive sufficiently rich environmental information as an input [10]. Simultaneously, the machine should be capable of efficient response and execution, which requires it to provide sufficiently rich forms of output. These inputs and outputs should be highly automated, minimizing the need for human intervention. Therefore, sensors play a crucial role as input devices, whereas actuators are essential output devices.

While smartphones boast significant computational power, they are equipped with a limited set of sensors, such as cameras, microphones, and inertial measurement units (IMUs). Additionally, the effectiveness of these sensors can be compromised when the smartphone is not actively in use. For example, a smartphone lying face up on a surface will have its rear camera blocked and the front camera facing the ceiling, rendering it unable to provide useful data. In contrast, the cockpit of an intelligent vehicle can host a more diverse array of sensors that remain operational as long as the vehicle is in use. Inside the cabin, sensors in seat cushions can detect the presence of passengers, cameras can observe user behavior and facial expressions, and steering angle sensors can assess driver fatigue. Microphone arrays are capable of picking up voices and identifying specific speakers. On the structure of the vehicle, wheel speed sensors and IMUs work together to accurately assess the vehicle's motion state, while the power system continuously monitors energy consumption. Externally, cameras and radar systems keep track of other vehicles, pedestrians, and obstacles, and specialized sensors can evaluate the current weather conditions, enhancing overall vehicle safety and functionality.

Smartphone output devices are notably limited, primarily comprising just the screen and speaker. These components do not directly influence the motion of any physical device nor are they categorized as actuators. In stark contrast, vehicles are equipped with a broad spectrum of actuators beyond mere screens and speakers. Each electrical component within a vehicle function as an actuator, facilitating adjustments in seat positions, mirror angles, trunk lid operations, climate control, and the speed of windshield wipers. Furthermore, the vehicle itself acts as a large actuator, maintaining safe operation by managing the outputs of the powertrain and chassis systems to prevent loss of control and collisions with other vehicles, pedestrians, and obstacles. In the realm of advanced autonomous driving, the vehicle transcends its traditional role, operating as a comprehensive actuator that efficiently transports users to their intended destinations.

Vehicles are equipped with numerous sensors and actuators, all of which are designed, calibrated, and managed cohesively to achieve a high degree of synergy. While smartphones are capable of connecting to various smart home devices, enabling them to interact with an extensive range of sensors and actuators, these configurations lack the level of integration and coordination found in vehicle systems. This sophisticated orchestration in vehicles allows for more precise and efficient performance, which is not attainable with the more fragmented systems typically used with smartphones.

The rich array of sensors and actuators in vehicles can create vast space for potential intelligent scenarios for automotive HMI. Especially when we are facing technology reformation, elements in automotive HMI human factors model are changing, which brings new opportunities, see Fig. 8.

4.2 AIGC Extends the Ability of HMI

Artificial Intelligence Generated Content (AIGC) refers to content that is autonomously created by AI systems, which can include text, images, audio, and interactive experiences. The development of AIGC began to gain traction with advancements in machine learning and natural language processing technologies. Early AIGC systems focused primarily on text-based content, such as automated news articles and basic content curation. Over time, the capabilities of AIGC systems expanded dramatically due to improvements in deep learning architectures, particularly with the introduction of models like GPT for text and DALL-E for images. These models leveraged vast amounts of data to generate high-quality, contextually relevant content that mimics human creativity and understanding.

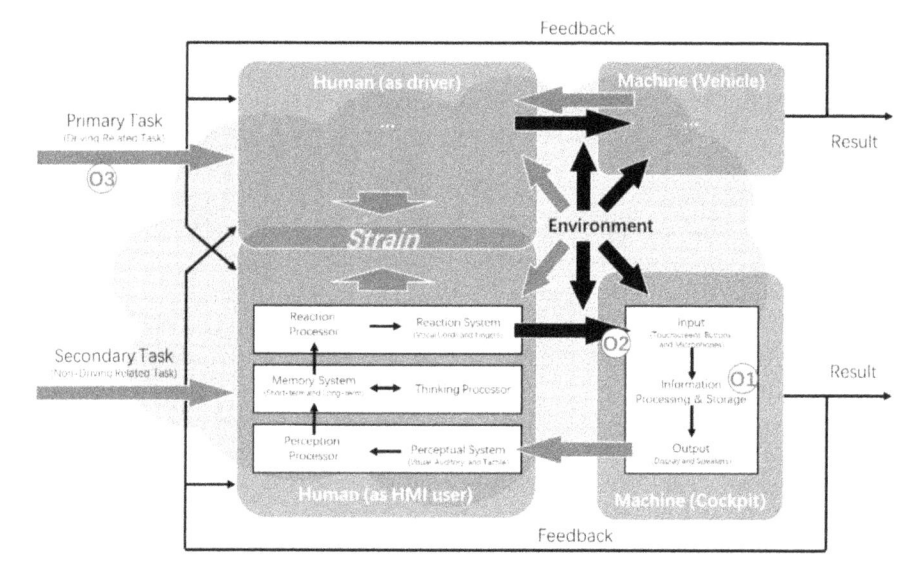

Fig. 8. Three opportunities from the automotive HMI human factors model.

In the automotive industry, AIGC has started to significantly influence the design and functionality of intelligent cockpits make them much stronger, see O1 marker in Fig. 8. These advanced systems enhance user interactions through personalized content, dynamic interface adaptations, and sophisticated voice-assisted functionalities. By integrating AIGC, automakers can provide a more intuitive, engaging, and adaptive user experience, thereby transforming the way drivers and passengers interact with their vehicles.

However, the application of AIGC in automotive HMI isn't simply a matter of transplanting PC and mobile-based conversational agents and image generation applications directly into vehicles. It's rare for someone to compose a paper or create a promotional poster using an automotive HMI system. Instead, AIGC must be tailored to the unique scenarios of automotive use, including assisting with vehicle settings, remembering past journeys, and predicting future destinations. This approach ensures that AIGC enhances the driving experience by providing contextually relevant assistance and information, leveraging the technology to serve specific needs and enhance safety and comfort for drivers and passengers alike.

To optimize AIGC for automotive HMI, it should evolve in the following six directions:

1. AI memory and understanding: The system should remember and understand users' behaviors, habits, and history. For instance, when a user says, "I want to go to the bank I visited last time," the system should automatically know the specific address.
2. Inter-app communication: Breaking down barriers between applications to avoid repetitive user input is crucial. For example, after AIGC recommends five restaurants, the user should be able to say, "Take me to the second one," without having to re-member and input the name into the navigation system.

3. Increased response speed: The response time of AIGC systems, which often rely on extensive cloud computing power, needs improvement as they currently lag behind traditional natural voice interactions.
4. Accuracy of generated content: It is vital that the content generated by AIGC is verifiable and accurate to avoid creating illusions, such as recommending a non-existent restaurant.
5. Conciseness and clarity: Answers should be concise and structured to deliver the most important information first, especially important when driving, where users prefer quick and relevant information over lengthy conversations.
6. Intuitive multimodal interactions: AIGC should leverage various sensors to gauge users' moods and intentions, enabling more natural and intuitive interactions that better understand human intent.

These advancements will make AIGC more practical and user-friendly within the automotive context, enhancing both functionality and user experience in intelligent cockpits.

4.3 Multimodal Interaction Reshapes the Form of Cockpit

Multimodal interaction changes how user interact with machine, see O2 marker in Fig. 8. Multimodal interaction for automotive HMI refers to a hybrid interaction approach where touchscreen or voice serve as the primary modality of interaction, supplemented by natural interaction modalities such as gestures, head movements, eye tracking, and facial expressions.

The trend toward multimodal interaction in automotive HMI is inevitable. From a technological perspective, natural interaction sensors—such as gesture recognition cameras, eye-tracking devices, and facial expression analyzers—are increasingly sophisticated. Artificial intelligence technologies have advanced to the point where they can predict and interpret user intentions more accurately. From a demand perspective, the volume of interaction data inside vehicles is growing, and existing single-mode interfaces are insufficient to handle this complexity effectively. Additionally, as market competition intensifies, there is a pressing need for products to innovate and differentiate. Multimodal interaction offers a compelling solution by enabling more intuitive, efficient, and user-centric interactions within the automotive environment.

When developing multimodal interaction for automotive HMI, several key considerations should be kept in mind:

1. Avoid technology overload: It's crucial to focus on user needs to enhance their experience rather than just stacking technologies for the sake of it.
2. Leverage strengths and mitigate weaknesses of natural interaction modalities: For example, natural interaction generally offers intuitive and easy-to-learn methods, but it can suffer from low precision and difficulty in determining start and end points of interactions.
3. Designers need a clear methodology: The possible combinations of different interaction modes are virtually endless. Design should be guided by methodologies rather than solely relying on the designer's inspiration.

4. Embrace the vast potential for product differentiation: Multimodal interaction opens up new possibilities for innovative cockpit layouts, such as remote screens and smart surfaces, offering significant opportunities for differentiation in the market.

4.4 Autonomous Driving Rebuilds the "Third Space"

In sociology, the third place refers to the social surroundings that are separate from the two usual social environments of home ("first place") and the workplace ("second place"). In his book The Great Good Place, Ray Oldenburg argues that third places are important for civil society, democracy, civic engagement and establishing feelings of a sense of place [11].

For many years, there has been a desire to make cars an important "third space," as for many people, hours are spent in their vehicle each day—more than other potential third spaces like libraries or cafes. However, the ability to engage in activities within this space is severely limited when the driver's primary focus must be on driving and avoiding accidents.

Level 3 autonomous driving (L3) is on the horizon, offering a solution to this limitation. Level 3 autonomy refers to a driving mode where the vehicle can handle all aspects of the driving task in specific conditions, allowing the driver to divert their attention from driving tasks, see O3 marker in Fig. 8. This shift enables drivers to engage in a broader range of non-driving related tasks, such as watching videos, reading books, or using computers and smartphones for work. This advancement significantly expands the functional utility of the vehicle, transforming it into a more productive and enjoyable third space.

The transition from a driving space to a "third space" has prompted designers to rethink the layout of automotive HMI. As traditional driving-related tasks become intermittent with the advent of autonomous driving, designers are considering whether components like the steering wheel and pedals could retract during autonomous modes. This retraction would allow for a more flexible use of space, facilitating non-driving related activities such as entertainment or office work. Ideally, screens could be positioned directly in front of the driver to prevent neck strain from prolonged sideways glances. Such concept introduced in concept cars over five years ago. These innovations were initially stalled due to the slower-than-expected rollout of autonomous driving technologies, but as adoption increases, these concepts are expected to further evolve.

However, until full autonomous driving is feasible in all scenarios, the cabin cannot be completely transformed into a living room space. Drivers must remain prepared to take over control in certain situations. Therefore, any work or entertainment resources provided to the driver should consider the potential need for sudden driver engagement. This means avoiding activities that might excessively tire or overly excite the driver, ensuring they remain alert and ready to take over when necessary.

5 Conclusion

Automotive HMI is a complex human-machine interaction system. To conduct an in-depth analysis, this paper introduces the automotive HMI human factors model and based on it, identifies three challenges and three opportunities for Automotive HMI. The challenges stem from the interaction between driving-related tasks and non-driving-related tasks, the diversity of interaction tasks and modalities, and the integration of software and hardware. The opportunities arise from the rapid development of AIGC technology, multimodal interaction technologies, and autonomous driving technologies. These challenges and opportunities merit serious consideration and exploration by researchers and practitioners in the field of intelligent vehicles. Furthermore, it is hoped that researchers will use the automotive HMI human factors model proposed in this paper to identify additional challenges and opportunities within automotive HMI.

References

1. Gong, Z., Ma, J.: Automotive HMI Evaluation Method. China Machine Press, Beijing (2022)
2. Hewett, Baecker, Card, et al.: ACM SIGCHI Curricula for Human–Computer Interaction. ACM SIGCHI (2014)
3. Ma, J., Gong, Z.: Automotive Human-Machine Interaction (HMI) Evaluation Method. Springer, Singapore (2024)
4. Bubb, H., Bengler, K., Grünen, R.E., Vollrath, M.: Automotive Ergonomics. Springer, Wiesbaden (2021)
5. Choudhary, P.: Mobile phone use during driving: effects on speed reduction and effectiveness of compensatory behaviour. Accid. Anal. Prev. **106**(6), 370–378 (2017)
6. Strayer, D.L., Watson, J.M., Drews, F.A.: Cognitive distraction while multitasking in the automobile. Psychol. Learn. Motiv. – Adv. Res. Theory **54**(54), 29–58 (2011)
7. Young, K.L., Salmon, P.M.: Examining the relationship between driver distraction and driving errors: a discussion of theory, studies and methods. Saf. Sci. **50**(2), 165–174 (2012)
8. Crundall, E., Large, D.R., Burnett, G.: A driving simulator study to explore the effects of text size on the visual demand of in-vehicle displays. Displays **43**, 23–29 (2016)
9. Godfrey, M.D., Hendry, D.F.: The computer as Von Neumann planned it. IEEE Ann. Hist. Comput. **15**(1), 11–21 (1993)
10. Wechsler, D.: The Measurement of Adult Intelligence. Williams & Wilkins Co (1939)
11. Oldenburg, R.: The Great Good Place. Da Capo Press, Boston (1999)

The History of Automotive Human-Machine Interaction: Seven Directions of Evolution

Zaiyan Gong[✉]

HVR Lab, Tongji University, Shanghai 201804, China
gongzaiyan@foxmail.com

Abstract. Automotive Human-Machine Interfaces (HMI) are increasingly crucial in modern vehicles, and understanding their evolution helps clarify past advancements and future directions. This article defines automotive HMI and analyzes its development through a structured review of 154 historical car models. It identifies three major goals—capability, interaction, and intelligence—and outlines seven evolutionary directions including function scope, online resources, ambiance creation, interface folding, interaction types, modality diversity, and intelligent decision-making. These concepts frame the discussion across five distinct phases of automotive HMI development: early phase, budding phase, explosive phase, diverse phase, and AI empowered phase. Concluding with a forward-looking perspective, the article forecasts the integration of AI Generative Content in automotive systems, proposing design recommendations that leverage AI to enhance the adaptiveness and intuitiveness of future automotive interfaces.

Keywords: Automotive HMI · AIGC · Interaction Modality

1 Introduction

Human-machine interaction (HMI) is the study of the design, evaluation, implementation, and other related aspects of interactive machine systems intended for direct use by humans [1]. HMI is applicable to not only computers, cell phones, and automobiles but also various other fields, including household appliances, industrial equipment, and large interactive facilities in public places. Therefore, the definition of HMI involves a certain vagueness. Nevertheless, for only automobiles, we can provide a precise definition to determine what automotive HMI is and what it is not [2].

Vasantharaj discussed modern HMI technologies and practices for automobile, detailing multimodal, multi-touch, and multi-zone systems that are being integrated into modern vehicles [3]. Tan defined automotive HMI as the communication between human and vehicle, mediated by an interface [4]. Bengler discussed a comprehensive HMI framework designed to cater to automated vehicles, analyzing types of HMIs and their influences on interaction within automotive systems. They emphasized the evolving need for interfaces that can manage complex interactions between drivers, vehicles, and external environments as automation increases [5]. Zhang categorized the phases of automotive HMI research into conceptual construction, system and technology refinement, and user perception studies. They highlighted the importance of integrating user feedback and technology advances to enhance interface effectiveness and safety [6].

However, prior research by scholars in the field often regards automotive HMI merely as an area of modern and futuristic technology application. This approach tends to overlook the need for a precise definition of HMI boundaries and lacks a comprehensive account of its evolution. Historically, the development of automotive HMI has been driven by advancements in technology and changing user demands, which necessitate a detailed exploration of these influences over time.

This paper begins by defining the scope and boundaries of automotive HMI, establishing a clear framework for analysis. It then explores the underlying principles and key strategic directions that have guided the planning and implementation of HMI systems in the automotive sector. With this foundation, the paper proceeds to trace the historical development of automotive HMI, examining how technological advancements, regulatory changes, and shifts in consumer expectations have influenced its evolution. Finally, leveraging the insights gained from the historical analysis, the paper offers predictions for the future development of automotive HMIs, highlighting potential technological innovations and market trends that could shape the next generation of user interfaces in vehicles.

2 Definition and Method

2.1 Definition of Automotive HMI

Automotive HMI is a system that enables the transmission of dynamic information and emotions between a human and a vehicle, except for the main driving task [7]. This definition we proposed has precise boundary for research.

Automotive HMI primarily facilitates the transfer of information, such as commands from the user and feedback from the vehicle. For instance, during navigation setup, the driver inputs a destination, selects it from displayed options, and then follows the provided route instructions on the display. When designing specific interactions, the information for each step in this example needs to be clarified in a more detailed manner.

Moreover, emotional interaction is an emerging function within automotive HMI, focusing less on conveying explicit information and more on expressing complex emotions like a sense of luxury or comfort through elements like dynamic ambient lighting and on-screen animations. While traditionally underemphasized, these emotional interactions are becoming increasingly crucial in automotive HMI.

It's important to note that automotive HMI only includes dynamic interactions. Static elements, such as text on a door sill or seat stitching, do not qualify as HMI because they do not involve active communication between the vehicle and its users.

Furthermore, primary driving tasks like the position and size of the steering wheel, the steering feel when driving, the foot feel on the clutch, gas and brake pedals, or the feel of shifting gears in a manual-gearbox vehicle, aren't considered part of HMI. These are integral to the vehicle's mechanical operation and handled by different engineering departments. However, the scope of automotive HMI is becoming wider. For example, interfaces for tasks like gear selection in automatic vehicles, though traditionally not included, are becoming relevant for HMI research when they incorporate innovative control methods, such as touch-based adjustments.

In expanding the scope of HMI, researchers should consider how static elements can be transformed into dynamic interactions. For example, an ambient light strip that adjusts its effects based on navigation cues qualifies as HMI. This broadens the focus beyond traditional buttons and screens to include a wider array of interactive technologies.

2.2 Evolutionary Directions

To understand how automotive HMI evolve, we should understand the evolution directions. And to understand the evolution directions, we should know how the HMI system works.

A typical system structure of a human-machine system is shown as Fig. 1 [8]. In the described HMI system process, the interaction begins with the human receiving a specific task. Upon receiving this task, the human evaluates the situation and makes a judgment on how to interact with the machine. This involves executing specific operations on the machine, such as inputting data or adjusting controls based on the task requirements.

Once the human has interacted with the machine, the machine processes these inputs and produces a result. This result can be a direct output of the task performed, such as a calculation, a physical response from a robotic arm, or any other actionable output depending on the nature of the machine and the task. Simultaneously, the machine provides feedback to the human. This feedback is crucial as it informs the human about the success of the initial interaction or the need for further adjustments. The feedback may come in various forms—visual displays, auditory signals, or even tactile responses—which help guide the human in refining their interactions with the machine or in making decisions for subsequent steps.

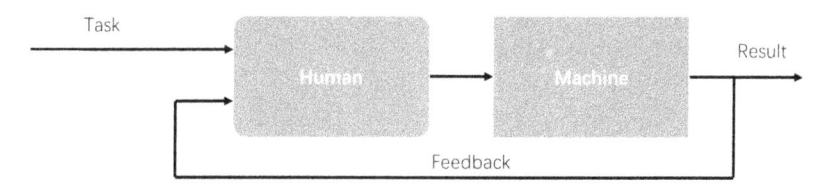

Fig. 1. System structure of a human-machine system.

To continuously evolve an HMI system, three clear strategies emerge. Firstly, the system can be given a richer variety of tasks to handle. This expansion allows the HMI to operate across a broader range of scenarios, enhancing its versatility and applicability. Secondly, enhancing the direct interaction between humans and machines is crucial. Improving this interface involves refining the user interface and feedback mechanisms to make them more intuitive and responsive. Thirdly, the system should generate greater outputs, which are partially based on the intelligence of the machine itself, rather than only on human inputs.

Specifically for automotive HMI, there are three goals in its evolution. The first is to expand the capability of controllable functions within the vehicle, allowing drivers and passengers to interact more comprehensively with their cars. The second goal is to optimize the interaction experience, making it smoother, faster, and more intuitive, thereby reducing cognitive load and enhancing safety. The third is to produce more intelligent outcomes, which means the system should not only react to inputs but also anticipate needs and adjust to contexts automatically, thereby increasing the vehicle's overall intelligence and efficiency.

To identify specific evolutionary directions in automotive HMI, a methodical approach was undertaken by analyzing press release articles from 154 typical car models spanning the years 1998 to 2024. This analysis was facilitated by the use of large language models which helped to sift through the extensive textual data, capturing trends and shifts in HMI features over this 27-year period.

Based on such analytical methods, we have identified seven specific evolutionary directions for automotive HMI, focusing on three main goals: capability, interaction, and intelligence.

Capability:

Function Scope: This involves determining which functions the automotive HMI system can control. It questions whether the system only manages the infotainment system or encompasses broader control over various systems throughout the vehicle, and even extends to remotely controlling external smart systems.

Online Resource: Considering the limitations of local information, which is often not real-time and confined by local processing power, there is a need for access to richer, real-time online information and cloud computing resources.

Ambiance Creation: As previously defined, automotive HMI is not only about conveying information but also emotions. It aims to influence the emotional state of the occupants, making them feel more relaxed or energized, enhancing the overall driving experience.

Interaction:

Interface Folding: Given the limited space inside a vehicle, it's crucial to maximize the functionality of available interfaces. This might involve 'folding' or layering the interface so that the same screen can toggle between climate controls, navigation, and other systems.

Interaction Type: This refers to whether interactions are directive or more natural and intuitive.

Modality Diversity: This concerns whether there are varied modalities of interaction available and if these modalities can seamlessly integrate with each other.

Intelligence:

Intelligent Decision-Making: The system should be capable of proactively offering comprehensive suggestions based on environmental data and personalized needs of the passengers. Alternatively, the system could require simpler inputs from the user because it integrates intelligent inputs from the system itself, thus simplifying user interaction.

These directions highlight the evolving complexity and capability of automotive HMI systems, underlining their pivotal role in enhancing user experience, system efficiency, and overall vehicle functionality.

3 Historical Phases of Automotive HMI

Based on the seven evolutionary directions, we can divide the history of automotive HMI into 5 phases: early phase, budding phase, explosive phase, diverse phase, and AI empowered phase. The key features of each phase are shown in Table 1, and the detailed history will be reviewed in this part.

Table 1. Key features of automotive HMI historical phases

Evolutionary Directions	Early phase	Budding phase	Explosive phase	Diverse phase	AI empowered phase
Function Scope	Low	Mid	Mid	High	High
Online Resource	Low	Low	Low	Mid	High
Ambiance Creation	Low	Low	Low	Mid	High
Interface folding	Low	Mid	Mid	Mid	High
Interaction types	Low	Low	Mid	Mid	High
Modality Diversity	Low	Low	Mid	Mid	High
Intelligent Decision-Making	Low	Low	Low	Mid	High

3.1 Early Phase (1920s – 2000)

Since the 1920s, radios, the first electrical device irrelevant with primary driving tasks, have been installed in automobile cockpits. The early phase of automotive HMI started. At that time, all evolutionary directions are in the low stages.

In 1923, Springfield, an American coachbuilder, and Daimler, a British motor company, were among the first to offer original car radios, which could cost up to 25% of the car's total price. In 1929, the first commercial car radio was the accomplishment of Paul Galvin and the Galvin Manufacturing Corporation. It was the Motorola 5T71, as shown in Fig. 2. Drivers would use knobs to change stations and control volume. By the late 1930s, car radios had evolved to include interactive features, such as preset buttons for favourite channels. Mercedes-Benz introduced its first radio with automatic station search in 1956, the first radio with digital display and stored stations in 1979 (see Fig. 3), and the first CD player in 1985.

The DIN 75490 standard was first published on November 1, 1979. This standard defined the installation space and general requirements for radio communication devices in motor vehicles, setting the groundwork for what would eventually be recognized internationally as the 1DIN size for car radios, and the double size for car radios, CD players or navigations is called 2DIN. In 1984, the DIN standard turned to ISO 7736 standard [9]. The standardization of head units increased the interoperability among car models, but it also means users can only control the head units themselves, rather than the whole car.

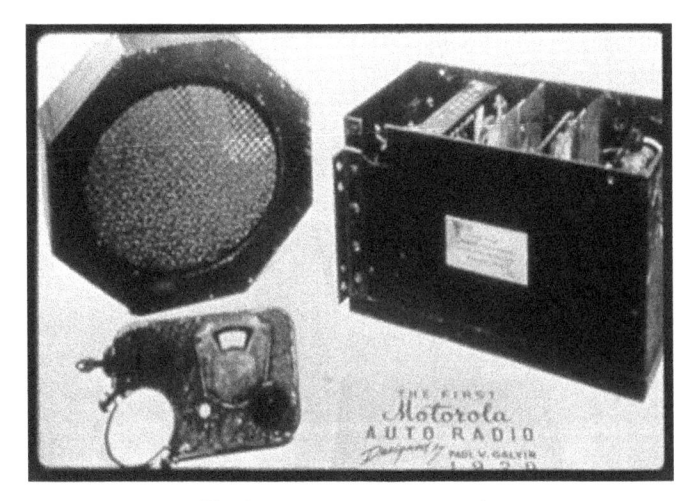

The History of Automotive Human-Machine Interaction   41

Fig. 2. Motorola 5T71 car radio.

Fig. 3. Mercedes-Benz S-Class Series 126 radio with digital display and stored stations.

There were some innovative automotive HMI in that phase. For example, in 1986, General Motors debuted the Buick Riviera with a touch-sensitive central screen, dubbed the "graphic control center," depicted in Fig. 4. This marked the beginning of HMI systems centered around touchscreens, but their popularity was initially limited due to the rudimentary state of electronic and communication technologies at the time.

Thus, although this phase also saw a rise in the integration of various electronic devices into cars, such as in-vehicle telephones and satellite navigation, automotive HMI cannot control powertrains, chassis, and electrical devices. The function scope of the early phase is still regarded as low stage. Besides, there was no interface folding, no digital ambiance, no digital online resource, and single interaction modality – the buttons.

Fig. 4. "Graphic Control Center," the central touchscreen in the Buick Riviera.

3.2 Budding Phase (2001 – 2011)

Automotive HMI entered intelligent era in 2001. From that time, premium car models provided a large central display to control various functions, including car settings. The function scope enlarged from the HMI system itself to the whole vehicle. At the same time, to show much more information, the interface on displays were folded, which means different pages can be shown at different times.

The first generation of BMW's iDrive system, introduced in 2001 on 7 Series, represented a groundbreaking advancement in car interface technology. iDrive was one of the first comprehensive infotainment systems in the automotive industry, designed to control a wide range of vehicle functions with a single interface, reducing the clutter of buttons typically found in luxury vehicles. iDrive was revolutionary in that it integrated the controls for the navigation system, climate control, audio systems, vehicle settings, and other features into one system. This integration was managed through a central console knob, which allowed users to navigate through menus displayed on a dashboard-mounted display screen. The operation of the iDrive system involved a combination of turning, pressing, and tilting the knob to navigate through a series of hierarchical menus. By rotating the knob, users could scroll through options, press down to select, and tilt to move across different menu levels. This allowed drivers to access a multitude of functions without taking their eyes off the road for extended periods, aiming to enhance safety alongside functionality, as shown in Fig. 5.

While iDrive was a pioneer in the car infotainment space, its initial complexity and the steep learning curve associated with its use received mixed reviews from both critics and consumers. However, it set the standard for the developments in automotive HMI systems since then, influencing not only subsequent iterations of iDrive but also the designs of other manufacturers' systems. Audi MMI system and Mercedes-Benz COMAND system launched later can all be seen in the shadow of iDrive's design.

Fig. 5. BMW 7 Series with the first generation of iDrive system.

However, at that time, screens of most car brands were always controlled by buttons or knobs, rather than touch. Thus, interaction types and modality diversity are still in a low stage. The system received GPS data, but little online digital data is available.

3.3 Explosive Phase (2012 – 2018)

Although touchscreens first appeared in some cars during the 1980s, for some decades, automotive HMI touchscreens mainly served as substitutes for physical buttons, offering limited control and interaction mostly through simple taps.

It was not until 2012 that a major innovation occurred with the introduction of the Tesla Model S. The Model S featured a 17-inch central control touchscreen that controlled virtually everything in the car, completely eliminating traditional physical buttons. This touchscreen integrated numerous functions such as climate control, navigation, music, and vehicle settings, centralizing control in a single interface, see Fig. 6. This approach not only enhanced the aesthetic cleanliness of the vehicle's dashboard but also significantly transformed how drivers interacted with their cars, setting new standards for automotive HMI design.

In addition to touchscreen, natural interactions like voice control and gesture control also developed fast in this phase. In 2011, the Ford Sync system, utilizing Nuance voice recognition technology, was capable of understanding more than 10,000 voice commands. This marked a significant evolution in voice control technology, shifting from basic command recognition to a more advanced understanding of natural language. In 2015, BMW introduced the first in-air gesture control on 7 Series. This innovative system allowed drivers to perform certain functions such as adjusting the volume, accepting or rejecting phone calls, and navigating multimedia menus through simple hand gestures.

Fig. 6. Tesla Model S with a 17-inch screen and no physical button.

Fig. 7. Roewe RX5 equipped with the Banma operating system.

This historical phase also witnessed the rise of Chinese automobiles in HMI, and their gradual transformation from followers to leaders. In 2016, SAIC Motor released the Roewe RX5, which was positioned as "the world's first mass-produced Internet-connected vehicle." The Roewe RX5 was equipped with the Banma operating system, which was jointly created by SAIC Motor and Alibaba and enabled maps and entertainment content to be online in real time, as shown in Fig. 7. This system put forward an interaction framework "maps as the desktop". Its voice control system that could comprehend natural language, and it provided users with OTA upgrade services.

In conclusion, during this historical phase, the types of interaction within automotive HMI expanded from traditional, directive interaction such as buttons and touchscreens to include more natural interaction modalities like voice and gesture control. This diversification allowed users to choose from various interaction methods to control specific tasks, significantly enhancing the diversity of interaction modalities. Additionally, online connectivity features became increasingly crucial, supporting services like navigation, voice commands, and OTA updates. However, during this phase, the development of automotive HMI in areas such as ambiance creation and intelligent decision-making was still in its low stages.

3.4 Diverse Phase (2019 – 2023)

In the past five years, automotive HMI has undergone rapid development, particularly in terms of capability.

Capability. The function scope has become more comprehensive, with nearly all systems within a vehicle, even including windows, seats, and windshield wipers, now integrated into centralized HMI systems. Additionally, screens for the front passenger and rear passengers have expanded entertainment options for more vehicle occupants.

Online resources have become indispensable to HMI systems, with in-car audio and video entertainment now largely sourced from online platforms, so many car models have moved away from offering interfaces for CDs and USB drives. Cloud computing enhanced navigation and voice control systems.

Ambiance creation started, because dynamic ambient lighting and scent diffusion systems have been introduced, which can change with the rhythm of the music and create varied atmospheres through different combinations. Moreover, anthropomorphic avatars are being used to enhance the emotional value for users.

More importantly, as the capabilities of automotive HMI expand, the role of the vehicle cabin has also become more diverse. It is no longer just a space for transportation; it has transformed into a shared entertainment space for family members, as well as a venue for meetings and office work.

Interaction. In terms of interaction, automotive HMI has evolved to show greater diversity during this phase, though compared to the previous explosive phase, the advancements have not been sufficient to propel it to the next stage.

As for interaction types, voice interaction has become increasingly powerful and the user experience more natural. However, gesture control has not seen further development.

Regarding interface folding, the concept has expanded beyond the central control screen to include the dashboard display and specialized control screens provided for either the front or rear seats. This expansion indicates a broader application of the folding interface concept, aiming to enhance user accessibility and interface efficiency across different areas of the vehicle's cabin.

Li Auto One introduced in 2018 is an early milestone of the diverse phase. The Li Auto One is a three-row, six-seater SUV that comes equipped with four screens in the front row, one of which is dedicated to providing video and other entertainment resources for the front passenger. The central control screen features an anthropomorphic

Fig. 8. Li Auto One has 4 screens in front row, positioned as a mobile home.

avatar that can display various facial expressions during voice interactions, mimicking human responses, as shown in Fig. 8. Following Li Auto, many car models provided entertainment screens for front passengers or rear passengers, like Xpeng G9, Mercedes-Benz EQS, Audi Q6 e-tron, Volkswagen Tiguan L, etc.

While the Li Auto One may not introduce many groundbreaking technical innovations in its HMI, its concept of a "mobile home" is revolutionary. This approach redefines the vehicle's purpose, emphasizing comfort and utility akin to a living space, which has resonated strongly with consumers in the Chinese market. This strategy highlights a significant shift in automotive design philosophy, focusing on creating a holistic and functional environment that extends beyond mere transportation, aligning with modern lifestyle needs and preferences.

Intelligence. In the realm of intelligent decision-making, automotive HMI has also begun to evolve during this phase. For instance, navigation systems are now capable of suggesting destinations and nearby parking options based on the user's historical travel patterns and current environmental conditions. Additionally, cabin devices are increasingly adapting vehicle settings in real time based on the occupants' conditions. For example, if the system detects that a child is sleeping, it can automatically lower the volume inside the vehicle. these advancements highlight how automotive HMI is moving towards a more context-aware system that not only responds to direct inputs but also anticipates needs and adjusts settings to enhance comfort and convenience for all passengers.

3.5 AI Empowered Phase (2024 – Future)

Some people think that there have been no significant technological innovations in automotive HMI in recent years, leading to a development bottleneck. However, it's important not to overlook the potential profound impact of artificial intelligence (AI) on automotive HMI. Since 2023, AIGC technology, such as ChatGPT, is changing the world, including automotive HMI. Some car models integrated AIGC to improve voice control ability and generate pictures.

Indeed, the automotive cabin is not a place for encyclopedic Q&A or crafting marketing copy. Implementing capabilities like ChatGPT's conversational abilities or Midjourney's image generation directly into automotive HMI might seem flashy but could lack meaningful engagement or user retention. This highlights that the development of AIGC within the automotive cabin depends not only on the capabilities of general AI models but also significantly on applications designed specifically for in-car scenarios.

Therefore, when thinking about how AIGC can empower the future of automotive HMI, it is crucial to consider the 7 evolutionary directions from the 3 goals.

Capability. In terms of capability, AIGC should enhance the utilization of online resources, not only by accessing real-time information but also by leveraging the substantial computational power of cloud computing to expand the potential of AIGC. This approach could enable more dynamic and responsive systems that tailor the driving experience to real-time conditions and user preferences.

Besides, AIGC holds immense potential in the realm of ambiance creation. For instance, it could dynamically generate display wallpapers, ambient lighting effects, and music playlists based on the vehicle's geographic location and the occupants' conditions, enhancing the overall in-car experience. By integrating these intelligent, context-aware systems, automotive HMI can offer a more personalized and enjoyable environment, significantly increasing the value and attractiveness of the vehicle's interactive features.

Interaction. In terms of interaction, expanding the array of natural interaction types—such as gesture recognition, facial recognition, eye tracking, and even brain-computer interfaces—could greatly enhance the diversity of interaction modalities in automotive HMI. Although these technologies have existed previously, they have not been widely adopted in vehicles due to challenges such as difficulty in accurately determining start and end points and recognizing user intentions. However, with the support of advanced AI capabilities, systems can now more accurately and proactively interpret users' intentions.

Besides, these natural interaction modalities can be integrated with existing mainstream interaction modalities like touchscreens and voice commands. For example, if a driver looks towards the right-side mirror, the central control screen could automatically display the adjustment interface for the right-side mirror, allowing the user to make adjustments with a simple touch.

As for interface folding, AI-powered enhancements could lead to significant breakthroughs. Currently, users face many choices on the screen, from which they need to control. With a more powerful AI, the system could more precisely predict a user's needs and present only a few relevant options. For instance, during a long drive, the system could proactively offer to make a reservation at a convenient and affordable restaurant at an upcoming service area, eliminating the need for the driver to browse through complex restaurant interfaces.

Furthermore, with the advancement of AI, an interesting question arises: do we still need large touchscreens when a significant amount of information no longer needs to be displayed directly in front of the user? The BMW Vision Neue Klasse concept car launched in 2024 provides some insights. It features a wide Panoramic HUD along the lower edge of the windshield that displays various types of information through a mirror-like mechanism. This interface is larger and positioned for easier viewing, but it is untouchable due to its distance, as shown in Fig. 9. With AI enhancements, more proactive and richer suggestions and options could be presented on this HUD, reducing the functional burden traditionally carried by the touchscreen control panel. While it's unclear if BMW's design was specifically intended to embrace the AI era, it certainly offers significant inspiration for future developments in automotive HMI.

Fig. 9. BMW Vision Neue Klasse with the Panoramic HUD.

Intelligence. In the current phase where AI is tasked with empowering automotive HMI intelligence, it's crucial to focus on how AI can specifically serve automotive scenarios beyond simple feature migration and sensationalism. Here are five suggestions for effectively integrating AI into automotive HMI.

AI Memory and Understanding: AI should remember and understand user behaviors, habits, and history. For example, if a user specifies a preference for parking at P6 at Hongqiao Airport, the system should automatically set P6 as the destination whenever the user plans a trip to the airport. This eliminates the need to display a variety of parking options, streamlining the decision-making process.

Seamless Application Integration: AI should break down barriers between applications to avoid redundant user inputs. If a user asks about locations, and AIGC provides suggestions, the user should be able to simply say, "Take me to the second one," without having to manually input the destination into the navigation system.

Increased Response Speed: AIGC in automotive contexts must handle dialogues and process information swiftly as the interaction involves complex computations which can be time-consuming. As drivers expect quick responses while driving, the system must be optimized to respond faster. For simple commands like "open the window," they should not require processing through the AIGC system.

Ensuring Accurate Information: It is vital that AI-generated content be accurate and reliable. Misinformation, such as recommending a non-existent restaurant, can lead to significant inconveniences and wasted time, which is particularly critical in driving contexts.

Conciseness and Relevance: When interacting with AI systems in vehicles, users typically seek quick and straightforward answers rather than detailed explanations. For instance, if a user asks about an issue like abnormal tire pressure, the immediate concern is whether it is safe to continue driving and how to get help, rather than an in-depth tutorial on tire pressure.

These guidelines aim to make AI a more effective and integral part of automotive HMI by focusing on practicality, efficiency, and user-centric functionality. By adhering to these principles, AI can enhance the driving experience, ensuring that technology serves as a helpful companion rather than a distracting or misleading element.

4 Conclusion

Automotive HMI is a complex human-machine interaction system. Reviewing its history and exploring the underlying forces of its development can help us understand the past, present, and future of automotive HMI development. This paper starts by providing a clear definition of automotive HMI, which serves as the basis for our exploration of its development trajectory. Then, based on the system structure of a human-machine system and a comprehensive analysis of press releases for 154 historical car models, we propose three major goals and seven evolutionary directions for the development of automotive HMI. Addressing five phases of automotive HMI development, the paper systematically analyzes the changes in these evolutionary directions and details the HMI systems of several typical vehicles in each historical phase. Looking towards the AI era, the paper further makes systematic predictions based on these evolutionary directions and outlines specific design recommendations for the application of AIGC in vehicles.

The analysis in this article focuses on the main thread of evolutionary directions, and thus inevitably overlooks some aspects of automotive HMI history, such as the development of colors and graphics inside screen interfaces. If readers wish to delve deeper and more comprehensively into automotive HMI, this article can serve as a starting point, encouraging further exploration into the various branches of this subject.

References

1. Hewett, Baecker, Card, et al.: ACM SIGCHI Curricula for Human–Computer Interaction. In: ACM SIGCHI (2014)
2. Gong, Z., Ma, J.: Automotive HMI Evaluation Method. China Machine Press, Beijing (2022)
3. Vasantharaj, G.: State of the art technologies in automotive HMI. SAE Technical Paper 2014-01-0258 (2014)
4. Tan, Z., Dai, N., et al.: Human-machine interaction in intelligent and connected vehicles: a review of status Quo, issues, and opportunities. IEEE Trans. Intell. Transp. Syst. **23**(9), 13954–13975 (2022)
5. Bengler, K., Rettenmaier, M., Fritz, N., Feierle, A.: From HMI to HMIs: towards an HMI framework for automated driving. Information **11**(2), 61 (2020)
6. Zhang, X., Liao, X.-P., Tu, J.-C.: A study of bibliometric trends in automotive human-machine interfaces. Sustainability **14**(15), 9262 (2022)
7. Ma, J., Gong, Z.: Automotive Human-Machine Interaction (HMI) Evaluation Method. Springer, Singapore (2024)

8. Bubb, H., Bengler, K., Grünen, R.E., Vollrath, M.: Automotive Ergonomics. Springer, Wiesbaden (2021)
9. ISO 7736:1984. International Organization for Standardization, 15 June 2019

How Do Different HMIs of Autonomous Driving Monitoring Systems Influence the Perceived Safety of Robotaxis Passengers? a Field Study

Yaoqin Gu[1,2], Youyu Sheng[1,3], Yujia Duan[1,2], and Jingyu Zhang[1,2]($\boxtimes$)

[1] CAS Key Laboratory of Behavioral Science, Institute of Psychology, Beijing 100000, China
zhangjingyu@psych.ac.cn
[2] Department of Psychology, University of the Chinese Academy of Sciences, Beijing 100000, China
[3] Thrust of Robotics and Autonomous Systems, The Hong Kong University of Science and Technology (Guangzhou), Guangdong 510000, China

Abstract. Despite their significant potential to transform urban mobility, passengers still harbor safety concerns regarding robotaxis. Effective Human-Machine Interfaces (HMIs) may enhance users' safety perceptions of these systems. Yet, strategies to improve such perceptions are not well-explored. To elucidate how system differences influence passenger perceptions, we conducted a field study involving a comparative analysis of two commercially operated robotaxi systems, System A and System B. Subsequently, we gathered data from passengers of both systems to assess their perceptions of safety. The results indicated that under normal operating conditions, passengers using both systems reported similar levels of safety. However, in the event of incidents, perceived safety significantly declined among passengers who used System B, whereas it remained stable for passengers using System A which provides more explanation on the nature of the incidents. These findings offer crucial insights for operators and provide a valuable resource for future transportation research.

Keywords: Robotaxis · HMIs · Autonomous driving · Perceived safety

1 Introduction

The integration of autonomous driving technology into taxi services has led to the emergence of 'robotaxis'—a term that blends 'robot' and 'taxi' [1]. Robotaxis essentially represent shared autonomous vehicles that leverage the benefits of the sharing economy, cost reduction, and advancements in AI technology to enhance operational automation [2]. Specifically, robotaxis are expected to alleviate traffic congestion by improving road throughput and reducing vehicular accidents through more efficient vehicle operations [1, 3].

Globally, many companies are striving to develop robotaxi technology. Governments around the world have adopted more liberal stances on robotaxis, providing clearer policy directions and increasingly focusing on their performance post-deployment [4]. In

2023, leading domestic autonomous driving technology companies in the United States, Cruise and Waymo, successively obtained operational licenses for all-weather commercial operation of driverless taxis in San Francisco [5]. In order to seize the commanding heights of the development of the autonomous vehicle industry, Until May 2024, seventeen countries around the world have formulated or revised laws and regulations related to autonomous vehicles, aiming to clear legal obstacles for the development of the autonomous vehicle industry [6].As of February 2024, China had issued local policies for autonomous driving tests in 21 cities, including Beijing, Wuhan, Shanghai, Guangzhou, and Shenzhen, with over 60 companies obtaining licenses for these tests [7].

Previous studies revealed significant concerns regarding the safety and security of autonomous vehicles (AVs), which may deter potential users from adopting this technology [8–11]. Perceived safety, crucial in fields such as Human-Robot Interaction (HRI), is defined as the user's perception of the level of danger and their comfort during interactions with AVs [12]. This factor is essential for AV acceptance and influences user interaction and adoption [13, 14]. Additionally, trust has been identified as a major hurdle, closely linked with concerns about safety, security, usability, accessibility, and comfort [9, 15]. Initially, users might perceive the automation system as trustworthy and reliable; however, their trust diminishes when they witness errors. Unless these errors are adequately explained, skepticism towards even reliable behaviors persists [16]. This underscores the need for further research into error management and communication strategies to enhance user trust and perceived safety.

However, as robotaxis near widespread deployment, it becomes critical to address how specific design elements of Human-Machine Interfaces (HMIs) can influence these perceptions. Moreover, the effectiveness of feedback designs in enhancing perceived safety may have been overlooked [17, 18]. By analyzing the products currently on the market, we identified two mainstream types of Human-Machine Interface (HMI) systems employed in robotaxis (see Figs. 1, 2 and 3 for details). In summary, System A provides detailed textual prompts for both safety officers and passengers, offering comprehensive situational awareness that likely enhances user trust and confidence by clearly explaining vehicle behaviors and road conditions. This approach is particularly beneficial in scenarios where understanding the context of vehicle operations is crucial for user reassurance. Conversely, System B employs a minimalist design that focuses primarily on the vehicle's current operational status without detailed contextual information, which might appeal to users who prefer simplicity and a less cluttered interface. However, this design may not meet the needs of users who require detailed explanations to feel safe, especially during complex or unexpected driving situations.

Providing information about how and why a vehicle behaves in a certain way is critical to gaining trust and safety in autonomous driving [19, 20]. Previous research has shown that, despite increased cognitive load, a full awareness of the vehicle's surroundings can help reduce the stressful experience. Furthermore, users who interacted with more information-rich interfaces showed greater willingness to test true self-driving systems [21]. To further explore the relationship between Human-Machine Interfaces (HMIs and perceived safety, and to identify which HMIs positively influence perceived safety, we conducted a field experiment.

This experiment involved collecting firsthand data from users who had experienced either of the two HMIs of robotaxis through field surveys. The study specifically compared the users' perception toward the systems when the incidents occurred. We hypothesized that System A, which offers more detailed information, would positively impact perceived safety more than System B when incidents occurred. By analyzing feedback from participants, this research aims to explore the effect of different HMIs on perceived safety in specific contexts, thereby contributing to a deeper understanding of how interface design can enhance user's perceived safety in autonomous transportation.

2 Literature Review

Psychological factors, rather than technological ones, are the primary obstacles to the adoption of autonomous vehicles (AVs), with trust being perhaps the most crucial barrier [22]. Another factor impacting the intention to use public transport is perceived safety, within the context of Astha perception of safety becomes even more critical due to the heightened concerns associated with this technology [23].The literature on Human-Robot Interaction (HRI) employs various terms to describe safety perception, including psychological safety (26,27), sense of safety and security (28), perceived safety (29), mental safety (30), and sense of security (31,32). Research emphasizes that predictable and expectation-aligned robot behaviors, which enhance perceived safety, are critical for integrating AVs into daily transportation systems, highlighting its importance for the successful adoption of these technologies [12–14].

Driverless autonomous vehicles (AVs; SAE levels 4 and 5 [29]) hold the potential to transform our mobility systems significantly. Therefore, enhancing user acceptance of autonomous driving technology represents a critical challenge. In this regard, research focused on Human-Machine Interfaces (HMI) in AVs can provide substantial insights and contributions. In the context of autonomous driving, the term Human-Machine Interface (HMI) is defined as the mechanism through which information is exchanged between a human agent and the vehicle's artificial intelligence system, typically through a user interface or dashboard [30], to facilitate human-computer collaboration [31].

In recent years, researchers and engineers have enhanced these interfaces to improve the flexibility of interaction between drivers and vehicles. With SAE levels between 1 and 3 (partial automation), the in-vehicle interaction grounds the seamless transfer and sharing of vehicle control between the human driver and the artificial intelligence to reduce the cognitive load and improve driving safety [17, 32]. With SAE levels between 4 and 5 (advanced automation), where all the driving subtasks (lateral and longitudinal vehicle motion control, and Object Event Detection & Response (OEDR)) fall to the autonomous driving system. In any of these scenarios, the transparency of the information conveyed by the automated system to the users in the car is essential [18] to gain trust.

To address the numerous issues stemming from insufficient transparency, methods that autonomously provide explanations of predictions and decisions to users have gained prominence, leading to the emergence of Explainable Artificial Intelligence (XAI) [33]. In this context, AI planning and scheduling are critical as they determine the sequence of actions an agent must perform to accomplish tasks, significantly influencing real-time decisions in dynamic environments [34]. This capability is particularly crucial for autonomous vehicles (AVs) that navigate through complex and unpredictable urban settings. Traffic conditions and road infrastructure are subject to frequent changes, necessitating that AVs regularly update their plans and adapt accordingly. AVs process a vast amount of data, exceeding human capabilities, which can lead to passenger confusion if the vehicle alters its course without a clear explanation. Therefore, explainable planning plays a vital role in helping users understand and trust the decision-making processes of AVs in these scenarios [35]. Additionally, providing "why" information is crucial to reassure users of the system's competence and to foster trust and situational awareness [36, 37].

3 Methodology

3.1 Participants

In this study, we collected 94 questionnaires, including 47 users who experienced System A and 47 users experienced system B in the past few days. The sample included 49 males (52.13%) and 45 females (47.87%), with an average age of 25.62 years (SD = 3.72). Educational backgrounds varied: 33 individuals (35.11%) held a postgraduate degree or higher, 49 (52.13%) had a bachelor's degree, and 12 (12.77%) possessed an associate degree or lower. All participants volunteered for the experiment and received a reward of 10 yuan upon completion.

3.2 Two Difference HMIs (System A and System B)

The two HMIs of the two brands of robotaxis were different in several terms. Figure 1 shows the interior view from a passenger's perspective, displaying the passenger interaction screens and safety officer interaction screens for both HMIs.

Fig. 1. The interior view from a robotaxis passenger's perspective

As shown in Fig. 2, from the passenger's HMIs at the intersection, the map displays from two systems reveal notable differences. System A offers an overhead view, allowing passengers to see the upcoming road and current traffic conditions on that road and its surrounding areas, while buildings on either side are dynamically represented with dot diagrams. Additionally, System A provides comprehensive auditory and textual prompts for actions such as lane changes and displays the speed of surrounding vehicles in meters per second. When the vehicle stops, a red line appears to indicate the vehicle is not in motion. A blue line indicates the distance to potential hazards ahead, contributing to the high understandability of the interface. The interface uses color-coded models of surrounding vehicles—red, yellow, and green—to represent varying levels of threat to the vehicle. In contrast, System B, despite providing a 3D map, only provide a proportional representation of the surrounding environment and architecture. In displaying the surrounding vehicles, System B used a simple green frame and does not display the operational processes of the system. This lack of detailed contextual information may affect the user's ability to fully comprehend the vehicle's status and the environment.

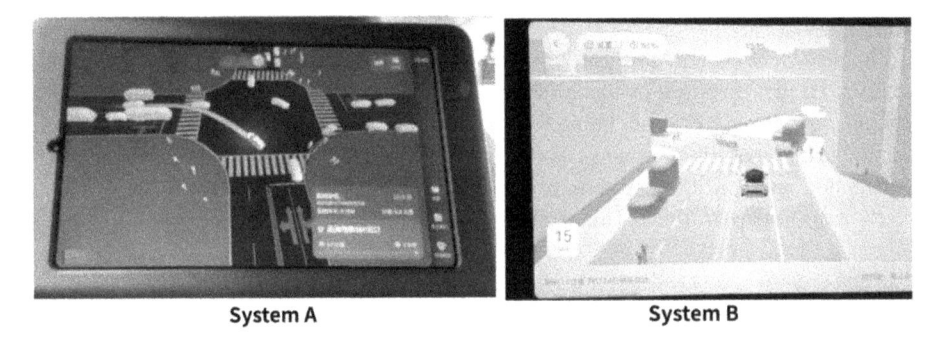

Fig. 2. Passenger HMIs display at intersection.

In abnormal conditions, System A would explain its actions in both the safety officer's interface and provided the in-car voice announcements such as "Swerving left to avoid, unable to connect across the line". On the other hand, System B only provides very limited information. No information would display on the safety officers' screen and the passenger's HMI interface only displays a text message "Securing safety". The lack of explanatory feedback in System B may leave passengers feeling less informed and potentially more concerned about their safety during such interventions.

In summary, whether in terms of map route displays or feedback experiences following incidents, System A surpasses System B in terms of interface understandability and explainability. Based on these observations, we hypothesize that passengers using System A will exhibit better performance in trust and safety perception compared to those using System B. To validate this hypothesis, further collection and analysis of actual passenger experiences and feedback data are required.

3.3 Measurement

The perception of the safety. A 7-point scale measured the perception of the safety, including three items such as "I can perceive the changes in the system after each update." (1: completely disagree-10: completely agree) [38].

System A	System B
Safety officer interaction screens	Passenger interaction screens
Text prompts road conditions and explanations	Text prompts vehicle control status

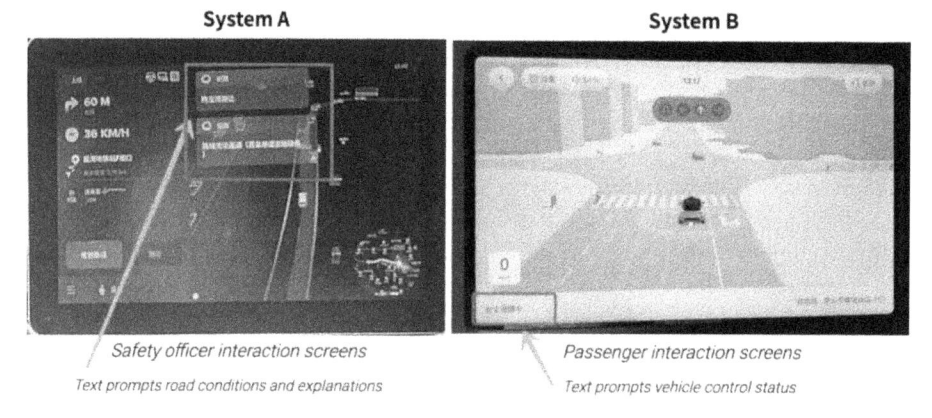

Fig. 3. Post-accident feedback comparison chart

Incident occurrence. The participants were required to mention any incident they experienced that is caused by the failure of the robotaxi. Specific issues included sudden braking, sudden acceleration, being too close to the vehicle in front, sudden changes in planned route, inability to change lanes, frequent lane changes, sudden disengagement of the autonomous driving system, or any other problems.

Demographic variables. This included age, gender, education background.

3.4 Procedure

This survey was conducted via one of the largest Chinese online survey platforms, Wenjuanxing(https://www.wjx.cn/). A link was disseminated through social networks and the Wenjuanxing platform itself. Respondents from different age groups and education levels were included in the sample. To control survey quality, a rule was set that people with the same IP address and username could access the link only once. Additionally, if the answer time was less than 5 min, the questionnaire was considered invalid. Moreover, several attention-check questions were included in the survey to identify whether a respondent was answering the survey carelessly. To make sure respondents have ridden in a robot taxi, everyone needs to upload screenshots of taxi rides at the beginning of the questionnaire. All survey questions were presented in Chinese. A total of 158 questionnaires were received, and 94 were validated to be satisfied.

4 Results

Two-way analysis of covariance (ANCOVA) was conducted to explore effect by controlling the factor of vehicle safety officer location. Our results indicate a significant interaction between system type and the occurrence of incident (F (1,89) = 8.14, p = 0.005, η_p^2 = .07, see Fig. 1). When no incidents occurred, passengers using the two systems reported similar level of safety. However, when an incident occurs, we witnessed a sharp drop on the perceived safety of passengers who experienced system B (F = 15.66, p 0 < .001), but not for those who experienced system A (F = 0.02, p = 0.88) (Fig. 4).

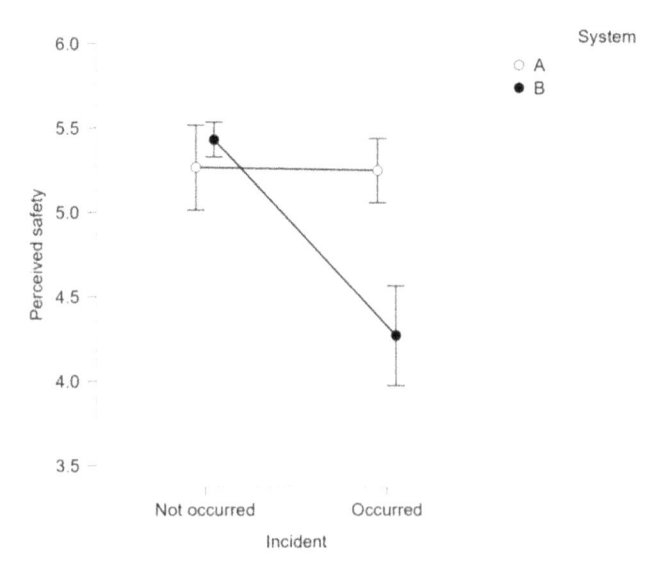

Fig. 4. The joint effect of system type and incident occurrence on perceived safety.

Further simple effect analysis found that, when an incident occurred, the perceived safety of passengers who experienced system A (M = 5.22, SD = 0.79) was significantly higher than that of system B (M = 4.32, SD = 1.35), t (36) = 2.60, p < 0.01, 95%CI = [0.19, 1.60]. However, when no incidents occurred, the perceived safety of passengers who experienced system B (M = 5.52, SD = 0.75) was higher than those in the perceived safety of system A (M = 5.16, SD = 0.99), t(54) = 1.55, p = 1.60.

5 Discussion

This study embarked on a field study to examine the effects of two human-machine interaction (HMI) designs in two commercially operating robotaxis. Among the two systems, system A provides passengers with a real-time god-view to show the vehicle's status and the surroundings. It also provides prompt explanations on the causes of any sudden events. On the other hand, system B provides less information.

Targeting individuals with experience in using robotaxis, we collected data from 47 passengers who experienced system A and 47 passengers who experienced system B. They were asked to provide their responses on their demographic information, perceived safety, vehicle safety officer location and whether they have experienced any incidents during the tour.

When no incidents occurred, passengers using the two systems reported similar level of safety. However, when an incident occurs, we witnessed a sharp drop on the perceived safety of passengers who experienced system B, but not for those who experienced system A.

This significant disparity highlights the crucial role of interaction design in robotaxis, especially during non-normative events. It appears that the assurance of a vehicle's state, conveyed through ongoing feedback, acts as a reassuring presence for passengers.

The maintenance of safety perception in the face of adverse conditions speaks to the ability of well-designed interaction interfaces to impart a sense of control and situational awareness, which is indispensable during moments of potential distress.

The implications of these findings extend beyond academic discourse into the practical realms of autonomous vehicle design and public policy. They suggest that for robotaxis to gain widespread acceptance, the design of interaction interfaces must prioritize not only the transmission of information but also the maintenance of passenger confidence during all phases of operation. Manufacturers and service providers should take heed of the need for interfaces that deliver continuous reassurance to passengers, thereby fostering an environment of trust and safety.

While we have provided an analysis of key findings and strategies for effective Human-Machine Interface (HMI) designs, our study's implications must consider two main limitations. Firstly, the limited sample size restricts the generalizability of our findings. To address this, future studies should aim to include a larger cohort or employ robust statistical methods to strengthen the validity of the results. Secondly, due to the nature of our field study, the HMIs were not uniformly controlled across different vehicles, which might affect the consistency of our data. Future research should standardize HMI settings or account for variations in HMI configurations in their analyses. Additionally, while we suggest employing controlled laboratory experiments using methods like the 'Wizard of Oz' to simulate and control experimental conditions, it is crucial to clarify the theoretical rationale and anticipated benefits of such methodologies in enhancing data reliability and better simulating user interactions with autonomous systems.

6 Conclusion

In conclusion, while autonomous driving is indeed the future, the journey there will be paved not only with advanced algorithms and sensors but also with the confidence and trust of the passengers who will use these services. Our study underscores the necessity for interaction interfaces that communicate not just data, but also security and reliability, particularly in times of unexpected trials on the road. It is these factors that will ultimately determine the successful integration of robotaxis into the fabric of daily transportation.

Funding. This Study Was Supported by Natural Science Fundation of China (T2192932, U2133209, 52072406), the Fundamental Research Funds of CAST (X242060302218) and the Key Project of Chongqing Technology Innovation and Application Development (Grant no. Cstc2021jscx-DxwtBX0020).

References

1. De Freitas, J., Censi, A., Smith, B.W., Di Lillo, L., Anthony, S.E., Frazzoli, E.: From driverless dilemmas to more practical commonsense tests for automated vehicles. Proc. Natl. Acad. Sci. U.S.A. **118**, e2010202118 (2021)
2. Merfeld, K., Wilhelms, M.P., Henkel, S., Kreutzer, K.: Carsharing with shared autonomous vehicles: uncovering drivers, barriers and future developments–a four-stage Delphi study. Technol. Forecast. Soc. Chang. **144**, 66–81 (2019)

3. Gogoll, J., Müller, J.F.: Autonomous cars: In favor of a mandatory ethics setting. Sci. Eng. Ethics **23**, 681–700 (2017)
4. Yun, Z., Zhao, W., Hua, J., Lei, S.: Trends in the commercialization of autonomous taxis (Robotaxi): Diverse co-progress, catalyzing new developments (2023). https://www.rolandberger.com/
5. CPUC approves permits for Cruise and Waymo to charge fares for passenger service in San Francisco. https://www.cpuc.ca.gov/news-and-updates/all-news/cpuc-approves-permits-for-cruise-and-waymo-to-charge-fares-for-passenger-service-in-sf-2023. Accessed 10 Apr 2024
6. Let self-driving cars enter the "fast lane" of the rule of law. https://www.szzg.gov.cn/2024/xwzx/szkx/202405/t20240510_4822001.html. Accessed 21 May 2024
7. "LuoboKuaipao" self-driving car travels across the river. https://www.hubei.gov.cn/hbfb/rdgz/202402/t20240228_5099301.shtml. Accessed 10 Apr 2024
8. Ahangar, M.N., Ahmed, Q.Z., Khan, F.A., Hafeez, M.: A survey of autonomous vehicles: enabling communication technologies and challenges. Sensors (Switzerland) **21**(3), 1–33 (2021). MDPI AG
9. Kaur, K., Rampersad, G.: Trust in driverless cars: Investigating key factors influencing the adoption of driverless cars. J. Eng. Technol. Manag. **48**, 87–96 (2018)
10. Panagiotopoulos, I., Dimitrakopoulos, G.: An empirical investigation on consumers' intentions towards autonomous driving. Transp. Res. Part C Emerg. Technol. **95**, 773–784 (2018)
11. Xu, Z., Zhang, K., Min, H., Wang, Z., Zhao, X., Liu, P.: What drives people to accept automated vehicles? findings from a field experiment. Transp. Res. Part C Emerg. Technol. **95**, 320–334 (2018)
12. Bartneck, C., Kulić, D., Croft, E., Zoghbi, S.: Measurement instruments for the anthropomorphism, animacy, likeability, perceived intelligence, and perceived safety of robots. Int. J. Soc. Robot. **1**(1), 71–81 (2009)
13. Lasota, P.A., Fong, T., Shah, J.A., et al.: A Survey of Methods for Safe Human-Robot Interaction. Now Publishers (2017)
14. Lichtenthäler, C., Lorenzy, T., Kirsch, A.: Influence of legibility on perceived safety in a virtual human-robot path crossing task. In: 2012 IEEE RO-MAN: The 21st IEEE International Symposium on Robot and Human Interactive Communication, pp. 676–681. IEEE (2012)
15. Pigeon, C., Alauzet, A., Paire-Ficout, L.: Factors of acceptability, acceptance and usage for non-rail autonomous public transport vehicles: a systematic literature review. Transp. Res. Part F Traffic Psychol. Behav. **81**, 251–270 (2021)
16. Dzindolet, M.T., Peterson, S.A., Pomranky, R.A., Pierce, L.G., Beck, H.P.: The role of trust in automation reliance. Int. J. Hum. Comput. Stud. **58**(6), 697–718 (2003)
17. Venkatesh, V., Brown, S.A., Bala, H.: Bridging the qualitative-quantitative divide: guidelines for conducting mixed methods research in information systems. MIS Q. **37**(1), 21–54 (2013)
18. Wu, P.F.: A mixed methods approach to technology acceptance research. J. Assoc. Inf. Syst. **13**(13), 172–187 (2012)
19. Jose, R., Lee, G.A., Billinghurst, M.: A comparative study of simulated augmented reality displays for vehicle navigation. In: Proceedings of the 28th Australian Conference on Computer-Human Interaction, ser. OzCHI 2016. New York, NY, USA, pp. 40–48. ACM (2016)
20. Lungaro, P., Tollmar, K., Beelen, T.: Human-to-AI interfaces for enabling future onboard experiences. In: Proceedings of the 9th International Conference on Automotive User Interfaces and Interactive Vehicular Applications Adjunct, ser. AutomotiveUI 2017, New York, NY,USA, pp. 94–98 (2017)
21. Morra, L., Lamberti, F., Pratticó, F.G., La Rosa, S., Montuschi, P.: Building trust in autonomous vehicles: role of virtual reality driving simulators in HMI design. IEEE Trans. Veh. Technol. **68**(10), 9438–9450 (2019)

22. Dillon, A., Morris, M.G.: User acceptance of information technology: theories and models. Annu. Rev. Inf. Sci. **14**(4), 3–32 (1996)
23. Delbosc, A., Currie, G.: Modelling the causes and impacts of personal safety perceptions on public transport ridership. Transp. Policy **24**, 302–309 (2012)
24. Kamide, H., Mae, Y., Kawabe, K., Shigemi, S., Hirose, M., Arai, T.: New measurement of psychological safety for humanoid. In: 2012 7th ACM/IEEE International Conference on Human-Robot Interaction (HRI), pp. 49–56. IEEE (2012)
25. Akalin, N., Kristoffersson, A., Loutfi, A.: Evaluating the sense of safety and security in human–robot interaction with older people. In: Social Robots: Technological, Societal and Ethical Aspects of Human-Robot Interaction, pp. 237–264. Springer
26. Matsas, E., Vosniakos, G.-C.: Design of a virtual reality training system for human–robot collaboration in manufacturing tasks. Int. J. Interact. Des. Manufact. (IJIDeM) **11**(2), 139–153 (2017)
27. Nonaka, S., Inoue, K., Arai, T., Mae, Y.: Evaluation of human sense of security for coexisting robots using virtual reality. 1st report: evaluation of pick and place motion of humanoid robots. In: IEEE International Conference on Robotics and Automation, 2004. Proceedings. ICRA 2004, vol. 3, pp. 2770–2775. IEEE (2004)
28. Nyholm, L., Santamäki-Fischer, R., Fagerström, L.: Users ambivalent sense of security with humanoid robots in healthcare. Inform. Health Soc. Care 1–9 (2021)
29. SAE International; ISO: J3016: Surface Vehicle Recommended Practice: Taxonomy and Definitions for Terms Related to Driving Automation Systems for On-Road Motor Vehicles; SAE International: Warrendale. PA, USA (2021)
30. Bischoff, S., Ulrich, C., Dangelmaier, M., Widlroither, H., Diederichs, F. (n.d.): Emotion Recognition in User-Centered Design for Automotive Interior and Automated Driving
31. Bevan, N., Carter, J., Earthy, J., Geis, T., Harker, S.: New ISO standards for usability, usability reports and usability measures. Lect. Notes Comput. Sci. (Including Subseries Lecture Notes in Artificial Intelligence and Lecture Notes in Bioinformatics) **9731**, 268–278 (2016)
32. Wu, J., Liao, H., Wang, J.W., Chen, T.: The role of environmental concern in the public acceptance of autonomous electric vehicles: a survey from China. Transp. Res. Part F Traffic Psychol. Behav. **60**, 37–46 (2019)
33. Burkart, N., Huber, M.F.: A survey on the explainability of supervised machine learning. J. Artif. Intell. Res. **70**, 245–317 (2021)
34. Mohseni, S., Zarei, N., Ragan, E.D.: A multidisciplinary survey and framework for design and evaluation of explainable AI systems. ACM Trans. Interact. Intell. Syst. (TiiS), **11**(3–4), 1–45 (2021)
35. Van Brummelen, J., O'Brien, M., Gruyer, D., Najjaran, H.: Autonomous vehicle perception: the technology of today and tomorrow. Transp. Res. Part C Emerg. Technol. **89**, 384–406 (2018)
36. Koo, J., Kwac, J., Ju, W., Steinert, M., Leifer, L., Nass, C.: Why did my car just do that? explaining semi-autonomous driving actions to improve driver understanding, trust, and performance. Int. J. Interact. Des. Manuf. **9**(4), 269–275 (2015)
37. Ekman, F., Johansson, M., Sochor, J.: Creating appropriate trust in automated vehicle systems: a framework for HMI design. IEEE Trans. Hum-Mach. Syst. **48**(1), 95–101 (2018)
38. Cao, J., Lin, L., Zhang, J., Zhang, L., Wang, Y., Wang, J.: The development and validation of the perceived safety of intelligent connected vehicles scale. Accid. Anal. Prev. **154**, 106092 (2021)

Better Together: 3D Anthropomorphic Assistant Avatars and Empathetic Voice Interventions on Emotion Regulation

Bofei Huang[1(✉)], Xinyue Gui[2], Chia-Ming Chang[2], and Haoran Xie[1]

[1] Japan Advanced Institute of Science and Technology, Ishikawa, Japan
s2310050@jaist.ac.jp
[2] The University of Tokyo, Tokyo, Japan

Abstract. Despite advancements in driver-assisted systems, human emotions significantly influence driving safety and behavior. Previous research has highlighted the impact of emotions like anger and anxiety on driving, suggesting the need for effective emotional regulation strategies. Our approach leverages the visually engaging 3D assistant avatars and the calming effect of empathetic voice cues to enhance the driver's emotional state, particularly in stressful scenarios such as traffic jams, encounters with uncivil driving behavior, and sudden pedestrian crossings. A video-based user study was conducted with 16 participants to evaluate the effectiveness of this combined approach. The study compared the proposed method against the baseline of empathetic voice alone across three specific driving situations. Using the Augmented Video testing platform, participants experienced simulated driving scenarios, followed by interventions from either the proposed or baseline method. Results from a two-item, 5-point Likert scale questionnaire indicate a preference for the combined method, highlighting its potential to improve driving safety and promote a more civilized driving experience. This research contributes to developing in-vehicle emotional regulation systems, offering significant insights into managing driver emotions to enhance overall road safety.

Keywords: Automotive Interface · Emotional Regulation · Empathic Voice Interventions · Assistant Avatars

1 Introduction

Driving is still tricky despite advances in Advanced Driver Assistance Systems (ADAS). Human behavior is the primary cause of accidents while driving. Recently, the role of emotions while driving has gained attention [13,16]. Emotional states such as anger, fear, depression, embarrassment, and urgency can significantly impact driving behavior [18]. Developing approaches to reduce drivers' negative emotions in specific driving conditions is essential. Considering emotional factors, providing advice and support in particular driving scenarios is crucial to ensure safety and a pleasant driving experience.

Emotional regulation has been explored during driving due to various driving scenarios that can trigger sudden emotions, potentially leading to dangerous and aggressive driving behaviors. Compared with the visual cues, ambient lighting, empathetic voice, and assistant voice, the compassionate voice was verified to be the most effective [5]. 3D anthropomorphic assistant avatars were adapted to a traditional voice assistant and placed on the steering wheel, improving users' perceptions of the car's drivability and safety [9].

However, most studies on 3D anthropomorphic assistant avatars have focused on users' trust while driving. These studies typically examine daily driving scenarios under positive emotions, such as overtaking and braking assistance during regular driving [22]. There is little research on how these avatars perform in specific driving situations, such as traffic jams, managing uncivil driving by others, and handling sudden incidents like a pedestrian running across the road. Moreover, the impact and role of driver emotional swings on the avatar's effectiveness have not been thoroughly explored.

Therefore, we propose a method that combines the 3D anthropomorphic assistant avatars with the empathic voice. This method uses 3D anthropomorphic assistant avatars to strengthen users' trust and an empathic voice to calm emotions. By visually and audibly calming users' negative emotions during special driving situations, we can improve driving safety and promote a more civilized driving experience.

In this research, we conducted a video-based user study (N = 16). To calm user emotions, we used 3D anthropomorphic assistant avatars with empathetic voice interventions in specific driving scenarios. We compared the effectiveness of our approach with the most effective method from previous research [5], which was empathetic voice intervention as a baseline in this study, to evaluate the impact of 3D anthropomorphic assistant avatars in specific situations (see Fig. 1):

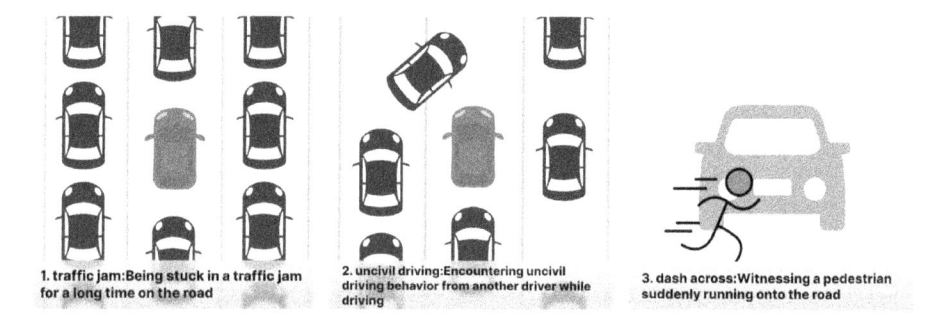

Fig. 1. Common scenarios in daily driving.

The study investigates the effectiveness and acceptability of the proposed methods and the baseline for providing emotional calm in our three scenarios. Valuable insights for developing in-vehicle emotional regulation systems are expected to be gained from these investigations. The main contributions of this work are listed as follows:

1) A video-based user study compared the driving emotion regulation system of a 3D anthropomorphic assistant avatar with an empathetic voice to a system with only an empathetic voice.
2) A detailed analysis of the effectiveness of driving emotion regulation under different negative emotions such as anxiety, anger, and panic among participants.

2 Related Work

2.1 Affective Interfaces

As the introduction states, emotions significantly impact user behavior and cognitive processes, particularly in driving scenarios where emotional triggers occur frequently [21]. The in-car interface plays a crucial role in influencing these emotional triggers. When the interface is unintelligent and lacks proper guidance, it can cause drivers to experience stress and frustration [24].

Braun et al.'s study explored how people in China and Germany feel about vehicle affective interfaces. [4] The study found that despite cultural differences, vehicles have a high demand for affective interfaces, as users believe that emotional awareness can improve their driving experience. For example, emotional navigation routes can enhance travel quality and mood.

Other researchers have also attempted to identify users' emotions through affective interfaces to provide better services and support. Silvia et al.'s study [6] aims to explore the development of an emotion-aware car interface that can detect the driver's emotional and cognitive states through facial expression analysis. Liu et al. [11] explore an emotion inference method based on the vehicle's Control Area Network (CAN-bus) and front-view camera data. It analyzes driver behavior and traffic context to enhance driving safety and comfort. Using these data streams allows for compelling emotional inference of the driver without infringing on privacy.

2.2 Emotion Regulation

Emotional regulation has become crucial in Human-Computer Interaction (HCI) with the development of emotion recognition technology. Given the significant impact of drivers' emotional states on road safety, several researchers have investigated techniques and effects of emotional regulation and intervention while driving. Paredes and Xin [15,25] have guided users through mindfulness and calming breathing exercises, helping them relax effectively. However, both methods have been facilitated through physical interaction and haven't yet explored more diverse scenarios that could trigger users' stress and frustration within a simulated setting.

Additionally, Various methods detect and regulate driver emotions, improving safety and acceptance of manual and autonomous driving. Studies show these methods can identify emotions such as frustration, aggression, fear, and joy. Appropriate measures like voice systems, music, or seat massage can counteract frustration and aggression in manual driving. In autonomous driving, cognitive and emotional regulation, relaxing movies, and music can assist anxious drivers [3].

2.3 Empathetic Assistant

Empathy is a traditional psychological concept that involves expressing experienced emotions and allows for rapid understanding of the target's emotional state. Moreover, the empathic response generated through empathy can effectively control and influence the other person's emotions and emotional experiences [7]. This ability is widely used in human-computer interaction, becoming a way to enhance user experience and even a method of user interaction [10]. The empathetic assistant in vehicles is a product developed in this background.

Anyasodo et al. [2]'s study explores how to design more human-like natural language interfaces for future vehicles by integrating empathy strategies from human-human interactions. Findings include adapting behavior and being aware of emotional context. However, practical implementations require rigorous testing to ensure effectiveness and user acceptance.

At the same time, some researchers try to make empathetic assistance come true. Okamoto and Sano's [14] study creates a humanoid AI agent called Yui to improve human-vehicle interaction and trust. Multimodal interaction tech captures driver emotions and intentions in real time. Yui enhances user experience and driving safety. Further testing is required to verify its effectiveness and user acceptance.

3 Method

3.1 Research Question and Hypotheses

As stated in the introduction, although visual assistance is commonly perceived as potentially distracting while driving, ambient lighting, HUDs, and other visual modalities have been shown to assist drivers effectively. Additionally, 3D anthropomorphic assistant avatars have significantly enhanced drivers' trust in the driving process. However, current research needs to explore the role of visuals in emotional regulation during driving, or the findings have been negative. Empathetic voice assistance has been recognized as effective in regulating emotions. As a branch of affective computing, it has also gained considerable popularity in Human-Computer Interaction (HCI). So, the research question is: **Can combining visual assistance with empathetic voice effectively reduce drivers' negative emotional responses to unexpected road events?**

So, we have the following hypotheses:

1. The proposed system is more effective than single empathetic voice assistance in reducing drivers' negative emotional responses to unexpected road events.

The proposed system enhances users' trust and strengthens the empathetic voice by effectively combining anthropomorphic assistant avatars with an empathetic voice's emotional regulation capabilities. Furthermore, this integration endows the empathetic voice with a tangible form, enhancing the vehicle's anthropomorphic characteristics and making the user perceive not just a mechanical assistive system but an emotionally interactive partner. Such a design strengthens emotional connections and significantly enhances the overall user experience by providing a more natural and intuitive interaction method. The system can more effectively guide users' emotions through dual stimulation of visual and auditory cues, particularly in stressful driving situations, helping them remain calm and focused.

3.2 Method

To verify our research hypothesis, we used an augmented video comparison approach to evaluate the proposed method. We selected several common negative emotions encountered during daily driving and designed corresponding scenarios for testing (see Fig. 2). The specific scenarios are as follows:

1. Being stuck in a traffic jam for a long time on the road with honking sounds (Fig. 3).
2. Encountering uncivil driving behavior from another driver while driving (Fig. 4).
3. Witnessing a pedestrian suddenly running onto the road, requiring emergency braking (Fig. 5).

These three situations represent negative emotions of anxiety, anger, and panic.

(a) scenario1 + baseline   (b) scenario1 + proposed

Fig. 2. The proposed interface and baseline in scenarios.

Fig. 3. Scenario 1: Being stuck in a traffic jam for a long time on the road.

Fig. 4. Scenario 2: Encountering uncivil driving behavior from another driver while driving.

Fig. 5. Scenario 3: Witnessing a pedestrian suddenly running onto the road.

We created the videos using real-life footage captured by online car cameras to capture more authentic participant reactions. After each video, we asked participants about their subjective satisfaction and the method's effectiveness. After all video tasks were finished, we interviewed participants about their overall impression of the two methods based on their driving experience.

3.3 Proposed System

Regarding the 3D anthropomorphic assistant avatars, we followed the previous work [5] to create a 3D anthropomorphic assistant with human-like behaviors. The appearance design features an anthropomorphic facial style with a medium level of realism and resolution to avoid the uncanny valley effect [12]. Additionally, a female agent was created based on the work [5], as gender positively contributes to the perception of anthropomorphism. Facial expressions were also included to build trusting relationships [23].

Our research primarily uses augmented videos in which all interactions between the 3D anthropomorphic assistant avatars and the empathetic voice are pre-recorded. We use Animaze [1] for facial motion capture. The videos start with our recorded 3D anthropomorphic assistant avatars displaying anthropomorphic behaviors such as gazing at the driver and making subtle facial movements like blinking and smiling. This helps establish a rapport with the user, creating a foundation of trust and ease. During critical moments in the video, such as unexpected driving events or when the video reaches 10 s, the avatars display tailored empathetic reactions, such as expressions of concern or surprise (see Fig. 6).

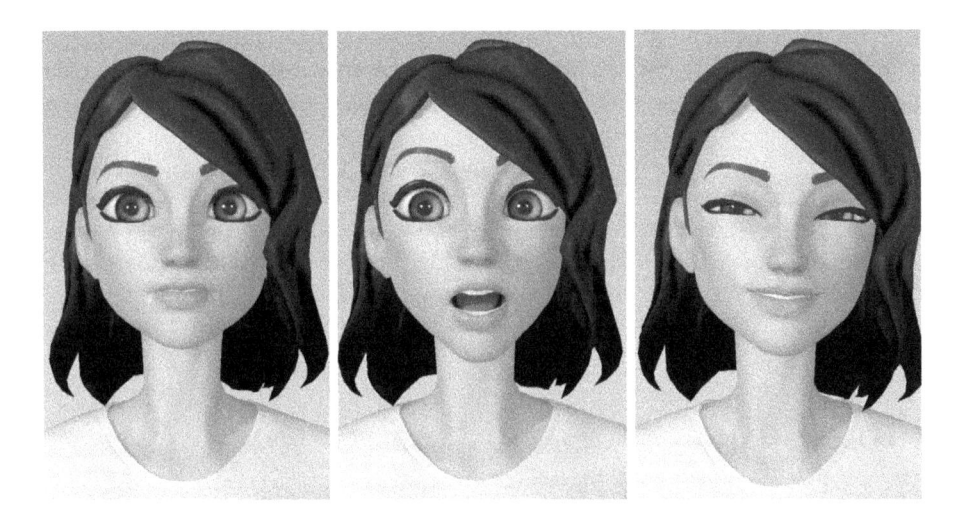

Fig. 6. Basic imagery and anthropomorphic facial expressions of 3D anthropomorphic assistant avatars. In the test videos, the avatar's expression will generally maintain a slight smile. When a special situation occurs, it will show a surprised look and then quickly switch to a warm, comforting expression. This pattern of expressions will be consistent across the three scenarios, with only timing differences.

These reactions are synchronized with the empathetic voice, providing a cohesive and supportive user experience. The avatars' lip movements and facial expressions are precisely tuned to match the tone and pace of the empathetic voice, making the interaction more realistic and ensuring that the emotional support is credible and compelling. These methods are used to create a more realistic 3D anthropomorphic assistant avatar.

We combine the designed 3D anthropomorphic assistant avatars with the empathetic voice to finalize the proposed system. For details on the specific design of the empathetic voice, both methods were evaluated under the same scenarios, using the same empathetic voice content. The text content of the empathetic voice is as follows:

1: *It seems we're caught in a bit of traffic. How about we use this time to listen to some music or perhaps a podcast to make it more enjoyable?*
2: *Looks like that driver was in a rush. It's important we keep our cool. Maybe some soft background music could help us stay relaxed and alert?*

3: *That was quite sudden, but you handled it well! We're safe, and that's what matters. Do you want to take a short break, or would some calming music be good for now?*

The text created for the empathetic voice was based on previous studies [5,19,20]. Different emotions were conveyed in each scenario, and slight modifications were made to the text to suit the three unique scenarios. The empathetic voice audio is from the huggingface Multi-voice-TTS-GPT-SoVITS model [8], creating a human-like voice. Unlike traditional voice assistants, an empathetic voice assistant emphasizes identifying the frustration from the participant's potential negative emotions and allaying these emotions through empathetic interaction.

Our study examined the short-term emotional changes that occurred following an accident. To ensure that users did not have to wait for long periods or feel rushed, the waiting periods were kept short, or sufficient time was provided to help users relax. It was observed that longer empathetic voice designs could lead users to perceive the voice as supervisory, which might cause aversion [5]. The empathetic voice interventions were designed to last only 10–15 s to avoid this.

4 User Study

We conducted a pure video experiment to compare the efficacy of empathetic voice interventions only and the proposed method, which combines 3D anthropomorphic assistant avatars and empathetic voice interventions.

We recruited 16 participants from the university, including 11 males and 5 females aged 23–34. Ten participants had driving experience, 5 had less than three years, 4 had more than three years, and 1 had exactly three years. Participants were informed about the data privacy policy and compensated with 1,000 yen for a 20-min in-person experiment.

4.1 Tasks and Conditions

Before the study started, we didn't tell the participants exactly what scenarios they'd encounter. They only knew that an Emotion Regulation system would intervene at some point during the video. We chose not to use the original environmental sounds from these clips to ensure they didn't interfere with our test of the empathetic voice intervention. Instead, we used just the drive footage and added a simulated driving environment for the audio. At the beginning of the study, we briefly introduced the participants to the research content and the outline of the experiment.

The test videos are divided into a 10-s particular driving scene and a 10-s video of the proposed methods or baseline, totaling 20 s. The video content includes real driving scenarios enhanced with a driving windshield frame and device frame (device frames are proposed methods only) to increase the immersion of the videos. We have three scenarios to describe different driving conditions that can influence a driver's emotions. Then, we had six types of videos. To increase data reliability and reduce bias, we repeated these videos three times and played them randomly to the participants. Each participant watched 18 videos in sequence. The test duration was approximately 5–6 min.

During the video test, participants had to hold the steering wheel controller throughout the viewing. The window closed after each video ended, and an interface with two drop-down questions appeared. Participants evaluated the method using a two-item, 5-point Likert scale, assessing its likability and effect on emotion regulation. Then, they pressed the "Next" button to proceed to the following video. If participants did not complete the questions, a prompt appeared, preventing the following video from playing to ensure the integrity of the data and the experiment. After all the video tests were finished, we recorded all the participants' responses and conducted a brief interview. The interview focused on which of the three test scenarios were more likely to trigger negative emotions, relating these to the negative emotions encountered during daily driving and discussing the pros and cons of the two methods used in the study. The specific questions were as follows:

Q1: In your daily driving experience, how often do you feel negative emotions arise? Which negative emotion is most common?
Q2: Facing negative emotions, would you consider using an emotion regulation method? If so, which method would you prefer?

These two questions are designed to validate the satisfaction and effectiveness of the two methods in the corresponding scenarios. Through this testing process, we aim to gain a deeper understanding of people's acceptance and the effectiveness of emotion regulation methods in driving scenarios.

4.2 Experimental Setup

We used a laptop (NVIDIA GeForce RTX 3070, i7-11800H) connected to a monitor and utilized a steering wheel controller to simulate the driving environment. Participants had to wear headphones throughout the test to ensure they could hear the audio content (see Fig. 7). We developed an Augmented Video [17] testing platform based on PYTHON+OPENCV, which evaluated the effectiveness of emotion regulation methods in specific driving scenarios. Participants experienced a driving environment through a steering wheel controller and screen. They imagined encountering driving scenarios that could cause them to experience negative emotions in three different scenarios. They also watched specially processed videos that simulated real driving scenarios. The within-factor empathy and the scenarios were counterbalanced.

5 Results

The accuracy of the video test was recorded, and feedback on satisfaction and effectiveness was collected using Likert scales. The Likert scale results were ana-

(a) The hardware setup for user study

(b) The appearance during user study

Fig. 7. User study environment.

lyzed using the Wilcoxon signed-rank test, revealing significant differences in results. Additionally, since the data in this study are ordinal Likert scale data, we chose to use the Kruskal-Wallis test for analysis. Although the results can only show differences, combining them with descriptive statistics can verify their validity.

5.1 User Preference and Actual Performance

The results indicate that all users prefer the proposed method for calming their emotions, supporting our hypothesis. Figure 8 illustrates that the proposed method has higher Participant satisfaction levels than the baseline method. The proposed method received a more significant number of "Agree" and "Strongly Agree" ratings, especially in the situations of "uncivil driving" (S2) (P-value < 0.05) and "Unexpected incursion" (S3) (P-value = 0.05). Both methods received high ratings in the "Traffic Jams" (S1) (P-value < 0.05), but the proposed method outperformed the baseline.

Better Together 71

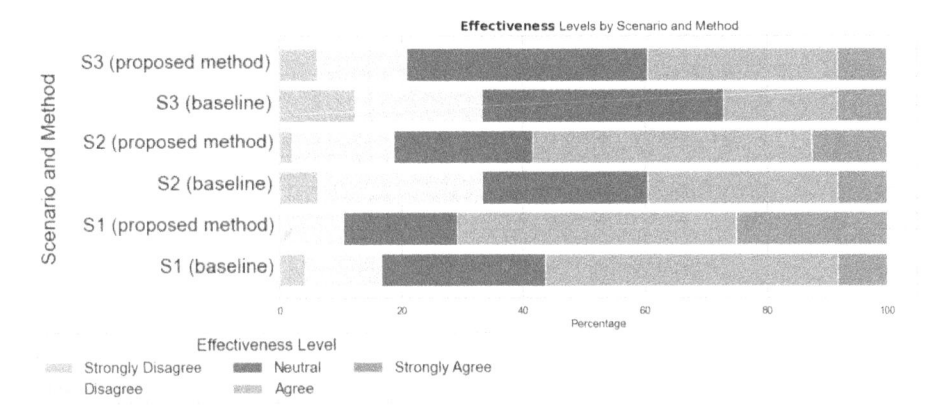

Fig. 8. Likert scale results of effectiveness levels for three scenarios comparing with the baseline and proposed methods.

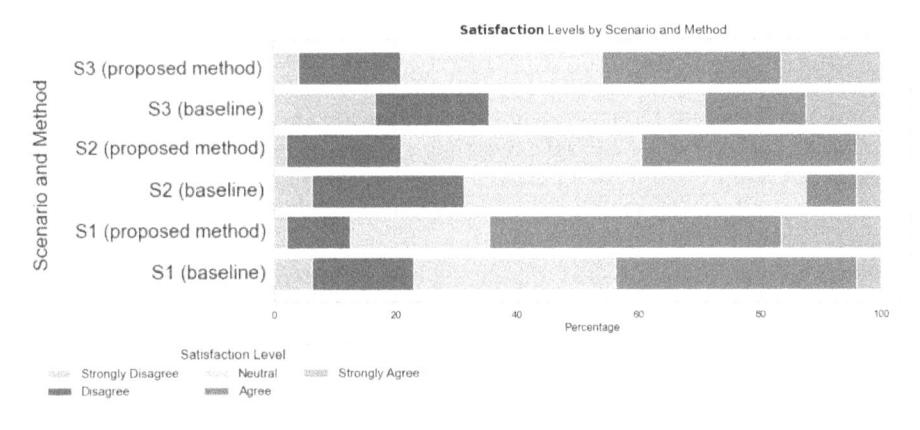

Fig. 9. Likert scale results of satisfaction levels for Three scenarios, comparing the baseline and proposed methods.

In terms of effectiveness, as shown in Fig. 9 and Table 1, the proposed method maintains a significant advantage in S1 (P-value < 0.05) and S2 (P-value = 0.05), far surpassing the baseline. However, in S3, the difference between the two methods is more minor (P-value = 0.135). Although the proposed method is more favored overall, some Participants have said that while it provides an excellent interactive experience and a sense of companionship in emergencies, it does not leave enough time to look at the avatar when someone suddenly runs into the road or incursion.

Based on the results, we can draw the following findings, which can be validated from Figs. 8 and 9, as well as the subsequent discussion:

F1 The proposed system had more effectively encouraged drivers to maintain positive emotions during prolonged driving or in high-stress environments.

Table 1. Kruskal-Wallis Test Results for Satisfaction and Effectiveness

Scenario	Metric	Method	Median	IQR	H-statistic	p-value
S1	Satisfaction	Proposed	4.0	1.00	5.758	0.016
		Baseline	3.0	1.00		
	Effectiveness	Proposed	4.0	1.25	4.470	0.034
		Baseline	4.0	1.00		
S2	Satisfaction	Proposed	3.0	1.00	6.092	0.014
		Baseline	3.0	1.00		
	Effectiveness	Proposed	4.0	1.00	3.724	0.054
		Baseline	3.0	2.00		
S3	Satisfaction	Proposed	3.0	1.00	3.753	0.053
		Baseline	3.0	2.00		
	Effectiveness	Proposed	3.0	1.00	2.230	0.135
		Baseline	3.0	2.00		

F2 Users had perceived the emotional support provided by the integrated system as more comprehensive and effective than that provided by empathetic voice assistance alone.

F3 Users had thought the proposed system was more reliable when making decisions.

F4 Users had been more satisfied overall and had preferred the integrated system over one that only used empathetic voice assistance.

After the video test, most participants also said they would consider trying similar products daily.

Fig. 10. Average baseline and proposed methods satisfaction in three scenarios by different driving experiences.

At the same time, we categorized the participants based on their driving experience into four groups: more than 3 years of driving experience, exactly 3 years of driving experience, less than 3 years of driving experience, and no driving experience.

While our experiment focuses on the driving environment, participants with driving experience may have biases due to their driving history. On the other

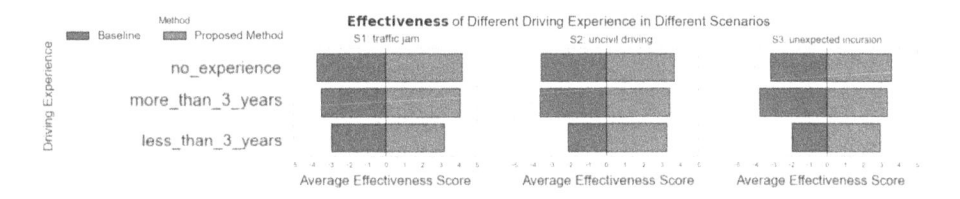

Fig. 11. Average baseline and proposed methods effectiveness in three scenarios by different driving experiences.

hand, participants with no driving experience may have a more genuine and focused perception of the emotional intervention and regulation aspects of driving scenarios. We had only one participant with exactly 3 years of driving experience, so we did not include this group in the statistical analysis of the grouped results.

In the analysis of overall satisfaction among different groups (Fig. 10), it was found that for participants with over 3 years of driving experience, the baseline either slightly outperforms the proposed method or performs similarly in various scenarios. In contrast, for participants with no driving experience and less than 3 years of driving experience, the proposed method consistently receives higher average satisfaction scores than the baseline method. This difference may be due to experienced drivers being more familiar with baseline as traditional driving assistance and better equipped to handle various driving situations. On the other hand, drivers with no experience or less than 3 years of experience may find it easier to accept the new proposed method as they have fewer established habits. When facing unexpected situations, they may be more inclined to rely on and trust the empathetic voice with a 3D anthropomorphic avatar, feeling a greater sense of companionship and shared responsibility.

Regarding effectiveness (Fig. 11), the situation is similar to the satisfaction analysis, with the distinction that almost all participants felt that the proposed method had an advantage in S1. The distribution in S2 and S3 is the same as in the satisfaction analysis.

5.2 Discussion

After the video testing, we conducted brief interviews with the Participants. Regarding the impact of different scenarios, we found that participants without driving experience believed that unexpected situations (S3) were most likely to trigger negative emotions. They felt that these negative emotions were more from the responsibility of being a driver, leading to feelings of self-blame and fright.

Participants with driving experience, on the other hand, considered other drivers' uncivil behavior (S2) to be more likely to cause anger, drawing from their daily driving experiences. While they would feel shocked by unexpected situations, they would quickly calm down, assess the situation, and take appropriate actions. Regardless of driving experience, participants reported fewer negative emotions during long traffic jams (S1).

Regarding method preference, participants with driving experience generally favored the proposed method (3D anthropomorphic avatar with empathetic voice) because it offered a richer interactive experience and more emotional support. Participants unanimously agreed that the 3D anthropomorphic avatar brought a sense of trust and robust interactivity towards the car itself. This trust and interactivity were the main reasons and core factors for calming their emotions, distinguishing it significantly from the single empathetic voice method. For example, a male participant (30 years old, less than 3 years of driving experience) believed that this method increased trust and companionship, effectively soothing emotions and providing a sense of companionship during incidents, preventing feelings of loneliness or sole responsibility.

Participants without driving experience had varying preferences for the two methods. They felt that in unexpected emergencies, especially S3, they would need more time to focus on visual displays. However, they believed the proposed method would be more effective in specific scenarios. For instance, a 27-year-old female participant thought an anthropomorphic avatar could alleviate boredom in S1 and increase trust in S3. However, she doubted she would have enough time to watch the visual display.

Meanwhile, some participants mentioned that long voice feedback could have adverse effects, especially in other drivers' uncivil behavior (S2), which could distract attention and increase negative emotions. A 23-year-old female participant pointed out that the baseline, in particular, lacked interaction and that long verbal content during negative emotional states could exacerbate negative feelings.

Finally, regarding the overall experimental design, several participants noted that the current methods of emotional regulation, including the text and avatar performance, felt too official and rigid. They hoped for more personalized options and emotional variations in the future. For example, a 24-year-old male participant (precisely 3 years of driving experience) said that although the proposed method was better, it still felt stiff, and he wished for more customizable choices.

6 Limitation and Future Work

In this experiment, we focused on comparing the emotional intervention effects of the two methods through augmented video. Although we obtained good results, there is still a lack of more objective methods for verification and experimental setup, such as monitoring participants' heart rates or recognizing facial expressions. Additionally, the videos used were pre-recorded, which made it nearly impossible to adapt the content based on participants' emotional changes and provide more interaction. The study also only broadly categorized the driving scenarios, while real driving situations are more complex and variable, as is the classification of emotions.

In future research, we plan to refine the experimental scenarios further and more carefully distinguish the corresponding emotions. For participants with different levels of driving experience, we will also attempt to classify the emotional stimulation levels of the experimental scenarios to obtain more insights into users' different perceptions and responses to the two methods.

7 Conclusion

In this study, we attempted to combine 3D anthropomorphic assistant avatars with empathetic voice interventions. We compared them to the baseline method of empathetic voice alone using an augmented video approach known for its sound, emotional, and soothing effects. The experiment showed that integrating 3D anthropomorphic assistant avatars with empathetic voices significantly enhances emotion regulation during driving. Participants generally preferred the combined method over the single empathetic voice. This indicates that the proposed method has higher satisfaction and perceived effectiveness, especially in scenarios involving traffic jams and uncivil driving behavior from others. However, the difference between the two methods was insignificant in unexpected emergencies.

Participants also unanimously agreed that the 3D anthropomorphic assistant avatars increased their trust and interaction with the vehicle, which was the main reason for soothing their emotions. This sense of trust and interaction was particularly evident among participants with less or no driving experience, who found these avatars more engaging and supportive. These findings provide insights for future researchers in designing in-car emotional intervention methods and contribute to developing more practical and realistic driving assistants.

References

1. Animaze: Animaze official website. https://www.animaze.us/
2. Anyasodo, B., Burnett, G.: Empathy consideration in the design of natural language interfaces for future vehicles (2021)
3. Bosch, E., et al.: Emotional garage: a workshop on in-car emotion recognition and regulation. In: Adjunct Proceedings of the 10th International Conference on Automotive user Interfaces and Interactive Vehicular Applications, pp. 44–49 (2018)
4. Braun, M., Li, J., Weber, F., Pfleging, B., Butz, A., Alt, F.: What if your car would care? Exploring use cases for affective automotive user interfaces. In: 22nd International Conference on Human-Computer Interaction with Mobile Devices and Services, pp. 1–12 (2020)
5. Braun, M., Schubert, J., Pfleging, B., Alt, F.: Improving driver emotions with affective strategies. Multimodal Technol. Interact. **3**(1), 21 (2019)
6. Ceccacci, S., et al.: A preliminary investigation towards the application of facial expression analysis to enable an emotion-aware car interface. In: Antona, M., Stephanidis, C. (eds.) HCII 2020. LNCS, vol. 12189, pp. 504–517. Springer, Cham (2020). https://doi.org/10.1007/978-3-030-49108-6_36

7. Dymond, R.F.: A scale for the measurement of empathic ability. J. Consult. Psychol. **13**(2), 127 (1949)
8. HuggingFace: multi-voice-TTS-GPT-soVITS. https://huggingface.co/spaces/Ailyth/Multi-voice-TTS-GPT-SoVITS
9. Knutzen, K., Weidner, F., Broll, W.: Talk to me! Exploring stereoscopic 3D anthropomorphic virtual assistants in automated vehicles. In: Proceedings of the 11th International Conference on Automotive User Interfaces and Interactive Vehicular Applications: Adjunct Proceedings, pp. 363–368 (2019)
10. Leite, I., Pereira, A., Mascarenhas, S., Martinho, C., Prada, R., Paiva, A.: The influence of empathy in human-robot relations. Int. J. Hum Comput Stud. **71**(3), 250–260 (2013)
11. Liu, S., et al.: The empathetic car: exploring emotion inference via driver behaviour and traffic context. Proc. ACM Interact. Mob. Wearable Ubiquitous Technol. **5**(3), 1–34 (2021)
12. Mori, M., MacDorman, K.F., Kageki, N.: The uncanny valley [from the field]. IEEE Robot. Autom. Mag. **19**(2), 98–100 (2012)
13. Nesbit, S.M., Conger, J.C., Conger, A.J.: A quantitative review of the relationship between anger and aggressive driving. Aggress. Violent. Beh. **12**(2), 156–176 (2007)
14. Okamoto, S., Sano, S.: Anthropomorphic AI agent mediated multimodal interactions in vehicles. In: Proceedings of the 9th International Conference on Automotive User Interfaces and Interactive Vehicular Applications Adjunct, pp. 110–114 (2017)
15. Paredes, P.E., et al.: Just breathe: in-car interventions for guided slow breathing. Proc. ACM Interact. Mob. Wearable Ubiquitous Technol. **2**(1), 1–23 (2018)
16. Roidl, E., Siebert, F.W., Oehl, M., Höger, R.: Introducing a multivariate model for predicting driving performance: the role of driving anger and personal characteristics. J. Safety Res. **47**, 47–56 (2013)
17. Soro, A., Rakotonirainy, A., Schroeter, R., Wollstädter, S.: Using augmented video to test in-car user experiences of context analog HUDs. In: Adjunct Proceedings of the 6th International Conference on Automotive User Interfaces and Interactive Vehicular Applications, pp. 1–6 (2014)
18. Stephens, A.N., Groeger, J.A.: Situational specificity of trait influences on drivers' evaluations and driving behaviour. Transport. Res. F: Traffic Psychol. Behav. **12**(1), 29–39 (2009)
19. Urakami, J., Moore, B.A., Sutthithatip, S., Park, S.: Users' perception of empathic expressions by an advanced intelligent system. In: Proceedings of the 7th International Conference on Human-Agent Interaction, pp. 11–18 (2019)
20. Urakami, J., Sutthithatip, S., Moore, B.A.: The effect of naturalness of voice and empathic responses on enjoyment, attitudes and motivation for interacting with a voice user interface. In: Kurosu, M. (ed.) HCII 2020. LNCS, vol. 12182, pp. 244–259. Springer, Cham (2020). https://doi.org/10.1007/978-3-030-49062-1_17
21. Wang, F., Chang, C.M., Igarashi, T.: Virtual horse: an anthropomorphic notification interface for traffic accident reduction. In: 13th International Conference on Automotive User Interfaces and Interactive Vehicular Applications, pp. 16–20 (2021)
22. Wang, F., Chang, CM., Igarashi, T.: Direct or indirect: a video experiment for in-vehicle alert systems. In: Krömker, H. (eds.) HCI in Mobility, Transport, and Automotive Systems, HCII 2023. LNCS, vol. 14049, pp. 245–259. Springer, Cham (2023). https://doi.org/10.1007/978-3-031-35908-8_17
23. Waytz, A., Heafner, J., Epley, N.: The mind in the machine: anthropomorphism increases trust in an autonomous vehicle. J. Exp. Soc. Psychol. **52**, 113–117 (2014)

24. Zepf, S., Dittrich, M., Hernandez, J., Schmitt, A.: Towards empathetic car interfaces: emotional triggers while driving. In: Extended Abstracts of the 2019 CHI Conference on Human Factors in Computing Systems, pp. 1–6 (2019)
25. Zhou, X., He, G., Zhu, H., Wang, Y., Zhang, W.: Evaluation of driver stress intervention with guided breathing and positive comments. Appl. Ergon. **114**, 104144 (2024)

Unlock Your Trust: Experiencing a Biophilic Autonomous Driving Through Gamification

Saeedeh Mosaferchi, Salvatore Cesarano, and Alessandro Naddeo[✉]

University of Salerno, Via Giovanni Paolo II, 132, 84084 Fisciano, SA, Italy
anaddeo@unisa.it

Abstract. This study looks at how integrating biophilic interventions into driverless cars can lower stress levels and increase passenger comfort and trust. Even though autonomous car usage is increasing, public trust in the technology is still low, which has an impact on consumers' acceptance and desire to buy them. Utilizing virtual reality and a dynamic driving simulator, the research used biophilic treatments in an entertaining game. A total of thirty students took part, divided into two groups and given varying game lengths. The findings indicated that a five-minute game decreased stress by 36.5% and raised trust by 38.46%, while a shorter three-minute game considerably lowered stress by 50.96% and increased trust by 64.9%. Additionally, the group with less exposure reported feeling more at ease. The results show that stress and trust are positively impacted by biophilic encounters, implying that shorter, more immersive virtual reality experiences could more successfully increase comfort and trust. To further corroborate these results, larger sample numbers and objective data like HRV and EEG should be included in future studies.

Keywords: Trust · Comfort · Gamification · Biophilic Autonomous Vehicles · Virtual reality

1 Introduction

Despite the increasing technological advancements in vehicles and the tangible improvements in the performance of self-driving cars, significant public trust in autonomous vehicles (AVs) remains lacking (1–3). People worry about possible hazards because self-driving cars lack human assistance in many driving activities, while being safer than conventional cars. Autonomous cars often like to retain control over a great deal of driving activity, depending on how automated they are (4, 5). However, numerous researches have demonstrated the strong correlation between people's perceptions of comfort and trust when utilizing an autonomous vehicle. In addition, stress and acceptance can be claimed as other crucial determinants on which driving an autonomous vehicle (6, 7). Thus, a lack of successful and effective interaction between humans and self-driving cars is observed, resulting in a significant reduction in the willingness to use and purchase these vehicles (8, 9). Accordingly, each factor that make this interaction smooth, would be helpful to create a trustworthy and comfortable atmosphere for an autonomous driving (8, 10).

So far, different researchers have raised and tried some efforts to improve end users' trust, acceptance, and comfort, in addition to lessening their stress. Anthropomorphism, the utilization of visual and auditory feedback, the development of interactive interfaces/feedback between people and self-driving cars as well as personalized interactions, and the improvement of interior design using specialized materials are all examples (11–15). Another technique has been used in the transportation industry to increase knowledge and awareness, enhance human-machine interaction, and optimize individuals' performance is gamification (16, 17). In the present study, therefore, the researchers aimed at developing a game using biophilic elements.

Both American biologist E.O. Wilson and German psychologist Erich Fromm separately invented the word "biophilia". Fromm defined biophilia as the psychological attraction to everything that is alive and vital, focusing on the development of a biophilic personality (18, 19). Also, Eduard Wilson, a biologist and naturalist emphasized that biophilia refers to "the innately emotional affiliation of human beings to other living organisms." The concept of "innate tendency" is used to express the qualities of "hereditary," while also serving as a "learning rule" that offers an insightful viewpoint on nature (19, 20). On the flip side, improving positive feelings such as calmness, well-being, trust, enjoy, and comfort, in addition to lessening negative emotions like stress and fear can be expressed as obvious consequences of applying Biophilia (21, 22).

Regarding the mentioned benefits of Biophilia and in order to ameliorate individuals' trust during riding a self-driving car, a biophilic environment was developed as a game and played using virtual reality to assess the probable positive effect of Biophilia for autonomous driving.

2 Methodology

Participants. Since females are more emotional and inclined in nature rather than men (23) and in order to control gender's effect as a confounding factor, only women volunteers were accepted to attend this experiment. Thirty Italian female students of the University of Salerno participated voluntarily, then they were randomly divided into 2 groups. Their average age was 23.93 years, and all of them were single. Among the participants, 50% were pursuing a master's degree, 43% were working towards a bachelor's degree, and only 7% were studied in a PhD program. 90% of the students had a driving licence, and 67% of them were studying engineering fileds.

Apparatus. A dynamic driving simulator, which is located in a closed and specific space inside the laboratory of Human Centred Design and Vehicle Design by Simulation at the University of Salerno in Italy, was utilized. Three 65-inch Hisense displays, creating a 120° horizontal field of view, projected the virtual predefined roads. The simulator featured an adjustable seat, a steering wheel, gas and brake pedals, and surround sound equipment. BeamNG software was used for the driving simulation.

Procedure. Initially, the research team outlined the objectives and procedures of the study to all participants, informing them that they could opt out at any time, even during the experiment. After that, participants filled out a nature scale (24) and a demographic questionnaire on a tablet. There was no need for participants to operate the any driving

Fig. 1. Dynamic driving simulator used for the experiments

task because the whole driving scenario was automated. They took a seat in the simulator, set the distance between the pedals and the steering wheel to their liking, and warmed up with two minutes of automated driving. The experiment was started by the researchers as soon as they said they were ready. To preserve realistic settings, no one else was allowed inside the simulation room during the experiment except the experimenters and the subject. Two groups (Group 1 and Group 2) were randomly assigned to the participants. The first three minutes of completely automatic driving were experienced by participants in both groups. Next, attendees utilized the tablet to answer two 10-point Likert scales assessing"stress" and"trust", pausing the experiment in the process. To carry out the experiment further, they were then given a virtual reality headset and two controllers. Then, they started playing the biophilic game while they were sitting in the simulator. Worth noting that the experimenters conducted a brief conversation at the end of the experiment to extract their opinions and suggestions.

Fig. 2. Playing the biophilic game using the virtual reality headset during the autonomous driving

In this game, participants had to walk in a forest to find dead trees and bushes with yellow leaves among all other green ones. A large waterfall and several birds that began to sing as they came into contact with or glanced at them could also be seen in the forest. Participants were required to remove the sprinkler pot from the vicinity of some trees and water the yellow trees. Upon successful watering, the yellow trees or bushes would become green, and they would be rewarded with ten cents. Tempo For the first group, the game lasted three minutes, and for the second, five minutes. The participants' scores were displayed in the headset upon the conclusion of the game, and they were informed that it had ended. Finally, they filled out the scales of trust, stress, and comfort (Table 1).

Questionnaires.

1. **Demographic Questionnaire:** Seven questions related to personal information were asked, such as age, gender, marital status, etc.
2. **Connectedness to Nature Scale:** Mayer et. al (24) have developed 14 questions related to people's feelings, perceptions, and relationships with nature and has developed as the "Connectedness to nature scale" and was utilised during the experiment to evaluate the probable effect of this characteristic on participants' trust and comfort. The questionnaire is given in the table below:

Table 1. Connectedness to nature scale

Num.	Phrase	Strongly disagree (1)	Disagree (2)	Neutral (3)	Agree (4)	Strongly Agree (5)
1	I often feel a sense of oneness with the natural world around me.					
2	I think of the natural world as a community to which I belong.					
3	I recognize and appreciate the intelligence of other living organisms					
4	I often feel disconnected from nature.					

(*continued*)

Table 1. (*continued*)

Num.	Phrase	Strongly disagree (1)	Disagree (2)	Neutral (3)	Agree (4)	Strongly Agree (5)
5	When I think of my life, I imagine myself to be part of a larger cyclical process of living.					
6	I often feel a kinship with animals and plants					
7	I feel as though I belong to the Earth as equally as it belongs to me					
8	I have a deep understanding of how my actions affect the natural world.					
9	I often feel part of the web of life.					
10	I feel that all inhabitants of Earth, human, and nonhuman, share a common 'life force'.					
11	Like a tree can be part of a forest, I feel embedded within the broader natural world.					
12	When I think of my place on Earth, I consider myself to be a top member of a hierarchy that exists in nature.					

(*continued*)

Table 1. (*continued*)

Num.	Phrase	Strongly disagree (1)	Disagree (2)	Neutral (3)	Agree (4)	Strongly Agree (5)
13	I often feel like I am only a small part of the natural world around me, and that I am no more important than the grass on the ground or the birds in the trees.					
14	My personal welfare is independent of the welfare of the natural world.					

3. **Trust, Comfort, and Stress Scales:** Three 10-point Likert scales of the participants' perception of trust, comfort, and stress were given to them before (initial), during (intermediate), and after (final) playing the game. Individuals' trust were assessed for these 3 steps, their stress were asked during and at the end, and comfort was evaluated only at the final stage.

3 Results

In the first group, the average age was 23.9, whereas in the second group, it was 24.90. In the following, the results of each group have been mentioned and then a comparison is expressed to show the differences among two experiments. Finally, scores related to connectedness to nature are also provided.

Group 1 results. Based on the results of group 1, participants' averages of initial, intermediate, and final trust scores were 5.2, 6.13, and 7.2. As the accompanying figure illustrates, there was a 17.88% gain in trust between the initial and intermediate scores, as well as a 17.45% increase between the intermediate and final values. Individuals' trust in self-driving cars has thus been clearly impacted by the biophilic game. However, the final trust increased by 38.46% comparing to the initial.

In addition, participants' stress levels also dropped, from 5.67 to 3.6, which can be claimed 36.5% of decrement in their stress. However, their stress levels during and at the end of the experiment are shown in the following figure.

Moreover, the mean of comfort for the first group was obtained 5.53, and 3.69 was the final score of connectedness to nature of 15 participants of the first group.

Group 2 results. 15 participants of the second group experienced 3 min of playing the game. Surprisingly, their final trust increased by 64.9% comparing to the initial trust.

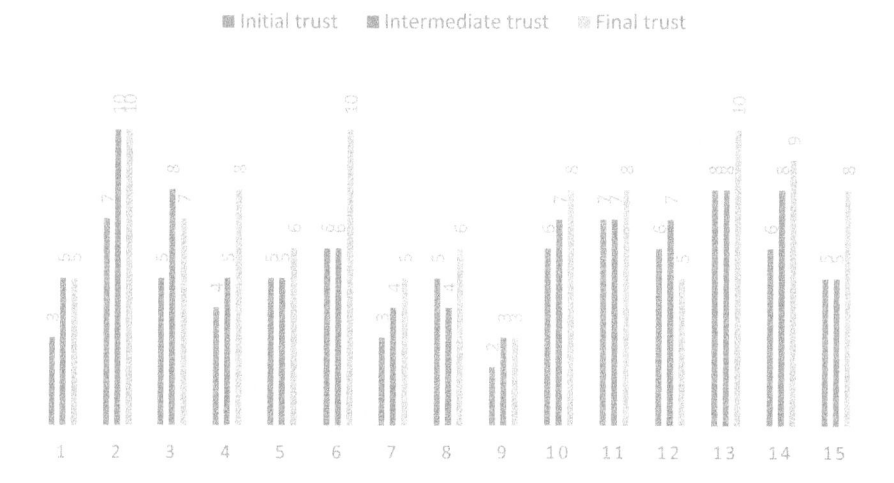

Fig. 3. Initial, intermediate, and final trust scores of groups 1.

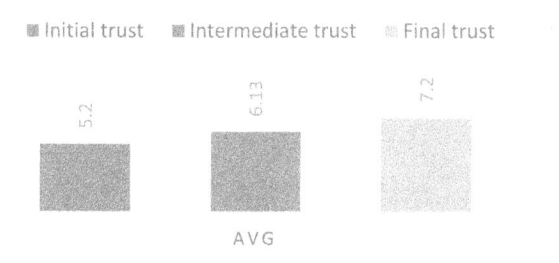

Fig. 4. Initial, intermediate, and final trust averages of group 1.

According to the following figure, participants' trust has dropped in the middle of the experiment, while at the end a significant increment had appeared.

Results showed 50.96% of decline in their perceived stress after playing the game.

In addition, 7.87 was the comfort average of the second group which declared at the end of the experiment. Worth mentioning that 3.68 was their connectedness to nature score which approximately doubles the score of group 1.

Comparison of group 1 and group 2. The following graphs depict the comparison between three levels of trust scores for both groups. For the final step, gamification gave group 2 a significant rise in trust, surpassing the group 1 data, but trust did not improve from the initial to the intermediate phase. Data comparison indicates a 12.92% improvement in ultimate trust in group 2.

Also shown are the stress graphs of the participants, which are 29.72% lower than those of group 1.

Two next figures express perceived comfort of all 30 participants and comfort average of both groups, respectively.

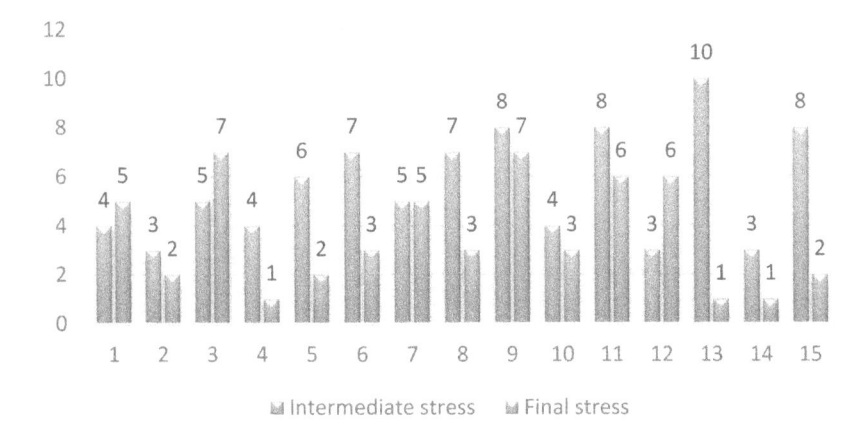

Fig. 5. Intermediate and final stress scores of group 1.

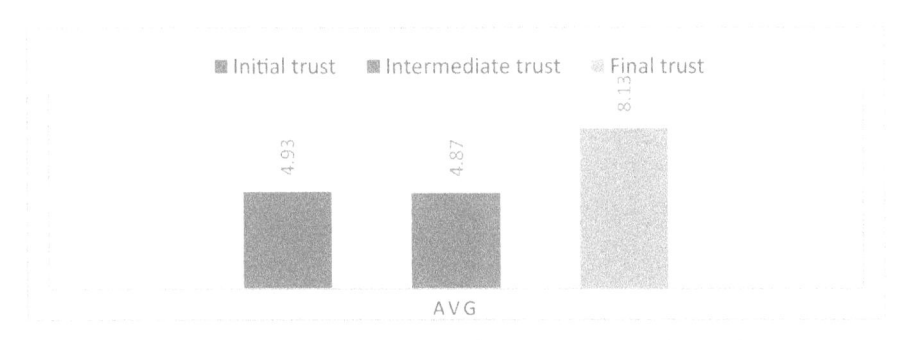

Fig. 6. Initial, intermediate, and final trust averages of group 2.

The correlations between nature scores with individuals' trust, stress, comfort, age, and mode, are shown in following figure (Figs 1, 2, 3, 4, 5, 6, 7, 8, 9, 10, 11 and 12).

In summary, we conducted a Kolmogorov-Smirnov test to confirm normality across all datasets. With normality verified, we performed paired sample t-tests. In Group 1, the post-game trust p-value was 0.02, while in Group 2, it was 0.000. For stress, Group 1 had a post-game p-value of 0.022, and Group 2's was also 0.000. All results were statistically significant, indicating that trust significantly increased and stress significantly decreased following the biophilic game experience.

4 Discussion

The study delved into the impact of Biophilic experiences on participants' levels of trust and stress, which are significantly influenced by exposure to natural elements. Interestingly, it was found that less exposure to such elements could lead to increased comfort levels and a heightened sense of trust, while simultaneously reducing stress

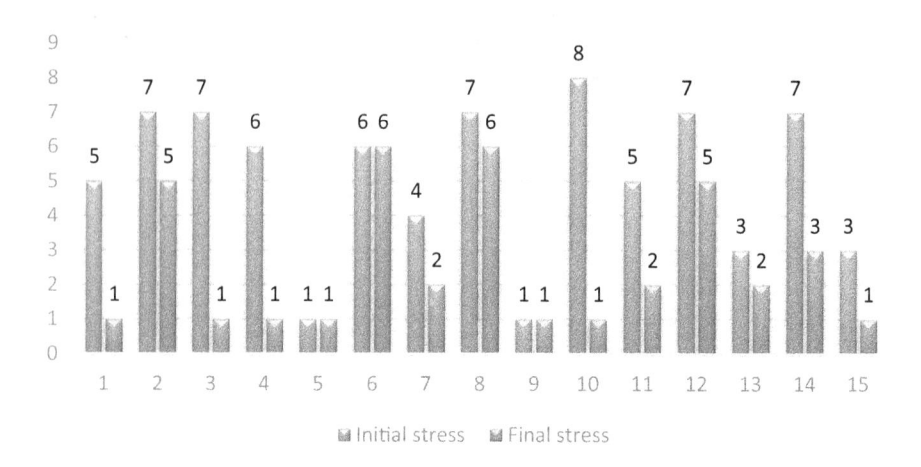

Fig. 7. Intermediate and final stress scores of group 2.

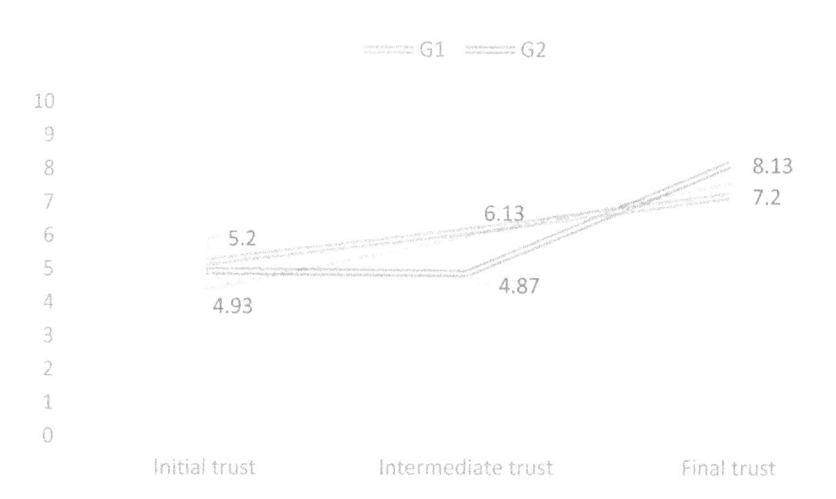

Fig. 8. Average trust comparison of 2 groups for the experiment

levels. However, the study also acknowledges potential negative effects associated with virtual reality usage, such as discomfort due to headset weight or motion sickness and cybersickness which may counteract the positive impact of Biophilic experiences (25, 26). Moreover, prolonged use of virtual reality technology can create a sense of detachment from the real environment, akin to being immersed in a video game atmosphere (27). Despite these potential drawbacks, individuals who reported feeling a stronger connection to nature tended to experience greater comfort, placed more trust in autonomous vehicles, and exhibited lower levels of stress. This finding underscores the importance

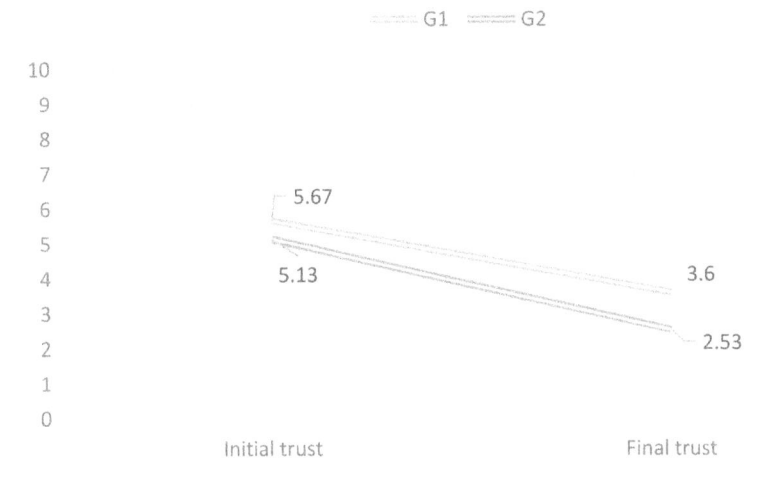

Fig. 9. Average stress comparison of 2 groups for the experiment

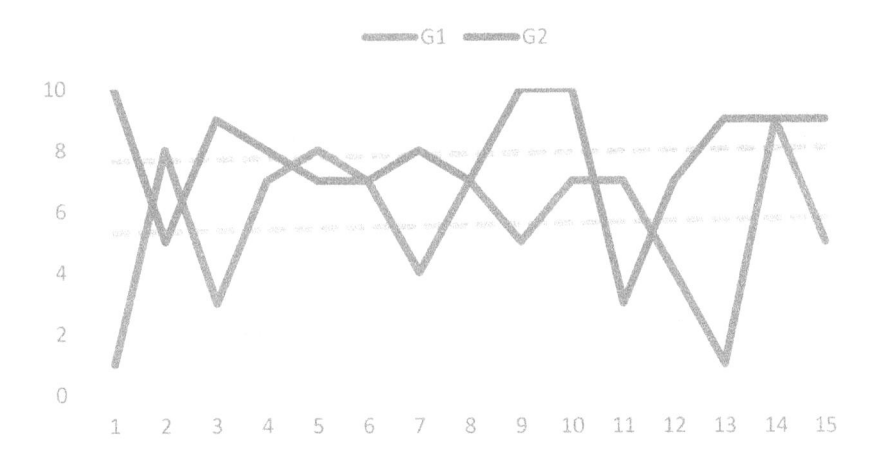

Fig. 10. Perceived comfort of all 30 participants.

of incorporating natural elements into various environments, including the automation sector.

Architects have been at the forefront of embracing Biophilia, recognizing its potential to enhance comfort and reduce stress (28). However, applying these principles in sectors like automotive design may seem counterintuitive, especially given the current emphasis on luxury interior designs. Nevertheless, the study suggests that human psychological needs often follow predictable patterns, and integrating natural elements into car interiors could lead to more satisfying and comfortable experiences for users. Despite the limitations posed by the small sample size of the study, the researchers anticipate

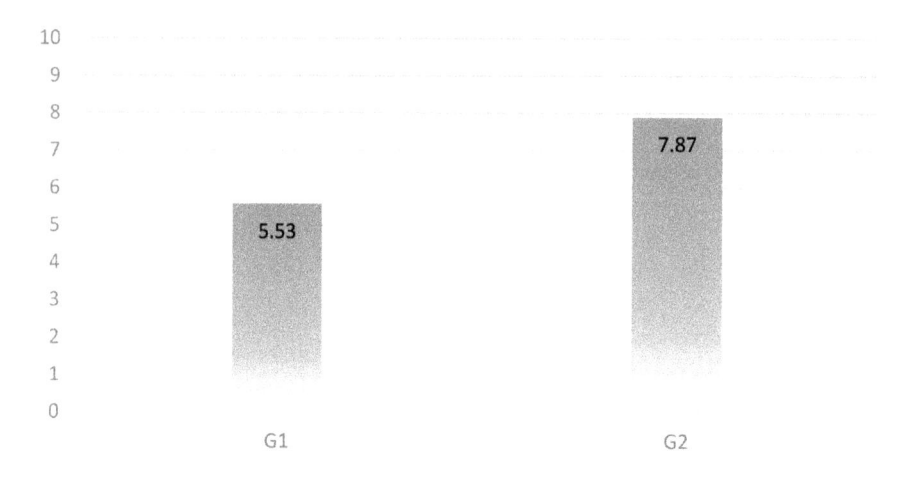

Fig. 11. Comfort average of both groups after the experiment

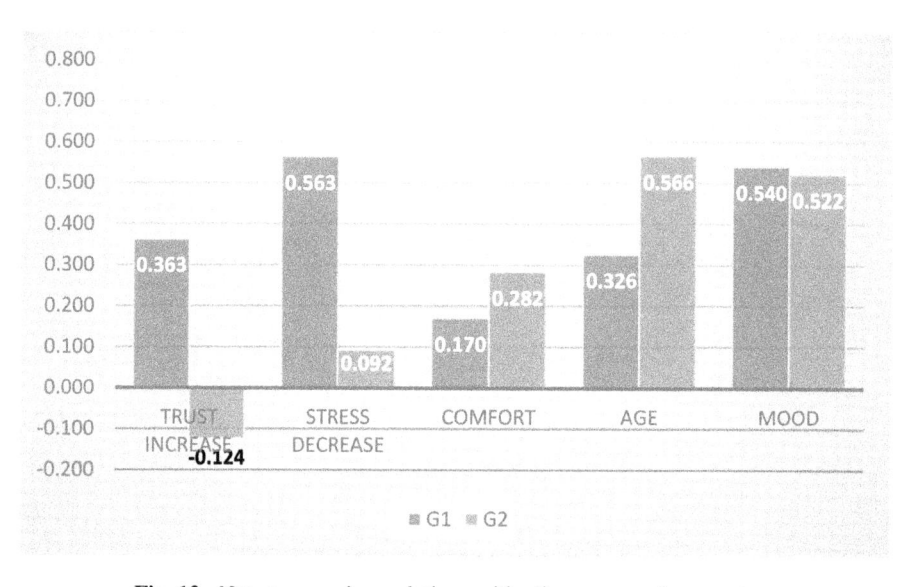

Fig. 12. Nature scores' correlations with other measured parameters

that further exploration of these concepts with a larger participant pool will yield more reliable results. Objective measures such as Heart Rate Variability (HRV) and Electroencephalography (EEG) data could provide valuable insights in future studies, enhancing our understanding of the relationship between Biophilic experiences and psychological well-being in various contexts.

5 Conclusion

The literature extensively discusses the prevalent distrust among people towards self-driving cars, as evidenced by numerous studies. In response, experts globally have undertaken various initiatives aimed at enhancing public trust in autonomous vehicles. However, despite these efforts, definitive solutions to address this issue remain elusive. Nevertheless, the findings of the present study offer a promising starting point for the development of autonomous vehicles, presenting a novel and potentially advantageous approach. It is important to note that although the study's findings offer insightful information, they also emphasize the need for more discussion on the timing and format of exposure to the ideas that underpin the development of trust in autonomous cars. This implies that in order to improve public trust-building tactics for self-driving technology, a more thorough investigation of these variables is necessary. The advancement of autonomous vehicle development and acceptability will depend heavily on ongoing research and stakeholder discussion. Policymakers, engineers, and academics can collaborate to develop creative solutions that effectively address public concerns and encourage the broad adoption of self-driving cars by expanding on the study's findings.

Limitations and future studies. Similar to other research projects, this one had a few limitations, one of which being the small participant pool. To improve the findings' robustness, a bigger sample size should be considered in future research. Furthermore, people's experiences with technology and their interactions with nature can be greatly influenced by their educational backgrounds. Therefore, it is necessary to make sure that participants with comparable educational backgrounds are compared in order to account for this aspect. Nevertheless, even though driving simulator research is quicker and less expensive than real-world research, it could produce results that differ from participants' perceptions and responses. Thus, it makes sense that in the future, experiments with real autonomous vehicles would supplement interventions employing driving simulations.

Acknowledgements. All students who participated with this study are greatly appreciated by the researchers. Their presence and insightful opinions made a big difference in getting the results that were desired.

References

1. Waung, M., McAuslan, P., Lakshmanan, S.: Trust and intention to use autonomous vehicles: Manufacturer focus and passenger control. Transport. Res. F: Traffic Psychol. Behav. **1**(80), 328–340 (2021)
2. Mosaferchi, S., Califano, R., Orlando, L., Pica, G., Pierri, V., Naddeo, A.: Developing an effective questionnaire for trust-investigation while using an autonomous vehicle. In: Comfort Congress, pp. 12 (2023 Sep 5)
3. Raats, K., Fors, V., Pink, S.: Trusting autonomous vehicles: an interdisciplinary approach. Transp. Res. Interdisc. Perspect. **1**(7), 100201 (2020)
4. Ha, T., Kim, S., Seo, D., Lee, S.: Effects of explanation types and perceived risk on trust in autonomous vehicles. Transport. Res. F: Traffic Psychol. Behav. **1**(73), 271–280 (2020)

5. Rödel, C., Stadler, S., Meschtscherjakov, A., Tscheligi, M.: Towards autonomous cars: the effect of autonomy levels on acceptance and user experience. In: Proceedings of the 6th International Conference on Automotive User Interfaces and Interactive Vehicular Applications, pp. 1–8 (2014 Sep 17)
6. Sun, X., et al.: Exploring personalised autonomous vehicles to influence user trust. Cogn. Comput. **12**, 1170–1186 (2020)
7. Su, H., Jia, Y.: Study of human comfort in autonomous vehicles using wearable sensors. IEEE Trans. Intell. Transp. Syst. **23**(8), 11490–11504 (2021)
8. She, J., Neuhoff, J., Yuan, Q.: Shaping pedestrians' trust in autonomous vehicles: an effect of communication style, speed information, and adaptive strategy. J. Mech. Des. **143**(9), 091401 (2021)
9. Reig, S., Norman, S., Morales, C.G., Das, S., Steinfeld, A., Forlizzi, J.: A field study of pedestrians and autonomous vehicles. In: Proceedings of the 10th International Conference on Automotive User Interfaces and Interactive Vehicular Applications, pp. 198–209 (2018 Sep 23)
10. Xing, Y., Lv, C., Cao, D., Hang, P.: Toward human-vehicle collaboration: review and perspectives on human-centered collaborative automated driving. Transp. Res. part C Emerg. Technol. **1**(128), 103199 (2021)
11. Tian, Y., Wang, X.: A study on psychological determinants of users' autonomous vehicles adoption from anthropomorphism and UTAUT perspectives. Front. Psychol. **16**(13), 986800 (2022)
12. Cheng, P., Meng, F., Yao, J., Wang, Y.: Driving with agents: investigating the influences of anthropomorphism level and physicality of agents on drivers' perceived control, trust, and driving performance. Front. Psychol. **15**(13), 883417 (2022)
13. Praveena, K., Manjunatha, M., Dutt, A., Khan, I., Maan, P., Hussien, R.A.: The future of transportation design: balancing aesthetics and functionality in autonomous vehicles. In: E3S Web of Conferences 2024, vol. 505, pp. 01010. EDP Sciences (2024)
14. Yardım, S., Pedgley, O.: Targeting a luxury driver experience: design considerations for automotive HMI and interiors. Int. J. Des. **17**(2), 45–66 (2023)
15. Wiegand, G., Eiband, M., Haubelt, M., Hussmann, H.: "I'd like an explanation for that!" exploring reactions to unexpected autonomous driving. In: 22nd International Conference on Human-Computer Interaction with Mobile Devices and Services, pp. 1–11 (2020 Oct 5)
16. Khakpour, A., Colomo-Palacios, R.: Convergence of gamification and machine learning: a systematic literature review. Technol. Knowl. Learn. **26**(3), 597–636 (2021)
17. Wang, W., Gan, H., Wang, X., Lu, H., Huang, Y.: Initiatives and challenges in using gamification in transportation: a systematic mapping. Eur. Transp. Res. Rev. **14**(1), 41 (2022)
18. Fromm, E.: The Heart of Man: Its Genius for Good and Evil. Open Road Media; 2023 Feb 28
19. Zhong, W., Schröder, T., Bekkering, J.: Biophilic design in architecture and its contributions to health, well-being, and sustainability: a critical review. Front. Architectural Res. **11**(1), 114–141 (2022)
20. Wilson, E.O.: Biophilia and the conservation ethic. In: Evolutionary Perspectives on Environmental Problems, pp. 250–258. Routledge (2017 Jul 5)
21. Wijesooriya, N., Brambilla, A.: Bridging biophilic design and environmentally sustainable design: a critical review. J. Clean. Prod. **10**(283), 124591 (2021)
22. Latini, A., et al.: Virtual reality application to explore indoor soundscape and physiological responses to audio-visual biophilic design interventions: An experimental study in an office environment. J. Building Eng. **15**(87), 108947 (2024)
23. Zelezny, L.C., Chua, P.P., Aldrich, C.: New ways of thinking about environmentalism: elaborating on gender differences in environmentalism. J. Soc. Issues **56**(3), 443–457 (2000)

24. Mayer, F.S., Frantz, C.M.: The connectedness to nature scale: a measure of individuals' feeling in community with nature. J. Environ. Psychol. **24**(4), 503–515 (2004)
25. Descheneaux, C.R., Reinerman-Jones, L., Moss, J., Krum, D., Hudson, I.: Negative effects associated with HMDs in augmented and virtual reality. In: Virtual, Augmented and Mixed Reality. Design and Interaction: 12th International Conference, VAMR 2020, Held as Part of the 22nd HCI International Conference, HCII 2020, Copenhagen, Denmark, July 19–24, 2020, Proceedings, Part I 22 2020, pp. 410–428. Springer International Publishing (2020). https://doi.org/10.1007/978-3-030-49695-1_27
26. Lavoie, R., Main, K., King, C., King, D.: Virtual experience, real consequences: the potential negative emotional consequences of virtual reality gameplay. Virtual Reality **25**(1), 69–81 (2021)
27. Diodato, R.: Virtual reality and aesthetic experience. Philosophies. **7**(2), 29 (2022)
28. Joye, Y.: Architectural lessons from environmental psychology: the case of biophilic architecture. Rev. Gen. Psychol. **11**(4), 305–328 (2007)

An Interactive Game for Improved Driving Behaviour Experience and Decision Support

Gonçalo Penelas, Tiago Pinto[✉], Arsénio Reis, Luís Barbosa, and João Barroso

Escola de Ciências e Tecnologia, University of Trás-os-Montes and Alto Douro, Vila Real, Portugal
`al68536@alunos.utad.pt`, {`tiagopinto,ars,lfb,jbarroso`}`@utad.pt`

Abstract. This paper presents an interactive game designed to improve users' experience related to driving behaviour, as well as to provide decision support in this context. This paper explores machine learning (ML) methods to enhance the decision-making and automation in a gaming environment. It examines various ML strategies, including supervised, unsupervised, and Reinforcement Learning (RL), emphasizing RL's effectiveness in interactive environments and its combination with Deep Learning, culminating in Deep Reinforcement Learning (DRL) for intricate decision-making processes. By leveraging these concepts, a practical application considering a gaming scenario is presented, which replicates vehicle behaviour simulations from real-world driving scenarios. Ultimately, the objective of this research is to contribute to the ML and artificial intelligence (AI) fields by introducing methods that could transform the way player agents adapt and interact with the environment and other agents decisions, leading to more authentic and fluid gaming experiences. Additionally, by considering recreational and serious games as case studies, this work aims to demonstrate the versatility of these methods, providing a rich, dynamic environment for testing the adaptability and responsiveness, while can also offer a context for applying these advancements to simulate and solve real-world problems in the complex and dynamic domain of mobility.

Keywords: Artificial Intelligence · Machine Learning · Reinforcement Learning · Deep Learning · Deep Reinforcement Learning · Game Theory

1 Introduction

Autonomous driving is a sophisticated technology that enables vehicles to navigate without human intervention. Although represents one of the most rapidly evolving areas in artificial intelligence (AI) and machine learning (ML), it's still a really challenging task, as it integrates multiple technologies to achieve its functionality, requiring substantial computing power to handle various tasks, such as vehicle positioning, environmental perception, path planning, and motion control [3]. To advance this field, simulation environments play a crucial role, offering safe and controlled settings for testing and training intelligent agents. This paper introduces an interactive game environment designed to enhance user experience in driving behavior simulations, leveraging cutting-edge ML techniques to replicate and improve upon real-world driving scenarios.

The core of our approach involves the use of the Unity Engine, a versatile and widely-used platform for creating interactive, real-time 3D content, and considered the best engine by some, as demonstrated in a study that compared Unity and Unreal engines across various computers, with Unity coming out on top [2]. Unity's robust capabilities and cross-platform support make it an ideal choice for developing complex simulations that can model dynamic and realistic driving environments. By utilizing Unity, we can create visually appealing and functionally rich simulations that provide a strong foundation for training AI agents.

In addition to Unity, we employ the Unity ML-Agents Toolkit, an open-source project that transforms Unity environments into training grounds for intelligent agents. This toolkit supports various ML methods, including reinforcement learning (RL), making it a powerful tool for developing and refining AI behaviors. The integration of ML-Agents with Unity allows for seamless interaction between the simulation and the learning algorithms, facilitating the development of sophisticated, adaptive agents.

Our focus is on DRL, particularly two prominent algorithms: Proximal Policy Optimization (PPO) and Soft Actor-Critic (SAC). These algorithms are chosen for their proven effectiveness in complex decision-making tasks [8], and their availability in the ML-Agents Toolkit. In this study, their potential will be explored and introduced for future work in training autonomous driving agents within our simulated environment.

The interactive game environment developed for this research features a detailed 3D car model equipped with various sensors to collect environmental data. This setup enables the simulation of diverse driving scenarios, providing a comprehensive platform for testing the adaptability and decision-making capabilities of AI agents. By focusing on the visual elements of the simulation, we aim to create a rich, dynamic environment that enhances the training process and contributes to the advancement of autonomous driving technologies.

Ultimately, this research aims to demonstrate the potential of advanced ML techniques in improving the realism and effectiveness of driving simulations. By leveraging state-of-the-art tools and methodologies, we strive to contribute to the fields of ML and AI, offering insights that could lead to more authentic and fluid gaming experiences as well as practical solutions to real-world mobility challenges.

2 Background

2.1 Unity Engine

Unity Engine [13], developed by Unity Technologies, is a leading platform for creating interactive, real-time 3D and 2D content. It is a cross-platform game engine that has significantly impacted various industries and continue to expand its support to include over 19 platforms, including desktop platforms, gaming consoles, mobile platforms, and virtual reality platforms. The engine offers an interactive simulation environment that provides a rich user experience [11]. Beyond their original purpose of video game development/designing, the versatility and robustness of modern game engines have extended their influence in designing realistic scenarios of various fields, making them invaluable across diverse sectors, including various applications, one of them simulated Connected and Autonomous Vehicles (CAVs) [16]. Unity's workflow stands out from most other game development environments. It offers an exceptionally productive visual process and extensive cross-platform support, making it a preferred choice for many developers. Unity packages are managed from a centralized shared location, providing excellent optional functionality without burdening every project with unnecessary features [4]. Unity is not only a powerful game engine but also a versatile tool that supports a wide range of applications across different industries. Its ease of use, comprehensive platform support, and productive visual workflow make it an excellent choice for both novice and seasoned developers.

2.2 ML-Agents Toolkit

The Unity Machine Learning Agents Toolkit (ML-Agents Toolkit) is an open-source project that transforms games and simulations into training environments for intelligent agents. Using a straightforward Python API, developers can train agents through methods like reinforcement learning, imitation learning, and neuroevolution. The toolkit includes PyTorch-based implementations of advanced algorithms, making it accessible for developers to train intelligent agents. These agents can be used for various purposes, such as controlling NPC behavior, automated game testing, and pre-release game design evaluations [12]. The primary training utility provided by the ML-Agents Toolkit is 'mlagents-learn'. This tool accepts numerous command-line options and utilizes a YAML configuration file containing all the necessary configurations and hyperparameters for training. The specific configurations and hyperparameters in this file can significantly impact training performance, always depending on the agents, environment and the training method intended to use [15]. The core components of this toolkit are:

- **Learning Environment**: The package allows to convert any Unity scene into a learning environment and train character behaviors using a variety of machine learning algorithms, and to embed these trained behaviors back into Unity scenes to control your characters [14]. More specifically, the Unity C#

SDK transforms any scene into a learning environment by defining agents and behaviors, where agents, attached to Unity GameObjects, manage observations, actions, and rewards, and behaviors define agent attributes and actions, identified by Behavior Name, based on Learning, Heuristic, and Inference types [12].
- **Python Low-Level API**: A Python interface for interacting with the learning environment, contained in the package. It communicates with Unity through the Communicator and is used for training and other purposes, like custom algorithms [12].
- **External Communicator**: Connects the Learning Environment with the Python Low-Level API [12].
- **Python Trainers**: Contains machine learning algorithms in the mlagents package, accessible via the mlagents-learn command-line utility [12].

This components interaction can be seen on the following example (Fig. 1).

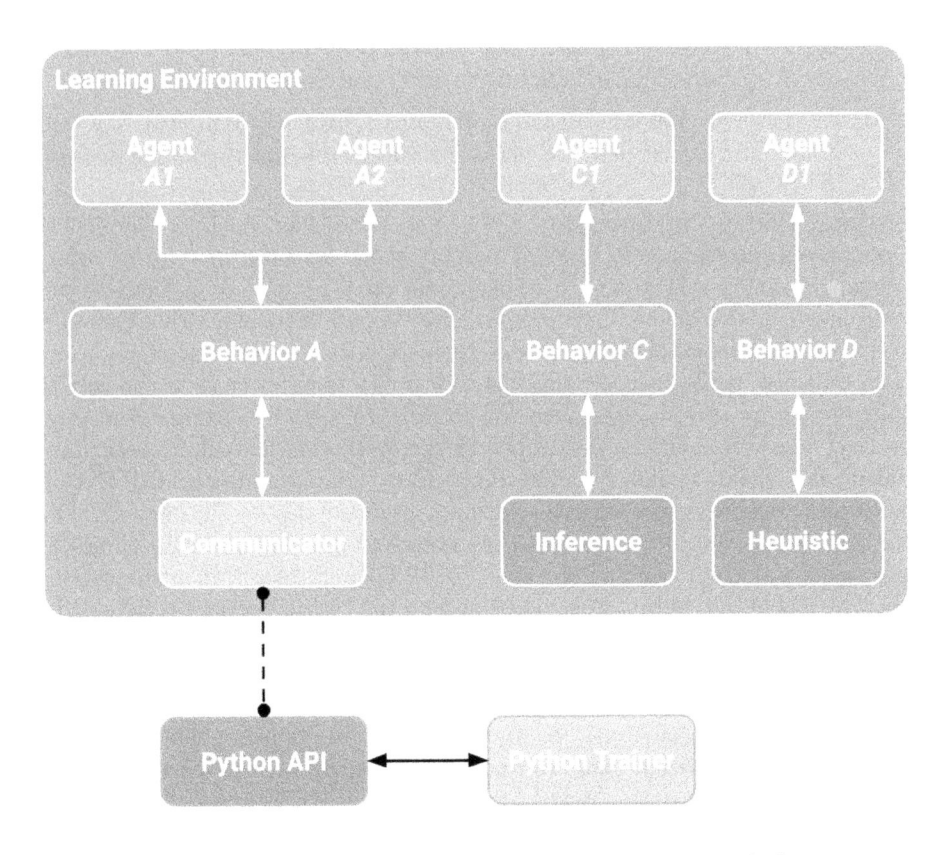

Fig. 1. Example block diagram of ML-Agents Toolkit [12]

2.3 Training Methods

The Unity ML-Agents Toolkit offers a variety of training methods, providing flexibility and efficiency in developing intelligent agents. The ML-Agents Toolkit provides three primary training methods that can be used independently or in combination:

- **Behavioral Cloning (BC)**: This method involves training agents to mimic demonstrations provided by human players or bots. BC can be employed on its own or as a pre-training step to accelerate learning in more complex methods such as GAIL or RL. Leveraging BC requires recording demonstrations as input for the training algorithms [12].
- **Generative Adversarial Imitation Learning (GAIL)**: GAIL integrates imitation learning with reinforcement learning, enabling agents to learn from demonstrations with or without extrinsic rewards. This approach can be used independently or alongside BC and RL to enhance the training process and improve agent performance [12].
- **Reinforcement Learning (RL)**: This fundamental method involves training agents by interacting with the environment to maximize cumulative rewards. RL can be implemented using PPO and Soft Actor-Critic [12].

Among these, we will be focusing on PPO and SAC, which are two key reinforcement learning algorithms that play a significant role in the training process.

Proximal Policy Optimization. PPO has established itself as the default on-policy optimization algorithm in reinforcement learning due to its robust performance and straightforward implementation. This success is theoretically underpinned by the policy improvement lower bound, although PPO itself does not directly maximize this lower bound. Instead, it focuses on maximizing a surrogate objective while ensuring that the new policy remains close to the current policy [9]. At its core, it uses a neural network to approximate an ideal function that maps an agent's observations to the optimal actions in a given state. Implemented within frameworks like TensorFlow, it communicates with Python processes to optimize step updates within a gradient descent framework. This approach has proven more effective than standard gradient descent, leading to more stable and faster training processes [7]. PPO operates within an actor-critic structure, where the "actor" selects actions and the "critic" evaluates them. This method combines current experiences with critiques to update the policy in a way that avoids the large, destructive updates characteristic of traditional policy gradient methods. It achieves this by alternating between sampling data from interactions with the environment and optimizing a clipped policy surrogate. This balance of simplicity, computational efficiency, and effective sample usage contributes to its status as a state-of-the-art method [1]. Moreover, it addresses the sensitivity of policy gradient algorithms to step sizes. By limiting the policy update at each training step, ensures stability and adaptability in new environments. This capability to adjust the objective function during training helps overcome the challenges associated with step size selection, making PPO a reliable choice for diverse and dynamic scenarios [10].

Soft Actor-Critic. SAC is an off-policy reinforcement learning algorithm, distinguishing itself from on-policy methods like PPO. It can learn from experiences collected at any time in the past by storing them in an experience replay buffer, from which samples are randomly drawn during training. This approach significantly enhances sample efficiency, often requiring 5–10 times fewer samples than PPO to achieve comparable performance. However, SAC typically necessitates more model updates, making it well-suited for environments where each step takes longer, around 0.1 s or more. Additionally, SAC is a "maximum entropy" algorithm, promoting intrinsic exploration through the maximization of entropy [12]. The core concept of SAC involves using approximation functions to learn continuous action space policies, categorizing it as a stochastic actor-critic method. SAC implements soft policy iteration, an algorithm that alternates between policy evaluation and policy improvement to learn optimal maximum entropy policies. During policy evaluation, SAC seeks an accurate value function for the current policy, while the policy improvement step updates the policy distribution towards the exponential distribution. SAC utilizes three neural networks: the actor network for policy approximation, the value network for state value approximation, and the critic network for Q-value estimation. These networks collectively predict actions, compute temporal-difference error signals, and aim to maximize both rewards and policy entropy, encouraging extensive exploration [5]. As an off-policy actor-critic algorithm based on the maximum entropy RL framework, SAC's training objective is to maximize both entropy and reward. This dual objective differentiates SAC from traditional actor-critic methods that solely focus on maximizing cumulative rewards. SAC modifies the objective function by incorporating the expected entropy of the policy, favoring stochastic policies and thus enhancing exploration [6,17]. Overall, SAC's off-policy nature, combined with its emphasis on entropy maximization, makes it an effective algorithm for environments requiring efficient sample usage and robust exploration capabilities. The integration of multiple neural networks to approximate policy and value functions further underscores its sophisticated approach to continuous action space learning.

3 Game Environment

The interactive game developed for this research is implemented using the Unity game engine, which provides a flexible and robust platform for creating dynamic and visually appealing simulations. The game environment is designed to simulate real-world driving scenarios within a structured grid layout, aimed at improving driving behaviour through targeted tasks.

The game environment consists of a large flat terrain, offering an expansive area for the vehicle to navigate, formed by 6 parallel roads intersected by another 7 parallel roads, creating a network of intersections. This grid structure is designed to mimic urban road layouts, offering a variety of paths for the car to navigate, as can be seen in the in Fig. 2.

The agent in the simulation is represented by a detailed 3D model of a car. This car model is equipped with two sensors for collecting data from the environment, the front-facing sensor (Fig. 3) to gather information about obstacles

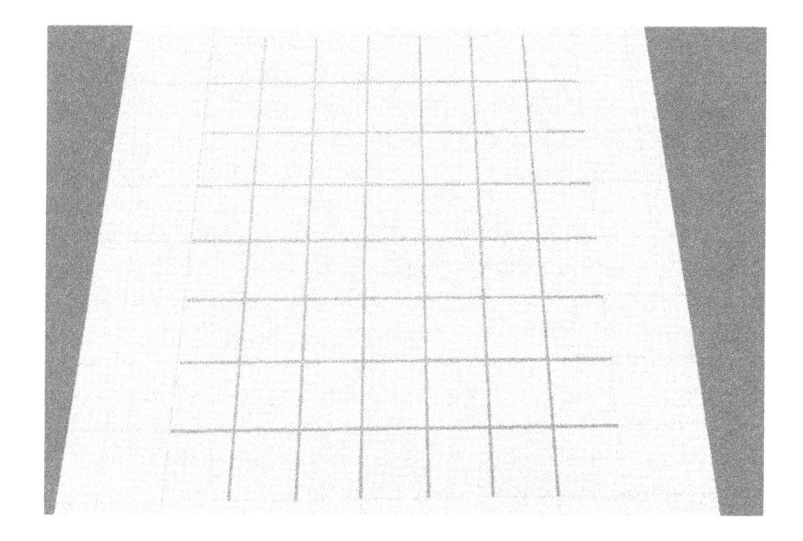

Fig. 2. Above view of the map

Fig. 3. Front-facing sensor in front of the target

(if applied) and target, and the 360-degree sensor (Fig. 4), to collect data from all directions, providing comprehensive situational awareness to the agent.

A designated target zone is marked within the environment, highlighted by a red transparent cylinder. This zone serves as a goal for the vehicle, challenging the agent to navigate the road and reach the specified location. The target and agent can be seen in Fig. 5.

Fig. 4. 360-degree sensor on the road

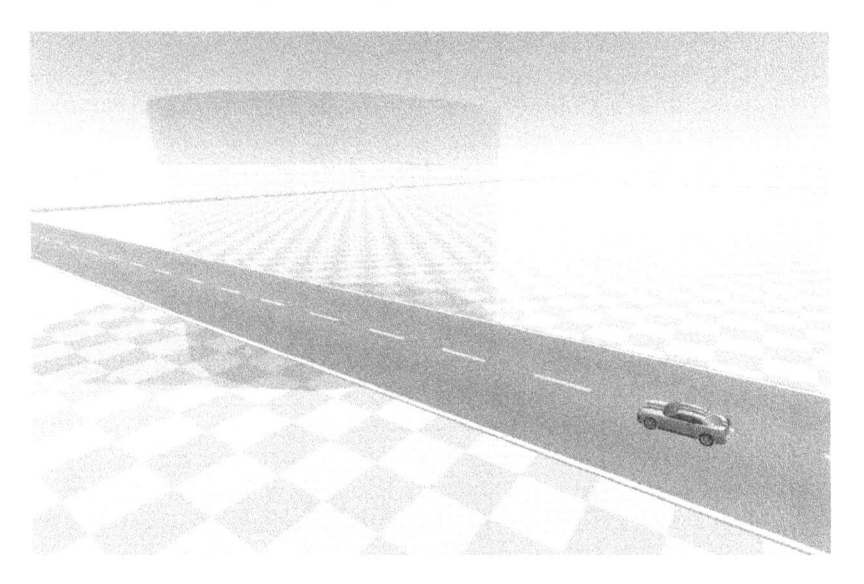

Fig. 5. Target and agent side by side view

Both the car and the target spawn randomly on the roads at the beginning of each session, ensuring that the learning process involves a wide range of scenarios and challenges. This randomization helps in creating a more comprehensive learning experience for the AI.

The future development and the main objective for the car is to learn how to navigate the grid efficiently to reach the target utilizing the previous studied approaches. By simulating a variety of driving scenarios within this structured yet dynamic environment, the game provides a rich platform for testing and improving the adaptability and decision-making capabilities of the AI, contributing to more realistic and fluid gaming experiences.

This environment provides a controlled yet versatile setting for testing autonomous driving algorithms. The combination of a straightforward road layout, detailed vehicle model, and configurable sensors allows for comprehensive evaluation and development of reinforcement learning techniques.

4 Conclusion

In this research, we have introduced an interactive game environment designed to enhance user experience in driving behavior simulations, focusing exclusively on the visual aspects of the project. Utilizing the robust and versatile Unity Engine alongside the Unity ML-Agents Toolkit, we created a dynamic and visually engaging simulation environment that mirrors real-world driving scenarios.

The environment features a structured grid layout representing urban road networks, with a detailed 3D car model equipped with front-facing and 360-degree sensors. These sensors are designed to collect comprehensive data from the environment, allowing the agent to navigate towards designated target zones randomly placed within the grid. This setup provides diverse scenarios to test and refine the agent's navigational capabilities.

We introduced two key reinforcement learning algorithms, PPO and SAC, which will be tested within this environment. PPO offers robust performance through effective policy updates within an actor-critic framework, while SAC enhances sample efficiency and exploration through its off-policy nature and entropy maximization.

Although this paper focuses on the visual setup of the project, it establishes a solid foundation for future work that can incorporate the full spectrum of machine learning and artificial intelligence techniques. By creating a visually detailed and interactive environment, we provide a powerful tool for advancing autonomous driving technologies. This environment facilitates extensive visual testing and refinement of machine learning algorithms, contributing to the development of more adaptive and intelligent autonomous systems.

The insights gained from this research can significantly influence how player agents adapt and interact within gaming environments, leading to more authentic and fluid gaming experiences. Furthermore, by using both recreational and serious games as case studies, this work highlights the versatility of these methods, offering a dynamic environment for testing agent adaptability and responsiveness. This research also provides a practical context for applying these advancements to solve real-world problems in the complex and dynamic domain of mobility.

Funding Information. The study was developed under the project A-MoVeR - "Mobilizing Agenda for the Development of Products and Systems towards an Intelligent and Green Mobility", operation n.o 02/C05-i01.01/2022.PC646908627-00000069, approved under the terms of the call n.o 02/C05-i01/2022 - Mobilizing Agendas for Business Innovation, financed by European funds provided to Portugal by the Recovery and Resilience Plan (RRP), in the scope of the European Recovery and Resilience Facility (RRF), framed in the Next Generation UE, for the period from 2021 -2026

References

1. Alagha, A., Singh, S., Mizouni, R., Bentahar, J., Otrok, H.: Target localization using multi-agent deep reinforcement learning with proximal policy optimization. Futur. Gener. Comput. Syst. **136**, 342–357 (2022). https://doi.org/10.1016/j.future.2022.06.015, https://www.sciencedirect.com/science/article/pii/S0167739X22002266
2. Ciekanowska, A., Kiszczak Gliński, A., Dziedzic, K.: Comparative analysis of unity and unreal engine efficiency in creating virtual exhibitions of 3D scanned models. J. Comput. Sci. Inst. **20**, 247–253 (2021). https://doi.org/10.35784/jcsi.2698, https://ph.pollub.pl/index.php/jcsi/article/view/2698
3. Gao, C., Wang, G., Shi, W., Wang, Z., Chen, Y.: Autonomous driving security: state of the art and challenges. IEEE Internet Things J. **9**(10), 7572–7595 (2022). https://doi.org/10.1109/JIOT.2021.3130054
4. Hocking, J.: Unity in Action, 3rd edn. Manning Publications, New York (2022)
5. de Jesus, J.C., Kich, V.A., Kolling, A.H., Grando, R.B., Cuadros, M.A.S.L., Gamarra, D.F.T.: Soft actor-critic for navigation of mobile robots. J. Intell. Robo. Syst. **102**(2), 1–11 (2021). https://doi.org/10.1007/s10846-021-01367-5
6. Kathirgamanathan, A., Mangina, E., Finn, D.P.: Development of a soft actor critic deep reinforcement learning approach for harnessing energy flexibility in a large office building. Energy AI **5**, 100101 (2021). https://doi.org/10.1016/j.egyai.2021.100101, https://www.sciencedirect.com/science/article/pii/S2666546821000537
7. Lukas, M., Tomicic, I., Bernik, A.: Anticheat system based on reinforcement learning agents in unity. Information **13**(4), 173 (2022). https://doi.org/10.3390/info13040173
8. Muzahid, A.J.M., Kamarulzaman, S.F., Rahman, M.A.: Comparison of PPO and SAC algorithms towards decision making strategies for collision avoidance among multiple autonomous vehicles. In: 2021 International Conference on Software Engineering and Computer Systems and 4th International Conference on Computational Science and Information Management (ICSECS-ICOCSIM), pp. 200–205 (2021). https://doi.org/10.1109/ICSECS52883.2021.00043
9. Queeney, J., Paschalidis, Y., Cassandras, C.G.: Generalized proximal policy optimization with sample reuse. In: Ranzato, M., Beygelzimer, A., Dauphin, Y., Liang, P., Vaughan, J.W. (eds.) Advances in Neural Information Processing Systems, vol. 34, pp. 11909–11919. Curran Associates, Inc. (2021)
10. Saikia, P., Pala, S., Singh, K., Singh, S.K., Huang, W.J.: Proximal policy optimization for RIS-assisted full duplex 6G-V2X communications. IEEE Transp. Intell. Veh., 1–16 (2023). https://doi.org/10.1109/TIV.2023.3275632
11. Singh, S., Kaur, A.: Game development using unity game engine. In: 2022 3rd International Conference on Computing, Analytics and Networks (ICAN). IEEE (2022) https://doi.org/10.1109/ican56228.2022.10007155

12. Unity Technologies: ML-Agents Overview - Unity ML-Agents Toolkit (2024). https://unity-technologies.github.io/ml-agents/ML-Agents-Overview. Accessed 22 May 2024
13. Unity Technologies: Unity Real-Time Development Platform | 3D, 2D, VR & AR Engine, May 2024. https://unity.com. Accessed 22 May 2024
14. Unity-Technologies: About ML-Agents package (com.unity.ml-agents) | ML Agents | 3.0.0-exp.1, October 2023. https://docs.unity3d.com/Packages/com.unity.ml-agents@3.0/manual/index.html. Accessed 22 May 2024
15. Unity-Technologies: ML-agents, May 2024. https://github.com/Unity-Technologies/ml-agents/blob/develop/docs/Training-ML-Agents.md. Accessed 22 May 2024
16. Wang, Z., Han, K., Tiwari, P.: Digital twin simulation of connected and automated vehicles with the unity game engine. In: 2021 IEEE 1st International Conference on Digital Twins and Parallel Intelligence (DTPI). IEEE, July 2021. https://doi.org/10.1109/dtpi52967.2021.9540074
17. Wong, C.C., Chien, S.Y., Feng, H.M., Aoyama, H.: Motion planning for dual-arm robot based on soft actor-critic. IEEE Access **9**, 26871–26885 (2021). https://doi.org/10.1109/ACCESS.2021.3056903

Analyzing Usage Behavior and Preferences of Drivers Regarding Shared Automated Vehicles: Insights from an Online Survey

Verena Pongratz(✉) [iD], Lorenz Steckhan [iD], and Klaus Bengler(✉) [iD]

Technical University of Munich, Boltzmannstr. 15, 85748 Garching, Germany
{verena.i.pongratz,lorenz.steckhan,bengler}@tum.de

Abstract. Studies show that shared automated vehicles (SAV) can increase public acceptance of automation and enable affordable on-demand mobility. However, the varying levels of knowledge about driver assistance systems (DAS) among users of automated vehicles can lead to their underuse or misuse. With the concept of vehicle sharing, familiarity with DAS varies depending on the individual user and the vehicle used. To address this issue, drivers of SAV need to be adequately informed about DAS and their intended use. This information could be provided before the trip through tutorials or during the trip through human-machine interfaces (HMI). Understanding user characteristics and expectations is essential to make these information concepts appealing. Accordingly, we conducted an online survey to gain insights into drivers' utilization patterns and preferences concerning shared vehicles and the use of automated driving features. The results indicate a desire for more information about the availability and intended use of DAS among users but a rejection of mandatory pre-driving introductions. The study highlights the importance of configurable and adaptive HMI concepts to provide information while driving, respecting the drivers' needs and preferences.

Keywords: Automated Driving · Shared Vehicles · Driver Assistance Systems · Intended System Use · Usage Behavior · Driver Preferences

1 Introduction

Vehicles equipped with an automated driving system have the potential to improve user mobility, comfort, traffic efficiency, and road safety [1, 2]. Several studies have shown that automated vehicles have a great potential to prevent traffic accidents or reduce damage [3, 4]. Despite its expected positive impact on people and road traffic, vehicle automation faces consumer resistance [5] and poses challenges, especially for automated vehicle drivers [6]. To address public concerns, Bansal et al. [7] emphasize that the successful integration of autonomous vehicles could be achieved mainly through car rental and car-sharing services. According to the literature, SAV could increase the acceptance of future automation and enable affordable on-demand mobility [8, 9]. The concept of shared vehicle use is characterized by different users with different backgrounds and varying levels of knowledge using different vehicles for different periods of time [10].

Consequently, the knowledge about DAS may vary depending on the user and the specific vehicle used. Given the frequent change between vehicles, it can be assumed that shared vehicle users are heterogeneously and often not sufficiently informed about the DAS of their SAV. This lack of familiarity with the systems may lead to their disuse or misuse, as drivers have too little system experience [2] and may not be aware of their dedicated functionality [11]. Additionally, the intended use of DAS may be compromised due to a lack of understanding or "misunderstanding of the systems' capabilities and limitations" [12, p.30]. Both scenarios contribute to a lack of use or incorrect use of DAS, potentially reducing their positive impact on road safety and user acceptance.

According to Koustanaï et al. [13], training and experience are necessary to better understand the system, including its capacities, benefits, and limitations. So, SAV drivers must be adequately informed about the available DAS and their intended use [14, 15] to ensure the correct use of system functions [13] and improve user acceptance of an in-vehicle system [2]. This could be achieved through various means, such as explanatory pre-drive tutorials or HMI concepts that provide information to the driver during the trip to encourage the intended use of DAS [6]. To make these attractive to users, it is crucial to understand their expectations and preferences regarding interaction with shared vehicles and their DAS. Therefore, we conducted an online survey to explore drivers' usage behavior and preferences regarding shared vehicle offerings (e.g., carsharing, short-term leasing, long-term rental, etc.) and their automated driving functions. The results presented in this paper serve as a basis for identifying drivers' requirements for future SAV and the use of DAS. It also aims to highlight the need for informative HMI concepts in future (shared) automated vehicles that provide assistance in the safe and intended use of DAS. Furthermore, the paper examines the reasons for not using shared vehicles and explores the potential impact of explanatory tutorials and information concepts on this decision.

2 Related Work

2.1 Influence of System Knowledge on Using Automated Driving Functions

Commercial vehicles are increasingly equipped with automated driving features such as Adaptive Cruise Control (ACC) or Lane Keeping Systems (LKS) to assist the human driver [16]. Although they should positively impact user comfort and safety [17], many drivers find it challenging to get used to them [16]. The development of training courses for learning how to interact with automated vehicles has been largely neglected but is necessary for the safe and efficient use of automated driving [14]. According to studies [18–20], many drivers are unaware of which DAS their vehicle has, what these systems can do, and how to use them correctly. Furthermore, drivers are often overwhelmed by the complexity of automated vehicles and their driving functions [6] or cannot associate the different system names with similar functions [21]. In addition, at least one-quarter of drivers are not informed about DAS when purchasing a vehicle [15, 22], and only a few are given the opportunity to try it out before buying [16]. However, studies show that drivers need several interactions with an automated system to understand and trust it properly [15, 23].

According to Carsten and Martens [11], current HMI concepts also encourage misinterpretation of system functions, as they often do not follow generally accepted guidelines for good human-machine interaction. Even when a vehicle is automated, the driver must be aware of the capabilities and limitations of the system in order to accomplish the driving task in the event of a takeover or cooperative control of the vehicle [16]. This becomes problematic when drivers of automated vehicles do not understand that system functions do not work under all conditions due to their lack of knowledge [11]. This lack of understanding of DAS can not only affect road safety [24, 25] and limit the expected benefits of automated driving [26]. It also leads to losing confidence in the system, causing users to choose not to purchase or use potentially helpful and safety-enhancing systems [11]. According to Trübswetter et al. [2], user acceptance is a decisive precondition for using DAS, as it is the user deciding whether to use a system or not. As a driver, knowing when it is safe or unsafe to use automated driving functions is, therefore, critical and should be supported by well-designed information systems and strategies.

2.2 Current Approaches to Information Concepts for Automated Driving

Understanding and correct use of system functions can be improved to some extent by appropriate pre-use instruction [15]. However, according to Ebinger et al. [6], the current methods by which drivers learn to understand and use automated driving do not lead to a sufficient understanding of the driving functions. Driver assistance systems and their intended use are usually described in detail in a vehicle's user manual. Therefore, drivers usually rely on these manuals as their primary source of information [22]. However, according to Boelhouwer et al. [27], the information found there is insufficient to improve the user's general understanding of the available driving functions and to adequately explain their intended use. Furthermore, manuals are not only long and complicated [14, 27] but also not understood by many readers due to the technical language used in them [28]. Therefore, reading manuals is not an efficient learning method [29]. Based on existing literature [30, 31], it can be assumed that users rarely use manuals for this reason. Instead, drivers often try to develop interaction strategies with DAS while driving [32]. However, this leads to an insufficient understanding of the relevant functions, e.g., safety-critical constraints, which remain unknown [33].

According to Ebinger et al. [6], tutoring is a better approach to prepare drivers for driving automated vehicles. Specifically, they show that driver tutoring effectively improves driver attention in the transition from automated to manual driving. Ebinger et al. [6, p.70] define driver tutoring as "technology-enhanced learning support focused on the safe use of automated vehicles". Different types of driver tutoring have already been investigated in the existing literature [6, 16, 34, 35], often in the context of takeover situations in automated driving. A distinction can be made between pre-drive and on-drive tutoring. For tutoring concepts that inform the driver while driving, the design and function of the HMI are crucial to enable driver to safely interact with the system functions of the automated vehicle [11]. As the primary means of communication, the HMI must help people understand the capabilities and limitations of automated system functions, especially when the driver cannot be completely decoupled from the driving task, as in semi-automated driving [11]. It is important to investigate the form of human-automation interaction and the type of information the human driver receives from an automated vehicle [36], as there is a fine line between information overload leading to stress and too little information leading to uncertainty [11]. Due to the changing role of humans in automated vehicles, information for monitoring and controlling automation becomes more important than information related to the driving task itself [23].

In particular, the information provided should offer system observability, reliability, and predictability of current and future system actions [11]. According to Beggiato et al. [23], it can be assumed that the driver's need for information decreases over the course of use and is not the same for every driver. Therefore, it is crucial to know the driver's individual characteristics and preferences to consider them in the information presented.

3 Methodology

This section outlines the survey details, questionnaire design, sample, and data analysis. The Ethics Committee of the Technical University of Munich reviewed and approved the study (reference number 2024–4-NM-KH).

3.1 Survey Design

The survey focuses on users' and non-users' suggestions for improvements and preferences regarding shared vehicle offerings and related DAS. It was conducted exclusively online to allow people to participate from a location of their choice. All participants were required to provide informed consent before the first question. In addition to demographic data, the online survey collected information on participants' theoretical knowledge, practical experience, and interest regarding automated vehicles and automated driving features in general. Participants were also asked if they owned a personal vehicle and if they had a Class B driver's license, as only individuals with a driver's license were to be included in the survey analysis. Next, participants were queried about their driving habits and frequency of use of shared vehicles, categorizing them as users or non-users of shared vehicle transportation.

Users were first asked to indicate how often they use shared vehicles on urban roads, country roads, and highways. Regarding the use of DAS, participants were asked to indicate whether they use DAS such as cruise control, ACC, or LKS in shared vehicles when available. Additionally, they were queried about their preparation time to familiarize themselves with shared vehicles and their frequency of informing about available DAS as well as their intended use. Furthermore, the primary medium used to inform about DAS should be identified. The choices were the user manual, the internet, the provided carsharing app, and testing functions while driving. In this context, they had to assess their need for information about DAS and decide whether they would prefer to receive more information about these systems. Preferences regarding pre-drive tutorials or on-drive HMI concepts were also asked. The last question addressed the desire for adaptive automatic adjustment of available driving functions in shared vehicles to the driver's own driving behavior.

After the demographic questions, non-users are primarily asked about the factors influencing their decision not to use shared vehicles. A lack of demand, low availability, low familiarity with shared vehicles, including their DAS, or too much effort to use them were possible answers. They were then asked to rate whether special scenarios could encourage their use of shared vehicles. Examples include a greater selection of DAS in shared vehicles or the availability of more information about existing DAS and their intended use.

Both users and non-users were asked if they would be more likely to use DAS if they were introduced to them in a brief introduction. This was followed by the question of whether they would take the time to be introduced to the available DAS and their intended use before the first drive. As an example, pictures and short videos were suggested as ways to introduce automated driving features. The last part of the questionnaire queried the general interest in information concepts for driving shared vehicles, such as tutorials or informative HMI, including mandatory introductions before driving.

3.2 Sample

The participants were recruited through distributing flyers at the Technical University of Munich, the Chair of Ergonomics subject database, and social media. To participate in the study, individuals were required to be at least 18 years of age and possess a Class B driver's license. Additionally, they should have sufficient knowledge of the German language and have access to the Internet, as the survey was conducted in German and entirely online. Participation in the study was voluntary and not remunerated.

A total of 164 individuals participated in the online survey. Of these, 86 were male and 78 were female, with an average age of 38.63 (standard deviation (SD) = 17.28). The age of the participants ranged from 18 to 80 years, with the majority aged between 25 and 34. They have held their driver's license for a mean (M) of 20.61 years (SD = 16.85). Additionally, 129 individuals own a private vehicle, while 34 do not. The test subjects' general theoretical knowledge of automated driving functions (cruise control, ACC, LKS, semi-automated, and fully automated systems) was found to average 3.43 (SD = 1.54) on a scale of 0 (none) to 6 (very much). The participants' general practical experience with automated driving functions averaged 2.74 (SD = 1.74) on the same scale. The highest levels of theoretical knowledge and practical experience were observed in the case of cruise control. The mean theoretical knowledge score was 4.31 (SD = 1.65), while the mean practical experience score was 4.62 (SD = 1.74). In contrast, the lowest levels of theoretical knowledge and practical experience were observed in the case of fully automated systems ($M_{theoretical} = 2.54$, $SD_{theoretical} = 1.85$; $M_{practical} = 0.71$, $SD_{practical} = 1.30$). On the same scale, the participants' interest in using automated driving functions and automated vehicles has a mean value of 3.90 (SD = 1.65).

In terms of shared vehicle usage, 87 individuals reported utilizing such a vehicle within the past 12 months, with the majority of them several times during this period. In contrast, 77 individuals had not done so. The group of SAV users is comprised of 51 men and 36 women, with an overall average age of 38.18 (SD = 15.47). Conversely, the non-user group comprises 35 men and 42 women, with an average age of 39.13 (SD = 19.22). Among those who used shared vehicles, 80% also possess a private vehicle, whereas for non-users, this percentage stands at 77.01%. The average driver's license ownership is 20.26 years (SD = 15.12) for users and 21.00 (SD = 19.22) years for non-users. The following figure illustrates the frequency with which users used shared vehicles in the last year. Due to the uneven distribution of the data, it is not sensible to differentiate between the individual categories for further analysis. However, they are relevant for the following discussion.

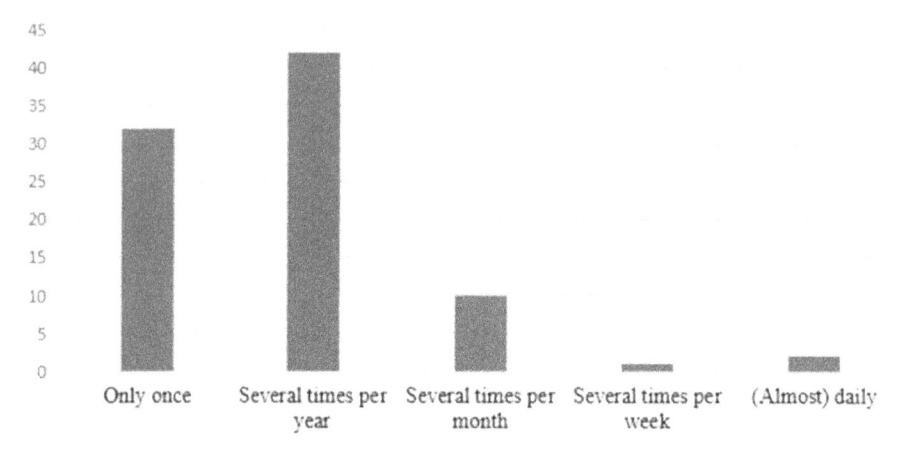

Fig. 1. Users' frequency of shared vehicle uses within the past 12 months.

3.3 Data Analysis

The survey data is evaluated through descriptive analysis, including calculating the mean value and standard deviation. Additionally, statistical methods, such as t-tests, are employed for mean value comparisons. The Welch test is used for samples that did not fulfill the requirements for applying a t-test, such as normal distribution or equality of variances. Cohen's d [37] is calculated to estimate the effect size of significant results and the related practical significance. The values d = 0.20, d = 0.50, and d = 0.80 are used to indicate the magnitude of the effect, with small, medium, and large effects, respectively. Finally, Spearman's Rho (ρ) was employed to calculate correlation analyses to determine whether there are links between individual factors. According to Cohen [11], the following effect limits are used for their evaluation: small correlation: $\rho = 0.10$, moderate correlation: $\rho = 0.30$, large correlation: $\rho = 0.50$.

The demographic data was initially analyzed descriptively, followed by t-tests for independent samples to statistically compare the calculated mean values of users and non-users. The responses regarding drivers' usage behavior and preferences were initially analyzed individually for each user group. T-tests for dependent samples were subsequently conducted to complement the descriptive analysis. Comparable questions were analyzed using t-tests for independent samples to compare the user groups' usage behavior and preferences. The significance level of 5% was applied for all inferential tests conducted.

4 Results

Comparing the two groups, namely users and non-users, no significant differences were observed in age (t (162) = 0.35, p = .728) or the number of years of driving license ownership (t (162) = 0.28, p = .779). Moreover, a comparable number of individuals own a private vehicle. A significant difference was found between the two groups in terms of their interest in automated vehicles (t (162) = -3.48, p = .001, d = 0.55).

On a scale of 0 (none) to 6 (very high), users (M = 4.31, SD = 1.47) displayed significantly higher interest in automated vehicles than non-users (M = 3.44, SD = 1.72).

Regarding automated driving functions and DAS in general, shared vehicle users showed significantly higher prior theoretical knowledge (M_{user} = 3.75, SD_{user} = 1.73; $M_{non-user}$ = 3.06, $SD_{non-user}$ = 1.95; t (162) = -2.91, p = .004, d = 0.46) and greater practical experience (M_{user} = 3.11, SD_{user} = 2.31; $M_{non-user}$ = 2.32, $SD_{non-user}$ = 2.21; t (162) = -3.61, p < .001, d = 0.56) than non-users. These findings apply to all driving functions queried (see Table 1), except for practical experience with fully automated systems. In the latter, no significant difference was found between users and non-users of shared vehicles.

Table 1. Results of the statistical mean value comparison regarding users' and non-users' theoretical knowledge and practical experience

Variable	User M (SD)	Non-user M (SD)	Statistics
Theoretical knowledge of cruise control	4.59 (1.43)	4.00 (1.81)	t (144.38) = −2.28, p = .024, d = .36
Practical experience with cruise control	4.89 (1.62)	4.31 (1.82)	t (162) = −2.13, p = .034, d = .33
Theoretical knowledge of ACC	4.11 (1.49)	3.30 (1.76)	t (162) = −3.21, p = .002, d = .50
Practical experience with ACC	3.76 (2.15)	2.79 (2.05)	t (162) = −2.94, p = .004, d = .46
Theoretical knowledge of LKS	3.98 (1.51)	3.29 (1.87)	t (162) = −2.62, p = .009, d = .41
Practical experience with LKS	3.80 (1.90)	2.79 (1.98)	t (162) = −3.33, p = .001, d = .52
Theoretical knowledge of partial automation	3.23 (1.78)	2.52 (1.96)	t (162) = −2.43, p = .016, d = .38
Practical experience with partial automation	2.21 (2.05)	1.22 (1.71)	t (161.39) = −3.36, p = .001, d = .52
Theoretical knowledge of full automation	2.83 (1.82)	2.21 (1.84)	t (162) = −2.16, p = .032, d = .34
Practical experience with full automation	0.89 (1.39)	0.51 (0.17)	t (162) = −1.87, p = .063

Furthermore, the frequency of use of shared vehicles is found to correlate significantly with theoretical knowledge ($\rho = 0.210$, $p = .007$), practical experience ($\rho = 0.286$, $p < .001$), and interest ($\rho = 0.239$, $p = .002$) in automated driving and DAS in general.

The following results are derived from statements rated by respondents on a scale of –2 (strongly disagree) to 2 (strongly agree). The results indicate that shared vehicle users exhibit a significantly higher use of available functions and DAS in their private vehicle (M = 1.22, SD = 1.28) compared to non-users (M = 0.35, SD = 1.60; t (116.65) = –3.39, p = .001). With an effect size of d = 0.60, this corresponds to a medium effect. The use of DAS in private vehicles is positively correlated with the frequency of use of shared vehicles ($\rho = 0.259$, $p = .003$). No significant difference was found when users and non-users were asked whether they would take the time for an introduction to the DAS of a shared vehicle (t (162) = –0.123, p = .902). The two groups independently rated this question similarly ($M_{user} = -0.13$, $SD_{user} = 1.50$; $M_{non\text{-}user} = -0.16$, $SD_{non\text{-}user} = 1.56$). The attitude towards taking the time for an introduction to the DAS of a shared vehicle before their first ride is positively correlated with age among users and non-users ($\rho = 0.178$, $p = .022$).

4.1 Users of Shared Vehicles

Shared vehicle users are predominantly young people aged 25–34, with a slight male predominance (58.6%). The survey results indicate that shared vehicles are mainly used on urban roads. The frequency of usage on urban roads is rated at M = 3.87 (SD = 1.75) on a scale of 0 (never) to 6 (very often), while country roads are rated at M = 2.97 (SD = 1.84) and highways at M = 2.93 (SD = 1.90). The analysis revealed significant differences between the usage of shared vehicles on urban roads and country roads (t (86) = 3.64, p < .001, d = 0.45), as well as between their usage on urban roads and highways (t (86) = 3.52, p < .001, d = 0.47). In addition, the correlation analysis showed a statistically significant correlation between the use of shared vehicles and driving on urban roads ($\rho = 0.458$, $p < .001$). No significant correlation was found between the use of shared vehicles and urban roads or highways. Furthermore, no significant difference was observed between country roads and highways (t (86) = 0.257, p = .798).

The average driver of a shared vehicle takes approximately three minutes to become acquainted with the vehicle before embarking on their first journey. The time required for familiarization exhibited a significant correlation with the age of the respondents ($\rho = 0.370$, $p < .001$). Regarding the use of DAS, statistical analysis indicates that users are significantly more likely to address the availability of DAS than to focus on their correct use (t (66) = 4.22, p < .001, d = 0.17). Upon closer examination, users of shared vehicles rarely concern themselves with the available functions (M = 2.56, SD = 1.73) and even less often with their correct use (M = 2.28, SD = 1.58). A total of 64.37% of users rarely or never engage in the available functions of their shared vehicle before their first trip. Regarding the intended use of DAS, the figure rises to 74.71%. Conversely, only 12.64% of respondents indicated that they frequently considered the available DAS of their shared vehicle, and only 6.90% considered the intended use of these functions.

Significant correlations were identified between user characteristics and users' attitudes toward the availability and intended use of DAS. These findings are presented in the following table (Table 2).

Table 2. Correlations between user characteristics and dealing with DAS availability and their intended use.

Variable 1	Variable 2	ρ	p
Age of users	Dealing with DAS availability	ρ = 0.373	p < .001
Theoretical knowledge about DAS	Dealing with DAS availability	ρ = 0.363	p < .001
Practical experience with DAS	Dealing with DAS availability	ρ = 0.499	p < .001
Interest in using DAS	Dealing with DAS availability	ρ = 0.400	p < .001
Age of users	Dealing with DAS intended use	ρ = 0.269	p = .012
Theoretical knowledge about DAS	Dealing with DAS intended use	ρ = 0.364	p < .001
Practical experience with DAS	Dealing with DAS intended use	ρ = 0.426	p < .001
Interest in using DAS	Dealing with DAS intended use	ρ = 0.289	p = .007

When queried about the preferred method of obtaining information about the DAS of a shared vehicle, 88.10% of users indicated a preference for hands-on experience by trying them out while driving. In total, 32.19% of users obtain information alternatively, such as consulting the vehicle's user manual, accessing the internet, or utilizing the carsharing provider's app. Almost three-quarters of respondents (74.71%) also discover the correct use of driving functions by trying them out while driving. In this case, 36.78% of respondents obtain information through another medium mentioned above.

The utilization of driving functions in shared vehicles exhibits considerable variability when available. While cruise control is rather frequently used by drivers (M = 3.93, SD = 2.07), ACC (M = 2.93, SD = 2.26), LKS (M = 2.69, SD = 2.14), and partial automation (M = 1.53, SD = 1.88) are rarely to very rarely used when available. Table 3 illustrates the significant correlations between users' theoretical knowledge, practical experience, and the utilization of DAS in shared vehicles.

The following results are derived from statements rated by users on a scale of –2 (strongly disagree) to 2 (strongly agree). The desire for a large selection of DAS in shared vehicles is trending slightly positively among the users (M = 0.10, SD = 1.48). The majority of users (58.21%) indicated that they have more functions and DAS in shared vehicles than in private vehicles. Compared to private vehicles (M = 1.22, SD = 1.28),

Table 3. Correlations between users' theoretical knowledge, practical experience, and using DAS in shared vehicles.

Variable 1	Variable 2	ρ	p
Theoretical knowledge about cruise control	Use of cruise control	ρ = 0.328	p = .003
Practical experience with cruise control	Use of cruise control	ρ = 0.363	p < .001
Theoretical knowledge about ACC	Use of ACC	ρ = 0.432	p < .001
Practical experience with ACC	Use of ACC	ρ = 0.582	p < .001
Theoretical knowledge about LKS	Use of LKS	ρ = 0.268	p = .021
Practical experience with LKS	Use of LKS	ρ = 0.604	p < .001
Theoretical knowledge about partial automation	Use of partial automation	ρ = 0.341	p = .004
Practical experience with partial automation	Use of partial automation	ρ = 0.511	p < .001

the use of DAS is significantly less frequent in shared vehicles (M = 0.39, SD = 1.45; t(66) = 4.22, p < .001; d = 0.61). However, there is a significant correlation between the use of DAS in private vehicles and their use in shared vehicles (ρ = 0.465, p < .001). The latter correlates with the interest of users in automated driving (ρ = 0.351, p < .001), their theoretical knowledge (ρ = 0.282, p = .008), and practical experience (ρ = 0.414, p < .001) with automated driving functions in general. Furthermore, a positive correlation was identified between the use of DAS and the time required for users to become familiar with the DAS of a shared vehicle (ρ = 0.213, p = .048).

Regarding the use of DAS in shared vehicles, over 60% of users indicated a desire for more information and a willingness to use DAS more frequently if provided with a concise introduction (e.g., by pictures or brief videos). The desire for information on the correct use of DAS (M = 0.39, SD = 1.31) slightly outweighs that for information on the pure availability of DAS (M = 0.30, SD = 1.36). However, nearly 70% of respondents reject a mandatory introduction before the first trip (M = –0.74, SD = 1.43). A slight majority of users preferred receiving information about available DAS while driving (M = 0.08, SD = 1.43). The desire for instructions during the drive is more pronounced for the intended use (M = 0.23, SD = 1.43) than for the availability of DAS. Furthermore, the use of adaptive systems that adjust information about DAS to the user's driving behavior is perceived positively by the surveyed users (M = 0.26, SD = 1.43).

4.2 Non-users of Shared Vehicles

The primary reason for the non-use of shared vehicles was the lack of necessity due to the availability of private vehicles or other forms of transportation, with 93.51% of non-users citing this as the reason for their non-use. 28.57% of respondents showed a desire for independence afforded by their own vehicle, which they perceived to be lacking in a shared vehicle. 22.08% of non-users indicated that the effort required to use shared vehicles was a deterrent. 15.58% of respondents stated that the lack of shared vehicles in their vicinity renders their use impractical and sometimes impossible. A lack of familiarity with shared vehicles or their driving functions and the resulting uncertainties were identified as reasons for non-use by 14.28% of respondents. While three people criticized the high costs of rental vehicles, a lack of additional equipment, such as a child seat, was cited by two people as a reason for non-use.

To ascertain the potential for promoting the use of shared vehicles, the following suggestions were evaluated by non-users on a scale of -2 (strongly disagree) to 2 (strongly agree). Non-users would not use shared vehicles more frequently, even with additional information about the available DAS ($M = –1.05$, $SD = 1.37$) or their correct use ($M = –1.04$, $SD = 1.36$). The same applies to the explanation of DAS in a brief introduction (e.g., by pictures or short videos) ($M = –0.99$, $SD = 1.37$) or a more extensive selection of DAS in shared vehicles ($M = –1.14$, $SD = 1.24$). Even a mandatory introduction to the available DAS does not improve the attitude of non-users toward shared vehicles ($M = –1.16$, $SD = 1.25$). Providing on-drive information about available DAS ($M = –0.90$, $SD = 1.33$) and their intended use ($M = –0.88$, $SD = 1.33$) cannot help either to encourage respondents to use shared vehicles. Adaptive systems that adjust information about DAS to the user's driving behavior are rated most positively on average and are more likely to be considered by non-users than all other suggestions. However, the average rating of adaptive systems to promote shared vehicles' use is also negative ($M = -0.42$, $SD = 1.54$).

5 Discussion

The presented study aimed to investigate drivers' current usage behavior and preferences regarding shared vehicle offerings (such as car sharing, short-term leasing, long-term rental, etc.) and their automated driving features. The surveyed population in this study was balanced in terms of age, gender, ownership of a private vehicle, and whether shared vehicles are used. Overall, slightly more men than women and more users of shared vehicles than non-users were surveyed. Nevertheless, no significant differences were found in the main characteristics of the two user groups. Therefore, the existing minor differences can be disregarded, and the groups can be compared.

5.1 Users and Non-users in Comparison

Shared vehicle users showed greater theoretical knowledge, more practical experience, and a stronger interest in automated vehicles and DAS than non-users. Moreover, the frequency of shared vehicle use is positively correlated with all three aforementioned variables. At the same time, almost 60% of shared vehicle users state that they have more DAS in shared vehicles than in their private vehicles. Considering these results, it could be inferred that users' high level of knowledge and experience is a consequence of their use of shared vehicles. However, this must be viewed cautiously, as shared vehicle users also use DAS significantly more frequently in private vehicles. Furthermore, the frequency of shared vehicle use correlates positively with using DAS in private vehicles. Consequently, the higher prior knowledge and experience may also be based on using DAS in private vehicles, which is promoted by a generally higher interest in this topic. It is impossible to determine whether higher knowledge and experience is derived from using DAS in shared or private vehicles, as correlations cannot be used to determine causality. However, it is striking that the differences between users and non-users are evident and significant across all DAS surveyed.

Consequently, this disparity should not be disregarded. The lack of a significant difference in practical experience with fully automated systems is to be mentioned at this point. As fully automated vehicles are currently difficult to access, neither users nor non-users have the opportunity to gain practical experience with such systems. The small number of individuals that stated experience may have had contact with fully automated systems due to their professional activities. It can be reasonably assumed that the use of shared vehicles is not a factor influencing this result.

Neither users nor non-users would take much time to inform about a vehicle's driving features and DAS before their first drive. The respondents' age is positively correlated with their general attitude toward taking the time to inform about DAS.

Consequently, older drivers appear more inclined to invest time learning about automated driving functions and DAS. The same applies in reverse to younger drivers. However, given the small correlation between the two variables, this assertion should be interpreted with caution. As stated by Abraham et al. [15], it is not the number of learning methods and the amount of time spent in training that are decisive for successful training. Rather, the type and quality of training, combined with individual learning preferences, is crucial for the drivers' understanding and use of in-vehicle systems. Since driver learning preferences are currently poorly considered in driver instructions on in-vehicle technologies [15], they should be considered for tutorial and HMI concepts informing about DAS. At this point, adaptive concepts could help to provide customized information strategies based on drivers' learning preferences.

It is striking that both groups reject the idea of a mandatory introduction to DAS for shared vehicles. However, before completely ruling out this option, it is important to investigate whether some form of mandatory introduction may positively affect the intended use of DAS despite their initial rejection. Concerning that appropriate pre-use instruction can enhance the understanding and intended use of system functions [6, 15], legal standardization requiring the introduction of available DAS before using automated vehicles may help to ensure that DAS are used correctly. Making the availability of DAS dependent on an introduction could also be considered. Such an optional introduction, leading to the activation of automated driving functions once a corresponding introduction has been completed, may also avoid incorrect use of DAS. However, the impact on user acceptance must be investigated and considered for future information concepts. It must be taken into account that this only provides an opportunity to prevent misuse and does not solve the problem of non-use. Therefore, approaches must also be developed to motivate drivers to use DAS and avoid their non-use.

5.2 Users of Shared Vehicles

The results indicate that the majority of shared vehicle users are male and young people aged 25–34 years. These findings align with those of Hu et al. [38], which also identified young males between the ages of 25 and 39 years as the primary users of car sharing. However, it is impossible to establish this with certainty based on the current online survey, as this age range also shows a peak across all test subjects (including non-users). As more men than women participated in the survey overall, this result should also be subjected to further scrutiny. The composition of the test population may have influenced the results. Another factor that may influence the study's outcome is the frequency of use of shared vehicles. It is notable that 85% of users have only used shared vehicles once or several times per year in the last 12 months (see Fig. 1). More frequent use was only reported by a few participants (14.94%). This point should be criticized regarding the objective of conducting a survey with a balanced study population. Given that the risk of misuse or disuse of DAS is most likely to occur with unfamiliar vehicles, the drivers' needs in the initial contact with a vehicle seem to be most relevant for developing tutorial and HMI concepts for shared vehicles. Due to the low shared vehicle usage of the respondents, the present data set particularly includes the preferences of drivers with little experience with shared vehicles. It thus forms a valuable foundation for the future development of tutorial and HMI concepts and is useful for further studies despite this uneven distribution in usage frequency.

The results indicate that shared vehicles are mainly utilized on urban roads. The high correlation between shared vehicle use and driving on urban roads and the significant difference to other road types may be explained by the higher availability of, for example, carsharing vehicles in urban environments. This result aligns with the study by Prieto et al. [39], which indicates that the demand for car sharing is higher in urban areas compared to rural areas. Consequently, it could be beneficial to direct particular attention to urban driving when designing tutorial concepts for DAS in shared vehicles.

Regarding the use of DAS, users of shared vehicles seldom ascertain the availability of DAS in their vehicles and, even less frequently, their intended use. However, it remains unclear whether the complexity of DAS influences how often information about them is obtained. Prior theoretical knowledge, practical experience, and interest in using them appear to be related to the willingness to inform about DAS. Prior theoretical knowledge and practical experience with DAS also seem to be connected to the frequency of DAS use. The high positive correlations, particularly concerning practical experience, indicate a mutual influence. It can be assumed that familiar systems, such as cruise control, are used more frequently due to previous experience and knowledge. The lack of familiarity with a system could result in uncertainty and, consequently, a lack of use. Conversely, frequent use of DAS can facilitate the acquisition of knowledge and experience with these systems. These findings go along with those of Carsten et al. [11]. Additionally, further indications suggest that the level of familiarity influences the use of DAS. For instance, the use of DAS is significantly higher in private vehicles than in shared vehicles. The principle of shared vehicles is determined by regular vehicle change. Consequently, DAS may be better known in private vehicles as they are used more frequently. The fact that the use of DAS in private and shared vehicles correlates positively with each other should not be neglected at this point.

The time required for users to become acquainted with a shared vehicle before embarking on their first drive is approximately three minutes. This result is comparable to the study by Mayer et al. [40], which identified two minutes as the time required for familiarization with the car-sharing vehicle. In summary, 53% of respondents indicated that they required between one and three minutes to familiarize themselves with the vehicle [40]. These results can serve as an orientation for future concepts that inform drivers using pre-drive tutorials. Regarding the present study, it is striking that the user's age is positively correlated with the time users take to familiarize themselves with a shared vehicle before the first drive. Older drivers appear to require more time to familiarize themselves with the vehicle, while younger drivers are quicker. This could be attributed to a natural age-related decline in mental capacity, which decreases absorption capacity. However, as Lambert et al. [41] have observed, not all older drivers exhibit a decline in working memory capacity. Similarly, not all young adults demonstrate better cognitive abilities. Consequently, these findings cannot be generalized but warrant consideration due to the significant positive correlation.

In general, users of shared vehicles rarely ascertain the availability of DAS in their vehicles and, even more rarely, the intended use. Theoretical prior knowledge, practical experience, and interest in using DAS appear to be significant factors influencing the willingness to inform oneself about DAS. Among those who want to inform about DAS in shared vehicles, nearly 90% utilize driving as a means of experimentation to gain information about their availability. This also applies to the collecting of information about the intended use. Only a small number of users consult the vehicle manual or the provider's app. This aligns with the findings of previous studies, which indicate that user manuals are rarely utilized [30, 31] and that users prefer to experiment with DAS while driving as an alternative to vehicle manuals [32]. The fact that most shared vehicle users would like to receive more information about DAS and would use them more often if introduced to them, illustrates the importance of well-designed information concepts. In addition to providing information about the availability of DAS, it is increasingly important to focus on their intended use. Furthermore, future information concepts should provide on-drive information about DAS, for example, through the vehicle's HMI. According to Feinauer et al. [42], training drivers while driving is a promising approach for introducing them to automated driving functions. Adaptive information concepts that adapt the information to the user also appear attractive to users of shared vehicles and should be considered for future research.

5.3 Non-users of Shared Vehicles

The main reason for the disuse of shared vehicles is the lack of necessity due to the availability of private vehicles or other means of transportation. In the study by Meyer et al. [40], respondents also identified a lack of need as the primary reason for the disuse of shared vehicles. The desire to be able to move independently with one's own vehicle was rated similarly in both studies. The same applies to the perceived insecurities associated with driving in shared vehicles. However, this reason accounts for only a small proportion of both studies. In contrast, the lack of availability close to the place of residence as a reason for non-use is rated very differently. However, this can be attributed to the different origins of the study population.

Despite the proposed enhancements, the non-users surveyed demonstrated a lack of inclination to utilize shared vehicles more frequently. All statements regarding the design of shared vehicle offerings were rated negatively by the non-users surveyed. More than 90% of respondents indicated that they have no requirement for shared vehicles, a figure that is unlikely to change even if shared vehicle equipment were to be altered. Even well-designed information concepts regarding DAS have not been able to change the lack of demand. Only the assessment of adaptive concepts that adjust provided information and DAS to the user's driving behavior or preferences was slightly more positive. As the average rating was nevertheless negative in total, it is difficult to assume that adaptive systems contribute to a complete change in mood and more frequent use of shared vehicles. However, they are less strongly rejected by non-users. The necessity of incorporating adaptive concepts into future research thus also becomes evident when examining non-users' responses. Transferring innovative information concepts from shared to private vehicles is similarly important. The survey findings indicate that individuals who do not require shared vehicles are unlikely to be persuaded to use them by improving the equipment and service. Instead, they will probably persist in utilizing their private vehicles. Consequently, the information concepts for private vehicles should also be revised. This appears to be the optimal way to disseminate information about DAS and their intended use to all drivers and ensure the safe and efficient use of DAS in all vehicles. To achieve this, further studies are required to gain information about the needs and preferences of drivers in their private vehicles.

6 Limitations

Online surveys offer a simple and anonymous means of data collection, with high cost and time efficiency, minimal experimenter effect, and rapid access to the data. Nevertheless, it is important to consider the potential drawbacks of online surveys [43, 44] to accurately interpret the results. As the participants respond to all questions independently, there is no opportunity for queries or problems to be clarified when completing the questionnaire. Consequently, online questionnaires cannot be considered an infallible data collection method since incorrect completion or random answers cannot be ruled out, particularly when incentives such as prizes or expense allowances are offered. As remuneration was not provided for participation in this study, the potential for this effect to be minimal is acknowledged. Additionally, it is impossible to ascertain whether test subjects have completed the survey on more than one occasion, compromising the results' integrity. As participation in the survey requires using a device with an internet connection, the study design does not consider individuals who do not have access to the internet, such as senior citizens. This may limit the sample's representativeness. In this study, participants aged between 65 and 80 years account for a relatively small proportion (14.6%) of the total sample, yet they are not entirely overlooked. Overall, the distribution of age groups is relatively uniform, with a single peak occurring at the age range of 25–34 years, representing 45.7% of the total population. The potential impact of this peak on the results is discussed in Chapter 5.2. Due to the large number of participants who utilized shared vehicles only once or a few times per year, this data primarily encompasses users' preferences following their initial contact with shared vehicles or with minimal prior experience. Future studies could focus on a test group with a higher frequency of shared vehicle use to gain further insight into the usage behavior of regular shared vehicle drivers and their associated preferences. A more balanced sample regarding this factor would benefit future studies.

7 Conclusion and Future Work

To counteract the disuse and misuse of DAS and to motivate using them as intended, drivers must be sufficiently informed about the functions of their vehicles. The survey results indicate that users would benefit from more information about the availability and intended use of a shared vehicle's DAS. Furthermore, the findings suggest that providing this information would encourage users to utilize DAS more often.

The majority of individuals who utilize shared vehicles do so in urban environments, and they learn about the vehicles' available DAS and their intended use while driving. A mandatory introduction before driving is a concept that has been met with resistance from both users and non-users of shared vehicles. A possible effect of mandatory introductions on the intended and safe use of DAS must be investigated in further studies. Additionally, the results underscore the necessity for well-designed HMI concepts to inform drivers during their journey while respecting their preferences and expectations. Beyond that, user-adaptive HMIs may assist in fulfilling individual user preferences and needs. The latter may change in response to changes in drivers' tasks, environment, or cognitive state. With the increased use of automated vehicles and DAS, drivers learn how to deal with them and adapt their mental models of the system based on their experiences [23]. At this juncture, these systems must alter their approach and provide the user with information that is responsive to their mental model. If adaptive systems are implemented correctly, they act as qualified human assistants that unobtrusively observe their users' actions and state of mind, record the situation, and provide appropriate support [45]. The adaptive and context-specific communication of information through intelligent systems can help drivers of automated vehicles comprehend system functions and utilize them more securely [6]. Therefore, future research on automated driving should consider implementing configurable and adaptive information displays and HMI concepts that enable individual adaptability and adaptivity, thereby meeting drivers' diverse preferences and needs. In the HMI design, a distinction must be made if disuse should be avoided, misuse shall be prevented, or usage shall be motivated. For every concept, increasing user acceptance of DAS should be a priority to motivate using DAS, promote their intended use in future SAV and private automated vehicles, and thus increase road safety.

Acknowledgments. This work is a result of the joint research project STADT:up.

The project is supported by the German Federal Ministry for Economic Affairs and Climate Action (BMWK), based on a decision of the German Bundestag. The author is solely responsible for the content of this publication.

Disclosure of Interests. The authors have no competing interests to declare that are relevant to the content of this article.

References

1. Ossig, J., Cramer, S., Bengler, K.: Concept of an ontology for automated vehicle behavior in the context of human-centered research on automated driving styles. Information (2021). https://doi.org/10.3390/info12010021
2. Trübswetter, N., Bengler, K.: Why should i use ADAS? Advanced driver assistance systems and the elderly: knowledge, experience and usage barriers. In: Proceedings of the 7th International Driving Symposium on Human Factors in Driver Assessment, Training, and Vehicle Design, Bolton Landing, New York, USA, 17–20 June 2013, pp. 495–501 (2013). https://doi.org/10.17077/drivingassessment.1532
3. Doecke, S., Grant, A., Anderson, R.W.G.: The real-world safety potential of connected vehicle technology. Traffic Inj. Prev. (2015). https://doi.org/10.1080/15389588.2015.1014551
4. Furlan, A., et al.: Advanced vehicle technologies and road safety: a scoping review of the evidence. Accid. Anal. Prev. (2020). https://doi.org/10.1016/j.aap.2020.105741
5. Merfeld, K., Wilhelms, M.-P., Henkel, S., Kreutzer, K.: Carsharing with shared autonomous vehicles: Uncovering drivers, barriers and future developments – a four-stage Delphi study. Technol. Forecast. Soc. Chang. (2019). https://doi.org/10.1016/j.techfore.2019.03.012
6. Ebinger, N., Trösterer, S., Neuhuber, N., Mörtl, P.: Conceptualisation and evaluation of adaptive driver tutoring for conditional driving automation. In: Waard, D. de, Hagemann, V., Onnasch, L., Toffetti, A., Coelho, D., Botzer, A., Angelis, M. de, Brookhuis, K. (eds.) Proceedings of the Human Factors and Ergonomics Society Europe Chapter 2023 Annual Conference, Liverpool, UK, pp. 69–81 (2023)
7. Bansal, P., Kockelman, K.M., Singh, A.: Assessing public opinions of and interest in new vehicle technologies: an Austin perspective. Transp. Res. Part C Emerg. Technol. (2016). https://doi.org/10.1016/j.trc.2016.01.019
8. Ambadipudi, A., Heineke, K., Kampshoff, P., Shao, E.: Gauging the Disruptive Power of Robo-Taxis in Autonomous Driving. Mckinsey & Company, London (2017)
9. Krueger, R., Rashidi, T., Rose, J.: Preferences for shared autonomous vehicles. Transp. Res. Part C Emerg. Technol. (2016). https://doi.org/10.1016/j.trc.2016.06.015
10. Nansubuga, B., Kowalkowski, C.: Carsharing: a systematic literature review and research agenda. J. Serv. Manag. (2021). https://doi.org/10.1108/JOSM-10-2020-0344
11. Carsten, O., Martens, M.: How can humans understand their automated cars? HMI principles, problems and solutions. Cogn. Technol. Work **21**(1), 3–20 (2019). https://doi.org/10.1007/s10111-018-0484-0
12. Kim, H., Song, M., Doerzaph, Z.: Is driving automation used as intended? real-world use of partially automated driving systems and their safety consequences. Transp. Res. Rec. (2022). https://doi.org/10.1177/03611981211027150
13. Koustanaï, A., Cavallo, V., Delhomme, P., Mas, A.: Simulator training with a forward collision warning system: effects on driver-system interactions and driver trust. Hum. Factors (2012). https://doi.org/10.1177/0018720812441796
14. Forster, Y., Hergeth, S., Naujoks, F., Krems, J., Keinath, A.: User education in automated driving: owner's manual and interactive tutorial support mental model formation and human-automation interaction. Information (2019). https://doi.org/10.3390/info10040143
15. Abraham, H., Reimer, B., Mehler, B.: Learning to use in-vehicle technologies: consumer preferences and effects on understanding. Proc. Hum. Factors Ergon. Soc. Annu. Meet. (2018). https://doi.org/10.1177/1541931218621359
16. Boelhouwer, A., van den Beukel, A., van der Voort, M., Verwey, W., Martens, M.: Supporting drivers of partially automated cars through an adaptive digital in-car tutor. Information (2020). https://doi.org/10.3390/info11040185

17. Adomat, R., Geduld, G.-O., Schamberger, M., Rieth, P.: Advanced driver assistance systems for increased comfort and safety - current developments and an outlook to the future on the road. In: Valldorf, J., Gessner, W. (eds.) Advanced Microsystems for Automotive Applications 2003. Innovation, pp. 431–446. VDI-Buch. Springer, Berlin, Heidelberg (2003)
18. Maier, F.: Wirkpotentiale moderner Fahrerassistenzsysteme und Aspekte ihrer Relevanz für die Fahrausbildung. Dissertation, Technische Universität München. Eigenverlag der Deutschen Fahrlehrer-Akademie e.V. (2013)
19. Harms, I., Dekker, G.: ADAS: from owner to user. Insights conditions breakthrough Adv. Driver Assistance Syst. Connecting Mobility Utrecht The Netherlands (2017). https://www.verkeerskunde.nl/Uploads/2017/11/ADAS-from-owner-to-user-lowres.pdf
20. McDonald, A., Carney, C., McGehee, D.V.: vehicle owners' experiences with and reactions to advanced driver assistance systems (technical report). AAA Foundation for Traffic Safety (2018)
21. Abraham, H., Seppelt, B., Mehler, B., Reimer, B.: What's in a name: vehicle technology branding & consumer expectations for automation. In: Proceedings of the 9th International Conference on Automotive User Interfaces and Interactive Vehicular Applications, Oldenburg Germany, 24–27 September 2017, pp. 226–234 (2017). https://doi.org/10.1145/3122986.3123018
22. Boelhouwer, A., van den Beukel, A., van der Voort, M., Hottentot, C., de Wit, R., Martens, M.: How are car buyers and car sellers currently informed about ADAS? an investigation among drivers and car sellers in the Netherlands. Transp. Res. Interdisc. Perspect. (2020). https://doi.org/10.1016/j.trip.2020.100103
23. Beggiato, M., Pereira, M., Petzoldt, T., Krems, J.: Learning and development of trust, acceptance and the mental model of ACC. a longitudinal on-road study. Transp. Res. Part F Traffic Psychol. Behav. **35**, 75–84 (2015). https://doi.org/10.1016/j.trf.2015.10.005
24. Dickie, D., Boyle, L.: Drivers' understanding of adaptive cruise control limitations. Proc. Hum. Factors Ergon. Soc. Annu. Meet. (2009). https://doi.org/10.1177/154193120905302313
25. Parasuraman, R., Riley, V.: Humans and automation: use, misuse, disuse Abuse. Hum. factors (1997). https://doi.org/10.1518/001872097778543886
26. Fagnant, D.J., Kockelman, K.: Preparing a nation for autonomous vehicles: opportunities, barriers and policy recommendations. Trans. Res. Part A Policy Pract. (2015). https://doi.org/10.1016/j.tra.2015.04.003
27. Boelhouwer, A., van den Beukel, A., van der Voort, M., Martens, M.: Should I take over? Does system knowledge help drivers in making take-over decisions while driving a partially automated car? Transp. Res. F: Traffic Psychol. Behav. (2019). https://doi.org/10.1016/j.trf.2018.11.016
28. Oviedo-Trespalacios, O., Tichon, J., Briant, O.: Is a flick-through enough? A content analysis of advanced driver assistance systems (ADAS) user manuals. PLoS ONE (2021). https://doi.org/10.1371/journal.pone.0252688
29. Viktorová, L., Šucha, M.: Learning about advanced driver assistance systems – The case of ACC and FCW in a sample of Czech drivers. Transport. Res. F: Traffic Psychol. Behav. (2019). https://doi.org/10.1016/j.trf.2018.05.032
30. Mehlenbacher, B., Wogalter, M.S., Laughery, K.R.: On the reading of product owner's manuals: perceptions and product complexity. Proc. Hum. Factors Ergon. Soc. Annu. Meet. (2002). https://doi.org/10.1177/154193120204600610
31. Rettig, M.: Nobody reads documentation. Commun. ACM (1991). https://doi.org/10.1145/105783.105788
32. Strand, N., Nilsson, J., Karlsson, I., Nilsson, L.: Exploring end-user experiences: self-perceived notions on use of adaptive cruise control systems. IET Intel. Transport Syst. (2011). https://doi.org/10.1049/iet-its.2010.0116

33. DeGuzman, C.A., Donmez, B.: Drivers still have limited knowledge about adaptive cruise control even when they own the system. Transp. Res. Rec. (2021). https://doi.org/10.1177/03611981211011482
34. Politis, I., et al.: An evaluation of inclusive dialogue-based interfaces for the takeover of control in autonomous cars. In: Berkovsky, S. (ed.) 23rd International Conference on Intelligent User Interfaces, Tokyo Japan, 07.03.2018–11.03.2018, pp. 601–606 (2018). https://doi.org/10.1145/3172944.3172990
35. Rukonić, L., Mwange, M.-A., Kieffer, S.: Teaching drivers about ADAS using spoken dialogue: a wizard of oz study. In: Proceedings of the 17th International Joint Conference on Computer Vision, Imaging and Computer Graphics Theory and Applications, 2022, pp. 88–98. Science and Technology Publications (2022). https://doi.org/10.5220/0010913900003124
36. Kyriakidis, M., et al.: A human factors perspective on automated driving. Theor. Issues Ergon. Sci. (2019). https://doi.org/10.1080/1463922X.2017.1293187
37. Cohen, J.: Statistical Power Analysis for the Behavioral Sciences, 2nd edn. Erlbaum, Hillsdale, NJ (1988)
38. Hu, B., Zhang, Y., Feng, C., Dong, X.: Understanding the characteristics of car-sharing users and what influences their usage frequency. Inf. Process. Manage. (2023). https://doi.org/10.1016/j.ipm.2023.103400
39. Prieto, M., Baltas, G., Stan, V.: Car sharing adoption intention in urban areas: What are the key sociodemographic drivers? Transp. Res. Part A Policy Pract. (2017). https://doi.org/10.1016/j.tra.2017.05.012
40. Mayer, E., et al.: Carsharing und Verkehrssicherheit. Nutzungs- und Sicherheitsverhalten von Carsharing-Nutzern in Österreich. Zeitschrift für Verkehrssicherheit **67**, 147–157 (2021)
41. Lambert, A.E., Watson, J.M., Cooper, J.M., Strayer, D.L.: The roles of working memory capacity, visual attention and age in driving performance. Proc. Hum. Factors Ergon. Soc. Annu. Meet. (2010). https://doi.org/10.1177/154193121005400207
42. Feinauer, S., Voskort, S., Groh, I., Petzoldt, T.: First encounters with the automated vehicle: development and evaluation of a tutorial concept to support users of partial and conditional driving automation. Transport. Res. F: Traffic Psychol. Behav. (2023). https://doi.org/10.1016/j.trf.2023.06.002
43. Nayak, M., Narayan, K.: Strengths and Weakness of Online Surveys. IOSR J. Humanit. Soc. Sci. (2019). https://doi.org/10.9790/0837-2405053138
44. Evans, J., Mathur, A.: The value of online surveys. Internet Res. (2005). https://doi.org/10.1108/10662240510590360
45. Feigh, K., Dorneich, M., Hayes, C.: Toward a characterization of adaptive systems: a framework for researchers and system designers. Hum. Factors (2012). https://doi.org/10.1177/0018720812443983

Research on Slow-Moving Transportation Scenarios in Large Suburban Campuses from the Perspective of Autonomous Vehicle-Based Mobility Service Design

Jintian Shi

Shanghai Academy of Fine Arts, Shanghai University, Shangda Road No. 99, Baoshan, Shanghai 200444, China
`shijintian1017@126.com`

Abstract. With the continuous reduction of available space resources and the constant intensification of spatial organization methods in China's big cities, many complex large-scale suburban university campuses continue to emerge. People's activities in these campuses are becoming increasingly rich, transportation needs are becoming increasingly diverse, and slow-moving transportation has become their main mode of transportation. In addition, the content, form, and problems of slow-moving transportation have also changed, and the design of service system based on shared autonomous vehicles can effectively respond to the above issues. This paper takes slow-moving transportation scenario of large suburban university campuses as the main research object. Through field observation, case studies and questionnaire surveys, a systematic campus scenario study from User sub-scenario, Environment sub-scenario to Task sub-scenario (UET Scenario Analysis) was conducted, including space types, transportation systems, users' travel needs and transportation behaviors. Two campus transportation space types suitable for building autonomous vehicle-based service system and Environmental sub-scenario characteristics were identified. Through the data quantitative analysis results of a questionnaire survey on users' slow-moving transportation conditions in university campus, the characteristics of User sub-scenarios (transportation demand) and Task sub-scenarios (travel behavior) were derived. A set of campus slow-moving transportation scenario characteristics were developed to provide the research basis for the analysis and design of slow-moving transportation service.

Keywords: Slow-Moving Transportation · Campus Mobility Scenario · Mobility Service Design · Autonomous Vehicle-based Mobility

1 Introduction

1.1 Concept and Classifications of Campus

Campuses generally refer to some exclusive areas delineated by walls for various activities of a specific educational unit (such as teaching interactions, sports activities, faculty-student activities, and daily activities of school-related personnel) [1]. Many universities worldwide have open campuses without walls or gates, where the campus and city space are not clearly differentiated. In contrast, most campuses in China are closed for management and security reasons. The campuses discussed in this paper primarily refer to university campuses.

In recent years, with the continuous expansion of university construction and the shrinking of urban land, many universities have established large new campuses in suburban areas of cities, even forming university or college towns. These new university campuses are often located outside the city center or in outskirts, with the need for further improvements in surrounding urban public transportation and supporting services. Most campuses are large and have well-developed internal road systems, also provide various types of living services, forming a new type of mixed-use urban slow transportation unit. To address internal transportation issues (meet the purpose of travel and improve the travel experience), there is a greater need to establish convenient and efficient travel service systems. Therefore, large closed-loop university campuses with independent ownership and a significant area in non-central areas or suburbs of major cities in China are the focus of this study.

1.2 Current Situation of Campus Slow Transportation

This paper conducted an analysis of the internal transportation conditions of more than 20 universities in China that met the research objectives using various research methods and found the following main characteristics and status of mobility services in campus transportation: (1) The implementation of pedestrian system and vehicle system-separation still needs to be further improved. (2) Non-motorized transportation is the main mode of mobility for most colleges and universities. (3) Compared to the total population of the entire campus, the utilization rate of the mobility service provided by campus buses is not high. (4) The comfort and experience of campus buses need to be improved. (5) University campus transportation travel has a sporadic and periodic spatial and temporal feature, with higher peak flow during class hours than after-class hours. (6) The overall mobility order of the main travelers in campus transportation is good, which is conducive to the promotion and operation of travel services. Therefore, it can be concluded that there is still room for improvement in the campus transportation system and the mobility experience of most college and university in China.

2 The Two Main Types of Campus Transportation Spaces

The campus transportation space encompasses road systems, boarding and alighting areas, parking facilities, and open spaces. It serves to facilitate internal connectivity between different building clusters within the campus as well as external communication with the surrounding city. The campus transportation space is the most dynamic and changeable functional organization among all campus spaces, significantly influencing travel efficiency and experience [2].

According to *"Architectural Design Reference Collection"*, the development of the campus transportation system will adhere to spatial layout forms such as linear, molecular, zoning, and radiating types [3]. Meanwhile, RenKe He in *"Campus Planning and*

Design for Colleges and Universities" categorizes the campus spatial form into linear, grid-based, central-focused, and molecular types [4]. Flexible planning from a dynamic development perspective suggests that college campuses' transportation structure will continuously evolve around core-centric networks or grid-based.

Considering characteristics of autonomous vehicle performance and features of service system design, autonomous vehicle travel services can maximize their performance advantages in large campuses where commuting distances are long. This can enhance various user experiences due to unmet campus mobility needs. Therefore, multi-core networked campuses along with grid-based campuses align with this paper's research focus on two types of campus transportation spaces.

This study will analyze slow-moving transportation scenarios in these two types of campuses based on case studies, field observation and surveys results from user perspectives considering environmental factors as well as travel task requirements.

2.1 Multi-core Networked Campus Transportation Space

Key Characteristics of Transportation Space. The multi-core networked transportation space in a campus usually consists of several independent functional zones, each of which can meet the daily teaching and living needs of faculty and students. Some non-daily campus behaviors or non-core functions that occur less frequently need to be shared with relevant buildings or facilities throughout the campus. The multi-core networked transportation space is also the main form of transportation space in most large-scale campuses. Through a survey of the multi-core campus planning and design of Zhejiang University Zijingang Campus, Wuhan University, and South China Agricultural University, it was found that the multi-core networked campus transportation space has a clear hierarchy of main and secondary zones, and the rich road system effectively connects multiple campus sub-centers. The secondary road structure within the group is clear, ensuring transportation flow within the sub-core and throughout the campus, making it suitable for the operation of autonomous vehicles.

Primary Challenges in Slow-moving Transportation

1. *Slow-Moving transportation is susceptible to disruptions caused by other modes of transportation and mobility subjects.* Congestion or unexpected incidents within the campus motor vehicle transportation system can have a cascading impact, extending to nearby slow-moving areas and potentially disrupting the overall operation of the entire campus slow-moving transportation system.
2. *The continuity of the slow-moving transportation system is compromised.* Bicycles and electric bicycles serve as prevalent means of mobility for many faculty and students on campus. However, increased usage of this less-efficient transport modes has led to heightened demand for parking spaces, resulting in a significant number of bicycles encroaching upon sidewalks, thereby severely impacting both safety and path continuity within the campus slow-moving transportation network.
3. *Inadequate overall space allocation for slow-moving transportation.* Given that most suburban multi-core large-area campuses adhere to traditional garden-style planning principles with lower building density distribution, motor vehicles remain integral as a mode of transport. To ensure the safety of slow-moving transportation subjects,

such campuses often incorporate clearly defined physical barriers or designated areas that spatially, functionally, and visually segregate motor vehicle transportation from slow-moving transportation activities—resulting in an occupation of substantial space within the slow-moving transportation network.

2.2 Grid-Based Campus Transportation Space

Key Characteristics of Transportation Spaces. The grid-based campus transportation space employs the "module" concept from engineering design to partition and quantify the campus space into units, serving as fundamental components for various functional zones and building sites. Grid-based campus planning is a prevalent spatial organization approach for large campuses, with the primary medium for grid division being the campus road network. The resulting campus space exhibits regularity, symmetry, and harmonious scale (Fig. 1).

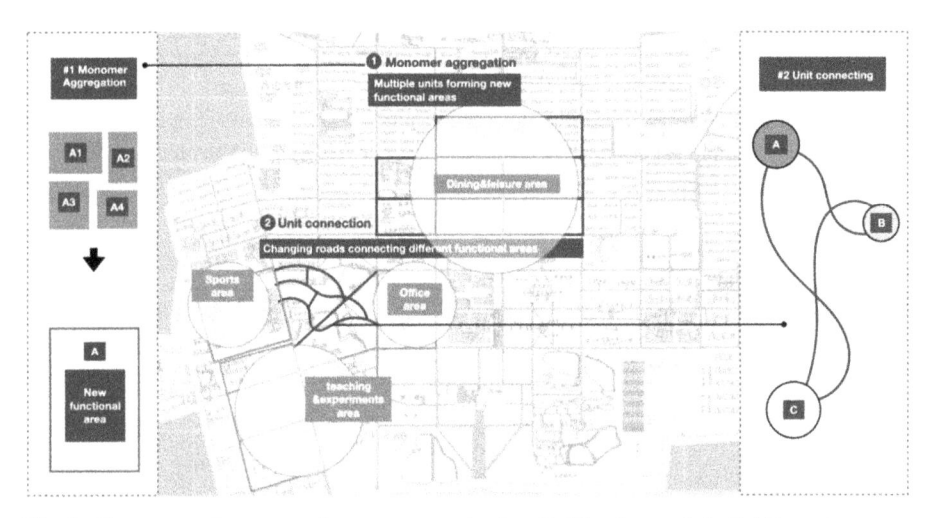

Fig. 1. Two ways of transportation space organization dividing by roads in Grid-based campus.

Huazhong University of Science and Technology exemplifies this approach by utilizing its road system as the basis for grid division in its campus layout. The entire campus is primarily divided into two east and west campuses, with particular emphasis on modularized planning in the west campus area. Here, multiple square ring roads formed by modular units connect and organize the campus space. The university's approach to campus planning involves an aggregation design technique - combining multiple units to create new spatial forms that establish functional groupings serving as primary and secondary functional areas within the campus; another planning method involves connecting different spatial units through diverse roadways to achieve functional extension and spatial innovation.

2.3 Primary Challenges in Slow-moving Transportation

1. *Extended Commuting Distances and Time.* The spatially uniform grid-based road network in campus often results in a balanced functional planning that increases the daily commuting distance and prolongs the average on-campus commuting time.
2. *Abundance of Transportation Nodes, Particularly at Intersections, Poses Potential Safety Hazards.* The proliferation of transportation nodes leads to various potential travel conflicts and safety hazards. For example, pedestrian and bicycle transportation entering an intersection can create an expanding flow that interferes with straight-through transportation [5]. However, autonomous vehicles equipped with vehicle-to-vehicle (V2V), vehicle-to-infrastructure (V2I), and intelligent networked systems can proactively plan routes and adjust speeds based on environmental information and real-time data to effectively mitigate safety hazards (see Fig. 2).
3. *Multiple Stakeholder Conflicts Exist within Slow-moving Transportation.* Grid-based campuses typically feature abundant internal service facilities, resulting in a high number of diverse transportation modes used by numerous transportation subjects within limited space. This situation gives rise to latent conflicts among stakeholders due to resource scarcity, spatial constraints, and diverse needs. Therefore, it is imperative to establish a dynamic on-demand intelligent slow-moving transportation service system tailored to specific times and locations based on the characteristics of multiple stakeholders.

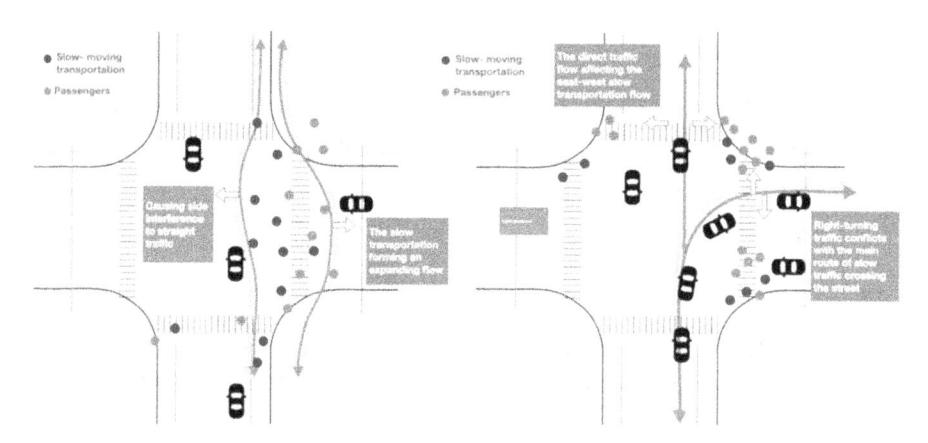

Fig. 2. The transportation nodes of grid-based campus are prone to potential conflicts with slow transportation.

3 Analysis of Environmental Scenarios for Campus Slow-Moving Transportation

3.1 Overall Functional Flowline

The distribution pattern of travel routes within the multi-core networked campus transportation scenario follows a "comprehensive control at the overall level, and regional enrichment at the local level" rule. The internal multi-level road network system clearly divides functional zones, to some extent lengthening students' commuting routes. In contrast, the functional flowline in grid-based campuses is relatively smooth with broad overall road scales, exerting a strong influence on multiple areas within the campus. However, it also brings about frequent transportation flow dispersion and potential conflicts among transportation subjects due to high connectivity.

3.2 Slow-Moving Transportation System

Campus Pedestrian System. The campus pedestrian system constitutes the core component of the slow travel system and represents the space unit with highest interaction between environmental scenarios and people [6]. In both multi-core networked and grid-based campus transportation scenarios, main and secondary roads are spacious with ample setback spaces around buildings; this allows for wide pedestrian areas along both sides of roads that possess high development flexibility. These spaces can undergo various forms of spatial transformation during different time periods based on diverse needs and scenarios under guidance from autonomous vehicle slow-moving transportation service stations as well as an overarching service framework.

Campus Cycling System. Cycling serves as a crucial mode of slow-moving transportation in large campuses—especially those without shuttle bus services. Research into multiple multi-core networked campus transportation systems revealed that certain universities have designated cycling-only or priority areas alongside pavement markings; however, in campuses where cycling-specific zones are not established but rather mixed-use areas shared by pedestrians and vehicles alike, cycling space is heavily encroached upon by motor vehicles—further infringing upon pedestrian walkways and static transportation spaces. To address these issues effectively requires implementing a comprehensive pedestrian-cycling system across campuses including pavement markings for cycling lanes while installing barriers at entry/exit points to delineate specific zones while providing functional reminders. In many functional compound university campuses where pedestrians share pathways with cyclists who further encroach upon walking paths as well as static transportation areas—the sidewalks flanking main thoroughfares become dedicated parking spots for bicycles—severely disrupting orderly operation within campus slow-moving transportation systems.

Therefore, in densely populated multi-core networked or grid-based campus environments characterized by diverse mobility demands—it's imperative not only to scientifically design cycling systems but also regulate cyclist behavior while analyzing user demographics to design relevant services meeting their needs—a background opportunity enabling intervention into slow-moving transit scenarios through service system design.

3.3 Static Transportation and Vehicle Systems

Static Transportation System

1. *Parking Space.* Static transportation refers mainly to school buses or personal vehicles boarding/alighting temporarily parked motorized/non-motorized vehicles over extended periods—all requiring rational management given ongoing spatial resource constraints resulting from increasing popularity surrounding pedestrian-vehicle system separation measures. Within multi-core networked or grid-based campus settings—parking spaces are typically situated near primary entrances/exits along select main arteries throughout key locations such as building perimeters/plazas—with occasional subterranean lots planned near primary entrances featuring "campus P + R" (Park & Ride) parking modes guiding immediate vehicle storage upon entering followed by transitioning towards walking/cycling-based intra-campus commutes.
2. *Campus Bus Stops.* Short-term pauses caused by boarding/alighting from motor vehicles represent another facet of static transportation—an analysis into universities offering bus services found most establishing simple stops along major thoroughfares whereas fixed bus routes/stops/fees lack informative signage detailing critical aspects like route information stop locations operating hours/service fees etc.—highlighting importance regarding real-time dynamic service status transmission using digital smart methods aiding users' decision-making processes when planning their travels.

Vehicle Transportation Systems. The utilization of motorized vehicles, including electric cars, motorcycles, and automobiles, is steadily increasing within campus environments. This trend is particularly pronounced in campuses featuring a multi-core network or grid-based layout, where the coverage of motorized vehicle travel extends across the entire campus. However, during peak travel periods such as class changes and mealtimes, motor vehicles are susceptible to creating transportation conflicts with pedestrians. The primary thoroughfares within the campus have effectively established a vehicular road system. These roads boast favorable conditions and wide surfaces, typically comprising dual or four-lane configurations with a minimum width of at least 7 m. Furthermore, certain secondary roads designed for mixed pedestrian and vehicular transportation feature widths exceeding 4 m. Such design facilitates future autonomous vehicle operations and may even allow for dedicated lanes and routes for autonomous vehicles while coordinating their operation with mixed-use lanes. Introducing shared autonomous vehicles into the campus's slow-moving transportation scenarios not only enhances overall travel experiences but also liberates substantial space currently allocated to vehicular transportation for use by slower-moving modes of transportation.

4 Analysis of User Scenarios for Campus Slow-Moving Transportation

4.1 Questionnaire Design and Validation Testing

Drawing from the scenario analysis framework in Sect. 2.3, the examination of campus pedestrian transportation scenarios can be approached through the lenses of users, environment, and tasks. Within user scenarios' sub-scenarios, personal attributes and connectivity attributes are closely intertwined with the travel context. Personal travel, particularly short-distance pedestrian journeys, is distinguished by substantial individual autonomy and variability. In accordance with the principle of *"Perfect Rationality"*, travel duration and distance significantly shape travelers' decision-making processes and conduct [7, 8]. Individual preferences, environmental awareness levels along routes, scenic encounters during travels, personal safety perceptions within environments as well as road congestion levels all exert influence on individuals' travel behavior and mode selections [9–11]. Furthermore, *"Bounded Rationality"* [12] posits that people's cognitive capacities and information sources impact their route choices while traveling.

Consequently, the author formulated a questionnaire titled "Survey on Pedestrian Travel Behavior in University Campuses" to undertake user research and scrutinize travel tasks for campus commuters based on demographic characteristics, connectivity attributes, journey features, and objectives. The sample distribution encompassed over ten major cities in China, encompassing 24 universities. A stratified proportional sampling approach was employed, resulting in a total selection of 378 samples, out of which342were deemed valid yielding an overall validity rate of 90.4%. The questionnaire collection methods included face-to-face interviews, telephone surveys, and online questionnaire submissions. Participants comprised college students and faculty members.

Before releasing the final questionnaire, the author conducted a preliminary survey by disseminating 31questionnaires, to ensure the soundness and scientific rigor of the questionnaire design through reliability and validity assessments (Cronbach α coefficient = 0.61; KMO value = 0).

4.2 Demographic Characteristics of the Survey Interviewees

Basic Characteristics of the Traveling People. A total of 254 (75%) undergraduate and graduate students and 83 (25%) faculty and staff from 24 universities across the country participated in this survey. There were 173 male and 169 female respondents (1.00 male to female ratio). Since pedestrian transportation is a type of transportation in which people interact extensively with their surroundings throughout the trip, the questionnaire focused on the survey of the respondents' familiarity with the campus environment. It was found that due to the fixed functions and scope of university campuses, as well as the repetitiveness of people's daily behaviors, most teachers, and students (64.33%) were familiar with the campus environment, with a Likert five-point scale average score of 3.85 and an SD of 0.91, indicating a low degree of dispersion. However, more than 35% of the respondents needed to enhance their interaction and communication with the campus environment through appropriate means (Table 1).

Table 1. Basic indicators of people's familiarity with campus environment

Items	Sample size	Min.	Max.	Average	SD	Median
familiarity with the campus	342	1.000	5.000	3.854	0.914	4.000

Satisfaction with Transportation and Intention to Use Autonomous Vehicle Services. In terms of "satisfaction with current campus transportation conditions," 38.01% of respondents found it acceptable, while 22.23% expressed dissatisfaction, indicating that over half believe there is a need for further improvement in the internal campus transportation situation. Regarding "intention to use autonomous vehicle services," 31.58% of respondents indicated a strong willingness, while 30.70% expressed moderate willingness; additionally, 27.78% stated their intention would depend on the circumstances, providing ample opportunities for service design to enhance the efficiency and user experience of campus autonomous vehicle travel at low speeds. Conversely, 7.02% were not very willing to use the service, and only 2.92% had no intention at all.

A total of 247 questionnaires were selected through questionnaire design from individuals who have access to on-campus shuttle services including faculty and students alike. In terms of "campus transportation satisfaction," over one-third of respondents held negative views (38.30%), highlighting an urgent need to address slow-paced travel issues on large campuses. Regarding "intention to use autonomous vehicle services," those expressing strong willingness accounted for 25.53%, while those expressing moderate willingness accounted for 34%. This provides a solid foundation for promoting autonomous vehicle services; meanwhile, nearly one-third (29%) indicated their decision would be contingent upon specific circumstances—indicating potential room for improvement through effective service design. Therefore, establishing a new model for autonomous vehicle slow-moving transportation services and cultivating trust and expectations among core target users regarding new campus travel services holds significant urgency and practical importance in this context within academic settings.

4.3 Transportation Connection Attributes

Group Connection Attributes. Humans are inherently social beings, and their travel behavior is not only driven by needs and objectives but also influenced by their connection attributes. These connections can be physical or relational, reflecting the sensitivity of individuals to changes in the external environment, information, and relationships during travel.

In examining group connection during travel, a survey question asked whether individuals prefer to travel alone or with others on campus. Initial results indicate that men (54.91%) seem to favor solo travel more than women (46.5%), while staff (51.19%) appear to prefer solo travel more than students (50.57%). However, after conducting a chi-square test, it was found that gender and academic status have no significant impact on solo campus travel. Overall data reveals that the ratio of choosing solo versus group campus travel is 51:49 respectively; slightly more people opt for solo trips over traveling with others. In scenarios involving slow-paced short-distance travels, users' group connection attributes do not exhibit strong tendencies.

External Environment, Information, and Relationship Connection Attributes. The survey also investigated users' connections with the external environment, information sources, and social relationships during their travels. When asked about behaviors engaged in during trips, "appreciating scenery along the way" emerged as the most popular choice (44.93%), followed by "focusing solely on traveling without engaging in other activities" (41.45%). The third most frequent behavior was "listening to music through headphones" (38.55%), while "observing pedestrians and events along the way" also occurred frequently (37.97%).

Additionally, "chatting or calling others via mobile phone" and "browsing news on mobile phones" were ranked fifth and sixth at 21.16% and 13.33%, respectively. Through chi-square tests analyzing differences between genders and academic statuses regarding these behaviors (see Table 2), it was observed that teacher-student identity significantly impacted both "observing pedestrians/events along the way" (chi = 19.699, p = 0.000 < 0.01) and "listening to music with headphones" (chi = 4.211, p = 0.040 < 0.05). These findings suggest potential adjustments in service content & interaction modes for autonomous vehicle services based on different user groups such as teachers & students when designing human-vehicle interactions.

Table 2. Cross (Chi-square) analysis results.

Variations	Name	Q2 status-staff/student		Total	χ^2	p
		1.0	2.0			
Q20_2 focusing on travel	0.0	59.30%	54.76%	58.19%	0.537	0.464
	1.0	40.70%	45.24%	41.81%		
Total		258	84	342		
Q20_1 appreciating scenery along the way	0.0	53.49%	60.71%	55.26%	1.338	0.247
	1.0	46.51%	39.29%	44.74%		
Total		258	84	342		
Q20_3 observing pedestrians &events	0.0	58.91%	71.43%	61.99%	4.211	0.040*
	1.0	41.09%	28.57%	38.01%		
Total		258	84	342		
Q20_7 listening to music through headphones	0.0	55.04%	82.14%	61.70%	19.699	0.000**
	1.0	44.96%	17.86%	38.30%		
Total		258	84	342		
Q20_8 chatting or calling others	0.0	76.74%	85.71%	78.95%	3.068	0.080
	1.0	23.26%	14.29%	21.05%		
Total		258	84	342		

(*continued*)

Table 2. (*continued*)

Variations	Name	Q2 status-staff/student		Total	χ^2	p
		1.0	2.0			
Q20_9 browsing news	0.0	87.21%	88.10%	87.43%	0.045	0.832
	1.0	12.79%	11.90%	12.57%		
Total		258	84	342		
Q20_10 watch short videos on phones	0.0	92.64%	95.24%	93.27%	0.684	0.408
	1.0	7.36%	4.76%	6.73%		
Total		258	84	342		

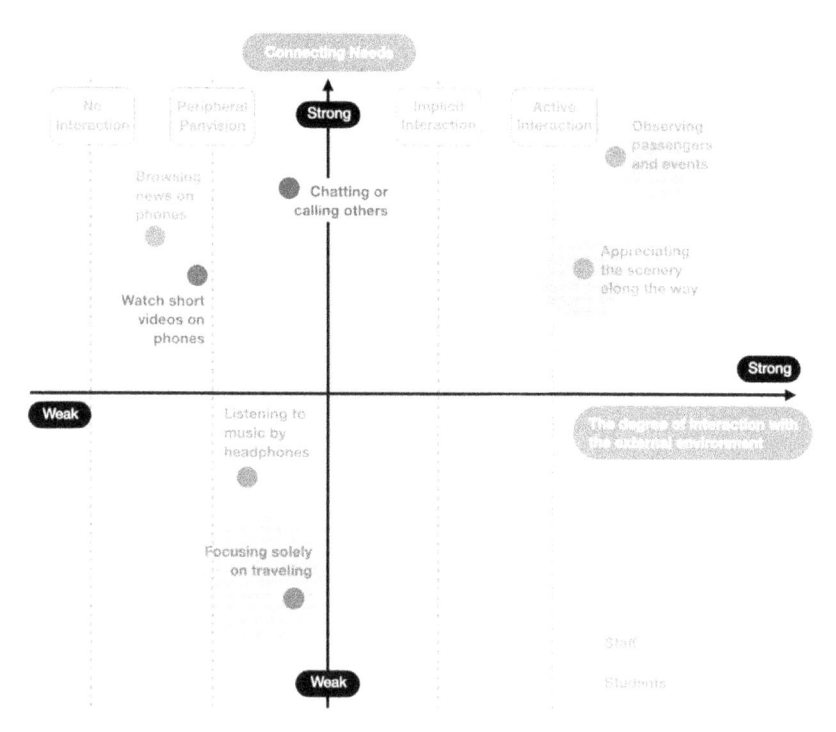

* $p < 0.05$ ** $p < 0.01$.

Fig. 3. Analysis of connection need and interaction degree of crowd behavior during campus transportation.

In the context of short-distance slow-moving transportation on campus, individuals maintain a relatively high level of connection with the external environment, primarily through visual communication. Faculty members are predominantly focused on their travel activities and engage in moderately interactive behaviors such as appreciating the scenery along the way. However, their overall sensitivity to changes in the external environment, information, and relationships is relatively weak. Conversely, students exhibit stronger connection attributes during their travels. They not only maintain personal connections with the outside world by observing pedestrians and events along their route but also gather environmental information through behaviors such as appreciating the scenery enroute. Additionally, creating a relatively independent experiential atmosphere by listening to music through headphones is a common behavior among student groups during campus travel, which significantly differs from that of faculty members (see Fig. 3).

5 Analysis of Task Scenarios for Campus Slow-Moving Transportation

5.1 Characteristics of Travel Behavior

Daily Average Travel Frequency and Single Trip Distance

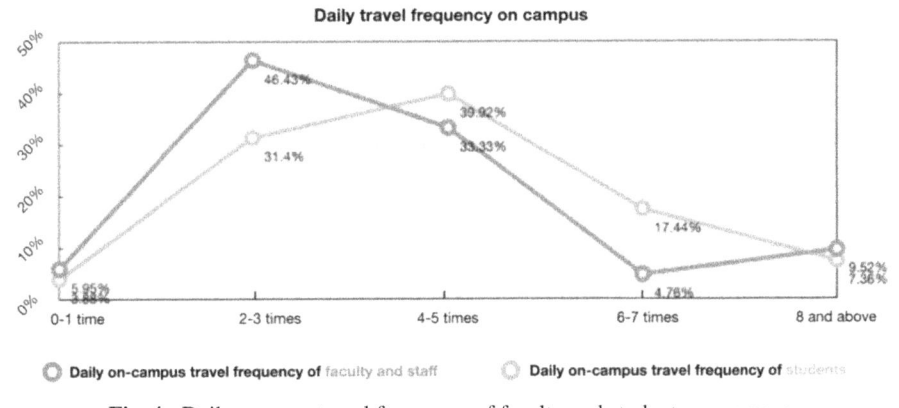

Fig. 4. Daily average travel frequency of faculty and students on campus.

1. *Daily Average Travel Frequency.* The daily average number of trips made by the subjects is an important indicator to describe travel characteristics, which needs to meet three conditions simultaneously: purposeful travel activities, walking or running on named roads, and one-way walking time exceeding 5 min [13]. As campus transportation mainly consists of high-frequency short-distance trips with frequent transfers, the research also specifically clarifies the interval between two trips. When the interval exceeds 10 min, it is counted as two separate trips. This survey investigates the daily average campus travel frequency among faculty and students in higher education institutions using a "trip" as a unit. Approximately 38.3% of respondents have a daily average campus travel frequency of 4–5 times, while 35.09% have a frequency of 2–3 times within the campus. Additionally, 14.33% reported making 6–7 trips per

day within the campus, while only 7.89% had a daily average frequency of more than eight trips per day within the campus; most faculty and students' daily average campus travel frequencies are concentrated between 2–5 times. Furthermore, upon analyzing data separately for faculty and student groups, it was found that faculty members generally have lower on-campus travel frequencies compared to students; nearly half of them make fewer than three trips within the campus each day whereas over sixty percent of students have a daily commute rate exceeding four trips within their campuses (see Table 3) (Fig. 4).

2. *Single Trip Distance.* Literature defines trips within 500 m on campus as short-distance trips, and those exceeding 500 m as long-distance trips [14]. Given that this study focuses on suburban large and medium-sized college campuses, the author has defined the following in this survey: trips within 500 m are considered short-distance, while those between 500–1000 m are categorized as medium-short distance, 1000–1500 m as mid-range distance, 1500–2000 m as medium-long distance, and over 2000 m as long-distance travel within the campus. T-test analysis of teachers' and students' identities, daily travel frequency, and single trip distances reveals differences in single trip distances within the campus. Students tend to have single trip distances distributed mostly between medium-short and medium-long ranges on campus, whereas faculty members engage more frequently in long-distance travels of over 2000 m within the campus.

Table 3. Analysis results of independent sample T-test.

	Q2-identity status (Mean ± SD)		t	p
	1.0(n = 258) students	2.0(n = 84) faculty		
Q16-single travel distance	2.25 ± 1.27	2.58 ± 1.47	−2.025	0.044*
Q13-travel frequency	3.16 ± 1.07	2.94 ± 1.20	1.465	0.145

* $p < 0.05$ ** $p < 0.01$.

Transportation Modes of Slow-Moving. The respective proportions of various modes of travel in the overall campus transportation volume not only effectively reflect the composition of transportation methods on campus, but also shed light on the characteristics, travel patterns, and diverse levels of transportation demand within the campus environment. The predominant mode of transport within campuses is walking (47.08%), complemented by a significant reliance on combined walking and cycling (25.73%) as well as electric vehicles (12.00%) for slow-paced commuting. Safety, convenience, and flexibility are identified as key factors influencing travel preferences within university campuses.

This study employs linear regression analysis to examine the relationship between five variables—gender, faculty/student status, age group, familiarity with campus surroundings, and current availability of shuttle services—and primary modes of travel within the campus setting (see Table 4). The resulting model yields an R-squared value of 0.114. Upon conducting an F-test on this model (F = 8.613; p = 0 < 0.05), it was found that at least one variable from Q2, Q8, Q9, Q1, and Q3 would have an impact on Q12; further investigation revealed that both current availability of shuttle services and respondent gender significantly influence individuals' selection of transportation modes within the campus environment.

Table 4. Results of linear regression analysis.

	Nonnormalized coefficient		Normalized coefficient	t	p	VIF	R^2	M-R 2	F
	B	Standard error	Beta						
constant	6.092	0.873	-	6.982	0.000**	-	0.114	0.1	F (5,336) = 8.613, p = 0.000
Q2-identity	0.074	0.621	0.011	0.119	0.905	3.381			
Q8-familiarity	−0.074	0.163	−0.024	−0.452	0.652	1.045			
Q9-campus bus	−1.629	0.31	−0.287	−5.251	0.000**	1.136			
Q1-gender	−0.604	0.303	−0.107	−1.992	0.047*	1.088			
Q3-Age span	0.253	0.162	0.149	1.565	0.118	3.454			

Dependent variable: Q12-transportation mode of campus slow-moving travel.
D-W value: 1.712.
*$p < 0.05$ **$p < 0.01$.

Travel Time and Unit Travel Time Consumption

Travel Time. Travel time refers to the specific times during a day when travel activities occur, with the minimum statistical unit typically being one hour. Analyzing travel time not only provides a visible distribution of peak and low travel volumes in an area but also allows for estimation of the purposes of travel during peak hours. The survey results from the question "At what time is your maximum on-campus travel volume?" indicate that the peak on-campus travel hours are 11:00–13:00 (31.58%) and 8:00–11:00 (28.95%), followed by 17:00–19:00 (19.59%). The number of people traveling in the afternoon to evening is relatively small (15.5%), and even fewer at night (0.88%).

Unit Travel Time Consumption. 35.67% of respondents have a unit travel time consumption between 11–15 min, while 32.46% spend between 5–10 min for their unit travels, and 10.82% take between 16–20 min for their unit travels. Only 4.97% have a unit travel time consumption of less than five minutes. This indicates that most people's on-campus travels fall within a fifteen-minute radius, yet there remains a minority facing prolonged commuting times within campus, necessitating efficient transportation systems and services to address this issue effectively in academic settings.

5.2 Purposes of Travel Behavior

Travel Purposes and Travel Chains

Travel Purposes. Campus travel can be categorized into essential, business, leisure, and special travel (see Table 6) based on different objectives. Essential travel primarily involves commuting for work or study (W), including trips related to work, self-study, or attending classes with the main goal of reaching the destination quickly and safely. Business travel (M) encompasses campus-related and personal affairs trips aimed at handling procedures or accessing services. Leisure travel (L) comprises journeys focused on recreational activities with a moderate sense of urgency and relatively flexible itineraries. Emergency travel (E) refers to unplanned trips due to unforeseen events. Essential travel accounts for the highest proportion (87.43%), followed by business-related travels at 59.65%, while leisure travels represent 36.55% of the total campus travels (Table 5).

Table 5. Purpose and classification of daily trips on campus.

	Essential Travel (W)	Business travel (M)		Leisure Travel (L)	Emergency Travel (E)
		Campus-related Business Travel (M-C)	Life-related Business Travel (M-L)		
Contents	Attending classes, go to work, self-study	Campus affairs and procedures	Lectures, training, events, etc.	Eating, shopping, showering, picking up delivery	Walking, entertainment, sports, visiting friends, etc.	Going out for medical treatment, emergency evacuation, etc.
Proportion	87.43%	23.98%	24.85%	59.65%	36.55%	2.34%

Trip Chain. The Trip Chain, also known as the travel activity chain, begins with the first purposeful stop and ends with returning home. It provides a visual representation of the traveler's journey and the sequence of activities [13]. Through research, the author has identified three main campus transportation Trip Chains: those related to work (W-C), life (L-C), and leisure (E-C). Each type of Trip Chain includes specific details encompassing different content and order (see Fig. 5).

The most frequent campus Trip Chain is "class attendance - life travel - class attendance - life travel - back to dormitory" (21.54%), followed by "class attendance - life travel - back to dormitory" (17.25%), and "class attendance - life travel - class attendance - leisure and entertainment - life travel - back to dormitory" (12.28%). This indicates that more frequent Trip Chains are associated with work-related trips (W-C). Furthermore, most campus travelers' behaviors exhibit functional complexity in terms of content and purpose. Each campus Trip Chain contains at least three travel purposes, while each Origin Destination pair involves at least three locations, demonstrating demand diversity and spatial richness (Fig. 6).

Research on Slow-Moving Transportation Scenarios in Large Suburban Campuses   137

Travel chain number	1	2	3	4	5	6	7	8	9	10
Proportion	21.64%	17.25%	12.28%	11.70%	9.94%%	9.06%	5.56%	5.26%	2.92%	0.58%
Contents of Travel chain	Class - Life travel - Class - Life travel - Dormitory	Class - Life travel - Class - Dormitory	Class - Life travel - Class - Entertainment - Life travel - Dormitory	Class- Life travel - Class - Dormitory	Class- Life travel - Class - Entertainment- Life travel - Class - Dormitory	Class - Dormitory	Life travel - Dormitory	Class- Life travel - Entertainment - Dormitory	Life travel - Entertainment - Dormitory	Entertainment - dormitory
Categories of travel chain	Work travel chain (W-C)	Work travel chain (W-C)	Work travel chain (W-C)	Work travel chain (W-C)	Work travel chain (W-C)	Work travel chain (W-C)	travel chain (-C)	Work travel chain (W-C)	travel chain (-C)	Entertainment travel chain (I -C)

Fig. 5. Contents and categories of campus slow travel chain.

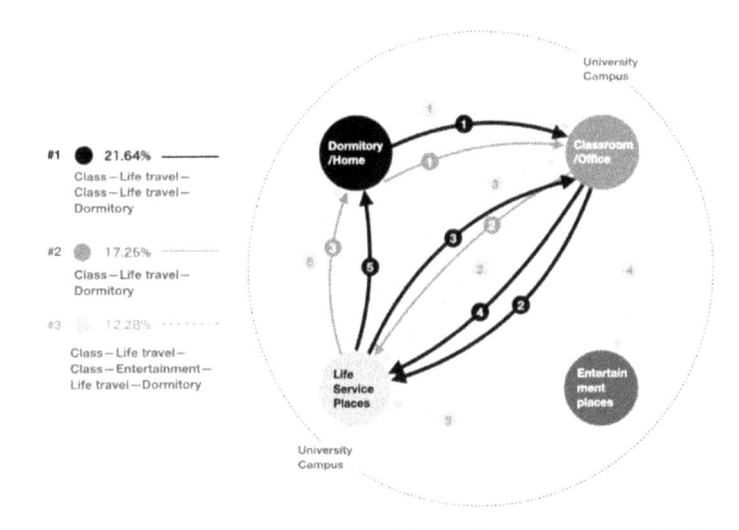

Fig. 6. Spatial distribution analysis of the top three campus travel chains.

An analysis of the spatial distribution of high-frequency travel chains on campus reveals that the path between classrooms/offices and living service facilities is particularly frequent, occurring at least once in each travel chain and up to three times. This suggests that most teachers and students have a rich and comprehensive daily activity scenario on campus. When constructing an autonomous vehicle service system on campus, it is advisable to plan for more service capacity and routes between classrooms/offices and living service facilities. Furthermore, in travel chains with the destination being the dormitory/home, the previous stop before reaching the destination is typically a living service facility. This makes the living service facility an important or even necessary transit point on the way home. Therefore, it may be feasible to extend the function space of living service facilities using autonomous vehicles as functional base stations, deploying autonomous convenience kiosk vehicles in their surrounding areas to expand their service range. The autonomous vehicles can adjust their routes based on real-time user needs and available services. In instances where there is excessive real-time capacity at a living service facility, autonomous vehicles can transport items to provide services for students and teachers at a distance, alleviating congestion. By utilizing intelligent means through a design approach focused on services, we can tap into spatial dynamism and functional mobility within the environment.

Travel Experience Needs. From an experiential perspective, user experience and demand value can be categorized into three dimensions: physical experience demand, psychological experience demand, and spiritual experience demand. Each dimension encompasses various sub-dimensions and specific elements of the user experience. Building upon previous research, the author has identified ten primary functional types and service content that cover the three dimensions of experiential demands for autonomous vehicles. A survey was conducted to gauge "user attention to different functions and services". The results indicate that concerning campus autonomous vehicle functions and services, users are most interested in being informed about the safety status of autonomous vehicle operations (81.34%), understanding the carrying efficiency of autonomous vehicle services (57.85%), as well as being aware of service fees (49.71%). Users also expressed interest in their riding experiences (40.12%), in-vehicle riding environments (33.72%), orderliness among other passengers inside the vehicle (26.16%). Additionally, there is some level of concern regarding whether the environment within the autonomous vehicle is quiet and private (13.66%). However, infotainment and social-related functionalities are not currently a primary focus for surveyed individuals with regards to campus autonomous vehicle services.

Through preliminary case studies and literature analysis, this paper divides user needs for campus autonomous vehicle services into four aspects based on perceived experiential levels and time development roadmap: environmental atmosphere needs, travel condition needs, infotainment needs, and intelligent needs (see Fig. 7). Environmental atmosphere needs emphasize factors such as in-vehicle equipment, space utilization, near-field environment considerations including decorum - all contributing to physical comfort perceptions during rides. Travel condition requirements necessitate effective display by autonomous vehicles of current operating conditions; environmental perception; decision-making processes; operational outcomes; along with informing passengers about potential key behaviors related to driving status. Infotainment requirements pertain to how passengers engage in activities like news browsing or watching videos while traveling via an autonomous vehicle after establishing trust in driving safety.

The focus on intelligent demands lies more on interaction modes through which people access these services rather than specific content itself – achieved through proactive perception by artificial intelligence systems catering to explicit/implicit user requirements while presenting adaptive content effectively communicating with passengers.

This enhances both autonomous vehicles' environmental perception capabilities alongside bolstering passenger trust - assisting realization of bodily comfort psychological security & emotional satisfaction goals within autonomous vehicle user experiences. It's important noting that initial three autonomous vehicle user experiences continue evolving from informational content & service type perspectives whereas intelligent demands serve as crucial means towards achieving these former objectives. Presently prevalent designs for autonomous vehicle travel service's User Experience predominantly concentrate on first two aspects such as cabin design & onboard screen human-machine interfaces displaying running statuses yet Information Entertainment Needs &

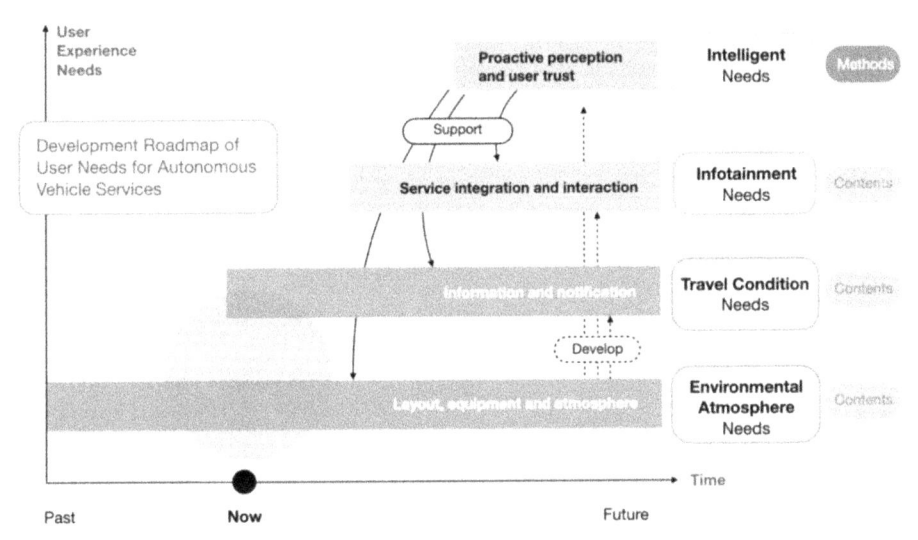

Fig. 7. Development roadmap of user experience needs for campus autonomous vehicle service.

Intelligent Demands remain largely unaddressed even by industry pioneer Waymo who only plans future provision for audiovisual entertainment within their driverless cars but hasn't implemented it yet at present stage despite its pioneering role within driverless travel sector industry.

Through the research, this paper has found that at this stage, the primary demands of most respondents for driverless car services are focused on driving safety perception and creating an environmental atmosphere. The demand for driverless car services is still primarily instrumental transport. The product life cycle of driverless car services is currently in the exploratory stage and should provide functional responses and service feedback to meet users' psychological safety perception needs. However, as the driverless car service gradually enters the growth and expansion period, users' demand for information entertainment and intelligent features will inevitably increase. Therefore, intelligent demand is also one of the important needs of campus driverless car travel service.

6 Summary

This study employs methods such as on-site investigation, literature review, and case analysis to conduct a three-dimensional analysis of the pedestrian transportation scenarios in university campuses, focusing on the environment, users, and tasks. It identifies and summarizes the fundamental issues present in pedestrian transportation within large suburban university campuses. Additionally, a survey questionnaire was designed to quantitatively analyze the pedestrian travel conditions of 378 faculty and students from 24 large universities across more than ten provinces in China. This preliminary research provides an understanding of the main characteristics of pedestrian transportation service scenarios in university campuses with regards to environment, user, and task aspects.

Consequently, it offers valuable insights for demand research and design direction for developing autonomous vehicle services tailored for pedestrian travel within university campuses.

6.1 Summary of the Current Situation of Slow-Moving Transportation in Campus

Table 6. Summary of problem characteristics of slow transportation system in target campus

NO	Categories		Problems	Severity	Applicability of shared driverless car service
1	the robustness of the system		easy to be disturbed by the travel behavior of motor vehicles and other slow transportation subjects	•••	•••
2	System inclusion	Travel inclusion	potential conflicts with other transportation modes and travel flows at traffic nodes	••○	•••
		Crowd Inclusiveness	travel behavior guidance and resource allocation among multiple slow transportation stakeholders	••○	••○
3	System continuity	Moving-line continuity	easily interrupted by pedestrians or sudden time	•••	••○
		Landscape experience continuity	the form of landscape node is single, and the function of landscape is insufficient	••○	••○

(*continued*)

Table 6. (*continued*)

NO	Categories	Problems	Severity	Applicability of shared driverless car service
4	System equilibrium	the spatial and temporal imbalance between slow traffic demand and resources of campus population	●●○	●●●
5	System effectiveness	longer travel distance, longer time, insufficient space, and poor experience	●●●	●●●

6.2 Characteristics of Slow-Moving Transportation in Campus

This paper focuses on the pedestrian transportation scenario in large suburban college campuses in China as the primary research subject, analyzing it from various perspectives including spatial types, functional flowlines, transportation systems, population characteristics, travel behavior and purposes. Through methods such as field observation, case analysis, and questionnaire surveys, the study ultimately summarizes the issues of campus pedestrian transportation systems and the characteristics of pedestrian transportation scenarios within these campuses. The paper begins by clarifying different types of campus concepts to specify its main research object and determine two main types of transportation space within this context. It then establishes an analysis framework from user, environment, and task perspectives. Environmental sub-scenarios are analyzed considering overall functional flowlines, pedestrian transportation systems, static transportation, and car transportation systems. Subsequently, quantitative data analysis is conducted on a survey questionnaire to study the characteristics and needs of primarily teachers and students who are traveling within campus grounds. This provides content parameters and specific characteristics for user sub-scenarios and task sub-scenarios. Finally, by combining conclusions drawn from analyses across three sub-scenarios; problems with campus pedestrian transportation system were summarized along with their associated characteristics. This not only offers new analytical perspectives for pedestrian travel design studies but also provides valuable insights into autonomous vehicle services in new slow-moving transportation scenarios such as suburban large university campuses (Fig. 8).

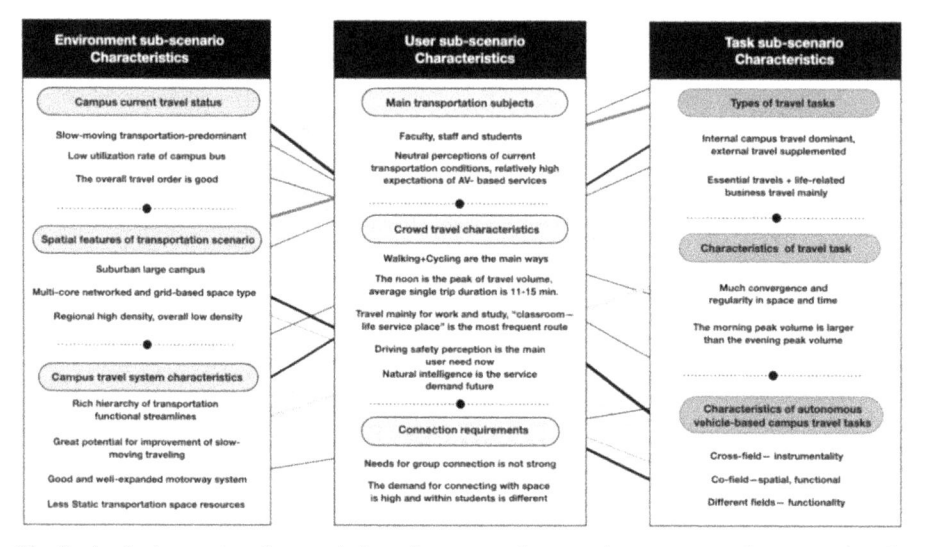

Fig. 8. Analysis on the characteristics of campus slow-moving transportation scenarios for autonomous vehicle services.

Disclosure of Interests. The authors have no competing interests to declare that are relevant to the content of this article.

References

1. Ying-Yi, L., Guan-Ping, L.: The discussion of environmental psychology and campus's landscape design. Guangdong Landscape Archit. (2006)
2. Kaplan, D.H.: Transportation sustainability on a university campus. Int. J. Sustain. High. Educ. (2015). https://doi.org/10.1108/IJSHE-03-2013-0023
3. Gang, F.: Analysis of campus planning and design of Chinese contemporary universities. Tianjin University (2005). https://doi.org/10.7666/d.y1531851
4. Lei, C.: Research on the development trend of University Campus Spatial planning and design. Zhejiang University (2016)
5. Jing, Z., Guangfu, Z.: Analysis of characteristics of urban road intersection traffic. J. China Municipal Eng. **2**, 3 (2010). https://doi.org/10.3969/j.cstp.2018.06.008. ISSN: 1004-4655.2010.02.004
6. Menini, S.E., Da Silva, T.O., Pitanga, H.N., et al.: Method for using nonmotorized modes of transportation as a sustainable urban mobility index in university campuses. J. Transp. Eng. Part A Syst. **2021**(2), 147 (2021)
7. Agrawal, A.W., Schlossberg, M., Irvin, K.: How far, by which route and why? A spatial analysis of pedestrian preference. J. Urban Des. **13**, 81–98 (2008)
8. Seneviratne, P.N., Morrall, J.F.: Analysis of factors affecting the choice of route of pedestrians. Transp. Plann. Technol. **10**(2), 147–159 (1985)
9. Simon, H.A.: A behavioral model of rational choice. Quart. J. Econ. **69**(1), 99–118 (1955)
10. Bekhor, S., Ben-Akiva, M.E., Ramming, M.S.: Evaluation of choice set generation algorithms for route choice models. Ann. Oper. Res. **144**, 235–247 (2006)

11. Yu, S., Zhang, H., Zhao, J.: Integrating shared autonomous vehicle in public transportation system: a supply-side simulation of the first-mile service in Singapore. Transp. Res. Part A Policy Pract. **113**, 125–136 (2018)
12. Albert, G., Toledo, T., Ben-Zion, U.: The role of personality factors in repeated route choice behavior: behavioral economics perspective. Eur. Transp. Trasporti Europei **48**, 47–59 (2011)
13. Yuhong, H.: Urban Transportation Sociology. Huazhong University of Science and Technology Press, Wuhan (2014)
14. Xiong, P.: Campus bus planning and design – a case study of Shenzhen university. J. Transp. Eng. Inf. **9**(01), 27–34 (2011)

Exploring the Perceived Cognitive Workload: The Impact of Various Scenarios and Emotions on a Driving Simulator

Buse Tezçi[1], Luca Tramarin[1], Edoardo Pagot[1], Marco Marchetti[2], Giuliana Zennaro[2], Paolo Denti[2], Stefano Giannini[3], Maura Mengoni[4], and Silvia Chiesa[1](✉)

[1] RE: LAB, Reggio Emilia, Italy
{buse.tezci,silvia.chiesa}@re-lab.it
[2] CRF, Rome, Italy
[3] Polito, Turin, Italy
[4] EMOJ, Rome, Italy

Abstract. Driver distraction due to emotional states gained attention in the last decades. Even though there are various studies examined and compared various emotions, so far changes in the emotional state was not examined. The aim of this paper was to explore the emotion-ordered effect on driver cognitive workload and contribute to the emotion distraction literature and draw practical implications for road safety. To study the effect, thirteen participants recruited for a driving simulator study and they were divided into two experimental groups in which they either tried Happy-to-Angry or Angry-to-Happy emotion transitions. Participants later assigned different driving scenarios. NASA-TLX data was collected after each scenario. Results reveal no statistically significant differences in perceived mental workload across different experimental conditions or their sequences, indicating consistent cognitive demands. However, observed trends suggest subtle variations that may require larger samples or more sensitive tools for detection.

Keywords: Driver distraction · Cognitive Workload · Affective distraction · Emotion order

1 Introduction

The multifaceted demands of the driving task, with its myriad of simultaneous actions and the constant need to monitor and react to both internal and external stimuli, increases the likelihood of impaired driving performance. Consequently, driver distraction stands out as a prominent contributor to accidents, as individuals may struggle to maintain focused attention on the various elements demanding awareness while navigating the road [1]. Understanding the intricate dynamics of driving distraction is crucial for addressing and mitigating the risks associated with it, ultimately improving overall road safety.

The most commonly studied distraction types in the literature come in various forms, including physical, visual, auditory and cognitive and their combination as they can occur simultaneously [2]. In the past fifteen years, in addition to the "classic" distraction types, a new category was added and increasingly recognized due to its great impact on drivers' performance is emotional distraction. The intricate interplay between emotions and driving behavior has been a subject of interest and concern in the field of transportation psychology [3].

1.1 Effect of Emotional Order on Driving Performance and Cognitive Workload

Numerous studies focused on comparing different emotional states, such as anger, boredom, sadness, happiness and examined their effect on driving behavior.

Initial and a limited number of studies on emotional distraction were conducted in mid-2010s. The main findings indicated that emotional valence of the content presented to drivers, whether a stimulus is positive or negative, had an influence on driving performance [4–7]. In the pioneer study done in emotional distraction research, Pêcher et al. [7] investigated the effect of emotional valence on driving behavior. Participants listened to happy, sad, and neutral music; neutral music served as a baseline where participants were most focused. Results showed that both sad and happy music led to deteriorations in driving behavior compared to neutral. These deteriorations varied between emotions: happy music caused more average speed decrease compared to neutral music and led to lateral control deterioration, while sad music, despite slightly decreasing mean speed, did not lead to longitudinal control deterioration. The participants reported to be aware of the distractive effect of happy music, but they were not aware of their reactions, such as following the rhythm of the song by tapping on the steering wheel. Authors suggested that especially, who are keen to be affected by happy music, might create a dual-task in which they increased their mental workload [7]. Similarly to auditory valence stimuli, visual stimuli with emotional content have been found to negatively impact driving behavior [8]. When participants were exposed to either negative or positive images before the hazard perception test, compared to neutral images, participants' subjectively reported perception of risk was reduced, electrodermal responses was reduced and eye-fixation duration was shortened significantly, suggesting a inhibition of a reduced sensitivity to potential road hazards [8]. Visual emotional stimuli are also very interesting to examine, due to their abundance on the streets. In fact, in another study authors reported that driving speed is lower when negative and positive stimuli (roadside billboards) is presented compared to neutral stimuli [4]. It indicates that independently from valence emotion inducing content is distractive to the drivers, however, authors also observed that the length of distraction lingered for positive stimuli longer than negative ones. Contrarily, in an additional memory recall tasks that drivers conducted while driving, they had better memory retention with negative stimuli. These two findings suggest that, even though emotional distraction can be caused by either positive or negative stimuli, the mechanism and implications on emotional distraction is different.

Even though various initial studies have taken a closer look at the deteriorating effects of emotions on driving behaviour, some articles also showed an opposite effect in which negative emotion induced by negative videos increased the risk perception of the participants, even though this was not reflected on driving behavior. This was especially prevalent compared to positive emotions [9]. This might be due to the peculiarity of specific emotions, such as anger. Anger is a specifically examined case as experiencing anger leads to deliberate aggressive behavior as opposed to committing unintentional driving error [10]. Studies showed that anger affective state might deteriorate driving behavior due to reduced situation awareness [11] and caused more driving errors [11, 12] and affected driving behavior negatively by leading to higher maximum speed compared to neutral state [11]. Emotional distraction, specifically anger, was found to degrade the driving performance equally or more than other distraction types, such as physical or cognitive distraction [2]. Despite anger's particularity and negative emotions deterioration effect found in the literature, not only negative emotions but also positive emotions affect driving behavior.

There is a considerable level of enthusiasm surrounding this subject, especially among those seeking a comprehensive understanding of Advanced Driver Assistance Systems (ADAS) and Driver Monitoring Systems (DMS). This heightened interest is driven by the recognition that exploring the emotional dimension of driving can significantly enhance the development and effectiveness of ADAS and driver monitoring technologies. By gaining insights into how emotions influence driver behaviour, not only manual but also during partial-autonomous driving [13], these systems can be refined to not only detect and respond to physical distractions but also to consider and respond to emotional states, thus advancing road safety to new level [14].

1.2 Perceived Workload

Perceived workload is a common metric that usually accompanies the affective distraction studies and often assessed using subjective scales, such as the NASA-TLX [15]. However, the findings from these studies are heterogeneous. For example, while anger has been shown to negatively impact driving behavior and situational awareness, it did not significantly affect perceived workload in some studies [2, 8, 11]. Conversely, another study reported a significant increase in workload levels among participants in an angry state compared to a neutral state [12]. In the same study similarly, when comparing workload scores between sad and neutral states, a significant difference was observed, despite both emotional states leading to a decline in driving performance. This discrepancy was attributed to the distinct cognitive appraisals associated with anger and sadness. Anger, being more closely linked to self-control, may result in a higher workload when individuals perceive a lack of control in a frustrating driving environment, whereas sadness, associated with situational control, may lead to a lower perceived workload as individuals attribute the difficulty to external factors [12]. Additionally, a study comparing a boring auditory condition to neutral and interesting conditions found a significant difference in workload scores, albeit not substantial [16] . Even though various studies indicate that emotional states, especially anger, might lead to increased levels of cognitive workload, these varied results highlight the need for more studies and experimental conditions that include complicated emotional situations to shed a light on other aspects of cognitive workload.

Moving forward, it is crucial to consider the dynamic nature of emotions and their potential residual effects on driving behavior. While previous studies have examined emotional states independently, future research should explore the effects of emotional changes within the driving context. This is also important as literature also indicated there might be residual effects stronger for some emotions, for example positive ones [4]. For instance, examining the transition from a happy to an angry state or vice versa and its impact on driving behavior, such as changes in speed, can provide valuable insights into the role of emotions in driving performance. By incorporating complex emotional scenarios and examining emotional changes in the vehicle, researchers can gain a deeper understanding of the factors contributing to driver distraction and develop effective interventions to enhance road safety [17].

Drivers experience varying levels of drowsiness under different ambient lighting conditions, which is expected due to the natural association between lighting levels, time of day, and daily wake/sleep cycles. Research shows that during the day, when ambient lighting is high, drivers exhibit lower percentages of drowsiness. This can be attributed to the fact that daylight hours align with periods of heightened alertness in our circadian rhythms. Conversely, at night, when ambient lighting is low, drivers tend to show higher percentages of drowsiness. This increase is likely due to the body's natural inclination towards sleep during nighttime hours, making it more challenging to stay alert and focused [18].

Furthermore, studies examined the impact of various weather conditions on driver drowsiness and secondary-task engagement. However, the total number of events and epochs recorded during adverse weather conditions such as sleet, snow, fog, mist, and others was quite small. This limited data set suggests that the sample size might not be large enough to provide a comprehensive understanding of how these specific weather conditions influence driver behavior and secondary-task engagement. As a result, further research with a larger sample size is necessary to adequately address these issues and determine the true impact of different weather conditions on driving performance and drowsiness levels [18].

1.3 Hypotheses

In the light of findings of the literature, the following hypotheses were developed to be tested with the experiment.

- Hypothesis 1: The inclusion of various elements in the scenario will increase the difficulty of driving.

For instance, adding elements such as complex road layouts, varying traffic densities, and different weather conditions can increase cognitive load on the driver. Complex road layouts require more attention and decision-making, leading to higher mental strain. High traffic densities demand constant vigilance and quick reactions, which can further escalate the difficulty. Adverse weather conditions like fog reduce visibility and road traction, challenging the driver's ability to maintain control and respond to unexpected events. Consequently, these factors collectively contribute to a more demanding and potentially stressful driving experience.

- Hypothesis 2: Perceived workload (*NASA-TLX* scores) in conditions with different emotional sequence (from happy to angry and from angry to happy) will be different.

The sequence in which these emotions are experienced can further impact the overall perceived workload. Transitioning from a happy to an angry state might result in a more pronounced increase in workload perception due to the sudden shift in emotional and cognitive demands. Conversely, moving from an angry to a happy state might lead to a significant reduction in perceived workload, as the positive emotions help mitigate stress and improve concentration. Therefore, both the type and order of emotions experienced play a crucial role in shaping the perceived cognitive demands of driving.

2 Method

2.1 Experimental Design

The experiment was designed as a 2 (Emotional state order: Happy-to-Angry, Angry-to-Happy) × 3 (Driving scenario complexity: Smooth, Moderate, Difficult) mixed design. Therefore, half of the participants were assigned to the so called "Happy-to-Angry" group and half were assigned to "Angry-to-Happy" group. Independent from the assigned group each participant tried three different driving scenarios in a random order.

2.2 Participants

Consequently, the final dataset for analysis comprised thirteen participants, consisting of 7 females and 6 males, with average age of 30.8 ($M = 27.1$, $Min = 19$; $Max = 41$). Regarding driving experience, 17% of the participants reported having less than three years of driving experience, while 58% indicated having between three to ten years of experience. The remaining 25% of participants reported having more than ten years of driving experience.

2.3 Materials

Driving Simulator. The experimental research employed a static driving simulator, developed by Oktal-Scaner and powered by AVSimulation Scaner's simulation software. This simulator is equipped with authentic vehicle controls, including a force-feedback steering wheel, pedals for acceleration, braking, and clutch, a manual gear shift, and a cluster with various levers, including indicators. The seat is adjustable to accommodate drivers of varying heights, and simulator sounds are delivered through a stereo audio system. The simulator's architecture includes a projector screen, which displays the simulated environment in 1080p resolution at 60 Hz. An LCD display behind the steering wheel presents the vehicle's instrument panel, while another touchscreen is positioned on the right side of the driver, mimicking a car's central console. Driving scenarios are designed using the Scaner Studio software suite, featuring a 3D terrain, a road network, traffic, and a storyboard of the scenario. The latter allows the user to program various custom actions by other traffic agents and to reproduce audio narratives to guide the testing subjects through the test.

Driving Scenarios. Two highway driving scenarios and one citizen scenario were developed, each varying in traffic intensity.

Independently from the order of the emotions, the duration of each scenario was seven minutes. Participant tried both sessions in a random order.

In each scenario, participants tried either a change from angry emotion to happy emotion or happy emotion to angry emotion.

Following the baseline period, the emotional event is given by the pre-registered voice followed by a song. The "Happy" event refers to the cancellation of a chore or work-related task, allowing one to enjoy a recreational event. Conversely, the "Angry" event involves receiving a request from one's boss, leading to the cancellation of a recreational event, encountering increased traffic, and facing negative consequences due to the traffic. The music selection was based on the Cowen et al.'s taxonomy (https://www.ocf.berkeley.edu/~acowen/music.html) [19].

In more details the Smooth condition is a scenario in highway. The driving simulation begins with an introduction where the participant is welcomed and instructed to drive and use the tablet and begin driving as they would normally. The simulation starts with free driving on a highway with medium traffic.

Next, in a joyful scenario, the participant drives on a highway with light traffic, informed that they are heading to the supermarket, which is about to close, but reassured that they will arrive on time.

The scenario then focuses on wellbeing, with the participant prompted to activate a speed camera alert. The highway remains lightly trafficked.

In the anger scenario, the participant encounters a slow-moving vehicle that they cannot overtake, risking the supermarket being closed before they arrive. This situation is designed to induce frustration.

A neutral state with visual distractions follows, where the participant is instructed to pick up and put down an object, say loudly some words and touch images on the tablet screen while driving.

The final segment involves coaching, where the participant is offered the option to use Adaptive Cruise Control.The moderate scenario involves driving on a highway with heavy traffic.

During the joyful scenario, the participant is informed that he is driving to a work training course and the driver decides to listen to cheerful music to distract himself.

The scenario then shifts to coaching. The participant is given the option to activate the Automatic Emergency Brake by pressing a button on the screen.

In the anger scenario, the participant is warned that the traffic conditions are critical, making it certain he/she will arrive late to the course, which will already be in progress.

Following this, a neutral state with visual distractions is introduced. The participant is instructed to pick up and put down a pen, loudly say some words, and touch images of on the tablet screen, all while driving on a heavily trafficked highway. Finally, the wellbeing segment begins. The participant is offered the option to entertain himself by reading a joke by pressing a button on the screen.

The Dangerous scenario involves driving in a city at night with low traffic and foggy conditions.

In the joyful condition, the participant is driving with low traffic at night in the fog while heading to a work training course and he decides to listen to cheerful music. The scenario then shifts to coaching. The participant is given the option to activate the auto hold feature, which keeps the vehicle stationary after braking, useful in traffic or on inclines, by pressing a button on the screen. The driving conditions remain the same, with low traffic at night in the fog.

In the anger scenario, the participant is warned that the traffic conditions are critical, making it certain they will not arrive on time to the course. This situation is designed to induce frustration.

Following this, a neutral state with visual distractions is introduced. The participant is instructed to pick up and put down a magazine, say some words aloud, and touch images on the tablet screen, all while driving in a city at night with low traffic and fog.

Finally, the wellbeing segment begins. The participant is offered the option to entertain themselves by reading a joke by pressing a button on the screen.

In the Angry-to-Happy condition the scenario is the same but with the emotion conditions in the opposite order.

Questionnaires

Demographic information. Demographic information is collected from participants including age, education level, and driving habits.

After-Session Questionnaires: NASA-TLX (NASA Task Load Index). NASA-TLX questionnaire was used after each driving session to obtain workload induced by each scenario on participants.

The questionnaire s a widely used subjective assessment tool designed to evaluate perceived workload in various tasks, including driving. The NASA-TLX assesses workload along six dimensions: mental demand, physical demand, temporal demand, performance, effort, and frustration level.

Participants rate each dimension on a scale from 0 to 5, where 0 represents "very low" and 5 represents "very high." These ratings provide insights into the subjective experience of workload associated with the task being evaluated.

2.4 Procedure

Participants were assigned to two groups with reversed orders of simulated emotions. The first group experienced the "Angry-to-Happy" scenario, while the second group underwent the "Happy-to-Angry" scenario.

To commence the study, participants filled out an entry questionnaire. Subsequently, participants provided information about their knowledge of ADAS, DMS systems, and sensors, along with any relevant experiences.

Once the entry questionnaires were finished, the experimenter exited the room, instructing participants to follow the pre-registered voice commands. Participants were left alone in the driving simulator room, where the emotion recognition software began registering their emotions throughout the experiment. Participants followed the voice prompts and completed the scenario. Following the conclusion of the first scenario, the experimenter re-entered the room and administered the after-session questionnaire.

Upon completion of the questionnaire, the second session commenced, followed by the second after-session questionnaire. Subsequently, the third session was conducted, accompanied by the third after-session questionnaire. Following the conclusion of all three sessions, participants filled out the end-questionnaire.

3 Results

Statistical analysis completed with IBM SPSS Statistics Version 29.0.2.0 (20) software.

3.1 NASA-TLX

The results of the NASA Task Load Index (NASA TLX) indicate that there is no statistically significant difference between the experimental conditions under investigation ($F(2,10) = 3.69; p = .06$). This lack of significance suggests that, based on the subjective workload assessments provided by the participants, the varying conditions did not result in perceptibly different levels of mental workload. This finding implies that the conditions, despite their differences, are not perceived as varying cognitive demands on participants.

Moreover, when comparing the specific sequences of conditions, A-H and H-A, the results similarly show no significant difference ($F(2,10) = 1.51; p = .23$). This consistency further supports the idea that the order in which these conditions are experienced does not affect the participants' perceived workload. Such a finding is important for experimental design, indicating that counterbalancing the conditions or the sequence in which they are presented does not introduce bias into the results.

However, it is worth noting that while the differences are not statistically significant, the data do exhibit a trend. This trend, although not robust enough to achieve statistical significance, suggests there might be subtle variations in how participants experience the workload under different conditions. These trends can be indicative of underlying patterns that could become significant with a larger sample size or with more sensitive measurement tools (Fig. 1).

4 Discussion

The NASA TLX results demonstrate no significant differences in perceived workload across the conditions or their sequences, implying consistency and reliability in the participants' workload assessment. This consistency is crucial as it suggests that the different experimental conditions, and the order in which they were presented, do not lead to varying levels of perceived cognitive demand. This reliability in workload assessment is essential for ensuring that the results are not influenced by extraneous variables or the sequence of the conditions.

However, despite the lack of statistically significant differences, the data exhibit trends that suggest there may be subtle variations in perceived workload that are not captured due to the current sample size or methodology. These trends are important as they hint at underlying differences that could become significant with further investigation.

For instance, increasing the number of participants could enhance the power of the study, making it more likely to detect small but meaningful differences in workload across conditions. A larger sample size would provide a more robust dataset, reducing the margin of error and increasing the confidence in the findings. Additionally, refining the methodologies used, such as employing more sensitive measurement tools or adjusting the experimental design, could help uncover these nuanced differences.

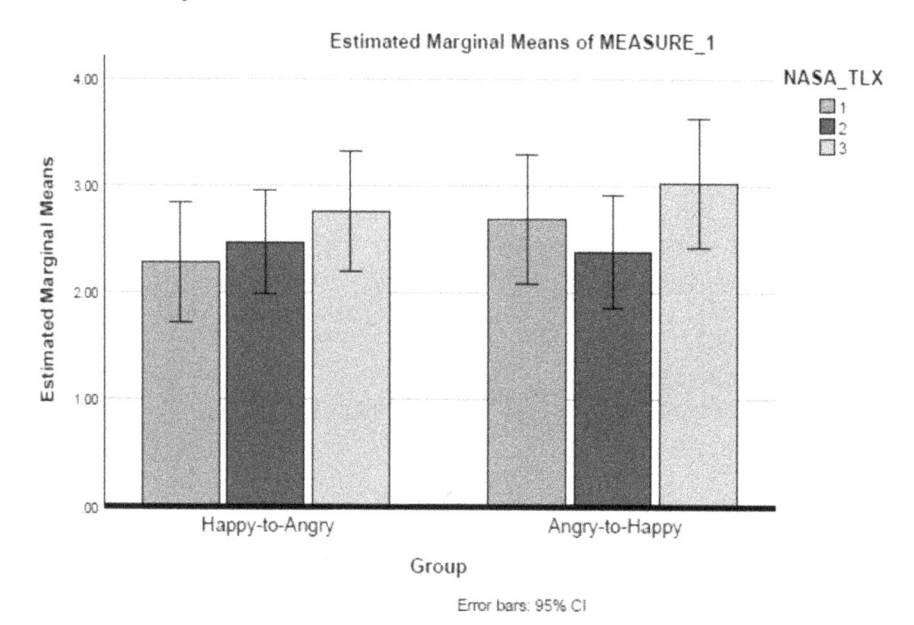

Fig. 1. Results of the Nasa-TLX in the three conditions (1: Smooth; 2: Moderate; 3: Dangerous)

Conducting further analysis with the gathered data is essential to comprehensively understand the nuances of the experiment. By incorporating additional sources of information, such as simulator data, emotional responses, and supplementary questionnaires, researchers can gain a more comprehensive understanding of the factors influencing the outcomes. This multifaceted approach allows for a more detailed exploration of potential differences and provides a more robust basis for drawing conclusions.

Simulator data, for instance, can offer insights into participants' behavior and performance in simulated environments, providing context to their subjective workload assessments. Emotion data can shed light on the emotional experiences associated with different experimental conditions, which may influence perceived workload. Additionally, supplementary questionnaires can capture additional variables or perspectives that may not have been addressed in the initial assessment.

Furthermore, it appears that the sequence or order in which the emotions are experienced does not have a discernible impact on the perceived cognitive workload, suggesting that the subjective assessments of workload remain consistent regardless of the emotional context in which they occur. This observation underscores the reliability and stability of the participants' workload evaluations, reinforcing the validity of the study's conclusions. Additionally, it implies that variations in emotional states do not significantly alter individuals' perceptions of the cognitive demands imposed by the experimental conditions.

4.1 Limitations

Based on the previous results, it is important to acknowledge limitations that may have influenced the study outcomes. These limitations should be addressed in future research to build upon the current findings and provide a more comprehensive understanding of the relationship between emotions, cognitive workload and driving behavior.

Lack of Neutral Group. While the study effectively controlled for the order of experienced emotions, and included a baseline driving period at the beginning of the driving session, the absence of a neutral group remains a limitation. To address this in future studies, it is recommended to incorporate a third neutral group that will undergo each driving scenario with a neutral stimulus that will not induce an emotion in the participants.

Driving Experience. Systematic studies indicated that novice drivers' hazard perception skills may not be as refined as those of experienced drivers [21, 22] potentially leading to a heightened tendency to feel nervous and uncomfortable during driving [3]. Consequently, even though only 17% of the sample consisted of drivers with less than three years of driving experience, lack of driving experience might have influenced driving behavior. Therefore, future studies, should aim for a more balanced sample to better compare and control for the effect of experience.

Number of Participants. One limitation of the study is the restricted number of participants, which could affect the robustness of the findings. With a limited sample size, the statistical analyses may not have sufficient power to detect subtle but potentially important trends. Increasing the number of participants in future research endeavors could enhance the reliability and generalizability of the results, potentially uncovering more definitive conclusions about the impact of emotional states on perceived cognitive workload in driving scenarios.

5 Conclusion

Our study investigates the connection between emotions, cognitive workload and driving behaviour. As we move forward in the pursuit of safer roads and the integration of autonomous vehicles, it is essential to consider the emotional dimension of driving. By doing so, we can develop more effective strategies to mitigate distractions, enhance driver safety, and, ultimately, reduce the incidence of road accidents [20, 21]. This research contributes to a growing body of knowledge that can inform policies and practices aimed at making our roads safer for all.

In conclusion, the NASA TLX findings indicate that the experimental conditions and their sequences do not significantly affect perceived mental workload, ensuring consistency in cognitive demands across different scenarios. While the lack of statistical significance suggests robustness in the experimental design, the observed trends point to potential subtle differences that merit further investigation with larger samples or more refined measurement methods. This insight is crucial for designing future studies and understanding the nuances of cognitive workload assessment.

Driver cognitive workload, a prominent contributor to accidents, necessitates a comprehensive approach to mitigate risks and enhance road safety. Understanding the methodologies to better study this aspect is important to grasp the effective impact of driving scenarios on cognitive workload, as well as the influence of emotions on driving performance. The interplay between emotions and driving behavior is a significant concern in transportation psychology, with research indicating that emotional states can elevate cognitive workload levels. Therefore, a nuanced understanding of these factors is essential for developing strategies to improve driver safety and performance.

Disclosure of Interests. The authors have no competing interests to declare that are relevant to the content of this article.

References

1. NHTSA: Distracted Driving. https://www.nhtsa.gov/risky-driving/distracted-driving
2. Sterkenburg, J., Jeon, M.: Impacts of anger on driving performance: a comparison to texting and conversation while driving. Int. J. Ind. Ergon. **80**, 102999 (2020). https://doi.org/10.1016/j.ergon.2020.102999
3. Jeon, M.: Emotions in driving. In: Emotions and Affect in Human Factors and Human-Computer Interaction, pp. 437–474. Elsevier (2017)
4. Chan, M., Singhal, A.: Emotion matters: implications for distracted driving. Saf. Sci. **72**, 302–309 (2015). https://doi.org/10.1016/j.ssci.2014.10.002
5. Chan, M., Singhal, A.: The emotional side of cognitive distraction: implications for road safety. Accid. Anal. Prev. **50**, 147–154 (2013). https://doi.org/10.1016/j.aap.2012.04.004
6. Cunningham, M.L., Regan, Micheal A: The impact of emotion, life stress and mental health issues on driving performance and safety (2016)
7. Pêcher, C., Lemercier, C., Cellier, J.-M.: Emotions drive attention: effects on driver's behaviour. Saf. Sci. **47**, 1254–1259 (2009). https://doi.org/10.1016/j.ssci.2009.03.011
8. Jones, M.P., Chapman, P., Bailey, K.: The influence of image valence on visual attention and perception of risk in drivers. Accid. Anal. Prev. **73**, 296–304 (2014). https://doi.org/10.1016/j.aap.2014.09.019
9. Hu, T.-Y., Xie, X., Li, J.: Negative or positive? The effect of emotion and mood on risky driving. Transp. Res. Part F Traffic Psychol. Behav. **16**, 29–40 (2013). https://doi.org/10.1016/j.trf.2012.08.009
10. Precht, L., Keinath, A., Krems, J.F.: Effects of driving anger on driver behavior – Results from naturalistic driving data. Transp. Res. Part F Traffic Psychol. Behav. 45, 75–92 (2017). https://doi.org/10.1016/j.trf.2016.10.019
11. Jeon, M., Walker, B.N., Gable, T.M.: Anger effects on driver situation awareness and driving performance. Presence Teleoperators Virtual Environ. **23**, 71–89 (2014). https://doi.org/10.1162/PRES_a_00169
12. Jeon, M., Zhang, W.: Sadder but Wiser? Effects of negative emotions on risk perception, driving performance, and perceived workload. Proc. Hum. Factors Ergon. Soc. Annu. Meet. **57**, 1849–1853 (2013). https://doi.org/10.1177/1541931213571413
13. Du, N., et al.: Predicting driver takeover performance in conditionally automated driving. Accid. Anal. Prev. **148**, 105748 (2020). https://doi.org/10.1016/j.aap.2020.105748
14. Presta, R., De Simone, F., Mancuso, L., Chiesa, S., Montanari, R.: Would I consent if it monitors me better? A technology acceptance comparison of BCI-based and unobtrusive driver monitoring systems. In: 2022 IEEE International Conference on Metrology for Extended Reality, Artificial Intelligence and Neural Engineering (MetroXRAINE),. IEEE, Rome, Italy, pp. 545–550 (2022)
15. Hart, S.G.: Nasa-Task Load Index (NASA-TLX); 20 Years Later. Proc. Hum. Factors Ergon. Soc. Annu. Meet. 50, 904–908 (2006). https://doi.org/10.1177/154193120605000909
16. Horrey, W.J., Lesch, M.F., Garabet, A., Simmons, L., Maikala, R.: Distraction and task engagement: how interesting and boring information impact driving performance and subjective and physiological responses. Appl. Ergon. **58**, 342–348 (2017). https://doi.org/10.1016/j.apergo.2016.07.011

17. Ceccacci, S., et al.: Designing in-car emotion-aware automation. Eur. Transp./Trasporti Europei **84**, 1–15 (2021)
18. Klauer, S.G., Dingus, T.A., Neale, V.L., Sudweeks, J.D., Ramsey, D.J.: The impact of driver inattention on near-crash/crash risk: an analysis using the 100-car naturalistic driving study data (2006)
19. Cowen, A.S., Fang, X., Sauter, D., Keltner, D.: What music makes us feel: at least 13 dimensions organize subjective experiences associated with music across different cultures. Proc. Natl. Acad. Sci. **117**, 1924–1934 (2020). https://doi.org/10.1073/pnas.1910704117
20. Presta, R., De Simone, F., Tancredi, C., Chiesa, S.: Nudging the Safe Zone: Design and Assessment of HMI Strategies Based on Intelligent Driver State Monitoring Systems. In: Krömker, H. (ed.) HCII 2023. LNCS, vol. 14048, pp. 166–185. Springer, Cham (2023). https://doi.org/10.1007/978-3-031-35678-0_10
21. Generosi, A., Ceccacci, S., Tezçi, B., Montanari, R., Mengoni, M.: Nudges-based design method for adaptive HMI to improve driving safety. Safety **8**, 63 (2022). https://doi.org/10.3390/safety8030063

Design of Automotive Interior and Human-Computer Interaction for Time-Sharing Rental: A Chinese Study

Hao Yang[1], Na Chen[2], Quanxin Jin[1], and Ying Zhao[3](✉)

[1] North China University of Technology, Beijing, China
`hao-yang12@ncut.edu.cn`
[2] Beijing University of Chemical Technology, Beijing, China
[3] Beijing Institute of Graphic Communication, Beijing, China
`wuyue8656@163.com`

Abstract. Due to the fact that time-sharing rental cars (TSRC) are not personal vehicles, users are prone to feeling unfamiliar or even uncomfortable. Compared to private cars, driving behaviors in TSRC are more likely to be influenced by the level of human-computer interaction (HCI) on the on-board computer and the road environment. The current article proposes to obtain main categories of driving experience of TSRC by the Grounded Theory. And the dimensionality of factors that affect the driving experience were reduced based on Factor Analysis. Common factors were extracted as the core research objectives, and the impact of each common factor on the willingness to use TSRC was analyzed. Then by means of the Analytic Hierarchy Process (AHP), the importance of different HCI methods in terms of meeting demands of using TSRC was evaluated. The results indicated that among the evaluation criteria, the most important one is that the on-board computer can provide sufficient intelligent prompt and driving assistance functions. And for HCI methods, physical buttons/knobs have the highest weight in matching the TSRC driver's demands, followed by voice interaction. The weights of touch screen and gesture recognition are relatively lower. And finally, the design implementation path for the car interior and HCI interface applicable to TSRC was formed.

Keywords: Time-sharing Rental Car · On-board Computer · HCI · Automotive Interior · Usage Willingness

1 Introduction

Time-sharing rental car (TSRC), as a new type of transportation mode that conforms to sharing transportation, has become important internationally. The interior of TSRC has also become an important mobile space. In order to provide a better user experience for car rental users, the cars launched by carsharing enterprises in recent years have shown a trend of lightweight, intelligent, interactive-friendly, and environmental-friendly. For example, AUTOLIB, a carsharing brand in Paris, France, has launched electric vehicles specially designed for time-sharing rental (TSR) by the Bollore Group (France). The entire interior is very simple and neat, without leaving too much storage space. Although the current TSR business model faces some problems in management and revenue, it has a large number of users and certain development prospect.

In the process of development, some problems that users may encounter during use are gradually exposed. Especially when driving in unfamiliar road environments, due to the fact that the vehicle is not privately owned by oneself, the driver's concern about the responsibility for collisions on road, the mismatch between the car interior and the driver's personalized subconscious behaviors, and the driver's unfamiliarity with the interior space can all trigger problems in human-computer interaction (HCI) or human-machine interaction (HMI). This directly affects the user experience and even poses security risks that need to be addressed, among which the more prominent problems include weak guidance for equipment operation, and low restrictions on dangerous behaviors [1]. Therefore, when deciding on car models to be launched in the carsharing market, it is important to emphasize the guidance, persuasion, and restriction to users through the interior elements such as marks, color and interior accessories. However, HCI problems are systematic and complex. They involve numerous variables and are difficult to study. Therefore, the current study proposes a set of methods to reduce the dimensionality of the systematic problem and simplify research focus. Then using the Analytic Hierarchy Process (AHP), the design criteria and HCI methods were evaluated, and the design basis for vehicle interior and HCI interfaces applicable to TSRC were explored.

2 Literature Review

Carsharing involves many business models, such as round-trip station-based (RTSB) mode, free-floating (FF) mode, business-to-consumer (B2C) mode and peer-to-peer (P2P) mode [2, 3]. A common service is to rent the cars out to registered users for a short period like three to five hours, rather than charging for a fixed period such as a whole day or a whole week. Such service could be called TSR service. Although FF mode seems more convenient, the influence on the decrease of car ownership is lower for FF than for RTSB services [4]. This has raised a new alarm for the carsharing industry: in addition to optimizing the service model, attention should also be paid to driver motivation and driving experience issues. Some Brazilian scholars have proposed a scale used to measure the experience of using shared cars, which involves issues such as convenience, trust, social identity, etc. [5], providing an important research foundation for this direction.

Many people with different preferences share a car, presenting a new usability challenge for the design of efficient HMI interface in the vehicle. Therefore, providing multiple adjustable functions that allow vehicle settings to achieve personalization is very important [6]. Some studies have also focused on HCI methods applicable to software and hardware installed in shared cars, such as gesture, voice, or eye movement interaction [7].

The interior design of a car is directly linked to the driver's experience [8]. With the popularization of modules such as intelligent driving assistance, fatigue monitoring, multimedia, and digital navigation, the interior has become an extension of the lifestyle of drivers and passengers. However, for TSRC, due to the driver's unfamiliarity with the interior environment, the design of the interior and HCI interfaces such as the digital instrument panel and central control screen has a more important guiding and restricting effect on the driving behaviors. Previous research indicated that a relationship existed between interaction performance and the modeling forms of instrument panel in shared cars [9]. There is also research revealing that the system usability scores of the central control screen interface with blue tone is always higher than that with red tone [10]. These researches provide a theoretical basis for the value of interior design in carsharing service. However, for the service providers, due to the large amount of vehicles they hold and the difficulty of management, they need to consider depreciation costs [11], cleaning costs, maintenance costs, etc. This determines that the optimization design of the interior of TSRC should not blindly focus on quality and beauty like private cars, which makes the implementation of interior design more complex. Key influencing factors need to be identified and prioritized in order to effectively conduct interior design suitable for TSRC users.

3 Method

3.1 Research on the Design Principles of TSRC Interior Combining Grounded Theory and Factor Analysis

Previous research has shown that interior design of B2C shared cars always faces problems caused by novice drivers who rent cars to practice driving skills, drivers who are not familiar with the rented car, Internet of Vehicles (IOV), and unmanned management system [1]. The user's unfamiliarity and lack of trust in the car's interior environment, as well as the lack of a service provider for direct consultation and communication, have become a major characteristic of TSRC service system. In addition, there are always some regular patterns in the demand for using shared cars for mobility [12]. Based on the above characteristics, this study developed an outline for semi-structured user interview, which was used to guide users to articulate meaningful opinions from five aspects: 1) regular functions, 2) optional functions, 3) vehicle performance, 4) platform services, and 5) in-vehicle environment. Part of the outline can be found in the appendix.

The purpose of the interview is to comprehensively evaluate the user experience issues that are commonly encountered in three TSRC travel scenarios, which are trips with storage services, airport-based long-distance travel, and traveling with family or friends in the home city [13]. A total of 16 people were interviewed, including 11 males and 5 females. According to the preliminary survey results, young people and college students are the main target audience. Therefore, for the selection of interviewees, young people were more favored. The finally determined interviewees include 11 people aged 21–30 and 5 people aged 31–42. The transcribed text consists of over 60,000 Chinese characters. After removing invalid corpus such as meaningless, irrelevant and semantically biased corpus, numbers were assigned to the remaining corpus data. Then, based on the Grounded Theory (GT), the corpora were coded and analyzed.

GT was proposed by Glaser et al. and is a process of constantly raising questions, making comparison, establishing classifications and connections, suitable for discovering and deriving theories from material research. This study used GT method to perform Open Coding and Axial Coding on the original interview text, and summarized the dimensions of TSRC usage willingness from user comments on TSRC driving experience. A coding team consisting of two individuals independently coded the interview text, and then verified and discussed each coding result. For divergent coding items, discussions from third-party of professors were introduced to help achieve consensus [14]. Finally, 10 main categories were obtained, which can serve as automotive interior design principles for TSR market. The main categories were:

M1: Convenient for users to locate targets and park vehicles;
M2: Provide guiding designs which are helpful to easily operating;
M3: Easy to maintain and manage;
M4: Extend the life of the cars;
M5: Feasible on complex road conditions such as multiple intersections and elevated bridges;
M6: Help users adapt to long waiting time caused by heavy traffic and congestion;
M7: Able to monitor driving fatigue and take corresponding measures;
M8: Rich auxiliary functions that can make users more convenient (but may increase maintenance costs);
M9: Enhance supervision and restrictions on the users;
M10: Reduce users' learning cost in the unfamiliar cabin space of the rental car.

Finally, Selective Coding was carried out with the aim of developing core categories from the main categories, and depicting the overall behavioral phenomena around the core categories. However, this process is relatively abstract and has certain limitations in terms of stability during operation. Therefore, the current study proposed to use Factor Analysis (FA) to extract common factors (CF) behind the main categories, so as to replace core categories with the CFs and use the CFs to summarize the overall behavioral phenomena. Moreover, there are certain advantage if the factor scores of the CFs are taken as independent variables to establish a multiple linear regression (MLR) model to explain the impact of interior design principles on TSRC usage willingness. Because this processing can reduce the number of variables included in the MLR model, solve multi-collinearity problems and improve the explanatory power of the model. As for the core categories developed in Selective Coding, they were only taken as a reference in the final determination of theories.

For these 10 main categories, 137 respondents were required to rate them with the Likert scale assignment method, and give a score ranged from 1 to 5, where 1 indicated complete disagreement and 5 indicated strong agreement. Due to the fact that respondents might not understand what a certain category meant, in addition to the main categories, some concepts and corresponding sub-categories extracted during the Open Coding and Axial Coding processes would also be provided as implementation means (Table 1) for that main category, so as to provide specific explanations for the main categories and guide participants to make judgments.

The basic idea of FA is to study the internal structure of the correlation coefficient matrix of the items (observation variables) in the scale, and group highly correlated items

Table 1. Main categories and corresponding concepts.

Main categories (design principles)	Examples of implementation means
M1	1) Shape design of the interior components is simple and has minimal visual interference 2) Customize the car infotainment system and enhance its suggestive design to highlight common functions such as navigation and reverse camera. Remove infrequently used functions to reduce information interference, and make users glad to use the in-vehicle infotainment system
M2	1) Add non-slip lines to the steering wheel, gear lever, etc. to increase friction, making them easy for users to grip 2) Provide a manual explaining the location of commonly used auxiliary functions such as self-adaptive cruise, adjustment of distance between cars, Auto Hold, etc. [15] 3) Stick arrow shaped shiny stickers at important HMI interfaces, such as the window lift button on the door trim panel and the switch buttons of the auxiliary functions mentioned above, to guide users to quickly find the targets
M3	1) Places that are prone to dirt and grime, such as door panels, the gear lever base, and the glove compartment, should have fewer grooves to prevent users from easily hiding garbage inside 2) Use materials like plastic that are easy to clean, and reduce materials such as felt which are prone to generating static electricity and adsorbing dust
M4	1) Use textile materials to cut down depreciation costs, and reduce expensive materials such as genuine leather 2) Regularly apply cleaning wax to the dashboard and door trim, to reduce phenomena such as aging, brittleness and cracking
M5	Provide an intelligent collision prevention system and display it reasonably on the on-board computer screen
M6	1) Enhance the computational and communication capacity of the on-board computer to support rich videos, movies, music, or images to increase the entertainment value of the interior space 2) Customize ambient lightings with different colors, to alleviate drowsiness when driving or being stuck on the road [16]

(*continued*)

Table 1. (*continued*)

Main categories (design principles)	Examples of implementation means
M7	Monitor driving fatigue and awaken the driver with sound and light stimulation
M8	1) Provide lost property storage boxes for later users to help collect items lost by previous users 2) Provide small trash cans to prevent users from littering
M9	Set up in-vehicle cameras to supervise user behaviors
M10	The layout of interior accessories and the in-vehicle color-matching schemes of all types of vehicles deployed by the TSR platform are uniformly reprocessed by the platform, forming sufficient recognizability, rather than directly deploying the original cars purchased from the market. Users can quickly adapt from one car to another.

according to a certain rule. Each group of items shares a CF. Therefore, the CF represents the basic structure of the items. That is to say, through FA, common influencing factors that cannot be directly observed but actually exist within the sample data $X_1, X_2,..., X_n$ can be extracted and named as P, which is a CF. And then the sample can be represented by a linear combination of P and the factor loading matrix A. P and A can be expressed as:

$$P = [P_1 P_2 \ldots P_k]^T \tag{1}$$

$$A = \begin{bmatrix} a_{11} & a_{12} & \ldots & a_{1k} \\ a_{21} & a_{22} & \ldots & a_{2k} \\ \ldots & \ldots & \ldots & \ldots \\ a_{n1} & a_{n2} & \ldots & a_{nk} \end{bmatrix} \tag{2}$$

where n refers to the dimension of the sample data; k is the number of CF.

In this study, FA was conducted on the 10 design principles listed in Table 1. Afterwards, a MLR model was established with the factor scores of each CF as the independent variables and the willingness to use TSRC as the dependent variable, to analyze the impact of recognition of the design principles on the usage willingness. For the issue of "willingness to use TSRC", quantification is still based on a 5-level Likert scale assignment method.

3.2 Evaluation System for TSR Service Considering Road Environment and Interior Design Principles

Impact of Road Environmental Factors on Interaction Experience. TSRC refers to a self-service system where rental enterprises own the vehicles and provide them to users at the parking points throughout the city [17]. The rented car is not privately owned by the user, so users are prone to feeling nervous and unfamiliar during the interaction with the car interior. The driving experience is also likely to be affected in specific road environments.

In terms of urban environment, existing research has shown that unlike ride-hailing which mainly runs in commercial districts with business centers distributing densely, TSRC does not primarily serve commuting [18]. A survey also showed that the two areas with the highest frequency and density of shared car usage were residential areas and work areas, presenting strong regularity [19]. Therefore, various driving environments may result in different user experiences for TSRC. Accordingly, the interior and information display design of the cars used for TSR should match the environmental characteristics to enhance the user experience. For example, providing car models with noise reduction and dust prevention designs for users to choose from, or adding customizable personalized accessories such as elbow rests in glove boxes or armrest boxes, etc., so as to reduce the user's sense of tension towards the environment and inadaptation with the rented vehicle, and enhance driving confidence. The current study focuses on the differences between TSRC driving experiences in public service ground (PSG) and that in commercial facility ground (CFG).

a) PSG refers to the land used to construct various facilities corresponding to the size of the residential population and serve the residents, involving government agencies, news and publishing, education, scientific research, medical and health, sports, public facilities, parks and green spaces, etc. Road accessibility is an indicator to reflect the difficulty of moving between points in the PSG network, and has become an important condition affecting the integration, connection, and development of urban areas [20]. Therefore, driving vehicles that are not privately owned by oneself on such kind of land requires drivers to pay special attention to driving safety, and "reducing mis-operation" is an important service goal for TSR enterprises.

b) CFG has obvious specificities compared with other types of urban lands. The radiation effect is strong; and the land is complex, diverse, and highly intensive, and can produce significant benefits [21]. These characteristics may cause that for driving in CFG, a car rented from TSR enterprises that one is not familiar with and may not be able to handle well can make it easier for the driver to panic and even helplessness to the road. Therefore, the configuration in the interior of cars for TSR service should accord with the impact of the characteristics of CFG on the driver's emotion, rather than just fulfilling basic functions.

Construction of the Evaluation System. This study proposes to construct an evaluation system of TSR service by means of AHP. AHP is a multi-objective evaluation method that combines qualitative and quantitative analysis. It can quantitatively describe non-quantitative events such as subjective judgments of humans, and is particularly suitable for large or complex systems involving multiple objectives, factors, or criteria.

The current study takes "A: meeting demands of using TSRC" as the overall objective, and takes representative HCI methods (C1: voice interaction, C2: gesture recognition, C3: touch screen interaction, and C4: physical buttons/knobs interaction) as the Plan layer elements, to build the AHP model. The middle layer of the model is the Criterion layer, which mainly includes three aspects of factors: 1) being able to adapt to typical road environments, 2) being easy to achieve vehicle-environment interaction, and 3) the interior design being reasonable.

Among the factors in the Criterion layer, "2) being easy to achieve vehicle-environment interaction" refers to whether the driver can easily and clearly observe other vehicles and pedestrians on the road during the driving process. Interior designs directly affect the cognition resource consumption of the driver and indirectly lead to different levels of attention to road conditions, which is important to TSRC drivers. Existing research revealed that good in-vehicle automated functions can reduce the driver's distraction on the road and allow the driver to focus more on secondary tasks in the cabin, thereby liberating the attention from monotonous observation to a certain extent [22]. Therefore, the level of vehicle-environment interaction, determined by the interior design of the TSRC, should be a criterion reflecting the degree to which the usage demand is met.

In addition, the interior design principles summarized in Table 1 are direct reflection of the service quality and interior reasonability of TSRC. Therefore, after extracting the CFs, they should also be included in the Criterion layer, as indicators of "3) the interior design being reasonable", to present the impact of car interior design on the degree to which the demand of using TSRC is met.

Considering that TSRC users are not very familiar with the interior space of the rented car, their inherent HCI behavioral habits are often difficult to continue. Therefore, it is necessary to evaluate the matching degree between representative HCI methods and the demand for TSRC usage, which is the reason for setting the Plan layer as being mentioned above. When organizing experts to construct judgment matrices for the Plan layer, the experts are invited to evaluate the four HCI methods from rationality, compatibility, and security in terms of each element in the Criterion layer. In this way, the impact of the HCI methods on the implementation of the criteria can be presented. Based on the group-decision evaluation matrix, the weights of the HCI methods can be calculated.

A total of five experts were invited, including two automotive design experts from enterprises and three long-term users of shared cars. The judgment matrices were constructed by the scaling method with a value range of 1–9 and their reciprocals. Using the personal judgment matrices of experts, the comprehensive judgment matrix can be obtained, by which the group decision-making is achieved. Geometric mean is adopted in this study to take the average of judgment decisions of several individuals. The calculation method is:

$$W_i = \prod_{k=1}^{n} W_{ki}^{\lambda_k} \qquad (3)$$

where λ_k refers to the weight values assigned by the evaluators. The sum of λ_k is $\sum_{k=1}^{n} \lambda_k = 1$. Due to the fact that average weights are adopted in this study, λ_k of all the evaluators are equal, $\lambda_1 = \lambda_2 = \ldots = \lambda_k = \frac{1}{5}$. W_{ki} represents the ranking weights of the ith element in the judgment matrix of the kth evaluator.

By the software yaahp (ver. 12.10.8257), model construction, calculation, and analysis are achieved. Consistency test of each matrix can also be directly completed using this software, which is to calculate the Consistency Ratio (CR) and ensure the values of all the judgment matrices are less than 0.1.

4 Results

4.1 Factor Analysis

Descriptive Statistic Results. Descriptive statistics were conducted on the scores of the design principles listed in Table 1 and the score of willingness to use TSRC, by the software SPSS (ver. 22.0). The results are shown in Table 2.

Table 2. Descriptive statistical results (n = 137).

Indicators	Mean	Standard deviation	Skewness	Kurtosis
M1	4.20	0.873	−0.800	0.065
M2	4.16	0.833	−0.852	0.655
M3	3.65	1.061	−0.681	−0.025
M4	3.61	1.196	−0.678	−0.404
M5	3.54	1.071	−0.671	−0.161
M6	3.64	1.253	−0.591	−0.603
M7	3.64	1.161	−0.523	−0.548
M8	3.50	1.151	−0.405	−0.588
M9	3.55	1.098	−0.342	−0.493
M10	4.26	0.814	−0.835	0.381
Willingness	3.78	0.638	0.225	−0.663

It can be seen that the means of all the indicators are between 3.5 and 4.4, and the standard deviations are also small. This reveals that the users' opinions on these design principles and on the willingness of TSRC usage generally tended to be positive, and acknowledged the importance of these design principles for TSRC. But the users also presented a relatively moderate attitude, without showing strong agreement or disagreement. The design principle with the highest degree of recognition is M10 ($m_{10} = 4.26$), and the one with the lowest degree of recognition is M8 ($m_8 = 3.5$).

The skewness coefficients of all the 10 design principles are negative, indicating a left-skewed distribution of the data and reflecting that most of the scores are on the high side. Among them, the absolute values of the skewness coefficients for M1, M2, and M10 are relatively large, while M6~M9 and the Willingness score tend to follow a normal distribution.

In terms of the kurtosis coefficients, generally speaking, Kurtosis = 3 means that the data are normally distributed. But in SPSS, the kurtosis coefficient of the normal distribution is set to 0. Therefore, the various indicators in this study generally follow a normal distribution. The kurtosis absolute values of the indicators are far less than 10, and the skewness absolute values are less than 3, indicating that although the data are not absolutely normal, it is generally acceptable to be seemed as a normal distribution when modeling the data [23].

Results of FA. In practical applications, KMO (Kaiser-Meyer-Olkin) and Bartlett's test are required to be conducted to verify whether the data are suitable for FA. The summary of the results is shown in Table 3.

Table 3. KMO measure and Bartlett's test.

KMO Measure of Sampling Adequacy	Bartlett's Test of Sphericity		
	Approx. Chi-Square	Df	Sig
0.744	700.397	45	0.000

The KMO value is 0.744 (>0.70), and the approximate Chi-square value of Bartlett's Test of Sphericity is 700.397, with a significance level of lower than 0.001, indicating that the sample data are suitable for FA.

After normalizing the data, the CFs are extracted. And their number k can be determined by the eigenvalues and cumulative variance contribution rate (VCR). The larger the eigenvalues and VCR, the stronger the CFs' ability to represent the overall data information. Generally, the standard is extracting factors with eigenvalues greater than 1 and cumulative VCR greater than 80%. Based on the above theories, three CFs were extracted through Varimax rotation. The results are shown in Table 4.

Table 4. Results of FA.

Factor	Design principles	Factor loading	VCR (%)	Cumulative VCR (%)
F1	M5	0.944	32.936	32.936
	M6	0.893		
	M7	0.878		
	M9	0.847		
F2	M3	0.919	23.640	56.576
	M4	0.881		
	M8	0.872		
F3	M1	0.792	18.029	74.605
	M2	0.784		
	M10	0.749		

According to the specific connotations of the 10 main categories derived from GT, namely the design principles of TSRC interior, the three CFs were named as: F1) intelligent prompt and driving assistance factor; F2) rental platform management factor; and F3) car interior universality factor. Using the factor scores of the three CFs as the independent variables and "willingness to use TSRC" as the dependent variable, an MLR model was established, as shown in Table 5. The overall model is significant ($p < 0.001$), and $R^2 = 0.662$, indicating that the goodness of fit of the model is acceptable. In addition, the effects of the three independent variables are all significant.

Table 5. The MLR model.

	Standardized Coefficient	Non-standardized Coefficient	t	p
Constant	3.781		117.871	0.000
F1	0.366	0.573	11.359	0.000
F2	0.295	0.462	9.165	0.000
F3	0.221	0.346	6.869	0.000

$R^2 = 0.662$, Adjusted-$R^2 = 0.654$,
$F = 86.738$, p<0.001.

The regression coefficients indicate that F1 has a greater impact on the willingness to use TSRC, while the impact of F3 is the weakest. But overall, the effects on the increase of willingness to use TSRC are all significant, effective and positive. Therefore, in car interior design for TSR, the effects of the above factors should be considered, and design of interior accessories and colors should be utilized to enhance the user's experience in universality and HMI, and optimize the efficiency of platform management.

4.2 Results of the Evaluation

According to the FA results, the CFs that affect interior design of TSRC are intelligent prompt and driving assistance factor, rental platform management factor, and car interior universality factor. By incorporating "adaptability to the road environment" and "being easy to achieve vehicle-environment interaction", an AHP model can be constructed as shown in Fig. 1.

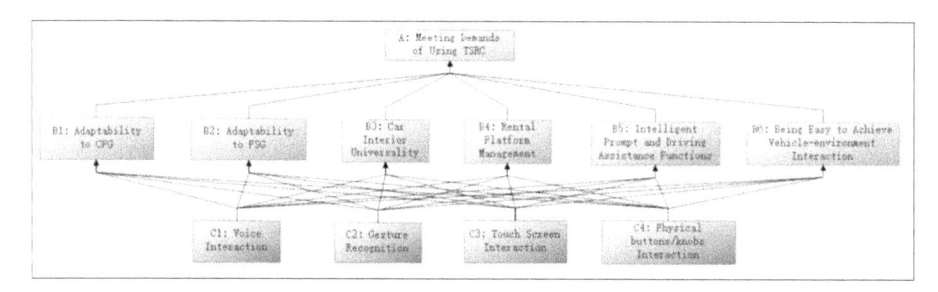

Fig. 1. The AHP model.

Due to factors such as subjectivity and experience, it is generally not possible to ensure judgment matrices of all experts achieve consistency directly. For the judgment matrices that did not meet the consistency requirement, corrections were made in the yaahp software based on the prompts given by the software. Researchers provided feedback to experts on the inconsistent matrix elements, and asked them to carefully analyze whether the logic before and after making judgement was consistent, and then make corrections. Finally, the CRs of all expert judgment matrices were less than 0.1, passing the consistency test.

Afterwards, the geometric means of the elements in the judgment matrices of all experts were taken to obtain the comprehensive judgment matrix, which was the group decision-making result. Then the ranking weights were calculated. The results are shown in Tables 6 and 7. The calculated matrices also passed the consistency test (CR < 0.1). Of course, due to the lack of logical significance in conducting consistency test on the calculated matrices, the CR values in the two tables are only for reference.

Table 6. Results of the Criterion layer.

Elements of the Criterion Layer	Weight	λmax	CR
B1	0.1388	6.1417	0.0225
B2	0.1074		
B3	0.1815		
B4	0.1414		
B5	0.2567		
B6	0.1743		

Table 7. Results of the Plan layer.

	B1	B2	B3	B4	B5	B6	Ranking Weight
C1: Voice	0.3025	0.2195	0.2953	0.2459	0.4118	0.2054	0.2954
C2: Gesture recognition	0.1754	0.1783	0.1152	0.2252	0.1163	0.1926	0.1597
C3: Touch screen	0.1279	0.3629	0.2306	0.2968	0.1609	0.2585	0.2269
C4: Physical buttons/knobs	0.3942	0.2393	0.3588	0.2321	0.311	0.3434	0.318
λmax	4.0335	4.0066	4.0479	4.0464	4.0253	4.0691	
CR	0.0125	0.0025	0.0179	0.0174	0.0095	0.0259	

From the results, it can be seen that for the overall objective, B5 (intelligent prompt and driving assistance functions) has the highest weight among elements in the Criterion layer, while C4 (physical buttons/knobs interaction) has the highest weight in the Plan layer. This reflects that providing necessary intelligent prompt and driving assistance functions is most important for meeting the demands of using TSRC. In addition, it should be noted that physical buttons/knobs play the most important role, rather than popular functions such as touch screen and voice interaction that are widely installed. This may be because the commonly used operations, such as air-conditioning control or adaptive cruise control, are relatively easy to obtain sufficient feedback through physical buttons.

5 Discussion

Due to the fact that the vehicle is not privately owned by individuals, users of TSRC may have a certain unfamiliarity with the interior environment. It takes some time to become familiar with the in-vehicle equipment, especially electronic devices. However, TSRC mostly charges by hour and day, so users do not have sufficient learning time. There may be a lack of operating instructions in existing cars deployed by TSR enterprises [1], or the provided operating instructions require the driver to spend a long time reading them. This is unreasonable, as it can lead to frequent misoperations by novice users, low usage efficiency, and inability to receive timely assistance when problems arise during operation [24]. In addition, some users have not developed good driving habits, and the service provider lacks effective supervision, resulting in poor vehicle condition and dirty interior [1], directly reducing the service life of the cars and affecting the use of other users. These issues pose challenges to the design of car interiors for TSR.

This study focuses on HCI and proposes design principles. Among the 10 design principles proposed through GT, M10 ($m_{10} = 4.26$) has the highest degree of agreement, followed by M1 and M2. The one with the lowest degree of agreement is M8 ($m_8 = 3.5$), followed by M9. To some extent, the results reflect the users' attitude. Users generally believe that car interior universality is very important for TSR, such as reducing visual interference, enhancing information reminders, etc., which is consistent with existing research findings [1]. On the contrary, the recognition degree to the installation of auxiliary accessories, such as small trash cans and lost property storage boxes, is very low. In addition, the installation of cameras to monitor driver behaviors has not received high recognition. From the interview, it can be inferred that this may be due to user concerns about privacy.

For TSRC, it is not suitable to use too many intelligent technologies, which may reduce the vehicle's universality. As research has shown, there is a certain contradiction between high intelligence and safety of first-time driving for B2C shared cars [24]. However, the current study revealed through MLR and AHP that intelligent prompt and driving assistance functions have the strongest impact on driving experience of TSRC.

The performance of such functions is related to the design level of the HCI interface. There is currently a large number of researches analyzing the design of on-board computer screen interface [25, 26]. However, considering the characteristics and demands of shared car drivers, no matter how beautiful the screen style design is or how rich the information is, it may not be suitable for being applied in TSRC. It should be noted that among typical interaction methods, physical buttons/knobs interaction is the most recognized one ($W_{C4} = 0.318$). Although touch screens have been applied widely and numerous functions exist on the screens, the sensitivity is relatively low and the tactile feedback is poor. Moreover, it is difficult for unfamiliar users to quickly read and understand the graphics and text on the user interface, which is apt to result in misoperations.

Many participants have reported that they never used the touch screen while driving, and only occasionally operated navigation or music while waiting for traffic signals or stopping driving. And other functions were almost not used. AHP analysis shows that for meeting the demands of using TSRC, touch screen interaction can only rank third. The same goes for voice interaction. The accuracy of speech recognition still needs to be improved, often requiring drivers to repeat commands in order to be understood, and can only execute simple commands. At present, the user experience of voice interaction is not very good and according to expert evaluations, it is not very suitable for TSRC users.

Sharing economy has been a hot topic in recent years. The innovation of Internet technologies and the progress of people's consumption concept make the sharing economy present a prosperous development. Accordingly, shared cars have also caused some controversy. Generally, people's sharing consumption scenarios are somewhat related to their cultural background [27]. The relation is inevitably very complex. Bucher et al. (2016) conducted a comprehensive study on the motives of consumers participating in Internet-mediated sharing economy, and revealed that materialism, sociability and volunteering are related to motives in different sharing contexts [28]. Under the cultural influence of different countries, the factors may vary and cannot be generalized. The current study investigates the needs and behaviors of Chinese TSRC users from the perspective of in-vehicle interaction performance and user experience, and proposes design principles and suggestions. This can provide a supplement to the research field of car-sharing, and help designers and service providers obtain more precise positioning when determining the vehicle types to be deployed or adding service items.

6 Conclusion

Using GT, a total of 10 main categories could be extracted through Open Coding and Axial Coding of user corpus. The categories reflect the user's demands for TSRC and can be used as interior design principles for cars deployed for sharing.

Through FA, the above 10 design principles can be summarized as three CFs, which are intelligent prompt and driving assistance, rental platform management, and car interior universality. The MLR model indicates that the factor scores of the three CFs can largely explain the willingness to use TSRC ($R^2 = 0.662$), in which F1 has the strongest impact.

Among the various criteria that should be implemented to meet the demands for TSRC usage, intelligent prompt and driving assistance functions have the highest weight. On the contrast, the weights of platform services provided to enhance adaptability to different types of road environments are very low, reflecting that people do not need to obtain such service information from the TSRC interior.

Among the four common HCI methods, physical buttons/knobs have the highest weight in matching the TSRC driver's demands, followed by voice interaction. The weights of touch screen and gesture recognition are relatively low, providing a reference basis for TSR enterprises to deploy cars and interior accessories.

Acknowledgement. This research was funded by Beijing Municipal Social Science Foundation, grant number 21YTC040.

Appendix: Part of the Outline of the Semi-structured Interview

1. **Regular functions:** What do you think of shared cars after driving them? Share your feelings about regular functions such as straight driving, turning, acceleration, and following cars.
2. **Optional functions:** If possible, do you think there are any auxiliary functions that need to be added to the car? (eg: self-adaptive cruise, adjustment of distance between cars, Auto Hold, etc.)
3. **Vehicle performance:** Do you think there are any shortcomings when driving the rented car?
4. **Platform services:** Since it's not your own car, do you feel lost, uncomfortable or unaccustomed (such as the sense of touch of the steering wheel, the layout of the buttons, etc.)? If available, do you need the TSR platform to provide any specific services through the on-board computer or voice broadcasting? Please speak freely based on your experience driving a private car.
5. **In-vehicle environment:** Are there any issues of dirt and mess in the cars you have rented?

References

1. Zhao, Y., Liu, G.: Research on the restriction design for interior space of B2C sharing. Zhuangshi 2018, pp. 117–119 (2018)
2. Münzel, K., Piscicelli, L., Boon, W., Frenken, K.: Different business models – different users? uncovering the motives and characteristics of business-to-consumer and peer-to-peer carsharing adopters in The Netherlands. Transp. Res. Part D Transp. Environ. **73**, 276–306 (2019)
3. Ramos, E.M.S., Mattos, D.I., Bergstad, C.J.: Roundtrip, free-floating and peer-to-peer carsharing: a Bayesian behavioral analysis. Transp. Res. Part D Transp. Environ. **115** (2023)
4. Becker, H., Ciari, F., Axhausen, K.W.: Measuring the car ownership impact of free-floating car-sharing – a case study in Basel, Switzerland. Transp. Res. Part D Transp. Environ. **65**, 51–62 (2018)
5. Dall Pizzol, H., Ordovás de Almeida, S., Do Couto Soares, M.: Collaborative consumption: a proposed scale for measuring the construct applied to a carsharing setting. Sustainability **9** (2017)
6. Kuemmerling, M., Heilmann, C., Meixner, G.: Towards seamless mobility: individual mobility profiles to ease the use of shared vehicles. IFAC Proc. Vol. **46**, 450–454 (2013)
7. Balogh, R., Lipková, M., Lučkanič, V., Ťapajna, P.: Natural notification system for the interior of shared car. IFAC-PapersOnLine **52**, 175–179 (2019)
8. Yang, E.J., Ahn, H.J., Kim, N.H., Jung, H.S., Kim, K.R., Hwang, W.: Perceived interior space of motor vehicles based on illusory design elements. Hum. Fact. Ergon. Manuf. Serv. Ind. **25**, 573–584 (2015)
9. Yang, H., Zhao, Y., Wang, Y.: Identifying modeling forms of instrument panel system in intelligent shared cars: a study for perceptual preference and in-vehicle behaviors. Environ. Sci. Pollut. Res. **27**, 1009–1023 (2020)
10. Yang, H., Liu, J., Guo, F., Chen, N.: In-vehicle heat-induced impact on the system usability of on-board computer interfaces considering the optimization of scheme presentation order. Urban Clim. **47**, 101387 (2023)

11. Wang, F.L.: Research on the operation mode of B2C shared automobile enterprises focusing on asset operation. J. Guiyang Univ. (Nat. Sci.) **16**, 44–47 (2021)
12. Fields, E., Osorio, C., Zhou, T.: A data-driven method for reconstructing a distribution from a truncated sample with an application to inferring car-sharing demand. Transp. Sci. **55**, 616–636 (2021)
13. Shaheen, S.A., Cohen, A.P.: Carsharing and personal vehicle services: worldwide market developments and emerging trends. Int. J. Sustain. Transp. **7**, 5–34 (2013)
14. Yanbo, Y., Dan, Z., Lei, H.: The concept of tourism enterprise's integrity and its construct dimensions: an exploratory research based on grounded theory. Nankai Bus. Rev. **17**, 113–122 (2014)
15. Yang, H., Zhang, J., Wang, Y., Jia, R.: Exploring relationships between design features and system usability of intelligent car human–machine interface. Robot. Auton. Syst. **143**, 103829 (2021)
16. Shoaib, Z., Akbar, A., Kamran, M.A., Kim, J., Jeong, M.Y.: A drowsiness reduction strategy utilizing visual stimulation with different colors of light: an fNIRS study. IEEE Access **9**, 105817–105830 (2021)
17. Cohen, B., Kietzmann, J.: Ride On! Mobility business models for the sharing economy. Organ. Environ. **27**, 279–296 (2014)
18. Xiaoou, C., Jiaqi, C., Jianhong, Y., Daoge, W.: Analysis of carsharing users and demand spatio-temporal characteristics. J. Tongji Univ. (Nat. Sci.) **46**, 796–803+841 (2018)
19. Li, Q.: Research on Interior Optimization Design of Shared Car Based on Synaesthesia Design. Jilin University, Changchun (2021)
20. Yu, X.: Research on Public Management and Service Land Grading of Central Nanchang City. Jiangxi Agricultural University, Nanchang (2020)
21. Jie, D.: The Research on the Urban Land Use Structure and Land Use Efficiency—Case Study of ChongQing GuanYinQiao. Chongqing University, Chongqing (2014)
22. Jamson, A.H., Merat, N., Carsten, O.M.J., Lai, F.C.H.: Behavioural changes in drivers experiencing highly-automated vehicle control in varying traffic conditions. Transp. Res. Part C Emerging Technol. **30**, 116–125 (2013)
23. Jiangmei, W., Zezhong, T., Haiyang, Z., Kaidi, L., Minzan, L., Yao, Z.: Remote sensing estimation method of carbon flux in farmland ecosystem. Trans. Chin. Soc. Agricult. Mach. **53**, 224–231 (2022)
24. Ying, Z.: Product service system design research of B2C carsharing based on Beijing. In: Proceedings of Conference of the Design Management Academy, Hong Kong (2019)
25. Li, R., Chen, Y.V., Sha, C.F., Lu, Z.P.: Effects of interface layout on the usability of in-vehicle information systems and driving safety. Displays **49**, 124–132 (2017)
26. Mitsopoulos-Rubens, E., Trotter, M., Lenné, M.: Effects on driving performance of interacting with an in-vehicle music player: a comparison of three interface layout concepts for information presentation. Appl. Ergon. **42**, 583–591 (2011)
27. Hang, S.: Research on the Consumers' Behavior Mechanism and Intervention Path of Sharing Economy. East China Normal University, Shanghai (2022)
28. Bucher, E., Fieseler, C., Lutz, C.: What's mine is yours (for a nominal fee) – exploring the spectrum of utilitarian to altruistic motives for Internet-mediated sharing. Comput. Hum. Behav. **62**, 316–326 (2016)

A Unified Framework for Hierarchical Pedestrian Behavior Generation in Urban Scenario

Zhengming Zhang[1], Vincent G. Duffy[1], Mark R. Lehto[1], Zhengming Ding[2], and Renran Tian[3(✉)]

[1] School of Industrial Engineering, Purdue University, West Lafayette, IN 47907, USA
[2] Department of Computer Science, Tulane University, New Orleans, LA 70118, USA
[3] Department of Industrial and Systems Engineering, North Carolina State University, Raleigh, NC 27606, USA

Abstract. Achieving fully autonomous driving systems hinges on the complex task of modeling pedestrian behavior, which is characterized by unpredictability and diverse actions. While significant progress has been made in predicting pedestrian trajectories and actions, the generation of interactive behaviors for realistic simulations remains underexplored. This study introduces an innovative unified framework designed to generate hierarchical pedestrian motion that not only responds to traffic dynamics but also reflects natural human movements. We utilize existing motion forecasting datasets as the high-level trajectory data and enhance this with egocentric datasets for detailed pose information. By synchronizing annotations from bird's-eye view and ego-view perspectives, we bridge the gap between macro-level paths and micro-level bodily movements, ensuring that the generated behaviors are coherent and integrated. The ultimate goal is to develop a system that enhances the authenticity of autonomous driving simulations and contributes to the overall safety and reliability of autonomous vehicle technologies.

Keywords: Pedestrian behavior modeling · Human motion · Autonomous driving

1 Introduction

Over the past decade, pedestrian safety has emerged as a pressing issue in traffic management and urban planning. The Insurance Institute for Highway Safety reports a significant rise in pedestrian fatalities from 2010 to 2021, highlighting the urgent need for enhanced safety measures and interventions [23]. Compounding this concern, the Governors Highway Safety Association (GHSA) projected over 7,500 pedestrian deaths in 2022-the highest since 1981-equating to about 20 fatalities daily [19]. These figures represent more than statistics; they reflect profound personal and communal losses, demanding urgent attention.

The disproportionate increase in pedestrian fatalities, which surged by 77% compared to a 25% rise in overall traffic deaths from 2010 to 2021, underscores the exceptional risks pedestrians face [20]. Unlike vehicle occupants, pedestrians lack protective barriers, making them especially vulnerable in traffic incidents [10]. This vulnerability necessitates more robust safety measures that go beyond conventional vehicle-centric approaches [11,41].

Pedestrian movements are difficult to predict and less regulated by traffic laws, complicating safety efforts [41,52]. Risky behaviors such as jaywalking, sudden road crossings, and distractions from electronic devices create complex challenges that require innovative, adaptable solutions. In densely populated urban areas, where pedestrians and vehicles frequently intersect, traditional traffic management methods often fall short. This scenario demands new strategies that seamlessly integrate into urban life, ensuring pedestrian safety while maintaining traffic flow.

Addressing these challenges involves a multifaceted approach that includes advancements in autonomous vehicle (AV) technology, urban planning that prioritizes pedestrian zones, and public education campaigns promoting safe pedestrian behaviors. AVs, equipped with advanced detection and predictive technologies, are central to reducing pedestrian fatalities. These systems can identify and respond to pedestrian movements, minimizing collision risks [23]. Urban design also plays a crucial role in enhancing pedestrian safety. The "complete streets" concept, which accommodates pedestrians, cyclists, and vehicles, can significantly improve safety. Infrastructure improvements like widened sidewalks, raised crosswalks, and dedicated pedestrian areas, along with traffic calming measures, create environments that discourage speeding and promote alertness among all road users. Finally, education remains vital for pedestrian safety. Campaigns highlighting the dangers of distracted walking, the importance of using crosswalks, and the benefits of mindful interactions between pedestrians and drivers are key to building a safety-oriented culture [51]. Driver education programs that focus on pedestrian safety and school curricula that teach safe practices from an early age are essential for fostering long-term behavioral changes.

Pedestrian behavior generation model emerges as a critical tool for enhancing the efficiency of all of these efforts. By simulating various pedestrian behaviors, these models help AVs navigate complex urban environments more safely, especially in unexpected situations involving erratic pedestrian actions. Urban planners can also use pedestrian behavior models to predict and refine the effects of proposed infrastructure changes before implementation. These simulations help identify potential safety issues, leading to more efficient and protective urban spaces for pedestrians.

In summary, addressing pedestrian safety requires a holistic pedestrian behavior generation model. Modeling pedestrian behavior not only enhances AV systems but also informs safer urban design and contributes to the education and training of both pedestrians and drivers. This generation model aims to create urban environments where technology, infrastructure, and human behavior work together to promote safety and harmony on the streets.

Building on these challenges and the need for innovative solutions, this paper proposes a novel unified framework for generating hierarchical pedestrian motion (Fig. 1). This framework aims to address the current gaps in existing research by generating both high-level (bird's-eye trajectory) and low-level (pedestrian pose) motion consistently. Although this work does not include experimental implementation of the proposed model, it provides valuable insights into the overall structure of such a generation system. This approach intends to bridge the gap between different levels of pedestrian motion generation, offering a comprehensive perspective that enhances the safety and efficiency of urban environments.

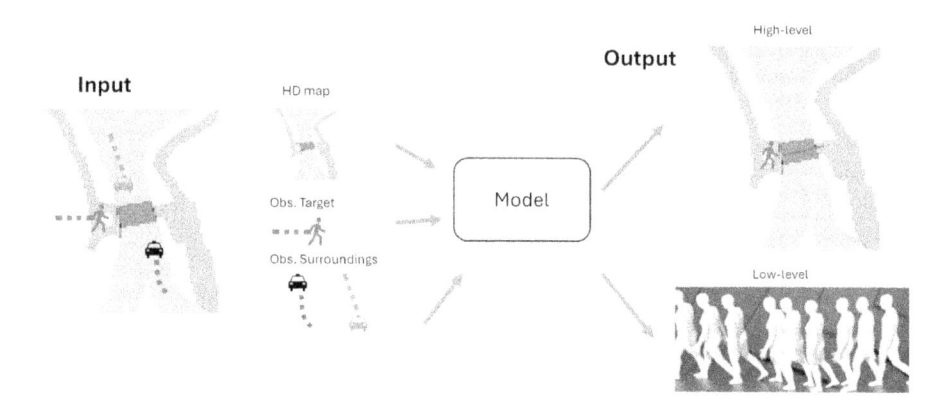

Fig. 1. Research Objective: Utilizing a diffusion model to develop a unified framework for generating both high-level and low-level pedestrian behaviors.

2 Literature Review

2.1 Naturalistic Data Collection for Pedestrian Behavior

In the modeling of pedestrian behavior, data acquisition plays a crucial role. The quality and type of data collected significantly influence the model's accuracy and applicability. There are several methods for collecting this data, each with its unique advantages and limitations.

One prevalent method is naturalistic driving data collection [4,8,12,14,18, 31,36,49]. In this approach, vehicles equipped with various sensors navigate through real-world environments to gather data. These sensors typically include cameras, LiDAR, and GPS systems, which collectively capture a rich dataset encompassing pedestrian behaviors, vehicle movements, and environmental conditions. After collection, the data undergoes extensive post-processing, including annotation and calibration, to ensure its usability for modeling purposes. This method's primary advantage is its realism, as it captures pedestrian behavior in natural settings, providing valuable insights into real-world dynamics.

Another approach involves using drones [7,40], or fixed cameras [27,34], such as those mounted on buildings, to observe pedestrian behavior. This method is particularly useful for studying pedestrian dynamics in specific areas, like sidewalks or public squares. However, datasets collected in this manner often feature less interaction between pedestrians and vehicles, as the focus is more on pedestrian-only zones. Additionally, the scenarios captured can be somewhat limited, as the camera's fixed position only allows observation of a specific area.

Besides the data collection environment, two commonly used perspectives are the bird's-eye view and the egocentric view. The bird's-eye view [6,17,22, 24,25,28,31,42,44], also known as the top-down view, provides a comprehensive overview of the scenario from above. This perspective is typically associated with a world coordinate system offering a broad, map-like representation of the environment. This view can either be a direct mapping of images to a world map, such as aerial images captured by drones [1,7,42,47,48], or a more abstracted representation that translates real-world dimensions into a scaled-down overview [5,12,16,31]. It allows for an encompassing visualization of spatial relationships and movements within a given area, making it ideal for tasks that require an understanding of layout and positional dynamics, such as urban planning or traffic flow analysis.

On the other hand, the egocentric view [9,29,32,35,38,45,46,50,53], or first-person view, offers a perspective from the viewpoint of an individual within the scenario. This view is more subjective and localized, providing a direct representation of the environment as seen from a specific vantage point. It is particularly useful in applications where individual experiences or interactions are of interest, such as in virtual reality settings [3], interaction systems [15], or studies of individual behavior within a larger context [37].

Each perspective offers unique advantages and is selected based on the specific requirements of the task. The bird's-eye view delivers a comprehensive overview, whereas the egocentric view yields detailed insights into individual experiences and interactions. Certain datasets, such as those referenced in [4,8,18], provide both viewpoints, enabling models to utilize information from each. However, typically, the output of the model is aligned with one of these perspectives.

2.2 Generative Models for Pedestrian Behavior

Generative models are a sophisticated class of tools designed to create new data points that convincingly mimic real-world phenomena. These models are crucial in simulating realistic pedestrian behaviors, aiding urban planning, autonomous vehicle training, and enhancing safety analysis. They replicate observed data and predict novel behaviors under hypothetical conditions, providing valuable insights into pedestrian dynamics.

Rule-based models are foundational in the domain of pedestrian behavior simulation [2]. These models use predefined sets of rules derived from empirical observations and statistical studies of pedestrian behaviors under various environmental conditions [13]. The primary strength of rule-based models lies in their simplicity and minimal computational resource requirements, making them highly efficient for real-time systems, such as traffic light control at intersections or pedestrian flow management in transport hubs [30]. They are particularly effective in predictable scenarios, such as regulated crosswalks, where pedestrian paths and behaviors follow known patterns.

However, rule-based models have significant limitations due to their rigidity. They struggle to adapt to unforeseen or novel situations, such as emergencies, unexpected social gatherings, or atypical urban configurations. This inflexibility highlights the need for more adaptive systems that can handle the complexity and variability of human behavior in less structured environments.

On the other hand, learning-based models offer a dynamic approach to simulating pedestrian behavior by adapting their predictions based on observed data. Techniques like supervised learning, or imitation learning, involve training models on datasets containing examples of pedestrian actions and their outcomes. This enables the models to learn and replicate complex behaviors observed in real-world settings, making them accurate in scenarios that mirror the conditions of the training data [21,43]. The effectiveness of imitation learning depends on high-quality, well-labeled data, which allows for detailed modeling of pedestrian interactions, such as navigating crowds and responding to traffic signals. However, this reliance on extensive datasets can limit the application of supervised learning models in environments not well-represented in existing data, potentially leading to errors in behavior prediction.

Reinforcement learning, another subset of learning-based models, addresses some of these limitations by enabling models to learn and optimize behavior through trial and error, guided by rewards and penalties. This method suits dynamic environments where pedestrian behavior constantly changes [33]. Reinforcement learning models adapt to new scenarios, such as varying pedestrian densities or environmental changes, making them ideal for smart city applications [26,39]. However, they require significant interaction data and are computationally intensive, involving numerous iterations to improve decision-making, which can be time-consuming and resource-demanding.

In conclusion, both rule-based and learning-based models are instrumental in simulating pedestrian behavior. Rule-based models excel in simplicity and efficiency, making them suitable for controlled environments with predictable patterns. Conversely, learning-based models offer the flexibility and adaptability needed for complex, dynamic settings where pedestrian behaviors evolve. Each model type has unique strengths and limitations, underscoring the necessity of selecting the right model based on specific application demands and constraints. Given our research focus on the variability of generating behavior, we have chosen imitation learning for this study to adaptively model and predict the diverse and changing patterns of pedestrian behavior.

3 Motivation

Current methods for generating pedestrian poses often depend heavily on physics-based models or rigid rule sets, which fail to capture the full range of human behavior. These methods lack the ability to reflect the true diversity and spontaneity observed in real-world pedestrian movements. To address this gap, there is a need to develop new frameworks that incorporate a richer set of data inputs, potentially sourced from real-world observations. Such frameworks would enable the modeling of pedestrian poses that more accurately represent the complexity of human behavior.

Integrating trajectory and pose data poses a significant challenge. The need for a unified approach that seamlessly combines these two aspects of pedestrian modeling is critical. Effective integration would not only improve the realism of these models but also enhance the predictive capabilities of autonomous systems operating in complex urban environments. Addressing these challenges could lead to substantial advancements in the field of autonomous driving, particularly in enhancing safety protocols and operational efficiency in densely populated areas.

3.1 Research Questions

Q1 How can pedestrian poses be generated without solely relying on physics or predefined rules, thus capturing a more comprehensive range of human movements?

Q2 How can high-level trajectory data be effectively linked and integrated with low-level pose data to ensure coherent and unified modeling of pedestrian behaviors?

3.2 Objective

To address these critical research questions, the objectives are designed to leverage advanced technologies and methodologies for enhancing pedestrian behavior generation in urban traffic environments.

O1 **Utilization of Imitation Learning Based on Naturalistic Pedestrian Behavior Data:** This objective aims to generate more realistic pedestrian poses by integrating detailed observations of real pedestrian movements. By utilizing a rich dataset that captures a wide range of behaviors and interactions within urban settings, the models developed will reflect the true diversity of pedestrian actions. This approach will improve the realism of simulations by grounding pose generation in authentic, observed behaviors.

O2 **Development of a Unified Framework for Behavior Generation:** This objective seeks to create a comprehensive framework that simultaneously generates both high-level trajectories and low-level poses. The framework will involve developing an intermediate representation that bridges the gap between the macroscopic movements of trajectories and the microscopic details of poses. By aligning these two levels of behavior within a single cohesive model, the framework aims to produce consistent and comprehensive outputs, effectively simulating the full range of pedestrian behaviors observed in urban traffic scenarios.

By addressing these objectives, the proposed research aims to fill existing gaps in pedestrian behavior generation. The use of imitation learning based on naturalistic data and the development of a unified framework for trajectory and pose integration will significantly enhance the realism and predictive capabilities of pedestrian models, ultimately improving safety and efficiency in autonomous driving systems.

4 Proposed Framework

This section presents our proposed framework, detailing its structure and the interplay between its components. Our methodology employs a two-stage approach that integrates high-level trajectory generation with low-level pose generation, seamlessly connected through a novel fuzzy transformation technique. This design facilitates a comprehensive generation process that accounts for both spatial dynamics and pose accuracy in complex environments.

4.1 Framework Overview

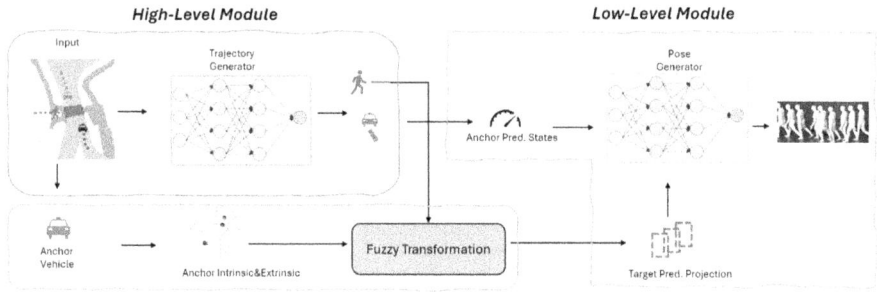

Fig. 2. The framework, as illustrated here, showcases the interconnected workflow starting from the bird's-eye trajectory generator, through the fuzzy transformation module, to the pose generator.

Figure 2 depicts our framework, consisting of three main components: the bird's-eye trajectory generator, the fuzzy transformation module, and the pose generator. These generators are powered by a generative model (such as GAN, CVAE, or DDPM) that reconstructs outputs from random noise, conditioned on specific inputs.

4.2 Trajectory Generator

The bird's-eye trajectory generation module is a key element of our framework, tasked with producing realistic, scenario-specific pedestrian trajectories from an overhead perspective. This process begins by collecting observed trajectories from various entities in the traffic environment, such as the ego vehicle, the target pedestrian, and other traffic participants. Although these bird's-eye trajectories provide a broad overview of the traffic scenario, they crucially capture the dynamics of all involved entities, offering a comprehensive dataset for trajectory prediction despite the lack of granular detail.

The initial step in trajectory generation involves a crucial coordinate transformation. Since the final outputs are the trajectories of the ego vehicle and the target pedestrian, it's necessary to transform the world coordinate system of all agents and map elements into a target-centered coordinate system. This transformation is accomplished using a transformation matrix, which reorients the spatial data to focus on the target pedestrian's perspective. This ensures that subsequent processing and trajectory prediction are relative to the target's position in the environment.

After the coordinate transformation, each agent's trajectory and each map element's polygon undergo a separate encoding process. This involves two distinct encoders designed to standardize the embeddings of similar types into a consistent shape and shared space, thereby normalizing data representation across different entities. This step prepares the spatial data for more complex integration and analysis, making it suitable for deep learning models.

Once the embeddings are standardized, a transformer encoder is used to integrate these embeddings within their respective categories. This allows for intra-category communication, enabling all traffic-related agents' trajectories, for example, to be considered in relation to each other. Following this integration, a cross-attention transformer decoder merges the two types of embeddings-those of the agents and the map elements. This fusion process is essential for understanding the interactions between dynamic agents and static environmental features, providing a rich contextual foundation for trajectory prediction.

The process concludes with the final, integrated encoding being input into a diffusion decoder. This advanced component is responsible for generating future trajectories for both the target pedestrian and the ego vehicle. By utilizing the power of diffusion models, which iteratively refine predictions towards higher probabilities based on the provided context, the decoder produces trajectories that are not only realistic but also deeply informed by the observed dynamics and spatial relationships within the traffic scenario.

Thus, this enhanced trajectory generator represents a sophisticated combination of coordinate transformation, encoding, integration, and diffusion decoding processes. Each step is carefully designed to contribute to the generation of accurate, scenario-specific pedestrian and vehicle trajectories, reflecting the complex interplay of movements in urban traffic environments. Through this comprehensive approach, our framework aims to significantly enhance the realism and predictive accuracy of pedestrian behavior modeling in the context of autonomous driving and urban traffic management.

4.3 Pose Generation

Fig. 3. Data preprocessing for egocentric pedestrian pose from dashcam video

To achieve realistic pedestrian poses, the process begins with acquiring video data from the BDD100K dataset (Fig. 3), which provides a comprehensive range of urban driving scenarios crucial for capturing diverse pedestrian behaviors. The next step involves detecting pedestrians within these videos using sophisticated object detection algorithms. Once the pedestrians are identified, their 2D poses are detected.

Following the detection of 2D poses, these poses are transformed into a 3D format. This transformation adds depth to the pose data, enabling more realistic simulations of pedestrian movements in three-dimensional space. To ensure the quality and accuracy of these 3D poses, a neural network-based discriminator evaluates the generated poses and filters out those that do not meet set standards of realism and accuracy. This multi-step process is essential for generating high-quality, naturalistic pedestrian poses necessary for advanced simulations and studies related to urban mobility and autonomous vehicle technologies.

Within our simulation framework, the pose generator plays a critical role, specifically tailored to produce realistic pedestrian poses by focusing on the nuances of an egocentric viewpoint. Unlike the trajectory generator, which incorporates a broad array of environmental observations and high-definition (HD) maps, the pose generator concentrates on a specialized set of conditional inputs. These inputs include the target pedestrian's egocentric trajectory, detailing the path observed directly from the ego vehicle's perspective, and the dynamics of the ego vehicle, providing context about its movement and speed relative to the pedestrian. Additionally, contextual text labels derived from advanced language model feature extraction further refine the inputs, allowing for nuanced adjustments to the pose based on descriptive scene elements.

This distinction highlights the adaptation to the unique requirements of egocentric versus bird's-eye views, recognizing the different coordinate systems and perspectives they offer. Using egocentric viewpoints necessitates understanding spatial relationships from the driver's perspective, significantly influencing how pedestrian poses are interpreted and generated.

The pose generator employs a sophisticated diffusion model during the inference stage, starting by sampling noise from a standard normal distribution. It then uses an encoder to integrate the conditioned inputs-predicted egocentric trajectory, ego vehicle dynamics, and text labels-into a coherent framework. These elements are iteratively processed to recover and refine pedestrian poses, ensuring that each generated pose accurately reflects the dynamic and often unpredictable nature of pedestrian movements in urban environments. This process is supported by robust datasets like BDD100K and Titan, which provide diverse scenarios of pedestrian interactions, and state-of-the-art 3D pose detectors pre-trained on datasets like H36m, ensuring high fidelity and realism in the simulated poses.

4.4 Fuzzy Transformation

The concept of fuzzy transformation builds on the intrinsic and extrinsic transformations that map an object's coordinates from an image to a world coordinate system. Here, "fuzzy" denotes the inherent uncertainty in both the intrinsic and extrinsic matrices and the variability in the sizes of traffic-related agents. This uncertainty exists because, although we have general estimates for parameters such as the dash camera's mounting position and orientation or the average size of pedestrians, precise values are often lacking. These specifics can vary based on the exact mounting position of the camera, the size of the ego vehicle, and natural variations in human dimensions.

Before diving into the details of intrinsic and extrinsic transformations, it is important to address the variability in human dimensions, which is relatively straightforward. Assuming a reasonable estimate of the transformation matrix, we can convert the bird's-eye view trajectory into an egocentric view trajectory. However, this trajectory only represents the center point of the egocentric view's bounding box due to the lack of detailed size information for agents in the bird's-eye view. To address this, we model pedestrian dimensions using a Gaussian distribution for height and width, based on the egocentric view dataset. For simplicity, we assume pedestrians are cuboidal, with equal width and length, and sample from these distributions to generate egocentric bounding boxes for pedestrians, centered on the points transformed by the intrinsic and extrinsic matrices.

In scenarios where intrinsic and extrinsic matrices are unavailable, we estimate these matrices by matching distributions. Specifically, we aim to align the features of transformed egocentric bounding boxes with those in the egocentric view dataset. This strategy is based on the assumption that two datasets of sufficient size and collected similarly (e.g., general traffic scenarios, not specific ones) will exhibit similar distributions of certain features, such as the location of bounding box centers, vertex positions, or movement directions. This approach leads to the formulation of an optimization problem aimed at minimizing the distance between the distributions for a selected feature. Constraints ensure that the transformation matrices remain within plausible limits, with the extrinsic matrix mirroring a typical dash cam setup and the intrinsic matrix approximating standard dash cam specifications. A robust initial guess for the extrinsic and intrinsic matrices is crucial, where the intrinsic might represent common camera settings, and the extrinsic typically involves a front cabin-mounted camera facing forward. Iteratively solving this optimization problem provides estimated ranges for the transformation matrices. When specifics of the camera setup are known for some egocentric view datasets, we can apply the known intrinsic matrix specifications and focus on estimating the extrinsic matrix, which often remains unknown. If both matrices are known, this estimation step is bypassed, with the stochastic variability primarily due to human size differences.

This fuzzy transformation approach provides flexibility in dealing with inherent uncertainties in camera setup and human dimensions, facilitating more accurate mapping of bird's-eye trajectories to egocentric views under varying conditions.

5 Discussion

5.1 Coherent and Consistent Behavior Generation

Our framework ensures coherence in simulation outputs by establishing a strong, logical connection between predicted trajectories and generated poses. This sequential integration is enhanced by fuzzy transformation techniques, maintaining consistency between bird's-eye and egocentric perspectives. As a result, high-level plans are accurately translated into detailed, contextually appropriate pedestrian poses.

5.2 Seamless Integration and Sophisticated Framework Development

A primary objective of our framework is to achieve seamless integration between high-level pedestrian trajectory planning and low-level pose generation. This integration is vital for producing realistic simulations that reflect pedestrian movement patterns across urban landscapes and the physical poses and gestures pedestrians exhibit in response to their surroundings and interactions with autonomous vehicles (AVs).

Our two-stage approach leverages an egocentric driving dataset for capturing naturalistic behavior and a pre-trained 3D pose detector for accurate pose extraction. This strategy effectively bridges the gap in dynamic pedestrian behavior generation. The framework aims to conceptualize and operationalize pedestrian behaviors in a technically sophisticated manner grounded in urban mobility realities. Successful integration of high-level trajectory planning with low-level pose generation will represent a significant advancement in creating realistic, interactive pedestrian behaviors essential for the next generation of autonomous vehicle technologies.

5.3 Data Efficiency

By leveraging existing datasets and pretrained models, our framework significantly reduces the necessity for extensive new data collection, thereby establishing itself as a cost-effective and resource-efficient solution for simulating pedestrian behaviors. This approach not only diminishes the time and financial burdens typically associated with large-scale data gathering but also accelerates the research and development process by utilizing readily available resources.

The use of these pre-existing, rich datasets and sophisticated models ensures that our simulation tool can immediately tap into a vast array of detailed pedestrian behaviors and scenarios without the delay imposed by the collection and preprocessing of new data. This is particularly advantageous in urban mobility studies where the variety and complexity of pedestrian dynamics are vast and multifaceted. The ability to quickly adapt and apply these datasets to new research questions or simulation environments enhances our framework's flexibility and responsiveness.

Furthermore, the integration of pretrained models such as advanced 3D pose detectors and natural language processing (NLP) feature extractors into our framework allows us to enrich the simulations without the overhead of training models from scratch. These models have been pretrained on diverse datasets, often larger and more comprehensive than what individual research projects could feasibly collect, ensuring high accuracy and generalizability of the simulation outputs.

This data efficiency not only promotes sustainability by reducing the redundant accumulation of similar datasets but also aligns with modern data science practices which emphasize the reuse and repurposing of existing digital resources. By optimizing the use of these resources, our framework supports the rapid iteration and scaling of pedestrian behavior models, facilitating ongoing improvements and enhancements with minimal resource waste.

5.4 Evaluation of Generative Model for High-Level and Low-Level Pedestrian Behavior

Evaluating the generative model for high-level pedestrian behavior involves assessing both the diversity and plausibility of the generated trajectories. Unlike prediction models, where the goal is to closely match observed data, generative models are evaluated on their ability to produce a wide range of realistic behaviors. Metrics such as Coverage, which measures how well the generated trajectories span the space of plausible pedestrian movements, and Novelty, which assesses the introduction of unique and realistic trajectories not present in the training data, are crucial. Additionally, the use of Inception Scores or Fréchet Inception Distance (FID) can help evaluate the quality and diversity of generated trajectories by comparing the distribution of generated samples to that of the real samples. Scenario-based evaluations, where the generative model is tested across various urban scenarios, can further illustrate its ability to produce contextually appropriate behaviors in different environments.

For low-level pedestrian behavior, evaluation focuses on the accuracy, naturalism, and diversity of the generated poses. While metrics such as Mean Per Joint Position Error (MPJPE) and Percentage of Correct Keypoints (PCK) are still relevant, they should be complemented with assessments of diversity and natural motion. Diversity metrics can include the number of distinct poses generated and the variability of joint angles across different poses. Temporal coherence is another critical factor, where the smoothness and continuity of poses over time are evaluated to ensure realistic motion. Qualitative assessments through expert reviews and user studies, where participants rate the realism and appropriateness of the generated behaviors in various contexts, provide additional validation. Combining these quantitative and qualitative methods ensures that the generative model not only produces accurate and realistic poses but also captures the variability and complexity of real pedestrian behaviors.

6 Conclusion

In this paper, we have presented a novel framework for generating hierarchical pedestrian behaviors that integrates high-level trajectory planning with low-level pose generation. Our approach employs a two-stage process that combines bird's-eye trajectory generation with egocentric pose modeling, connected through a fuzzy transformation technique. This framework not only enhances the realism and contextual appropriateness of simulated pedestrian behaviors but also provides a robust tool for advancing the capabilities of autonomous vehicle technologies in urban environments.

Our evaluation strategy includes metrics for both high-level and low-level behavior assessment, emphasizing the importance of diversity, plausibility, and temporal coherence. By leveraging existing datasets and pre-trained models, we have demonstrated a cost-effective and resource-efficient method for simulating pedestrian behaviors. This framework's ability to generate realistic and varied pedestrian movements is crucial for improving safety protocols and operational efficiency in autonomous driving systems.

7 Future Work

Future work will focus on implementing this framework and using experiments to validate its effectiveness. This involves setting up comprehensive experimental studies to test the framework's performance in various urban scenarios and environments. Following the evaluation discussion outlined in this paper, we will develop a more specific evaluation protocol to rigorously assess the generated models. This protocol will include both quantitative metrics, such as coverage, novelty, and temporal coherence, and qualitative assessments through expert reviews and user studies.

By systematically evaluating the framework using these protocols, we aim to refine and enhance its capabilities, ensuring that the generated pedestrian behaviors are both diverse and realistic. The insights gained from these experiments will be crucial for further optimizing the model and adapting it to new and complex urban conditions. Through this iterative process of implementation, experimentation, and evaluation, we hope to establish a solid foundation for the practical application of our framework in real-world autonomous driving systems, ultimately contributing to safer and more efficient urban mobility solutions.

References

1. Amirian, J., Hayet, J.B., Pettre, J.: Social ways: learning multi-modal distributions of pedestrian trajectories with GANs. In: 2019 IEEE/CVF Conference on Computer Vision and Pattern Recognition Workshops (CVPRW), Long Beach, CA, USA, pp. 2964–2972. IEEE (2019). https://doi.org/10.1109/CVPRW.2019.00359, https://ieeexplore.ieee.org/document/9025550/
2. Anvari, B., Bell, M.G., Sivakumar, A., Ochieng, W.Y.: Modelling shared space users via rule-based social force model. Trans. Res. Part C Emerg. Technol. **51**, 83–103 (2015)
3. Bhagavathula, R., Williams, B., Owens, J., Gibbons, R.: The reality of virtual reality: a comparison of pedestrian behavior in real and virtual environments. In: Proceedings of the Human Factors and Ergonomics Society Annual Meeting, Los Angeles, CA, vol. 62, pp. 2056–2060. SAGE Publications (2018)
4. Bhattacharyya, A., Reino, D.O., Fritz, M., Schiele, B.: Euro-PVI: pedestrian vehicle interactions in dense urban centers. In: CVPR. IEEE Computer Society (2021)
5. Biktairov, Y., Stebelev, M., Rudenko, I., Shliazhko, O., Yangel, B.: PRANK: motion Prediction based on RANKing. Adv. Neural Info. Process. Syst. **33**, 2553–2563 (2020)
6. Blaiotta, C.: Learning generative socially aware models of pedestrian motion. IEEE Robot. Autom. Lett. **4**(4), 3433–3440 (2019). https://doi.org/10.1109/LRA.2019.2928202, https://ieeexplore.ieee.org/document/8760356/
7. Bock, J., Krajewski, R., Moers, T., Runde, S., Vater, L., Eckstein, L.: The inD dataset: a drone dataset of naturalistic road user trajectories at German intersections. In: 2020 IEEE Intelligent Vehicles Symposium (IV), pp. 1929–1934. IEEE (2020)
8. Caesar, H., et al.: nuScenes: a multimodal dataset for autonomous driving. In: Proceedings of the IEEE/CVF Conference on Computer Vision and Pattern Recognition, pp. 11621–11631 (2020)
9. Cai, Y., et al.: Pedestrian motion trajectory prediction in intelligent driving from far shot first-person perspective video. IEEE Trans. Intell. Transp. Syst. **23**(6), 5298–5313 (2022)
10. Camara, F., et al.: Pedestrian models for autonomous driving part i: low-level models, from sensing to tracking. IEEE Trans. Intell. Transp. Syst. **22**(10), 6131–6151 (2020)
11. Camara, F., et al.: Pedestrian models for autonomous driving part ii: high-level models of human behavior. IEEE Trans. Intell. Transp. Syst. **22**(9), 5453–5472 (2020)
12. Chang, M.F., et al.: Argoverse: 3D tracking and forecasting with rich maps. In: Proceedings of the IEEE/CVF Conference on Computer Vision and Pattern Recognition, pp. 8748–8757 (2019)
13. Chen, M.Y., Linkens, D.A.: Rule-base self-generation and simplification for data-driven fuzzy models. Fuzzy Sets Syst. **142**(2), 243–265 (2004)
14. Chen, T., et al.: PSI: a pedestrian behavior dataset for socially intelligent autonomous car. arXiv preprint arXiv:2112.02604 (2021)

15. Deb, S., Strawderman, L.J., Carruth, D.W.: Investigating pedestrian suggestions for external features on fully autonomous vehicles: a virtual reality experiment. Transport. Res. F: Traffic Psychol. Behav. **59**, 135–149 (2018)
16. Fang, L., Jiang, Q., Shi, J., Zhou, B.: TPNet: trajectory proposal network for motion prediction. In: 2020 IEEE/CVF Conference on Computer Vision and Pattern Recognition (CVPR), Seattle, WA, USA, pp. 6796–6805. IEEE (2020). https://doi.org/10.1109/CVPR42600.2020.00683, https://ieeexplore.ieee.org/document/9156890/
17. Fridovich-Keil, D., et al.: Confidence-aware motion prediction for real-time collision avoidance. Int. J. Robot. Res. **39**(2–3), 250–265 (2020)
18. Geyer, J., et al.: A2d2: audi autonomous driving dataset. arXiv preprint arXiv:2004.06320 (2020)
19. Governors Highway Safety Association: New projection: U.S. pedestrian fatalities reach highest level in 40 years (2022). https://www.ghsa.org/resources/news-releases/pedestrians21
20. Governors Highway Safety Association: Pedestrian traffic fatalities by state: 2022 preliminary data (2023). https://www.ghsa.org/resources/Pedestrians23
21. Hu, A., et al.: Model-based imitation learning for urban driving. Adv. Neural. Inf. Process. Syst. **35**, 20703–20716 (2022)
22. Hu, Y., Chen, S., Zhang, Y., Gu, X.: Collaborative motion prediction via neural motion message passing, pp. 6319–6328 (2020)
23. Insurance Institute for Highway Safety: Pedestrian fatalities by state (2021). https://www.iihs.org
24. Jain, A., et al.: Discrete residual flow for probabilistic pedestrian behavior prediction. In: Proceedings of the Conference on Robot Learning, pp. 407–419. PMLR (2020). ISSN 2640-3498. https://proceedings.mlr.press/v100/jain20a.html
25. Katyal, K.D., Hager, G.D., Huang, C.M.: Intent-aware pedestrian prediction for adaptive crowd navigation. In: 2020 IEEE International Conference on Robotics and Automation (ICRA), , Paris, France, May 2020, pp. 3277–3283. IEEE (2020). https://doi.org/10.1109/ICRA40945.2020.9197434, https://ieeexplore.ieee.org/document/9197434/
26. Kulkarni, N., et al.: Nifty: neural object interaction fields for guided human motion synthesis. arXiv preprint arXiv:2307.07511 (2023)
27. Lerner, A., Chrysanthou, Y., Lischinski, D.: Crowds by example. In: Computer Graphics Forum, vol. 26, pp. 655–664. Wiley Online Library (2007)
28. Li, K., Eiffert, S., Shan, M., Gomez-Donoso, F., Worrall, S., Nebot, E.: Attentional-GCNN: adaptive pedestrian trajectory prediction towards generic autonomous vehicle use cases. In: 2021 IEEE International Conference on Robotics and Automation (ICRA), Xi'an, China, pp. 14241–14247. IEEE (2021). https://doi.org/10.1109/ICRA48506.2021.9561480, https://ieeexplore.ieee.org/document/9561480/
29. Liu, B., et al.: Spatiotemporal relationship reasoning for pedestrian intent prediction. IEEE Robot. Autom. Lett. **5**(2), 3485–3492 (2020). https://doi.org/10.1109/LRA.2020.2976305, https://ieeexplore.ieee.org/document/9013045/
30. Liu, S., Lo, S., Ma, J., Wang, W.: An agent-based microscopic pedestrian flow simulation model for pedestrian traffic problems. IEEE Trans. Intell. Transp. Syst. **15**(3), 992–1001 (2014)
31. Mandal, S., Biswas, S., Balas, V.E., Shaw, R.N., Ghosh, A.: Motion prediction for autonomous vehicles from Lyft dataset using deep learning. In: 2020 IEEE 5th International Conference on Computing Communication and Automation (ICCCA), Greater Noida, India, pp. 768–773. IEEE (2020). https://doi.org/10.1109/ICCCA49541.2020.9250790, https://ieeexplore.ieee.org/document/9250790/

32. Neumann, L., Vedaldi, A.: Pedestrian and ego-vehicle trajectory prediction from monocular camera. In: 2021 IEEE/CVF Conference on Computer Vision and Pattern Recognition (CVPR), Nashville, TN, USA, pp. 10199–10207. IEEE (2021). https://doi.org/10.1109/CVPR46437.2021.01007, https://ieeexplore.ieee.org/document/9577864/
33. Pan, L., et al.: Synthesizing physically plausible human motions in 3D scenes. arXiv preprint arXiv:2308.09036 (2023)
34. Pellegrini, S., Ess, A., Schindler, K., Van Gool, L.: You'll never walk alone: modeling social behavior for multi-target tracking. In: 2009 IEEE 12th International Conference on Computer Vision, pp. 261–268. IEEE (2009)
35. Quan, R., Zhu, L., Wu, Y., Yang, Y.: Holistic LSTM for pedestrian trajectory prediction. IEEE Trans. Image Process. **30**, 3229–3239 (2021). https://doi.org/10.1109/TIP.2021.3058599, https://ieeexplore.ieee.org/document/9361440/
36. Rasouli, A., Kotseruba, I., Kunic, T., Tsotsos, J.K.: PIE: a large-scale dataset and models for pedestrian intention estimation and trajectory prediction. In: Proceedings of the IEEE/CVF International Conference on Computer Vision, pp. 6262–6271 (2019)
37. Rasouli, A., Kotseruba, I., Tsotsos, J.K.: Understanding pedestrian behavior in complex traffic scenes. IEEE Trans. Intell. Veh. **3**(1), 61–70 (2017)
38. Rasouli, A., Rohani, M., Luo, J.: Bifold and semantic reasoning for pedestrian behavior prediction, pp. 15600–15610 (2021)
39. Ren, J., Zhang, M., Yu, C., Ma, X., Pan, L., Liu, Z.: InsActor: instruction-driven physics-based characters. Adv. Neural Info. Process. Syst. **36** (2024)
40. Robicquet, A., Sadeghian, A., Alahi, A., Savarese, S.: Learning social etiquette: human trajectory understanding in crowded scenes. In: Leibe, B., Matas, J., Sebe, N., Welling, M. (eds.) ECCV 2016. LNCS, vol. 9912, pp. 549–565. Springer, Cham (2016). https://doi.org/10.1007/978-3-319-46484-8_33
41. Robin, T., Antonini, G., Bierlaire, M., Cruz, J.: Specification, estimation and validation of a pedestrian walking behavior model. Transport. Res. Part B Methodol. **43**(1), 36–56 (2009)
42. Scholler, C., Knoll, A.: FloMo: tractable motion prediction with normalizing flows. In: 2021 IEEE/RSJ International Conference on Intelligent Robots and Systems (IROS), Prague, Czech Republic, pp. 7977–7984. IEEE (2021). https://doi.org/10.1109/IROS51168.2021.9636445, https://ieeexplore.ieee.org/document/9636445/
43. Tai, L., Zhang, J., Liu, M., Burgard, W.: Socially compliant navigation through raw depth inputs with generative adversarial imitation learning. In: 2018 IEEE International Conference on Robotics and Automation (ICRA), pp. 1111–1117. IEEE (2018)
44. Tao, C., Jiang, Q., Duan, L., Luo, P.: Dynamic and static context-aware LSTM for multi-agent motion prediction (2020). arXiv arXiv:2008.00777 [cs]
45. Yao, Y., Atkins, E., Roberson, M.J., Vasudevan, R., Du, X.: Coupling intent and action for pedestrian crossing behavior prediction. arXiv preprint arXiv:2105.04133 (2021)
46. Yin, Z., Liu, R., Xiong, Z., Yuan, Z.: Multimodal transformer network for pedestrian trajectory prediction (2021)
47. Yu, C., Ma, X., Ren, J., Zhao, H., Yi, S.: Spatio-temporal graph transformer networks for pedestrian trajectory prediction (2020). arXiv arXiv:2005.08514 [cs]
48. Yue, J., Manocha, D., Wang, H.: Human trajectory prediction via neural social physics. In: Avidan, S., Brostow, G., Cissé, M., Farinella, G.M., Hassner, T. (eds.) Computer Vision, ECCV 2022. LNCS, vol. 13694, pp. 376–394. Springer, Cham (2022). https://doi.org/10.1007/978-3-031-19830-4_22

49. Zhang, Z., et al.: Implementation and performance evaluation of in-vehicle highway back-of-queue alerting system using the driving simulator. In: 2021 IEEE International Intelligent Transportation Systems Conference (ITSC), pp. 1753–1759. IEEE (2021)
50. Zhang, Z., Tian, R., Ding, Z.: TrEP: transformer-based evidential prediction for pedestrian intention with uncertainty. In: Proceedings of the AAAI Conference on Artificial Intelligence, vol. 37 (2023)
51. Zhang, Z., Tian, R., Duffy, V.G.: Trust in automated vehicle: a meta-analysis. In: Duffy, V.G., Landry, S.J., Lee, J.D., Stanton, N. (eds.) Human-Automation Interaction. Automation, Collaboration, and E-Services. vol. 11, pp. 221–234. Springer, Cham (2023). https://doi.org/10.1007/978-3-031-10784-9_13
52. Zhang, Z., Tian, R., Sherony, R., Domeyer, J., Ding, Z.: Attention-based interrelation modeling for explainable automated driving. IEEE Trans. Intell. Veh. **8**(2), 1564–1573 (2022)
53. Zhong, J., Sun, H., Cao, W., He, Z.: Pedestrian motion trajectory prediction with stereo-based 3D deep pose estimation and trajectory learning. IEEE Access **8**, 23480–23486 (2020)https://doi.org/10.1109/ACCESS.2020.2969994, https://ieeexplore.ieee.org/document/8972435/

HCI in Aviation, Transport and Safety

RPAS Over the Blue: Investigating Key Human Factors in Successful UAV Operations

Felix Adams[✉] and Maria Hagl[✉]

German Aerospace Center (DLR), Braunschweig, Germany
{felix.adams,maria.hagl}@dlr.de

Abstract. The use of drones in the maritime sector has not been extensively explored yet. A collaborative project between the German Federal Police and the German Aerospace Center is investigating the potential use of a drone launched from a patrol boat. This prompts the following question: Which human factors are key for safe drone operations while efficiently accomplishing the mission objectives? To answer this question, we conducted literature research and analyzed twelve relevant studies. A total of twenty factors were identified. The five most frequently mentioned factors relate to situational awareness, judgment/decision-making, communication, teamwork, and manual flying skills. The relevance of each human factor for successful deployment is explained and analyzed in detail. The results of this study may serve as a foundation for the incorporation of human factors into a training concept for future maritime drone crews.

Keywords: Maritime RPAS · UAS · UAV · human factors · safety

1 Introduction

The production and use of remotely piloted aircraft systems (*abbr.* RPAS) is considered one of the fastest-growing and most dynamic industries worldwide see [1]. According to estimates by the Financial Service Monitor Worldwide [2], the global market for public unmanned aircraft systems (*abbr.* UAS) is expected to reach USD 1.1 billion in 2023 and rise to USD 2.0 billion by 2028, with an annual growth rate of 13.0%. It is important to emphasize that this sector has various applications, including also military and law enforcement agencies, on land and at sea.

1.1 RPAS in a Maritime Context

The discussed applications of governmental maritime RPAS include search and rescue missions, surveillance of ports and their infrastructure, maritime patrols to detect smuggling, piracy, or illegal fishing, seaworthiness checks, and forensic monitoring of ship exhaust [3, 4].

Since 2016, the German Aerospace Center (DLR) and the Federal Police of Germany have been conducting research as part of a joint project called Maritime RPAS Operations (MaRPAS). The research aims to explore the potential applications of RPAS in maritime operations, as well as the challenges they may encounter. One of the main goals consists of capturing automated situational information in the aforementioned areas of application with a fast response time, analyzing safety-critical situations and reacting quickly if necessary [5]. So far, ship-based navigation of the RPAS via a ground control station and a newly developed cable-guided landing aid have been successfully tested at sea [6]. However, further clarification is required regarding the design of the training concept for the crew. While various areas of RPAS applications on land have been discussed in the research literature, there are only a few scientific papers on use cases that deal with the challenges of maritime RPAS missions.

1.2 General Information and Variety in Unmanned Aviation

The global markets for the production, distribution, and development of software and systems for unmanned aerial vehicles (*abbr.* UAV) are North America (USD 4.5 billion), Asia (USD 4.4 billion) and Europe (USD 4.0 billion) in 2018 [7]. According to an estimate by Castellano [8], the industrial drone sector in Europe and the US is estimated to reach a market value of USD 50 billion by 2050. Military UAVs are used in over 100 nations worldwide [9], and the budget for this technology is constantly increasing [10].

Given the expected increase in demand for unmanned aerial vehicles and technical progress, especially concerning new technologies such as the introduction of artificial intelligence for automated flight guidance [11], a large number of UAVs are being offered for various application areas.

The most commonly utilized UAVs are multi-copter rotorcraft, which are employed for recreational activities, aerial photography and filming, as well as government disaster management [12]. These UAVs belong to the open category with a maximum take-off mass of 25 kg under European law [13]. This category also includes small, hand-guided, and autonomously deployable civilian or military fixed-wing aircraft such as the RQ-11 Raven drones of the U.S. Army [14]. Conversely, heavy-duty helicopter UAVs incorporate the SwissDrone [15], which is equipped with a jet engine. The area of application may include reconnaissance and search-and-rescue missions [16], transportation of goods and medical supplies, monitoring of high-voltage power lines, and operations in agriculture [17]. The lesser-known Fire Scout helicopter UAV comprises a combustion engine [14] and is deployed by the U.S. Coast Guard for maritime supervision [18]. Pure-wing drones possess the advantage of longer flight duration and higher speed, which enables them to cover greater distances in a search and rescue mission [16]. However, take-off and landing are more challenging due to their design [17].

The complexity and diversity of mission concepts vary depending on the application, whether for military or civilian operations [19]. These can be low-altitude missions within or outside the pilot's field of vision or missions that are integrated into civilian airspace [20]. In a search and rescue mission, the tasks include planning the flight route, dividing operational tasks to coordinate multiple UAS and pilots, and avoiding collisions with obstacles [16]. The exact military mission content and objectives are generally not publicly known. It is assumed that one of the main tasks is the surveillance of geographical sectors, the reconnaissance of unclear situation pictures, and the precise provision of weapons support for ground-based combat units (see [21]).

1.3 Standardization Issues and the Human Factor

The diverse applications of RPAS pose a challenge when introducing uniform operating regulations. European legislators are seeking to create a regulatory framework aimed at integrating UAV flights into the established air traffic network within a single operational area, such as the U-Space concept [22]. According to the European Commission Regulation 2019/947 issued by the European Aviation Safety Agency (EASA [23]), commercial operators of unmanned aerial vehicles are required to have a concept of operations. This concept includes a manual on operational procedures and general operating rules as well as an operational safety management system. The licensing of operations and personnel requires extensive training depending on the size of the UAV, its certified category, and intended areas of use. Among other things, operators in the certified category must demonstrate theoretical knowledge of the technical capabilities of their UAVs and pass a flight test. Drone pilots must complete a theory course and study the manufacturer's operating manual based on the subclass of the open category. The course includes topics such as aviation law, privacy, data protection, and human performance.

Hagl et al. [24] have already investigated the question of a uniform training design. The competencies and training of drone operators differ based on the type of UAV and mission, the area of operation, the degree of automated flight guidance, or the crew constellation. Various training methods are also discussed that integrate the knowledge, skills, and attitudes of drone pilots. Examples include scenario or event-based training approaches [25]. According to Schmidt et al. [26], it is recommended to teach competencies such as air law compliance in a one-time basic training and to regularly train other skills such as flying beyond visual range and teamwork to ensure safe and efficient RPAS operations. Requirements for prospective military drone pilots vary: some branches of the armed forces require conventional flight training first [1], while others, such as the U.S. Air Force, have developed a unique 9-month course that allows non-pilots to enter directly as RPAS operators [27]. However, little information on military training is publicly available. According to EASA requirements [23], commercial drone pilots and drone operators certified in the specific category should have the following competencies: the skills mentioned, such as the application of standard procedures in unmanned aerial vehicles inspection, flight planning, and the application of emergency procedures, proficiency in aeronautical communication and automated flight guidance, leadership, teamwork, and self-management, problem-solving and decision-making, situational awareness, workload management, and coordination or handover of tasks. Qi [28] emphasizes that human factors play a significant role in the incorrect operation of remotely piloted aircraft systems. Cummings et al. [29] come to a similar conclusion by examining the high level of automated flight guidance of modern drones and the risk posed by the automation bias applied by the operator. According to a recent study, two-thirds of drone mishaps and accidents are caused by human error, while one-third are due to technical problems [30].

1.4 Assumptions for Maritime RPAS Operations and Research Question

We estimate that a successful RPAS mission can be assessed based on the safety and efficiency of an operation. In this context, safety means that the UAV does not move outside the permissible operating limits and does not cause any damage or personal injury during the mission. The efficiency of a RPAS mission is determined by the successful completion of all mission parameters within a specified time frame.

Derived from the aforementioned paragraphs, the following factors are assumed to be general success competencies for RPAS missions in a maritime context: (1) Drone pilots are expected to have a comprehensive overview of the technical condition of the UAV and the external environmental conditions such as climate zone, weather, swell, or obstacles on the flight path ahead. (2) Drone pilots are expected to be able to fly in manual, semi-automatic, or automatic flight mode in both normal and emergency operations, even when technical systems are not functioning properly. (3) A level of conscientiousness and mental resilience is required to maintain a high level of concentration during a monotonous maritime mission over an extended period of time. (4) The crew is expected to work well together in a multi-crew concept, or in the single-operator case, to ensure effective coordination with the mission commander.

In current research, there is limited information about the factors that determine the success of a maritime RPAS mission. This study aims to draw insights from the current literature to identify relevant human factors in the field of maritime RPAS training that could lead to successful drone missions.

2 Method

2.1 Literature Review

A literature review was conducted to identify potential human factor-related aspects that could contribute to successful RPAS missions within a maritime environment. The information was accessed via the database quick search tool of the electronic library FernUniversität Hagen, EBSCO host, and Google Scholar. The following keywords were used by applying the Boolean operation AND: UAV training, competency. As a result, 35 references were identified and two papers were selected. The keywords Human Factors and military UAV operation were used to identify 38 references. Among them, one study for examination and one additional study from their respective literature citation were selected. Research of the working environment with the Boolean operation AND by the keywords maritime UAV, UAV operation, identified 148 references of which five studies were selected and one study was selected from an article's literature references. The full-text search option was utilized to conduct a prompt search in FernUniversität Hagen's database tool. A search for drone pilot selection assessment resulted in one study eligible for this review, while UAS operator competencies produced two research papers for further analysis. Additionally, eleven scientific articles were provided by DLR and one additional study was identified from one of the article's reference list.

2.2 Identification of Human Factors in Successful RPAS Missions

Of the 25 pre-selected and read articles, thirteen articles were excluded from further analyzing human factors that might lead to successful RPAS missions within a maritime environment. The reasons for this were, for example, articles that were too technically oriented and did not sufficiently address human factors, or too specific use cases that did not relate to a maritime context.

The remaining twelve articles [10, 24, 26, 27, 30–37] focus on general recommendations regarding RPAS missions, training, operational challenges, and selection criteria for UAV operators. We do not differentiate between air vehicle operator (*abbr*. AVO) and sensor operator (*abbr*. SO), as operators are usually trained for both positions for mutual role understanding and safety reasons in perturbation training.

In each article, all human factors that contribute positively to successful RPAS missions were individually assigned a numerical code. Human factors that occur in at least a quarter of the articles (n = 3) are described in the results.

3 Results

The most commonly identified human factors are listed in Table 1. The five most frequently encountered factors are (1) situational awareness, (2) judgment/decision-making, (3) communication, (4) teamwork, and (5) manual flying skills. An individual task focus was identified in most of the studies.

Situational awareness (SA) [10, 24, 26, 30, 31, 33–35] is described in the literature as a cognitive construct of information processing, which is divided into three processes: The perception and assimilation of information, the processing and understanding of the information, and the prediction of the development of future events through the results of the information processing process [38]. Or to put it more simply: "knowing what is going on" [39, p. 73]. This includes analyzing the environmental conditions, the state of the UAV, and how it is moving in space and time. According to Martins [39], a lack of SA is linked to several aircraft accidents in manned aviation, resulting from an overreliance on automation. Some pilots reported that they were "out of the loop" and did not understand the actions and analysis of the system (see [40]). It could be that the SA accident cause also applies to UAV operations. As early as 2006 [41], an analysis of the US Air Force database showed that situational awareness played a role in 18% of recorded UAV accidents. Study results of Rahmani and Weckman [30] seem to confirm these findings: Two-thirds of the causes of drone accidents were due to errors in SA and decision-making. Situational awareness and decision-making are closely related because once all the information is understood and processed, a decision can be made to respond to the situation [39, 42].

Judgment/decision-making [10, 24, 26, 27, 30, 31, 33, 35]: Recent aviation psychology literature discusses judgment and decision-making as the final step in the information-processing process [40, 43]. Rautenstrauch [44] suggests that this process can be guided by a FORDEC process structure. This involves assessing the time available, deciding if rapid intervention is required, gathering evidence, reviewing options, assessing risks, deciding and reviewing the outcome. In a recent study of military and civilian UAV accidents worldwide over the past decade, decision-based errors were found to be a leading human factor causing UAV accidents [45]. It was further found that drone pilots sometimes acted according to plans that were inadequate for the situation at hand.

Communication [10, 24, 26, 27, 31–33] is described in the encoder-decoder model by Shannon and Weaver [46] as a process of information transfer between senders

Table 1. Identified human factors contributing positively to successful RPAS missions in descending order of frequency

Identified Human Factors	n	Percent	Task focus
Situational awareness	8	66.6%	individual
Judgment/decision-making	8	66.6%	individual
Communication	7	58.3%	crew
Teamwork	6	50.0%	crew
Flight skills	5	41.6%	individual
Deductive reasoning	5	41.6%	individual
Monitoring systems	5	41.6%	individual
Handling crisis/emergencies	5	41.6%	crew
Inductive reasoning	4	33.3%	individual
Spatial orientation	4	33.3%	individual
System knowledge	4	33.3%	individual
Oral comprehension	3	25.0%	individual
Category flexibility	3	25.0%	individual
Estimation of time to contact	3	25.0%	individual
Organization/time management	3	25.0%	individual
Attention	3	25.0%	individual
Reasoning	3	25.0%	individual
Conscientiousness	3	25.0%	individual
Navigation	3	25.0%	individual
Hand-eye coordination	3	25.0%	individual

Note. Percentages as of reference to evaluated studies ($n = 12$).

and receivers. The successful transmission of a message requires mutual attention, the same knowledge of the communicated facts, the same coding, and an interference-free communication process. Feedback by repeating what has been said or by asking the recipient can help to avoid translation errors and ambiguities in the received message [47]. According to Wittmer and Roth [48, p. 378], effective communication skills can be crucial to the success of a mission. The authors recommend using clear and concise language, especially when under pressure. It is also important to remain calm, listen actively, and clarify any misunderstandings immediately. Communication in the multi-crew concept between the pilot and system operator should be standardized (see [10]). Lercel and Andrews [35, p. 239] further emphasize that poor communication among crew members can lead to confusion, blame, and fixation.

Teamwork is analyzed in half of the studies [10, 24, 26, 31, 33, 35], as it is mentioned in the context of safe RPAS operations. Salas et al. [49] define teamwork as the collaboration of two or more people to effectively achieve a common goal. In doing so, the team shares operational challenges and uses communication and coordination skills (see [50]). In terms of flight crew collaboration, Salas et al. [51] emphasize that knowledge of a task, a problem, and an understanding of the task-specific roles are important team factors. The knowledge, skills, and attitudes of UAV crews are currently context and mission-specific. Consequently, team competence in RPAS operations is dependent on the type of team and the specific mission task [51]. In manned aviation, insufficient cooperation of the crew was identified as one of the accident causes in the Air France 447 flight. According to de Wit & Cruz [52, p. 50], the crew had not adhered to the correct operational procedures and their actions were not mutually transparent. Comparable analyses for the operation of UAVs are obsolete as of this article.

Flight skills were identified as a relevant factor in five of the studies examined [24, 26, 30, 36, 37]. It should be noted that this factor is listed in the context of the respective study design as take-off/landing and cruise skills [36], flight training [24, 26], and skill-based errors [30]. According to several authors [53, 54], manual flight can be characterized as a psychomotor process divided into three main phases of information processing: perception, cognitive processing, and execution. Data from manned aviation show that flight accidents in the last 20 years have occurred more frequently during cruise flight and twice as frequent during landing compared to take-off [55]. This finding could be an indication of the challenges to be expected in automated UAV operations, especially concerning the landing on a ship. Automated assistance systems exist for RPAS landing guidance, utilizing mechanical [6] or sensory [56] technology. These systems have been successfully tested, but their validity is yet to be proven. In challenging environmental conditions or failures in automated landing systems, it is advisable to have manual flight skills [57, pp. 1265–1267].

Deductive and inductive reasoning [10, 32–34, 37] represent two forms of hypothetical thinking (see [58]). In deductive reasoning, a result is inferred by specifying an assumption and rule. Consider the following scenario in which a maritime RPAS possesses a jet turbine. It is a known fact that all jet turbines run on kerosene. Hence, it can be concluded that maritime RPAS are powered by kerosene. Inductive conclusions are not based on general validity but rather evaluate the likelihood of a conclusion. For example, if we consider maritime RPAS, we can assume that they are powered by kerosene because all jet turbines are powered by kerosene [59]. If a specific occurrence transpires during a mission, the crew will take specific action to resolve the situation. Alternatively, if the event has already occurred, the crew will take the necessary measures to resolve the issue [60].

In Monitoring systems [24, 26, 31, 35, 36], two use cases are distinguished. (1) Monitoring the UAV involves continuously observing various displays, data sets, and flight instruments. The goal is to interpret and recognize values and figures, detect any deviations in the system, and prevent any trajectory deviations or possible flight accidents [61, 62]. (2) Monitoring the environment can be done by using specific sensors (e.g., onboard cameras, etc.). In a maritime context, vessels can be tracked and identified (see [63]), or pollution by ship exhaust could be assessed [3].

In manned aviation, automation can lead to over-reliance on the system [64]. In Asiana Flight 214, the flight crew overlooked the fact that the automatic thrust control was no longer linked to the stabilization of the airspeed. As a result, the aircraft descended below the official glide path and collided with a seawall on approach to San Francisco in July 2013 ([65] National Transportation Safety Board, 2014). Similarly, automation of drone operations could lead to over-reliance on the system. As a consequence, safety would be compromised if flight parameters were not properly monitored in UAV missions ([61] Peysakhovich, 2018).

Handling crises and emergencies [24, 26, 27, 30, 37] requires effective error management based on good communication skills [66]. For example, in manned aviation, this involves a timely response to a standardized procedure such as an engine failure and a thorough problem analysis through information gathering, risk assessment, and decision-making. The decision-making process should include defining the problem, selecting a course of action, implementing the decision, and evaluating the outcome [40].

The definition of spatial orientation [24, 27, 33, 34] is not consistent in the existing research literature. In the context of aviation, spatial perception refers to the accurate detection of an aircraft's position, movement, and orientation relative to the Earth's surface [67]. Caraballo et al. [68] make a distinction between egocentric and allocentric representations. The former is described as self-object-centered, whereas the latter focuses on environmental information by object references. The authors postulate that the navigational performance of test subjects increases when both elements are combined. The cognitive representation of spatial perception in drone pilots is presumably influenced by distal factors that can be perceived directly by the pilot in manned aviation [34, p. 39]. According to Self et al. [67], the operator platform (mobile or stationary), the visual reference (external, egocentric, or exocentric), and the control mode of the drone (fully autonomous, manual, or semi-autonomous) are mentioned as influencing factors on the navigational performance of drone pilots. Approximately 5% of all unsafe UAV-Crew actions are assumed to be due to perceptual errors [45].

Within the included studies system knowledge [24, 26, 31, 37] refers to the basic theoretical knowledge of the drone's technical systems, including the engine, fuel system, electrical power supply, automatic control system, and elements of the navigation system. Furthermore, Irwin and Kelly [69, p. 56] cite proper system operation, knowledge of UAS operating limitations, as well as previous experience with system failures, maintenance personnel, and procedures. The manufacturers of drone systems provide this information, for example, in an operating manual for self-study or in the form of classroom seminars (see [15]). System knowledge training aims to qualify the crew to understand various engine and system displays and to recognize the proper system operations. Furthermore, the crew should be able to assess the safe operation of the UAV, considering system failures and malfunctions [69].

The ability to listen is also referred to as oral comprehension [10, 31, 33]. It involves understanding what is heard. The listener takes in words and sentences from which a story is formed. In a deeper sense, the listener creates a mental model of the narrated content [70]. The International Civil Aviation Organization (abbr. ICAO) adds that the spoken accent or variety should be sufficiently intelligible to an international community of users [71]. Linguistic or situational complications as well as unexpected turns of events can lead to delays in the comprehension process or the need for clarification strategies (see [71]). Estival and Molesworth [72] point out that communication within the cockpit and with ATC is a factor in aviation accidents. The results of the aforementioned study show that understanding other pilots is the greatest communicative challenge for the pilots surveyed. In a study conducted by Grindley et al. [45], it was found that any communication by drone pilots was responsible for 23.1% of the mishaps reported between 2012 and 2022.

As to category flexibility [10, 27, 33], Howse [33] describes a cognitive information processing method in which categories are organized flexibly. This involves the ability to create rules that specify how a set of items can be regrouped. In later publications [10, 27], this definition is supplemented by the property of mental adaptability. At the time of this report, no significant studies are available that establish a relationship between category flexibility and safe drone operation. However, there is scientific evidence in the area of solving complex problems with a high degree of system automation: Kessler et al. [73] demonstrate that the flexible application of conceptual and procedural knowledge enables the transfer of known solution models to novel situations.

The estimation of the time required to reach a flight target is referred to as the estimation of time to contact [24, 27, 33]. In their 2017 study, Carretta et al. [27] refer to the estimation of time and distance, whereas Hagl et al. [24] discuss the evaluation of visual data. This capability is crucial for planning and executing maritime RPAS operations, as it addresses two common challenges encountered: specifying the time required to reach a mission objective, such as the search area for a missing person [16], and determining the time required to cover flight distances. An example of this is a mission abort with the drone flying back along an unforeseen flight route [24]. Given that autonomous in-flight replanning is not yet a fully operational system [74, 75], the drone pilot must estimate the required flight path time. Subordinate cognitive processes may include the correct assessment of flight information such as location, distance, and remaining power [57].

Volkov et al. [36] define organization/time management [10, 33, 36] as the creation of a schedule for the allocation of resources. In an alternative interpretation, time management refers to the prioritization of upcoming activities based on their urgency [33]. Based on interview analysis with experienced drone pilots, Doroftei et al. [76] found that critical factors influencing human performance include the difficulty, complexity, duration, and nature of the task. One crucial countermeasure is the prioritized management of broken-down subtasks. This entails the task management behavior with the prioritization of the most effective cost/benefit sub-tasks [77].

The ability to ignore irrelevant targets and recognize relevant ones is referred to as attention [31, 33, 34]. This purely visual attention selection is enhanced by vigilance for acoustic information. Sustained and divided attention is provided for visual and auditory sources [33]. The focus of attention on selective perception can be regarded as a sub-aspect of situational awareness, which in turn is one of the most frequently cited human factors for causing drone accidents [30].

Reasoning [27, 33, 35] refers to a cognitive information processing process that monitors one's logical thinking [35]. Sub-processes include tasks such as general reasoning, real-time problem-solving, prioritizing tasks, evaluating risks, and assessing potential consequences [33]. The "inductive reasoning" and "deductive reasoning" skills analyzed above are components of reasoning [58]. Together, they form the basis of decision-making [58], which in turn was identified as the most frequently mentioned competence for safe drone operation [45].

Conscientiousness [10, 27, 33] is a personality trait associated with the attributes of organization, self-discipline, and reliability [10, 27]. In manned aviation, a high level of conscientiousness is seen as a predictor of pilots' attitude to flight safety (see [78]).

To our knowledge, no comparable studies are currently available for RPAS crews.

Gyagenda et al. [79] define navigation [10, 24, 36] as a meta-skill consisting of the skills of perception, localization, movement planning, and movement control. Consideration of the complexity of the environment and the mission is required to avoid obstacles, as might be mapping these. Navigating a drone in a maritime context can be challenging due to the lack of geographical reference points. Locating an emergency landing area is also difficult in this environment.

Hand-eye coordination [10, 27, 32] is a crucial skill for UAV operators. Drone pilots must be able to master the psychomotor process of flying, which requires a precise interplay of take-off and landing procedures [80, 81]. This process is an important safety measure to prevent drone crashes or incidents [57]. In situations where the drone's flight behavior exceeds the logical thinking of the operator, it may be necessary to intervene manually to safely achieve the mission objectives [82] or perform an emergency landing. The latter scenario illustrates the challenges that drone pilots may face at sea, as emergency landing sites may not be available [83].

4 Conclusion

It is predicted that the commercial, private, and public use of drones will increase significantly in the coming years [1, 2, 8]. The required competencies of drone operators vary according to aspects such as the type of UAV used, the mission, and many more [24]. One area that has not been discussed so far is the use of drones in maritime applications. This study aimed to explore human factors that might contribute positively to maritime drone missions. Most currently available drone systems are highly automated in their operation [17]. The human complementary influencing factor of automated systems is situational awareness [39]. Situational awareness, in turn, is an essential competence frequently identified in this literature review, which is described by the authors Rahmani and Weckmann [30] as one of the decisive factors for drone accidents. Drone operators stationed at a ground control station must have a clear understanding of the drone's flight path and its surroundings from the drone's perspective. They must also maintain constant awareness of the operational situation to ensure successful drone operations. If unforeseen events such as bad weather or technical system errors occur, the situation must be reassessed and, if necessary, a decision made on how to proceed (e.g., aborting the search for a missing person at sea). The skills of decision-making, communication, and teamwork can be fundamental aids in this process. Although automation takes place, the drone pilot's manual flying skills are considered to be the last chance to be able to land the drone safely in the event of a total loss of control of the automated control system. Other areas of competence covered in this literature overview primarily include cognitive sub-processes of the five most common competencies: situational awareness, judgment/decision-making, communication, teamwork, and manual flying skills. For example, inductive and deductive reasoning can be assigned to decision-making skills. Furthermore, hand-eye coordination can be seen as a characteristic of flying skills.

One limitation of the review is the lack of precision in the measurement of the competencies. For instance, the monitoring status of UAVs and system monitoring is uniformly coded as monitoring systems. Additionally, studies of human factors in UAV operations have been published by a limited number of authors and have primarily focused on military personnel selection [27]. It is also important to note that we did not conduct comprehensive and systematic literature research, which may have resulted in the omission of certain sources.

The human factors presented in this article were identified mainly for the use of drones over land – simply because there was not sufficient literature to scan concerning maritime missions. It can be assumed that these factors apply to an even greater extent to crews in a maritime context. The operational structure is fundamentally the same, with the exception that single events or a combination of specific factors occurring at sea can lead to a more restricted situation. These include rapidly changing weather conditions, a lack of emergency landing areas, limited orientation, and difficult take-off and landing situations. In this context, it remains to be investigated whether the human factors presented, in particular the five most frequently mentioned, can be confirmed in an empirical evaluation as significant predictors of safe drone operation in maritime use. Our review presents essential human factors for UAV operators that can serve as a basis for the design of a future training concept for maritime drone crews.

Acknowledgments. The authors would like to thank the project partners and reviewers for their contribution to this work.

Disclosure of Interests. The authors have no competing interests to declare that are relevant to the content of this article.

References

1. Li, S., Cummings, M.L., Welton, B.: Assessing the impact of autonomy and overconfidence in UAV first-person view training. Appl. Ergon. **98**, 103580 (2022). https://doi.org/10.1016/j.apergo.2021.103580
2. WISO: Public Safety Drone Market Growth, Trends Global Forecast 2028. https://www.wiso-net.de/document/FSM__134670469?ZG_PORTAL=portal_ebsco. Accessed 24 Feb 2024
3. Wang, J., Zhou, K., Xing, W., Li, H., Yang, Z.: Applications, evolutions, and challenges of drones in maritime transport. J. Mar. Sci. Eng. **11**(11), 2056 (2023). https://doi.org/10.3390/jmse11112056
4. EMSA: EMSA remotely piloted aircraft flying over North Sea for enhanced maritime surveillance in support of Danish Authorities. https://emsa.europa.eu/newsroom/press-releases/item/4940-emsa-remotely-piloted-aircraft-flying-over-north-sea-for-enhanced-maritime-surveillance-in-support-of-danish-authorities.html. Accessed 12 Aug 2023
5. DLR: MaRPAS 3 (Maritimer RPAS-Betrieb 3). https://www.dlr.de/fl/desktopdefault.aspx/tabid-1149/1737_read-77205. Accessed 24 Feb 2024

6. Schuchardt, B.I., Dautermann, T., Donkels, A., Krause, S., Peinecke, N., Schwoch, G.: Maritime operation of an unmanned rotorcraft with tethered ship deck landing system. CEAS Aeronaut. J. **12**(3), 3–11 (2021). https://doi.org/10.1007/s13272-020-00472-9
7. Kapustina, L., Izakova, N., Makovkina, E., Khmelkov, M.: The global drone market: main development trends. SHS Web Conf. **129**, 11004 (2021). https://doi.org/10.1051/shsconf/202 112911004
8. Castellano, F.: Commercial Drones Are Revolutionizing Business Operations. https://www.toptal.com/finance/market-research-analyst/drone-market. Accessed 12 Aug 2023
9. Sonenshine, T.D.: Debating drones in the global information age. Fletcher Forum World Aff. **46**(2), 33–45 (2022)
10. Rose, M.R., Arnold, R.D., Howse, W.R.: Unmanned aircraft systems selection practices: current research and future directions. Mil. Psychol. **25**(5), 413–427 (2013). https://doi.org/10.1037/mil0000008
11. Aibin, M., et al.: Survey of RPAS autonomous control systems using artificial intelligence. IEEE Access **9**, 167580–167591 (2021). https://doi.org/10.1109/access.2021.3136226
12. Krystosik, A.: The use of drones in the maritime sector - areas and benefits. Sci. J. **67**, 139 (2021). https://orcid.org/0000-0003-2123-161x
13. Carippo, F., et al.: Unmanned aircraft systems integration into European airspace and operation over populated areas. http://www.europarl.europa.eu/thinktank/en/document/IPOL_S TU(2023)733124. Accessed 12 Aug 2023
14. Aabid, A., et al.: Reviews on design and development of unmanned aerial vehicle (drone) for different applications. J. Mech. Eng. Res. Dev. **45**(2), 53–69 (2022)
15. SwissDrones: Unmanned Aircraft Flight Manual SDO 50 V 2, SDO 50 V 3. (unpuplished document). SwissDrones Operating AG (2021)
16. Lyu, M., Zhao, Y., Huang, C., Huang, H.: Unmanned aerial vehicles for search and rescue: a survey. Remote Sens. **15**(13), 3266 (2023). https://doi.org/10.3390/rs15133266
17. Mohsan, S.A.H., Othman, N.Q.H., Li, Y., Alsharif, M.H., Khan, M.A.: Unmanned aerial vehicles (UAVs): practical aspects, applications, open challenges, security issues, and future trends. Intel. Serv. Robot. **16**, 109–137 (2023). https://doi.org/10.1007/s11370-022-00452-4
18. Duan, G.J., Zhang, P.F.: Research on application of UAV for maritime supervision. J. Shipping Ocean Eng. **4**, 322–326 (2014)
19. Telli, K., et al.: A comprehensive review of recent research trends on unmanned aerial vehicles (UAVs). Systems **11**(8), 400 (2023). https://doi.org/10.3390/systems11080400
20. Hobbs, A., Lyall, B.: Human factors guidelines for unmanned aircraft systems. Ergon. Des. Q. Hum. Fact. Appl. **24**(3), 23–28 (2016). https://doi.org/10.1177/1064804616640632
21. Fahlstrom, P., Gleason, T., Sadraey, M.: Introduction to UAV Systems. 5th edn. Wiley, New York (2022)
22. Lavallée, C.: The EU policy for civil drones: the challenge of governing emerging technologies. Inst. Eur. Stud. Policy Brief **1**, 1–7 (2019)
23. EASA: Commission Implementing Regulation (EU) 2019/947 of 24 May 2019 on the rules and procedures for the operation of unmanned aircraft. https://easa.europe.eu/en/document-library/regulations/commission-implementingregual-tion-eu-2019947. Accessed 7 Jan 2024
24. Hagl, M., Stolz, M., Papenfuß, A., Biella, M., Dwinger, K.: Mission flexible – minimum general requirements for a UAV training concept. In: 14th AHFE International Conference on Applied Human Factors and Ergonomics, pp. 191–201. AHFE International, San Francisco (2023). https://doi.org/10.54941/ahfe1003165

25. Pavlas, D., Burke, C.S., Fiore, S.M., Salas, E., Jensen, R., Fu, D.: Enhancing unmanned aerial system training: a taxonomy of knowledge, skills, attitudes, and methods. Proc. Hum. Fact. Ergon. Soc. Annu. Meet. **53**(26), 1903–1907 (2009). https://doi.org/10.1518/107118109X12524444083159
26. Schmidt, R., Schadow, J., Eißfeldt, H., Pecena, Y.: Insights on remote pilot competences and training needs of civil drone pilots. Transp. Res. Procedia **66**, 1–7 (2022). https://doi.org/10.1016/j.trpro.2022.12.001
27. Carretta, T.R., Rose, M.R., Bruskiewicz, K.T.: Selection methods for operators of remotely piloted aircraft systems. In: Cooke, N.J., Rowe, L.J., Bennett, W., Joralmon, D.Q. (eds.) Remotely Piloted Aircraft Systems: A Human Systems Integration Perspective, vol. 2017, pp. 137–162. Wiley, New Jersey (2017). https://doi.org/10.1002/9781118965900.ch7
28. Qi, S., Wang, F., Jing, L.: Unmanned aircraft system pilot/operator qualification requirements and training study. MATEC Web Conf. **179**, 03006 (2018). https://doi.org/10.1051/matecconf/201817903006
29. Cummings, M., Huang, L., Zhu, H., Finkelstein, D., Wei, R.: The impact of increasing autonomy on training requirements in a UAV supervisory control task. J. Cogn. Eng. Decis. Making **13**(4), 295–309 (2019). https://doi.org/10.1177/1555343419868917
30. Rahmani, H., Weckman, G.R.: Working under the shadow of drones: investigating occupational safety hazards among commercial drone pilots. IISE Trans. Occup. Ergon. Hum. Fact., 1–13 (2023). https://doi.org/10.1080/24725838.2023.2251009
31. Bennett, W., Bridewell, J.B., Rowe, L.J., Craig, S.D., Poole, H.M.: Training issues for remotely piloted aircraft systems from a human systems integration perspective. In: Cooke, N.J., Rowe, L.J., Bennett, W., Joralmon, D.Q. (eds.) Remotely Piloted Air-Craft Systems: A Human Systems Integration Perspective, vol. 2017, pp. 163–176. Wiley, New Jersey (2017). https://doi.org/10.1002/9781118965900.ch7
32. Carretta, T.R., Rose, M.R., Barron, L.G.: Predictive validity of UAS/RPA sensor operator training qualification measures. Int. J. Aviat. Psychol. **25**(1), 3–13 (2015). https://doi.org/10.1080/10508414.2015.981487
33. Howse, W.R.: Knowledge, skills, abilities, and other characteristics for remotely piloted aircraft pilots and operators. Defense Tech. Inf. Center (2011). https://doi.org/10.21236/ada552499
34. Johnsen, B.H., et al.: Selection of Norwegian police drone operators: an evaluation of selected cognitive tests from "The Vienna Test System." Police Pract. Res. **25**(1), 38–52 (2024). https://doi.org/10.1080/15614263.2023.2179052
35. Lercel, D., Andrews, D.H.: Cognitive task analysis of unmanned aircraft system pilots. Int. J. Aerosp. Psychol. **31**(4), 319–342 (2021). https://doi.org/10.1080/24721840.2021.1895797
36. Volkov, O., Komar, M., Synytsya, K., Volosheniuk, D.: The UAV simulation complex for operator training. In: Proceedings of the International Conference on e-Learning 2019, pp. 313–316. IADIS Press, Porto (2019). https://doi.org/10.33965/el2019_201909R044
37. Zhou, C., Zhao, T., Hu, K.: Research on pilot control ability of drones in medium and large branch logistics. In: 2nd International Conference on Big Data Engineering and Education (BDEE), pp. 125–128. IEEE, Chengdu (2022). https://doi.org/10.1109/BDEE55929.2022.00027
38. Endsley, M.R.: Situation awareness in aviation systems. In: Garland, D.J., Wise, J.A., Hopkin, V.D. (eds.) Handbook of Aviation Human Factors, 1st edn., pp. 257–276. Lawrence Erlbaum (1999)
39. Martins, A.P.G.: A review of important cognitive concepts in aviation. Aviation **20**(2), 65–84 (2016). https://doi.org/10.3846/16487788.2016.1196559
40. Haider S.: Ensuring aircraft safety in single point failures, automation and human factors. In: 2020 Annual Reliability and Maintainability Symposium (2020). https://doi.org/10.1109/rams48030.2020.9153682

41. Tvaryanas, A.P., Thompson, W.T., Constable, S.H.: US military unmanned aerial vehicle mishaps: assessment of the role of human factors using human factors analysis and classification system (HFACS). Am. Psychol. Assoc. (2006). https://doi.org/10.1037/e448052006-001
42. Endsley, M.R.: Toward a theory of situation awareness in dynamic systems. Hum. Fact. **37**(1), 32–64 (1995). https://doi.org/10.1518/001872095779049543
43. Karyotakis, M., Braithwaite, G.: Human factors and human performance in UAS Operations. The case of UAS pilots in UAM operations. In: Harris, D., Li, W.C. (eds.) Engineering Psychology and Cognitive Ergonomics, 1st edn., vol. 14018, pp. 254–279. Springer, Heidelberg (2023). https://doi.org/10.1007/978-3-031-35389-5
44. Rautenstrauch, T.: Datenbasierte Entscheidungsfindung im Rahmen des FORDEC-Modells. Controller Magazin **4**, 52–56 (2023)
45. Grindley, B., Phillips, K., Parnell, K. J., Cherrett, T., Scanlan, J.P., Plant, K.L.: A decade of UAV incidents: a human factors analysis of casual factors (2023). https://doi.org/10.2139/ssrn.4631986
46. Shannon, C.E., Weaver, W.: The Mathematical Theory of Communication. Urbana (1949)
47. Röhner, J., Schütz, A.: Psychologie der Kommunikation, 2nd edn. Springer, Cham (2016). https://doi.org/10.1007/978-3-658-10024-7
48. Wittmer, A., Roth, M.: Human factors in aviation. In: Wittmer, A., Bieger, T., Müller, R. (eds.) Aviation Systems, 2nd edn., pp. 355–386. Springer, Cham (2021). https://doi.org/10.1007/978-3-030-79549-8_12
49. Salas, E., Dickinson, T.L., Converse, S.A., Tannenbaum, S.I.: Toward an understanding of team performance and training. In: Swezey, R.W., Salas, E. (eds.) Teams: Their Training and Performance, 1st edn., pp. 3–29. Ablex, New York (1992)
50. Greilich, P.E., et al.: Team FIRST framework: identifying core teamwork competencies critical to interprofessional healthcare curricula. J. Clin. Transl. Sci. **7**(1) (2023). https://doi.org/10.1017/cts.2023.27
51. Salas, E., Burke, C.S., Cannon-Bowers, J.A.: Teamwork: emerging principles. Int. J. Manag. Rev. **2**(4), 339–356 (2000). https://doi.org/10.1111/1468-2370.00046
52. de Wit, P.A., Moraes Cruz, R.: Learning from AF447: human-machine interaction. Saf. Sci. **112**, 48–56 (2019). https://doi.org/10.1016/j.ssci.2018.10.009
53. Haslbeck, A., Kirchner, P., Schubert, E., Bengler, K.: A flight simulator study to evaluate manual flying skills of airline pilots. Proc. Hum. Fact. Ergon. Soc. Annu. Meet. **58**(1), 11–15 (2014). https://doi.org/10.1177/1541931214581003
54. Childs, J.M., Spears, W.D.: Flight-skill decay and recurrent training. Percept. Mot. Skills **62**(1), 235–242 (1986). https://doi.org/10.2466/pms.1986.62.1.235
55. Kuskapan, E., Çodur, M.Y.: Examination of aircraft accidents that occurred in the last 20 years in the world. Düzce Üniversitesi Bilim ve Teknoloji Dergisi **9**(1), 174–188 (2021). https://doi.org/10.29130/dubited.754339
56. Ross, J., Seto, M., Johnston, C.: Autonomous landing of rotary wing unmanned aerial vehicles on underway ships in a sea state. J. Intell. Rob. Syst. **104**(1), 1–9 (2022). https://doi.org/10.1007/s10846-021-01515-x
57. Peng, L., Li, K.W.: Perceived difficulty, flight information access, and performance of male and female novice drone operators. Work **72**(4), 1259–1268 (2022). https://doi.org/10.3233/WOR-210862
58. Stephens, R.G., Dunn, J.C., Hayes, B.K.: Are there two processes in reasoning? The dimensionality of inductive and deductive inferences. Psychol. Rev. **125**(2), 218–244 (2018). https://doi.org/10.1037/rev0000088
59. Maurer, P.M.: Teaching induction and deductive reasoning. In: 2022 International Conference on Computational Science and Computational Intelligence (CSCI), pp. 2049–2053. IEEE, Las Vegas (2022). https://doi.org/10.1109/CSCI58124.2022.00368

60. Gazzo Castañeda, L.E., Sklarek, B., Dal Mas, D.E., Knauff, M.: Probabilistic and deductive reasoning in the human brain. Neuroimage **275**, 120180 (2023). https://doi.org/10.1016/j.neuroimage.2023.120180
61. Peysakhovich, V., Lefrançois, O., Dehais, F., Causse, M.: The neuroergonomics of air-craft cockpits: the four stages of eye-tracking integration to enhance flight safety. Safety **4**(8), 1–15 (2018). https://doi.org/10.3390/safety4010008
62. Sumwalt, R., Cross, D., Lessard, D.: Examining how breakdowns in pilot monitoring of the aircraft flight path. Int. J. Aviat. Aeronaut. Aerosp. **2**(3), 1–25 (2015). https://doi.org/10.15394/ijaaa.2015.1063
63. Marques, M.M., et al.: An unmanned aircraft system for maritime operations: the automatic detection subsystem. Mar. Technol. Soc. J. **55**(1), 38–49 (2021). https://doi.org/10.4031/mtsj.55.1.4
64. Parasuraman, R., Riley, V.: Humans and automation: use, misuse, disuse, abuse. Hum. Fact. J. Hum. Fact. Ergon. Soc. **39**(2), 230–253 (1997). https://doi.org/10.1518/001872097778543886
65. National Transportation Safety Board: Aircraft Accident Report, Descent Below Visual Glidepath and Impact with Deawall, Asiana Airlines Flight 214, Boeing 777–200ER, HL7742, San Francisco, California 6 July 2013 (Report No. AAR-14/01)
66. Malakis, S., Kontogiannis, T.: Refresher training for air traffic controllers: is it adequate to meet the challenges of emergencies and abnormal situations? Int. J. Aviat. Psychol. **22**(1), 59–77 (2012). https://doi.org/10.1080/10508414.2012.635127
67. Self, B.P., Ercoline, W.R., Olson, W.A., Tvaryanas, A.P.: 10. spatial disorientation in uninhabited aerial vehicles. Human factors of remotely operated vehicles. In: Self, B.P., Ercoline, W.R., Olson, W.A., Tvaryanas, A.P. (eds.) Advances in Human Performance and Cognitive Engineering Research, vol. 7, pp. 133–146. Elsevier, Amsterdam (2006)
68. Caraballo, I., Lara-Bocanegra, A., Bohórquez, M.R.: Factors related to the performance of elite young sailors in a regatta: spatial orientation, age and experience. Int. J. Environ. Res. Public Health **18**(6), 2913 (2021). https://doi.org/10.3390/ijerph18062913
69. Irwin, W., Kelly, T.: Airline pilot situation awareness: presenting a conceptual model for meta-cognition, reflection and education. Aviation **25**(1), 50–64 (2021). https://doi.org/10.3846/aviation.2021.14209
70. Hogan, T.P., Adlof, S.M., Alonzo, C.N.: On the importance of listening comprehension. Int. J. Speech Lang. Pathol. **16**(3), 199–207 (2014). https://doi.org/10.3109/17549507.2014.904441
71. Read, J., Knoch, U.: Clearing the air: applied linguistic perspectives on aviation communication. Aust. Rev. Appl. Linguist. **32**(3), 21.1–21.11 (2009). https://doi.org/10.2104/aral0921
72. Estival, D., Molesworth, B.: A study of EL2 pilots' radio communication in the general aviation environment. Aust. Rev. Appl. Linguist. **32**(3), 24.1–24.16 (2009). https://doi.org/10.2104/aral0924
73. Kessler, F., et al.: Promoting complex problem solving by introducing schema-governed categories of key causal models. Behav. Sci. **13**(9), 701 (2023). https://doi.org/10.3390/bs13090701
74. Wang, X., et al.: A mini review on UAV mission planning. J. Ind. Manag. Optim. **19**(5), 3362–3382 (2023). https://doi.org/10.3934/jimo.2022089
75. Usach, H., Vila, J.A.: Reconfigurable mission plans for RPAS. Aerosp. Sci. Technol. **96**, 105528 (2020). https://doi.org/10.1016/j.ast.2019.105528
76. Doroftei, D., De Cubber, G., De Smet, H.: Reducing drone incidents by incorporating human factors in the drone and drone pilot accreditation process. In: Zallio, M. (ed.) Advances in Human Factors in Robots, Drones and Unmanned Systems, pp. 71–77. Springer, Heidelberg (2020). https://doi.org/10.1007/978-3-030-51758-8_10

77. Rusou, Z., Amar, M., Ayal, S.: The psychology of task management: the smaller tasks trap. Judgm. Decis. Mak. **15**(4), 586–599 (2020). https://doi.org/10.1017/s1930297500007518
78. Ali, M.A., Malik, A.A.: Personality traits and safety attitude among aviators: a correlational study. Pak. J. Clin. Psychol. **21**(2), 3–31 (2022)
79. Gyagenda, N., Hatilima, J.V., Roth, H., Zhmud, V.: A review of GNSS-independent UAV navigation techniques. Robot. Auton. Syst. **152**, 104069 (2022). https://doi.org/10.1016/j.robot.2022.104069
80. Linga, O.: Automatic landing of multi-rotor on a floating maritime platform. Master's thesis, Norwegian University of Science and Technology (2020). https://hdl.handle.net/11250/2780954
81. Edney, A.J., et al.: Best practices for using drones in seabird monitoring and research. Mar. Ornithol. **51**, 265–280 (2023)
82. Reddy, P., Richards, D., Izzetoglu, H.: Evaluation of UAS operator training during search and surveillance tasks. In: 20th International Symposium on Aviation Psychology, pp. 211–216 (2019)
83. Ambroziak, L., et al.: Experimental tests of hybrid VTOL unmanned aerial vehicle designed for surveillance missions and operations in maritime conditions from ship-based helipads. J. Field Rob. **39**(3), 203–217 (2021). https://doi.org/10.1002/rob.22046

Piloting Continuous Neurophysiological Monitoring for Adapted Training of Public Safety Officers

Danielle Benesch[1](✉)[⬤], Tanya S. Paul[1][⬤], Alexandre Marois[2][⬤], Simon Paré[3][⬤], and Gregory P. Kratzig[4][⬤]

[1] Thales Research and Technology Canada, Quebec City, Canada
{danielle.benesch,tanya.paul}@thalesgroup.com
[2] École de psychologie, Université Laval, Quebec City, Canada
alexandre.marois@psy.ulaval.ca
[3] Public Safety Canada, Ottawa, Canada
simon6449@smtp.gc.ca
[4] Department of Psychology, University of Regina, Regina, Canada
gregory.kratzig@rcmp-grc.gc.ca

Abstract. Designing training programs such that students are fully prepared for real-world scenarios can be challenging, particularly when preparing individuals for safety-critical roles that necessitate performing under conditions of high stress and mental workload. A possible avenue for improving training programs is to adapt them according to the stress and mental workload experienced by trainees during each training scenario. However, self-assessments can disrupt the training process and may not always be accurate. To address this, the project proposes a continuous neurophysiological monitoring system that tracks each trainee's stress and mental workload, allowing instructors to view their development during training scenarios. The deployment of the system was piloted with four participants at the same time as they performed several conditions of the Revised Multi-Attribute Task Battery. Stress was induced by increasing the number of events, adding unpleasant sounds, and informing participants their tasks will be graded by the experimenters, while increased workload was induced by asking participants to perform more subtasks at the same time. After each task, participants provided subjective measures of stress and mental workload. Throughout the experiment, cardiorespiratory and brain activity were collected via a near-infrared spectroscopy headband, a smartshirt, and a smartwatch. These signals were processed in real time by the Sensor Hub system, running previously developed models of stress and mental workload for all four participants. The pilot data demonstrate the feasibility of instructors monitoring multiple students simultaneously using wearable sensors and real-time signal processing, with the potential to better prepare individuals for high stress and workload roles.

Keywords: Functional near-infrared spectroscopy (fNIRS) · Electrocardiography (ECG) · Real-time signal processing

1 Introduction

In safety-critical roles such as law enforcement, the capacity to handle high levels of stress and mental workload is of paramount importance. Stressors that may be faced in these roles include managing multiple information sources, dealing with incomplete or conflicting information, navigating rapidly changing scenarios, coordinating within a team under pressure, enduring adverse physical conditions, handling performance and time pressures, dealing with high workloads, auditory overload or interference, and physical threats [10]. Therefore, including such stressors in training could help prepare for safety-critical roles. Through controlled exposure to situations representative of their future roles, trainees may learn to manage their stress levels and mental workload more effectively [29]. However, designing training scenarios such that they elicit the appropriate amount of stress and mental workload at the right stage of the training is challenging [13].

One approach to address this challenge is to use self-reports or task performance to inform training [24,36]. However, self-report measures, such as the NASA Task Load Index (NASA-TLX) [18], can be impractical for real-world training environments by disrupting the training and only providing a snapshot dependent on the trainee's state at the time of the measurement [37]. Depending on the nature of the task, performance may also only be assessed infrequently, missing fluctuations in a trainee's state that occur between assessments. Furthermore, performance metrics may fail to explain why a trainee is struggling, or conversely, to identify that a trainee has exhausted their cognitive resources despite satisfactory performance [12]. This limitation can be particularly problematic in safety-critical roles where trainees must be prepared for additional stressors not present in the training environment. If a trainee is already at the limits of their cognitive resources during training, additional stressors in real-world scenarios could lead to mission failure.

In order to obtain a more comprehensive assessment of training, various neurophysiological measures have been explored, including functional Near-Infrared Spectroscopy (fNIRS) [7,22,25], electroencephalography (EEG) [4,9,12], eye-tracking [7], electrooculography (EOG) [9], Electrodermal Activity (EDA) [7], respiration [7,13,38], and heart activity [4,7,9,13,22,37,38]. Thanks to advances in wearable sensing technology, these measures can be taken with relatively little disruption to the training program and enable trainees and instructors to have increased awareness of the cognitive demands experienced in real time during training sessions. By analyzing data from neurophysiological measures alongside contextual information about the training environment, instructors can tailor their feedback and interventions to meet the specific needs of each trainee. Additionally, aggregating data from trainees and teams could inform the design of future training programs and workflows, with the potential to better prepare individuals for stressors commonly experienced in their roles.

The current study builds on previous work designing a near real-time neurophysiological monitoring system tailored for training, termed *Sensing Humans for Augmented Debrief (SHAD)*. Responding to needs identified by two

Canadian public safety organizations, the SHAD dashboard was developed to track trainees' neurophysiological responses and contextual data during various stages of training, with views for live monitoring, post-scenario analysis with video playback, and data retrieval of multiple trainees and sessions [26]. In order to have higher-level actionable information available to the instructors, beyond the raw neurophysiological signals, machine learning models to predict stress [5] and mental workload [30] were developed and integrated into the monitoring system.

The objective of the current work is to pilot the deployment of the monitoring system under conditions aiming to induce fluctuations in stress and mental workload. More specifically, this study aims to demonstrate the feasibility of using such an approach to measure multiple neurophysiological features related to stress and workload in real time, while collecting behavioral measures from a realistic task imposing demands typical of several operational domains, with potential applications to various training contexts. To this end, four participants carried out an experimental protocol with different conditions of the Multi-Attribute Task Battery II (MATB-II) cognitive task while wearing sensors connected to the monitoring system. In the next sections, we describe in details all the components of the task carried out by the participants as well as the neurophysiological measure components. Descriptive pilot data from the four participants collected are presented to demonstrate the full system's capacity, and potential improvements to the system are discussed.

2 Monitoring System

The SHAD monitoring system developed for public safety personnel training is based on the Sensor Hub solution, a near real-time, sensor-agnostic data integration, synchronization, and processing nexus that allows sampling data from multiple sensors and users. To facilitate the processing of the data of multiple sensors and users, the system uses a microservices architecture where data is shared over a common bus. Data sharing is implemented using the Message Queuing Telemetry Transport (MQTT) protocol. MQTT allows sensors and application components to publish and subscribe to data topics, promoting system modularity and extensibility.

For the pilot data collection described in this paper, all sensors worn by an individual were connected to a mobile phone, as shown in Fig. 1a. The Sensor Hub mobile application on the phone processes the data and runs machine learning models to extract higher-level features. The relevant data, features, and model predictions can then be published on MQTT and persisted in a database containing all the timestamped data from each user. The unified raw data from the sensors, extracted features, and model predictions are available both in (near) real-time for immediate visualization as well as saved in Comma Separated Value (CSV) format for further analysis.

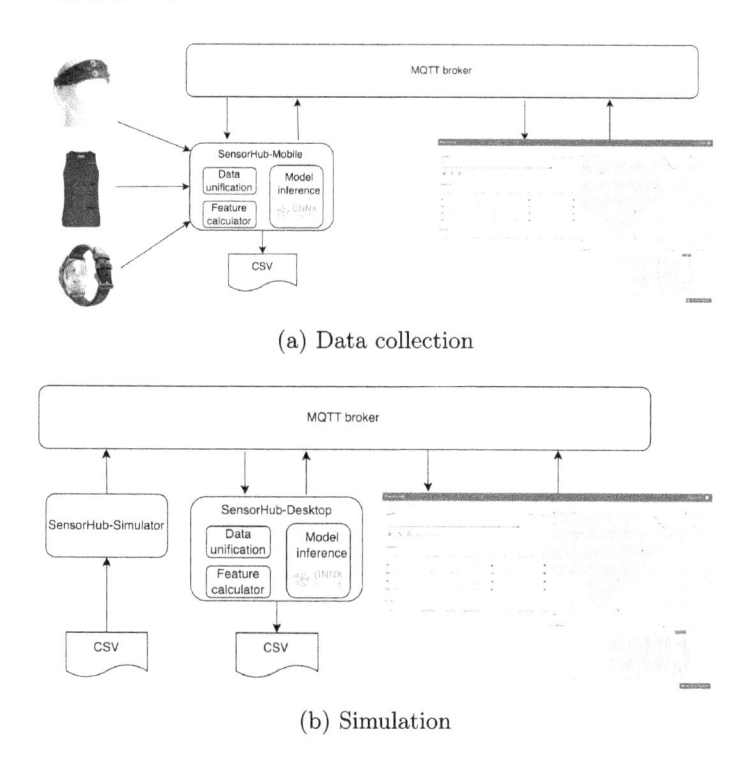

Fig. 1. Architecture of SHAD monitoring system.

The Sensor Hub also includes a simulation functionality to publish and subscribe to existing data via MQTT, allowing services to operate in near real time. This functionality is particularly useful for testing adjustments without having to collect new data each time. As shown in Fig. 1b, previously collected CSV files are processed with a desktop application running the same components that run on the mobile application, e.g., feature extraction implemented in Java and machine learning models running with Open Neural Network Exchange (ONNX) Runtime. As in a data collection setup, the extracted features and model predictions are available both in CSV format and in real time, where they can be streamed to dashboards such as the one developed for SHAD.

Sensor Hub can be configured with different sensors, feature extraction algorithms, and machine learning models. The specific choices and features developed for the SHAD monitoring system are detailed further in this section.

2.1 Sensors

The following devices are integrated into SHAD to collect various neurophysiological data:

- **Hexoskin Smart Shirt:** The Hexoskin garment (Carré Technologies Inc., Montreal, Canada) captures acceleration, respiration, and electrocardiography (ECG) data. Additionally, respiration rate, heart rate and R-R intervals

(the exact number of milliseconds between heartbeats) are calculated in real time by the Hexoskin device.
- **Wear OS Smart Watch:** Heart rate based on Photoplethysmography (PPG) recorded from the wrist was recorded from either the TicWatch or Fossil smart watches, both running Wear OS. The watch was used as a supplementary sensor for heart rate measurements, as data redundancies can improve the reliability of ambulatory physiological data recordings [33].
- **Octamon fNIRS:** Continuous wave fNIRS were recorded using either the Octamon headband or Octamon+ headcap (Artinis Medical Systems, Netherlands). Both devices include two receivers (Rx) and eight transmitters (Tx), transmitting two wavelengths (± 760 nm and ± 850 nm). The OxySoft software provided by Artinis (running on a laptop connected to the Octamon via Bluetooth) recorded the raw data and applied an algorithm based on the modified Beer-Lambert law to calculate concentration changes in oxy-hemoglobin and deoxy-hemoglobin.

Each participant had a Pixel 4a smartphone, which included a GPS, a camera and a microphone. The phone connected to all sensors worn by the participant. The Hexoskin smart shirt and Wear OS smart watch were connected directly via Bluetooth to the phone, while a laptop running the fNIRS OxySoft software was connected to the phone via Transmission Control Protocol (TCP) socket.

2.2 Algorithms

All algorithms were executed in near real time on the phone, with each feature extraction algorithm and model running approximately every second. The feature extraction algorithms were implemented in Java, and all supervised machine learning models were implemented with the Sci-kit learn library and exported to the ONNX format. The specific models included:

- **Stress:** This model's inputs were the baseline-normalized respiration rate and heart rate, both normalized by dividing the current rate by mean values recorded during a baseline phase [5]. The model was a binary Random Forest (RF) classifier predicting high vs. low stress. However, in order to have a continuous variable representing stress level, one approach that can be used is taking the probability of predicting the high stress class [27]. For RF classifiers implemented in Scikit-learn, this probability represents "the mean predicted class probabilities of the trees in the forest. The class probability of a single tree is the fraction of samples of the same class in a leaf" [31].
- **Mental Workload:** This model used features extracted from fNIRS data as input. First, the oxy-hemoglobin and deoxy-hemoglobin signals passed through a third-order digital Butterworth filter with a low cut-off of 0.008 Hz and high cut-off of 0.2 Hz. Mean, kurtosis, and skewness calculated with the filtered signals from each channel, using 20-second windows. The model took three features as input: the mean and kurtosis for the deoxy-hemoglobin from Tx8 and the kurtosis for the deoxy-hemoglobin from Tx3 [30]. Like the stress

model, the mental workload model was a binary RF classifier and provided the probability of predicting high mental workload as an output.
- **Activity Recognition:** This model was developed based on previous work [33], using features calculated from acceleration data to identify user activities. The dashboard displayed the output of the model icons representing the predicted class (e.g., running, walking, standing). While the model was included in SHAD to provide additional contextual information for scenarios in which trainees are moving, the current work does not focus on this model, as the experimental protocol only included tasks during which the participants remained relatively static.

3 Protocol

3.1 Task

The MATB-II [34] cognitive task was used under multiple conditions. Developed by NASA, the MATB-II is a computer-based tool used for assessing human performance and cognitive workload. It encompasses four main subtasks: system monitoring, resource management, tracking, and communications. These tasks simulate complex, multi-tasking environments and evaluate an individual's capacity to perform multiple tasks simultaneously. The number of events in MATB-II can be configured, allowing for the manipulation of task difficulty.

Participants went through experimental conditions aiming to manipulate stress and mental load. In the low-load conditions, participants performed two subtasks of the MATB-II task: system monitoring and resource management. In the high-load conditions, participants performed all four subtasks of the MATB-II task. Table 1 provides a summary of the MATB-II parameters used to manipulate the stress condition. In the low-stress conditions, participants performed the MATB-II with less frequent events. In the high-stress conditions, participants performed the MATB-II with more frequent events, as well as with further stressors added: (1) participants were asked to perform all four subtasks with unpleasant auditory stimuli [23], and (2) participants were told that their performance would be graded. These stressors were added with the aim to be more representative of some of the challenges that may be simultaneously experienced in law enforcement (rapidly changing scenarios, performance pressure, auditory overload/interference, etc.) [10].

This resulted in the following four conditions, which each participant did in a randomized order:

1. High stress + High load: four subtasks, more events (i.e., the high-stress parameters in Table 1), with additional auditory stimuli, participants told that their performance would be graded.
2. Low stress + High load: four subtasks, fewer events, without additional auditory stimuli, participants told that their performance would not be graded.
3. High stress + Low load: two subtasks, more events, with additional auditory stimuli, participants told that their performance would be graded.

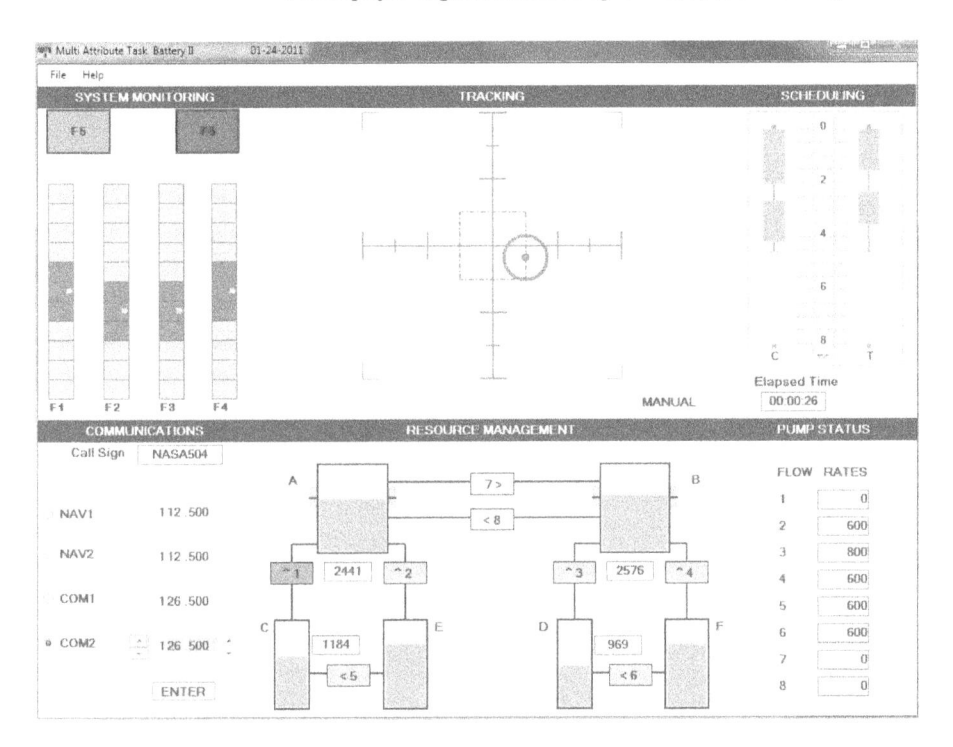

Fig. 2. A screenshot of the MATB-II task, which consists of the subtasks system monitoring, resource management, tracking, and communications.

Table 1. MATB-II parameters used to manipulate the stress condition.

Subtask	Parameter	High-stress	Low-stress
All subtasks	Seconds between events	[10, 35]	[20, 70]
Resource Management	# of pump failures	6	3
Communications	# of own call sign	6	2
Communications	# of other call sign	6	3
System monitoring	# of green-red issues	7	3
System monitoring	# of up-down issues	7	3
Tracking	Total minutes in auto mode	3	6

4. Low stress + Low load: two subtasks, fewer events, without additional auditory stimuli, participants told that their performance would not be graded.

3.2 Procedure

A diagram of the order of each experimental phase is shown in Fig. 3.

214   D. Benesch et al.

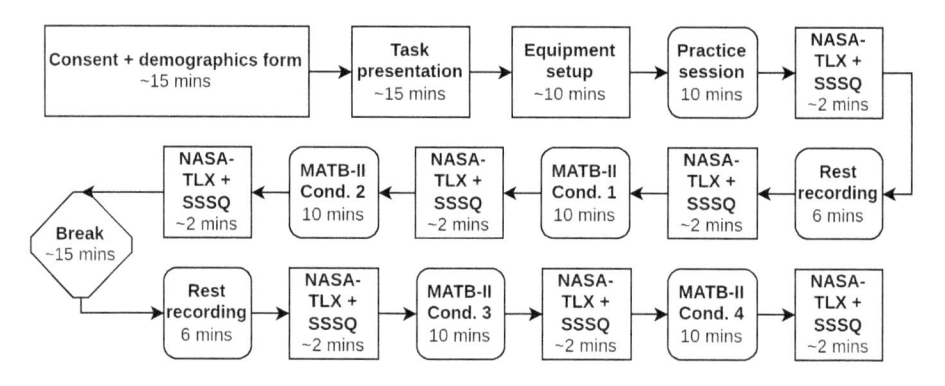

Fig. 3. The sequence of events during the experiment. The MATB-II conditions were randomized for each participant.

Practice Session. After a presentation with an explanation of task, participants did the task for 10 minutes. They were asked to do all four subtasks, and the number of events was the same as the low stress conditions (see Table 1). Then, they completed the NASA-TLX [18] and Short Stress State Questionnaire (SSSQ) [19], to assess their mental load and stress, respectively. After completing these questionnaires, participants had a final opportunity to ask questions about the task before a rest recording.

Rest Recordings. There were two rest recordings: (1) after the practice session and before the first MATB-II condition, and (2) after the break and before the third MATB-II condition. During the rest recording, participants were asked to focus on a black fixation cross shown on a white background for six minutes until the screen faded to black. After each rest recording, participants completed the NASA-TLX and SSSQ. The six-minute duration was chosen to have sufficient length for heart rate variability recordings, while also accounting for anticipation and recovery of stress tasks.

MATB-II Conditions. The sequence of the MATB-II conditions was randomized for every participant. After each condition, participants were asked to complete the NASA-TLX and SSSQ scales.

The Python code used to generate the Extensible Markup Language (XML) configuration files for the various conditions of MATB-II, the auditory stimuli sequences, and the video of the fixation cross used for the baseline recording can be found at https://github.com/ThalesGroup/requin-2023-experiment.

4   Pilot Deployment

4.1   Participants

The pilot study involved four participants (two female and two male; age ranging from 23 to 37), all of whom were employed at Thales Research and Technology.

These participants did not have specific expertise related to public safety, as the goal of this pilot testing was to evaluate the developed monitoring system and experimental protocol before testing them on the target population.

Due to limitations in available equipment, not all participants used the same monitoring devices. This also tested for the possibility to manage data from multiple sensors. One participant was equipped with the Octamon headband, and another with the Octamon Plus headcap. All participants wore Hexoskin smart shirts and TicWatch or Fossil smartwatches, which collected data on their cardiorespiratory activity and movement. Also note that one participant had to stop the experiment early after completing the first two sessions of MATB-II.

4.2 Stress and Mental Workload Predictions

Throughout the pilot study, the models developed for predicting stress and mental workload were run approximately once every second. The output of these models was the probability of a participant experiencing high stress or high workload at that moment. These probabilities were then multiplied by 100 and displayed in the dashboard as continuous values representing stress and workload levels as percentages, aiming to make the data more interpretable beyond the binary classification of high or low stress/workload. However, during the pilot study, it was observed that levels frequently reached their maximum values.

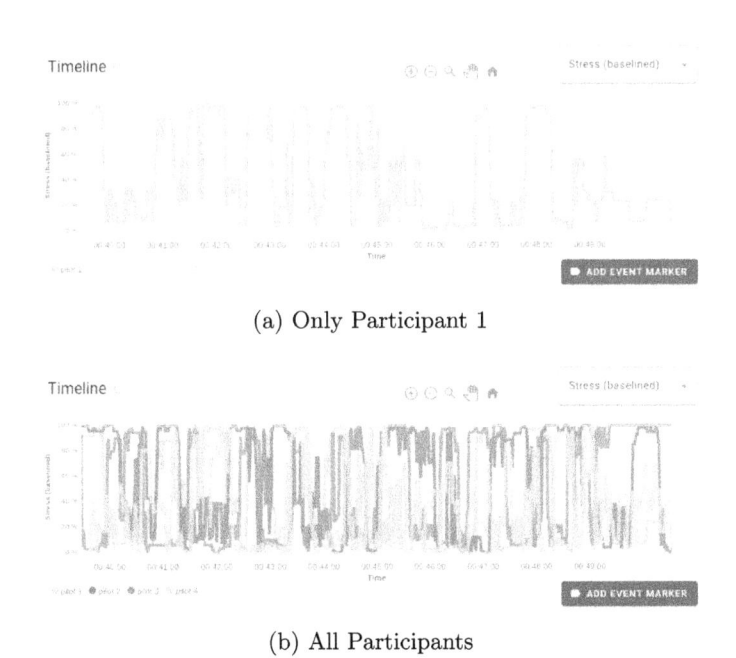

(a) Only Participant 1

(b) All Participants

Fig. 4. Detected stress levels (probability represented as a percentage) shown in dashboard. Each color corresponds to the data one participant.

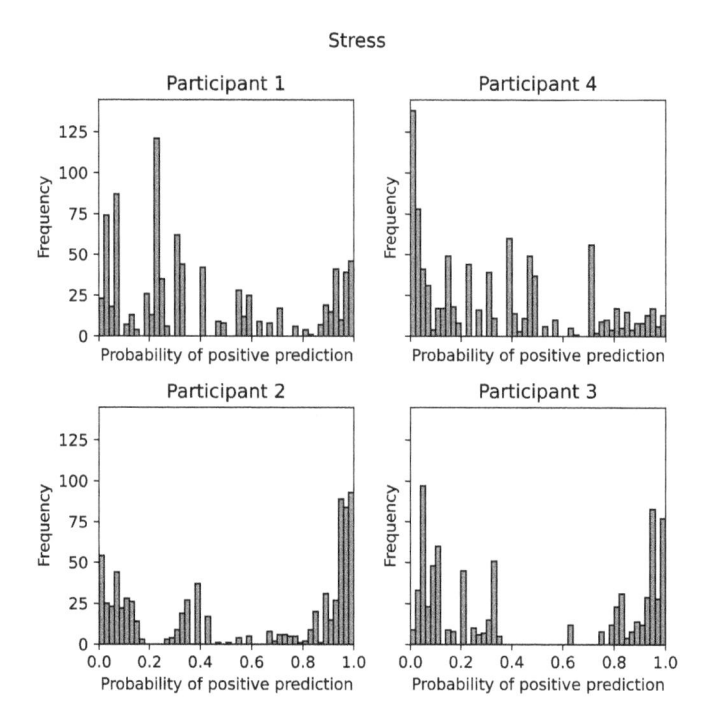

Fig. 5. Histogram showing the distribution of the probability of predicting high stress for each participant.

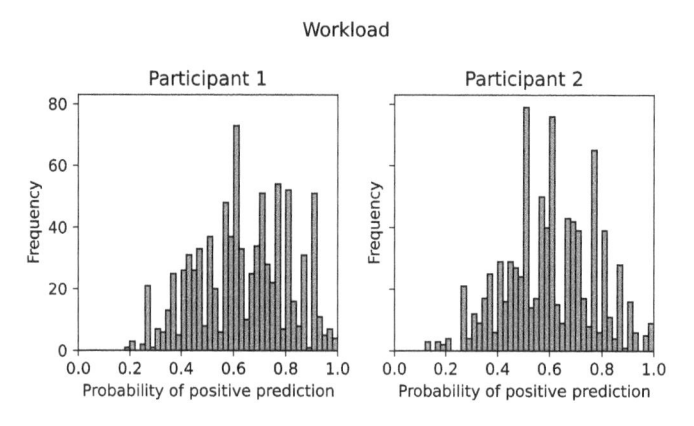

Fig. 6. Histogram showing the distribution of the probability of predicting high mental workload for each participant who wore the fNIRS device.

In particular, frequent sharp transitions between high and low probabilities created challenges in comparing measures between participants in the dashboard, as illustrated in Fig. 4.

Figures 5 and 6 illustrate the distribution of predicted stress and workload probabilities for each participant. Each probability value was grouped into bins to visualize the frequency of predictions falling within specific ranges. It was observed that all participants reached the maximum bin (probability of at least 0.98, displayed as 98% on the dashboard) for both stress and mental workload during the experiment. This high-frequency maximum bin indicates periods where the dashboard indicated that participants were under the maximum possible level of stress and workload.

4.3 Simulation and Model Adjustments

To better understand the observed probabilities, the influence of the input features on model output was analyzed. Given the well-established relationship between cardiorespiratory features and stress [17], including in the context of public safety [2,3,7,22,38], the probabilities of predicting high stress were plotted as a function of baseline-normalized heart and breathing rates. Two initial models were considered: the original RF model used the pilot study, as well as a Logistic Regression (LR) model, since it is more interpretable and had only slightly lower mean cross-validation performance on the training dataset (80.16 accuracy for logistic regression vs. 80.86 accuracy for the original RF model, see [5]). Figure 7 illustrates the decision boundaries and probabilities of high stress for both models. It can be seen that the decision boundaries of both models were primarily influenced by the baseline-normalized heart rate, with the decision boundary being approximately at 1.0, corresponding to whether the heart rate increased (more than 1.0) or decreased (less than 1.0) relative to the baseline heart rate. Both models also show similar trends for the probability of high stress: for the range of features displayed, the majority of the probabilities saturate to 0 or 1 after reaching a certain baseline-normalized heart rate. For example, it can be seen that a baseline-normalized heart rate of 1.25 results in

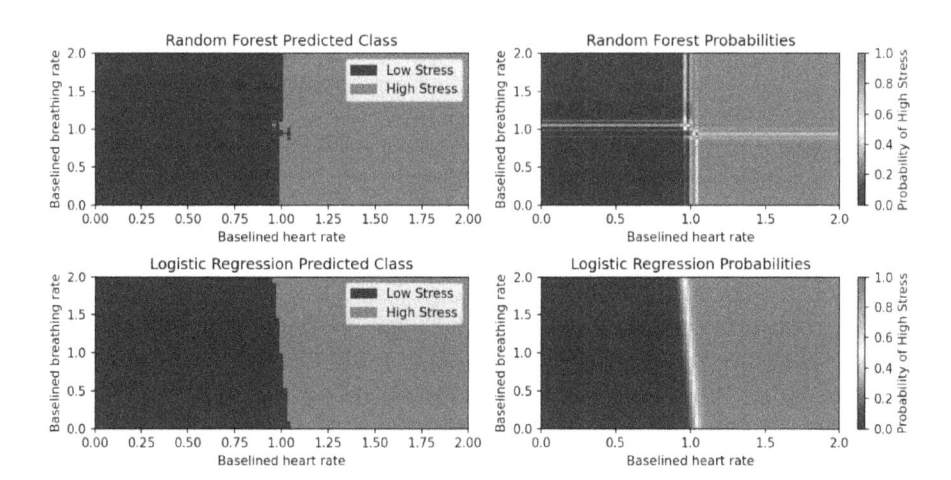

Fig. 7. Predicted class and probabilities of predicting high stress for the original RF and LR models.

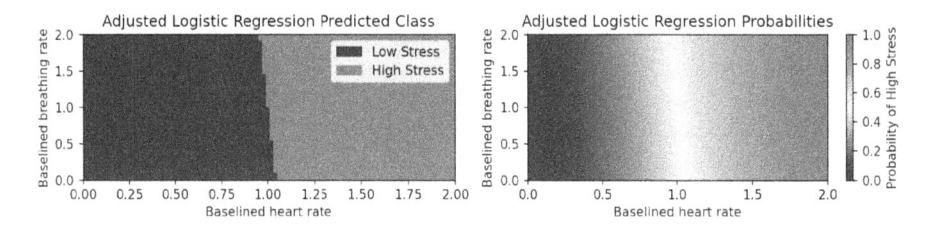

Fig. 8. Predicted class and probabilities of predicting high stress for the LR model with adjusted coefficients.

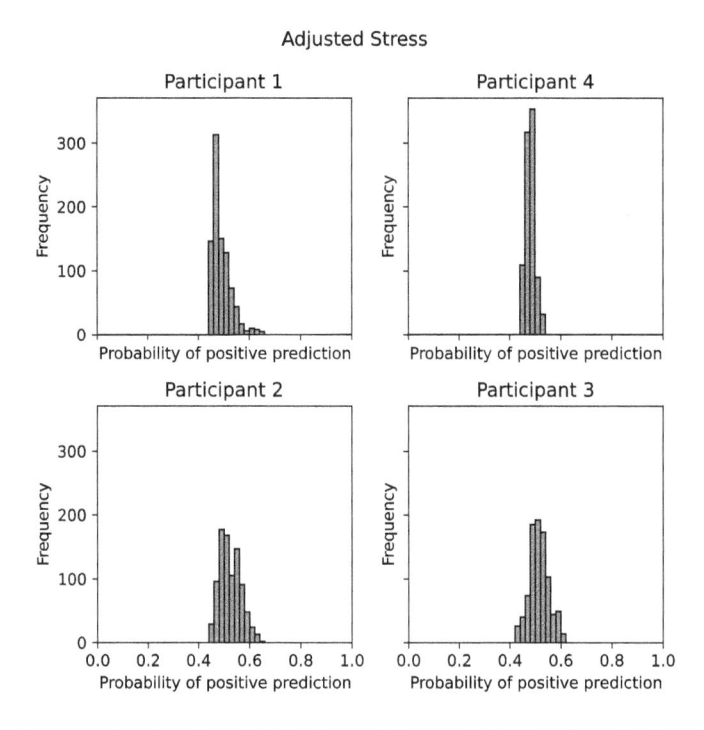

Fig. 9. Histogram showing the distribution of the probability of predicting high stress for each participant, following model adjustments.

the same probability as a baseline-normalized heart rate of 2 (i.e., double the heart rate compared to the baseline period). Using these probabilities to represent stress levels could pose challenges for applying the monitoring system in training scenarios aiming to represent a real-world public safety context, where the heart rate of officers can often more than double compared to resting heart rate when they are faced with the most stressful tasks of their shift [2]. Therefore, in order to distinguish between different levels of stress expected in a public safety officer training program, it may be more useful to increase the range of feature values where the probability of high stress is neither 0 nor 1.

(a) Only Participant 1

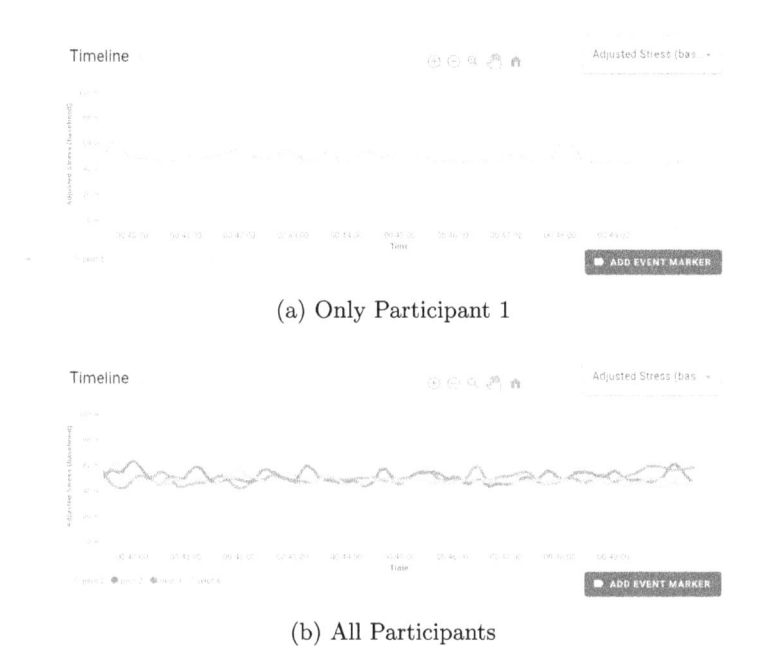

(b) All Participants

Fig. 10. Detected stress levels shown in dashboard, following model adjustments.

To explore possible model adjustments, several modifications were tested in the Sensor Hub simulator (shown in Fig. 1b), running modified feature calculation algorithms and models on the pilot data streamed in real time. A modified version of the logistic regression model was generated, multiplying its original coefficients by the same value. In this work, a factor of 0.075 was chosen, with the objective of avoiding saturation in the probabilities for the expected range of heart rates in public safety officers. For example, for a change in heart rate from a baseline of 63.1 to 147.6 (see Table 3 of [2]), the probability of high stress would range from approximately 0.978 to 0.989 in the modified model (depending on the breathing rate), rather than 1 in the original model. The adjustment aimed to provide a more gradual probability distribution without altering the original decision boundary, as illustrated in Fig. 8. Additionally, a windowing function was implemented to calculate the mean heart and breathing rates over a configurable window. This approach aimed to smooth the output probabilities, both to improve interpretability of the visualization in the dashboard and reduce fluctuations in model predictions caused by changes in the features that are not necessarily due to an increase in stress, such as momentary increases in heart rate due to respiratory sinus arrhythmia [6]. A simulation was run with the adjusted logistic regression model using input features averaged over a 10-second window, which has been found to accurately estimate average heart rate calculated over 5 minutes [1]. Figure 9 depicts the distribution of the probability of predicting high stress for each participant following the model adjustments, showing a more concentrated and lower range of predicted stress probabilities for all participants, compared to the probabilities obtained with the original model (Fig. 5). The model adjustments visibly reduced the sharp transitions in stress level previously noted in the dashboard. Figure 10 shows a screenshot from the dashboard displaying stress levels resulting from this adjusted model for a segment of the pilot data.

5 Discussion

In this pilot study, we tested the deployment of SHAD, a continuous neurophysiological monitoring system designed to assess stress and mental workload in public safety officer training. Four participants completed tasks from the MATB-II under conditions intended to manipulate stress and workload. Neurophysiological signals were recorded using wearable sensors, and machine learning models were employed to predict stress and workload levels. The pilot deployment demonstrated the feasibility of using the system to monitor multiple participants in near real time, but it also highlighted challenges in adapting models to provide meaningful information in the envisioned continuous monitoring context. Although the models were trained and validated on binary data ("high" vs. "low"), the dashboard displayed stress and mental workload levels based on the probability of predicting the positive class, an approach that has been applied in previous work to obtain more granular continuous values [27,39]. However, during the pilot deployment, the dashboard showed frequent maximum readings (i.e., indicating a probability of 1). Such saturation can make it difficult to distinguish between varying levels of stress and workload, complicating the identification of the most challenging parts of a training program. This could be particularly problematic considering that for certain critical tasks, some physiological activation is a normal reaction and not necessarily indicative of imminent failure to perform [14].

To understand the range of the levels shown in the dashboard, the relationship between input features and probabilities was visualized. Analysis of a simple LR-based stress model, primarily relying on heart rate relative to a baseline, suggested that the maximum probability would be shown well before heart rates reached levels common in public safety officers [2,3]. To qualitatively demonstrate how addressing this saturation could improve dashboard interpretability, we modified the stress model and ran a simulation with the same data from the pilot deployment. However, empirical evaluation and refinement of the models are needed, focusing on both their predictive accuracy and the relevance of the metrics shown to instructors. Future work will aim to validate and adapt the models based on data collected from the target population (i.e., trainees) following the same experimental protocol. The further development and evaluation of the models will be key to fully realize the potential of the monitoring system, in order to compute meaningful higher-level metrics that go beyond raw data, providing actionable information to instructors [15].

Although primarily targeted at instructors, the monitoring system could have multiple applications. For instance, trainees could be directly alerted about their cognitive state, a strategy that has been used to improve the efficiency training in the context of marksmanship [4]. Additionally, insights from stress and workload data could inform the design of training scenarios. By understanding the cognitive states induced by different tasks, training programs can be tailored to incrementally increase difficulty, better preparing trainees for real-world conditions without imposing excessive stress and workload [8]. Moreover, since stress and mental workload are potentially linked to cybersickness [16,21,28,35], a discomfort experienced by users exposed to simulation environments [20], such measures could be especially informative when designing simulation training. If these models are directly integrated into simulators, they could enable closed-loop adaptive training, automatically adjusting relevant parameters such as the number of stressors, based on the individual's state [11,12]. Lastly, the real-time monitoring system tested in this work could also be adapted to monitor public safety personnel in action, improving situational awareness and tracking health, particularly when model outputs are combined with other contextual information collected by the system like geo-location data [32].

6 Conclusion

This work contributes to the development of a real-time monitoring system which could provide a more comprehensive understanding of trainees' stress and mental workload levels with minimal disruption to training. With model predictions available in real time, as well as saved over time, the system could be used to improve training live for individual students and to inform the design of future courses. Ultimately, a neurophysiological monitoring system specifically designed for training could pave the way for more effective and personalized training experiences, better preparing individuals for safety-critical fields.

Acknowledgments. The authors would like to thank the participants in this pilot study, as well as acknowledge the work of the Thales development team. Special thanks are due to Jonathan Richard for his assistance with data collection and simulation testing. This financial support received from the Canadian Safety and Security Program (CSSP) is gratefully acknowledged.

Disclosure of Interests. Alexandre Marois was previously employed by Thales Research and Technology Canada, while Danielle Benesch and Tanya S. Paul are currently employed by the same organization, which has developed the monitoring system described in this article. The authors declare no other competing interests that are relevant to the content of this article.

References

1. Baek, H.J., Cho, C.H., Cho, J., Woo, J.M.: Reliability of ultra-short-term analysis as a surrogate of standard 5-min analysis of heart rate variability. Telemed. e-Health **21**(5), 404–414 (2015). https://doi.org/10.1089/tmj.2014.0104
2. Baldwin, S., Bennell, C., Andersen, J.P., Semple, T., Jenkins, B.: Stress-activity mapping: physiological responses during general duty police encounters. Front. Psychol. **10**, 2216 (2019). https://doi.org/10.3389/fpsyg.2019.02216
3. Baldwin, S., et al.: A Reasonable officer: examining the relationships among stress, training, and performance in a highly realistic lethal force scenario. Front. Psychol. **12**, 759132 (2022). https://doi.org/10.3389/fpsyg.2021.759132
4. Behneman, A., et al.: Neurotechnology to accelerate learning: during marksmanship training. IEEE Pulse **3**(1), 60–63 (2012). https://doi.org/10.1109/MPUL.2011.2175641
5. Benesch, D., Paul, T.S., Marois, A.: Training stress models on open-access data for a continuous human state monitoring platform. In: International Conference on Applied Human Factors and Ergonomics (2024)
6. Berntson, G.G., Cacioppo, J.T., Quigley, K.S.: Respiratory sinus arrhythmia: autonomic origins, physiological mechanisms, and psychophysiological implications. Psychophysiology **30**(2), 183–196 (1993). https://doi.org/10.1111/j.1469-8986.1993.tb01731.x
7. Bishop, A., MacNeil, E., Izzetoglu, K.: Cognitive workload quantified by physiological sensors in realistic immersive settings. In: Schmorrow, D.D., Fidopiastis, C.M. (eds.) Augmented Cognition, vol. 12776, pp. 119–133. Springer, Cham (2021). https://doi.org/10.1007/978-3-030-78114-9_9
8. Bong, C.L., Fraser, K., Oriot, D.: Cognitive load and stress in simulation. In: Grant, V.J., Cheng, A. (eds.) Comprehensive Healthcare Simulation: Pediatrics, pp. 3–17. Springer, Cham (2016). https://doi.org/10.1007/978-3-319-24187-6_1
9. Borghini, G., et al.: Quantitative assessment of the training improvement in a motor-cognitive task by using EEG, ECG and EOG signals. Brain Topogr. **29**(1), 149–161 (2016). https://doi.org/10.1007/s10548-015-0425-7
10. Cannon-Bowers, J.A., Salas, E.: Individual and team decision making under stress: theoretical underpinnings. In: Making Decisions Under Stress: Implications for Individual and Team Training, pp. 17–38 (1998). https://doi.org/10.1037/10278-001
11. Coyne, J.T., Baldwin, C., Cole, A., Sibley, C., Roberts, D.M.: Applying real time physiological measures of cognitive load to improve training. In: Schmorrow, D.D., Estabrooke, I.V., Grootjen, M. (eds.) Foundations of Augmented Cognition. Neuroergonomics and Operational Neuroscience, vol. 5638, pp. 469–478. Springer, Cham (2009). https://doi.org/10.1007/978-3-642-02812-0_55
12. Dey, A., Chatburn, A., Billinghurst, M.: Exploration of an EEG-based cognitively adaptive training system in virtual reality. In: 2019 IEEE Conference on Virtual Reality and 3D User Interfaces (VR), pp. 220–226. IEEE, Osaka, Japan, March 2019. https://doi.org/10.1109/VR.2019.8797840
13. Ferrari, V., Gagnon, J.F., Camachon, C., Kopf, M.: Psycho-physiological evaluation of the pilot: a study conducted with pilots of the French air force. In: Harris, D. (ed.) Engineering Psychology and Cognitive Ergonomics, vol. 10906, pp. 285–295. Springer, Cham (2018). https://doi.org/10.1007/978-3-319-91122-9_24
14. Friedl, K.E.: Military applications of soldier physiological monitoring. J. Sci. Med. Sport **21**(11), 1147–1153 (2018). https://doi.org/10.1016/j.jsams.2018.06.004

15. Friedl, K.E., Buller, M.J., Tharion, W.J., Potter, A.W., Manglapus, G.L., Hoyt, R.W.: Real time physiological status monitoring (RT-PSM): accomplishments, requirements, and research roadmap. US Army research Institute of environmental medicine technical note Tn16-02, biophysics and biomedical modeling division. Natick, United States (2016)
16. Garrido, L.E., et al.: Focusing on cybersickness: pervasiveness, latent trajectories, susceptibility, and effects on the virtual reality experience. Virtual Reality **26**(4), 1347–1371 (2022). https://doi.org/10.1007/s10055-022-00636-4
17. Giannakakis, G., Grigoriadis, D., Giannakaki, K., Simantiraki, O., Roniotis, A., Tsiknakis, M.: Review on psychological stress detection using biosignals. IEEE Trans. Affect. Comput. **13**(1), 440–460 (2022). https://doi.org/10.1109/TAFFC.2019.2927337
18. Hart, S.G., Staveland, L.E.: Development of NASA-TLX (Task Load Index): results of empirical and theoretical research. In: Advances in Psychology, vol. 52, pp. 139–183. Elsevier (1988). https://doi.org/10.1016/S0166-4115(08)62386-9
19. Helton, W.S.: Validation of a short stress state questionnaire. Proc. Hum. Factors Ergon. Soc. Annu. Meet. **48**(11), 1238–1242 (2004). https://doi.org/10.1177/154193120404801107
20. Ihemedu-Steinke, Q.C., Rangelova, S., Weber, M., Erbach, R., Meixner, G., Marsden, N.: Simulation sickness related to virtual reality driving simulation. In: Lackey, S., Chen, J. (eds.) Virtual, Augmented and Mixed Reality, vol. 10280, pp. 521–532. Springer, Cham (2017). https://doi.org/10.1007/978-3-319-57987-0_42
21. Kim, Y.S., Won, J., Jang, S.W., Ko, J.: Effects of cybersickness caused by head-mounted display-based virtual reality on physiological responses: cross-sectional study. JMIR Serious Games **10**(4), e37938 (2022)
22. Krätzig, G.P., Hembroff, C.C., Ahlgrim, B.: Comparison study of attention between training in a Simulator vs. Live-fire range. In: Schmorrow, D.D., Fidopiastis, C.M. (eds.) Augmented Cognition, vol. 12776, pp. 178–197. Springer, Cham (2021). https://doi.org/10.1007/978-3-030-78114-9_13
23. Kumar, S., Forster, H.M., Bailey, P., Griffiths, T.D.: Mapping unpleasantness of sounds to their auditory representation. J. Acoust. Soc. Am. **124**(6), 3810–3817 (2008). https://doi.org/10.1121/1.3006380
24. Luong, T., Argelaguet, F., Martin, N., Lecuyer, A.: Introducing mental workload assessment for the design of virtual reality training scenarios. In: 2020 IEEE Conference on Virtual Reality and 3D User Interfaces (VR), pp. 662–671. IEEE, Atlanta, GA, USA, March 2020. https://doi.org/10.1109/VR46266.2020.00089
25. Mark, J.A., Kraft, A.E., Ziegler, M.D., Ayaz, H.: Neuroadaptive training via fNIRS in flight simulators. Front. Neuroergonomics **3**, 820523 (2022). https://doi.org/10.3389/fnrgo.2022.820523
26. Marois, A., Salvan, L., Lemaire, N., Gagnon, J.F.: User-centered dashboard for sensors-enabled human state monitoring: two operational use cases. In: 14th International Conference on Applied Human Factors and Ergonomics (AHFE 2023) (2023). https://doi.org/10.54941/ahfe1003191
27. Mishra, V., et al.: Evaluating the reproducibility of physiological stress detection models. Proc. ACM Interact. Mob. Wearable Ubiquit. Technol. **4**(4), 1–29 (2020). https://doi.org/10.1145/3432220
28. Moinnereau, M.A., Benesch, D., Paré, S., Krätzig, G.P., Falk, T.H.: A Survey on the relationship between stress, cognitive load, and movement on cybersickness. In: International Conference on Applied Human Factors and Ergonomics (2024)

29. Nieuwenhuys, A., Oudejans, R.R.D.: Training with anxiety: short- and long-term effects on police officers' shooting behavior under pressure. Cogn. Process. **12**(3), 277–288 (2011). https://doi.org/10.1007/s10339-011-0396-x
30. Paul, T.S., Salvan, L., Kopf, M., Benesch, D., Marois, A.: Towards edge-computing assessment of cognitive workload using fNIRS data. In: 2023 IEEE International Conference on Systems, Man, and Cybernetics (SMC) (2023)
31. Pedregosa, F., et al.: Scikit-learn: machine learning in Python. J. Mach. Learn. Res. **12**, 2825–2830 (2011)
32. Rodrigues, S., et al.: Ambulatory assessment of psychophysiological stress among police officers: a proof-of-concept study. Occup. Health Sci. **2**(2), 215–231 (2018). https://doi.org/10.1007/s41542-017-0008-y
33. Salvan, L., Marois, A., Kopf, M., Gagnon, J.F.: Sensors-enabled human state monitoring system for tactical settings. In: 2022 IEEE Conference on Cognitive and Computational Aspects of Situation Management (CogSIMA), pp. 55–83. IEEE, Salerno, Italy, June 2022. https://doi.org/10.1109/CogSIMA54611.2022.9830666
34. Santiago-Espada, Y., Myer, R.R., Latorella, K.A., Comstock, J.R.: The Multi-Attribute Task Battery II (MATB-II) Software for human performance and workload research: a user's guide. Technical report, National Aeronautics and Space Administration (2011)
35. Sepich, N.C., Jasper, A., Fieffer, S., Gilbert, S.B., Dorneich, M.C., Kelly, J.W.: The impact of task workload on cybersickness. Front. Virtual Reality **3**, 943409 (2022). https://doi.org/10.3389/frvir.2022.943409
36. Siu, K.C., Best, B.J., Kim, J.W., Oleynikov, D., Ritter, F.E.: Adaptive virtual reality training to optimize military medical skills acquisition and retention. Mil. Med. **181**(5S), 214–220 (2016). https://doi.org/10.7205/MILMED-D-15-00164
37. Strang, A.J., Best, C., Funke, G.J.: Heart rate correlates of mental workload in a large-scale air-combat simulation training exercise. Proc. Hum. Factors Ergon. Soc. Annu. Meet. **58**(1), 2325–2329 (2014). https://doi.org/10.1177/1541931214581484
38. Tiwari, A., Cassani, R., Gagnon, J.F., Lafond, D., Tremblay, S., Falk, T.H.: Prediction of stress and mental workload during police academy training using ultra-short-term heart rate variability and breathing analysis. In: 2020 42nd Annual International Conference of the IEEE Engineering in Medicine & Biology Society (EMBC), pp. 4530–4533. IEEE, Montreal, QC, Canada, July 2020. https://doi.org/10.1109/EMBC44109.2020.9175414
39. Zhang, X., Krol, L.R., Zander, T.O.: Towards task-independent workload classification: shifting from binary to continuous classification. In: 2018 IEEE International Conference on Systems, Man, and Cybernetics (SMC), pp. 556–561. IEEE, Miyazaki, Japan, October 2018. https://doi.org/10.1109/SMC.2018.00104

A Pilot Approach and Landing Workload Assessment Method for Flight Crew Workload Airworthiness Certification

Nongtian Chen[✉], Ting Ma, Yiyang Han, and Kai Chen

Civil Aviation Flight, University of China, Guanghan 618307, Sichuan, China
chennnongtian@hotmail.com

Abstract. The verification of crew workload airworthiness compliance is one of the core contents of civil aircraft airworthiness certification. This paper takes the workload assessment of pilot approach and landing as the research object, and attempts to establish a pilot approach and landing workload evaluation method for crew workload airworthiness certification. Firstly, interpret the airworthiness clause CCAR25.1523 for crew workload and attempt to establish a compliance verification method that combines subjective evaluation with physiological evaluation. Through experimental design, Tobii eye tracking device and NASA-TLX scale were used to collect physiological indexes of eye movement and subjective survey data of participants. Four arithmetic operations were used for indicator blending and correlation analysis. The homogeneity of variance test analysis showed that the two indexes of gaze time smoothness ratio and average pupil rate of variation were statistically significant. The conclusion indicates that the smoothness ratio of gaze time and the average rate of pupil variation can be used to evaluate the workload of pilots during approach and landing. It shows that as the workload increases, the fluctuation amplitude of the smoothness ratio of gaze time is smaller, and the ratio is also smaller. Conversely, as the workload decreases, the fluctuation amplitude and ratio of the smoothness ratio of gaze time are larger. When the workload is higher, the fluctuation area of the average pupil variation rate coincides with the normal workload area, which is smaller. Conversely, the fluctuation area of the average pupil variation rate coincides with the normal workload area, which is a characteristic of the law.

Keywords: Approach and Landing · Workload Assessment · eye tracking · NASA-TLX · Airworthiness Certification

1 Introduction

With the rapid development of the aviation industry, pilot workload has become an important research field for optimizing airworthiness certification and verification of civil aircraft design and manufacturing systems, as well as human factors related to civil aircraft operation safety. In flight missions, especially during the approach and landing phase, pilots need to face various challenges and complex situations, such as aircraft performance requirements, traffic control, meteorological changes, and airport operating conditions. Pilots need highly focused attention, fast and accurate decision-making ability, and good flying skills in these environments. However, excessive workload may have a negative impact on the performance and decision-making of pilots, thereby increasing the risk of flight accidents. Therefore, it is crucial to evaluate and manage the workload of pilots. In the past few decades, researchers and the aviation industry have realized the importance of pilot workload assessment in improving flight safety and enhancing work efficiency, and have therefore conducted extensive research and exploration in this field.

At present, most of the methods for assessing pilot workload by scholars are in the theoretical stage, including subjective evaluation methods and physiological signal based evaluation methods. The subjective evaluation method usually uses a scale to evaluate the workload of participants. The NASA-TLX scale is a subjective measurement method widely used in post flight evaluations of pilots. It uses a two-level grading method to evaluate workload from six dimensions through weighted averaging [3]. In addition, the SWAT (Subjective Workload Assessment Technique) [4] and the Cooper Harper scale [5] are also commonly used to evaluate pilot workload. In the SWAT scale theory, workload is seen as a combination of three factors: time load, psychological stress load, and effort load. The SWAT scale is less sensitive to low workload levels and is often used for evaluating high workload levels. Cooper Harper scale is mainly applied in the design and development of human-machine operation interfaces for new or improved aircraft. It adopts the form of decision trees to evaluate workload based on control performance, to evaluate the difficulty of aircraft driving and make optimization.

Physiological measurement is a traditional method that reflects changes in the workload of operators by measuring changes using certain physiological indexes [6]. Scholars have studied the relative complexity and data sensitivity of workload in four dimensions: EEG measurement, ECG measurement, respiratory measurement and eye movement measurement [7]. In EEG measurement, Zhou Lingxiao proposed a method to evaluate brain workload during driving. The experimental results showed that when the brain workload was low, the frequency of high potential microstates in the left frontal lobe in the theta frequency band increased; When the workload of the brain is high, the frequency decreases [8]. In electrocardiogram measurement, Wilson studied the relationship between various physiological indexes and working mental load during flight training tasks, and the results showed that heart rate and heart rate variability changed significantly at different stages of the task [9]. Dong Mingqing found through experiments that there is a significant difference in heart rate between tasks of different difficulty levels, while there is no significant difference in heart rate variability. This indicates that although heart rate and heart rate variability are related to mental load, they cannot be directly used as direct indexes of changes in mental load, but can only be used as reference indexes [10]. In respiratory measurement, Sirevaagd found that both relative visual response and heart rate variability decreased as communication mental load increased, leading to the conclusion that communication affects relevant respiratory indexes [11]. Eye tracking measurement is currently the most widely used physiological measurement method in workload assessment. Researchers have analyzed the principle and found that vision is the fastest and most efficient way of searching for information among all senses, and is also the most sensitive to information changes [12, 13].

Many scholars have conducted extensive research on workload and have achieved rich results. This article intends to interpret the airworthiness regulation CCAR25.1523 on crew workload and attempt to establish a compliance verification method that combines subjective evaluation with physiological evaluation. Using Tobii eye tracking instrument and NASA-TLX scale to collect physiological indexes and subjective survey data of subjects, analyze the physiological characteristics of pilots during approach and landing stages, and select key indexes that can be used for evaluating pilot workload during approach and landing.

2 Interpretation and Compliance Verification of Airworthiness Regulation for Crew Workload

2.1 Interpretation of CCAR25.1523 Regulation

CCAR25.1523 of the airworthiness regulations provides a detailed arrangement for the minimum number of flight crew members, taking into account not only the accessibility and simplicity of operating equipment for crew members, as well as the approved operational types in accordance with Article 25.1525, but also the factors affecting the workload of each crew member. In Appendix D, detailed guidelines and requirements for crew workload are proposed [14]:

1. The accessibility and ease of operation;
2. The accessibility and visibility of all devices;
3. The number, urgency, and complexity of operating procedures;
4. The resources consumed for normal task execution;
5. The degree of real-time monitoring of equipment (including instruments) during flight mission execution;
6. Off seat work;
7. The degree of automation of aircraft systems refers to the ability of the system to automatically cut off and isolate obstacles caused by faults or failures, thereby reducing the actions required by the flight crew to prevent the loss of energy (hydraulic and power sources of flight control systems or other major systems);
8. The workload of communication and navigation;
9. The possibility of increasing workload due to any emergency situation leading to other emergency situations;
10. When the applicable operating rules require a minimum flight crew consisting of at least two pilots, one crew member is unable to work due to unforeseen circumstances.

Among the workload factors considered above, items (1) and (2) mainly consider the comprehensive efficiency of human-computer interaction interface, while the remaining eight items consider various indexes of flight crew workload. For example, item (3) mainly considers the time pressure of workload, and item (6) considers the utilization of spatial resources. The airworthiness regulations impose relevant constraints on the operational and safety performance of the flight crew from various aspects of design and arrangement, making human-machine communication more efficient and reducing the workload level of the flight crew.

2.2 Compliance Verification of Flight Crew Workload

Compliance verification is used in the design and development stage of aircraft, which is in the initial airworthiness certification stage. It is a procedure for conducting initial airworthiness certification for aircraft and its subcomponents, systems, structures etc. [15]. By using one or more compliance verification methods to verify whether the required verification objects have airworthiness and meet the corresponding airworthiness regulations issued by the authority, compliance verification runs through the entire design and development process of the aircraft, verifying the compliance of the verification objects with airworthiness regulations, and evaluating the airworthiness quality of the aircraft. Only when all compliance verifications are completed that the aircraft can apply for and obtain an airworthiness certificate. Compliance verification requires different procedures and methods, which are collectively referred to as compliance verification methods. The commonly used compliance verification methods range from MC0 to MC9, as shown in Table 1.

Table 1. Conformance verification methods MC0 ~ MC9.

Compliance work	Method coding	Compliance verification method	Corresponding documents
Engineering review	MC0	Declaration of conformity Cite model design documents Selection of formulas and coefficients definition	Model design documents Compliance Record Form
	MC1	Supporting paper	Instructions, drawings, technical documents
	MC2	Analysis/Calculation	Comprehensive explanation and verification report
	MC3	Safety assessment	Safety analysis
Test	MC4	Laboratory test	Test task book Test program Test report Experiment Result Analysis
	MC5	Ground test	
	MC6	Test flight	
	MC8	Simulator test	
Inspect	MC7	Aircraft inspection	Observation/Inspection Report Manufacturing compliance inspection records
Equipment identification	MC9	Equipment qualification	May include all previous compliance verification methods

When conducting compliance verification, one or multiple methods can be used, and there is also a principle when using compliance verification method that is meet airworthiness requirements at the lowest cost. This means that the more compliance verification methods are, the better, and they should be as few and simple as possible. Compliance verification methods are not mutually exclusive, so their number of uses is not limited to one. Multiple combinations can be formed for verification. These verification methods range from simple to complex, from local to comprehensive, from simulation to actual operation. Choosing a matching compliance verification method is of utmost importance. By considering the characteristics of the object to be verified, the type of human factor problem, etc., it is helpful to choose a matching compliance verification method. The compliance verification methods in terms of workload mainly include analysis and experimentation. At present, the airworthiness evaluation method for workload can be evaluated using subjective evaluation method combined with physiological evaluation method.

3 Experimental Implementation

3.1 Experimental Equipment and Scenarios

The main experimental equipment includes Tobii eye tracker and flight simulator. The Tobii eye tracker uses infrared or near-infrared cameras to track eye movements, accurately measuring eye movement indexes such as eye position, fixation point, fixation duration, and scanning path. In addition to the above prepared instruments, the experimental setup of the experimental scene, including temperature and humidity presets, should also be prepared. At the same time, participants should experience the experimental environment and equipment in advance. Figure 1 shows the first perspective of the participant's experience.

According to the eye movement scanning view obtained through experiments, it can be seen that outdoor interface has the highest attention ratio among the three interactive interfaces during approach and landing, followed by the flight data display interface, and finally the control interface.

3.2 Experimental Procedures

The experimental subjects include one instructor with rich flight experience and three students who have only received brief understanding and have a theoretical foundation. Before the experiment, participants need to familiarize themselves with the experimental equipment and its operation in advance. After entering the laboratory, check the integrity of the equipment and ensure that the testing equipment is working properly. Set the current indoor temperature and humidity to fully restore the airborne flight environment. Preparing a SWAT scale and record it during the simulation process, allowing subjects to perform approach and landing flight tasks in a normal simulated aircraft environment. Collect relevant data using an eye tracking device; Randomly insert common emergencies during the execution of flight missions and collect eye tracking data of the tested personnel. Within five minutes after each simulation, record the NASA-TLX scale on

(a) Outdoor and flight data display interface

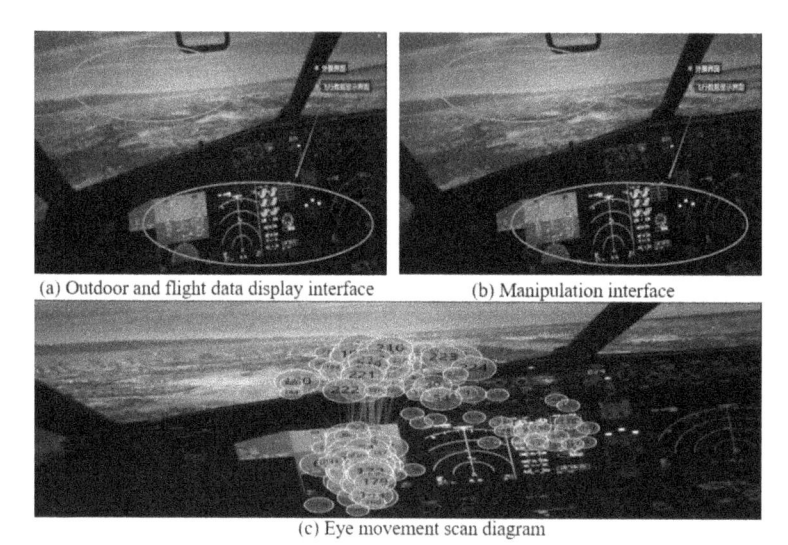

(b) Manipulation interface

(c) Eye movement scan diagram

Fig. 1. Participant eye movement and visual characteristics.

the subjects and record the pilot's comments. After completing the approach and landing phase mission, regardless of whether the mission is successful or not, the data is effectively recorded.

3.3 Experimental Measurement Indexes

Eye movement indexes refer to indexes that reflect dynamic changes in the eyes, including fixation, scanning, blinking, and pupil [16]. Among them, gaze index refers to the time the eyes stay in a specific area, used to measure the degree of concentration of attention [17]. The blinking index refers to the frequency and duration of blinking, which can reflect the attention level and fatigue level of the observed person [18]. The scanning index refers to the trajectory and speed of the eyeball's rapid movement during the observation process. By analyzing the scanning path and dwell time, one can understand the information processing methods and key focus of the observed person during reading or observation [19]. The pupil index refers to the size and variation of the pupil. The size of the pupil is influenced by factors such as light, emotion, and cognitive load. In tasks with high cognitive load, the pupil will expand to increase the amount of light entering the eye, thereby improving visual sensitivity and attention [20].

Based on the actual situation of the pilot during the approach and landing phase and the experimental environment, this experiment selected gaze index, scanning index, and pupil index as evaluation criteria. The subjective evaluation of pilot workload in the experiment was conducted using the NASA-TLX scale (used after simulation), SWAT scale (recorded during simulation), and pilot evaluation record form (used in conjunction with the NASA-TLX scale after simulation).

The indexes used in this experiment depend on flight experience [21] and the eye movement data of the subjects during the approach and landing phases. The NASA-TLX scale values of the subjects after completing the flight mission were calculated and subjective load values were obtained. All subjects were screened for data, and to ensure effective measurement, data that could not simultaneously measure left and right pupil diameters were deleted to obtain experimental preprocessing data. Finally, 10 indexes were selected (Table 2).

Table 2. Initial index

Number	Index	Number	Index
1	Fixation frequency	6	Average diameter of right pupil (total)
2	Scan frequency	7	Mean diameter of left pupil (fixation)
3	Average fixation duration	8	Average diameter of right pupil (fixation)
4	Average scan time	9	Mean diameter of left pupil (scan)
5	Average diameter of left pupil (total)	10	Average diameter of right pupil (scan)

3.4 Data Processing

Conduct workload assessment for the approach and landing phase, import three subjective evaluation values of workload into SPSS, and use ANOVA to analyze the significance of measurements under the same flight mission, the same measurement indicator, and different time periods, as shown in Table 3:

Both Instructor 1 and Student 1 successfully approached and landed, while Student 2 and Student 3 failed to approach and land. According to the analysis results, there are significant differences in the three subjective evaluation values and workload. Further processing the 10 proposed indexes resulted in 7 indexes as shown in the table below. The indexes were imported into SPSS and ANOVA was used to analyze the significance of measurements for the same flight mission, measurement indexes, and stage. The analysis results are shown in Table 4:

From Table 4, it can be seen the 7 indexes above all have significant differences and statistical significance.

4 Experimental Results and Validation

By using four arithmetic operations to combine indexes, when measuring pupil diameter, gaze is more accurate than scanning. Therefore, the target of indicator selection is shifted to gaze related indexes. In response to this research idea, the following plan is proposed to attempt to combine and analyze:

Table 3. Significance analysis of subjective evaluation

Test object	Subjective evaluation	F	P
Instructor 1	NASA-TLX form	5.724	<0.05
	SWAT form	14.167	<0.05
	Pilot description	14.643	<0.05
Pilot student 1	NASA-TLX form	15.712	<0.05
	SWAT form	3.458	<0.05
	Pilot description	2.547	<0.05
Pilot student 2	NASA-TLX form	15.257	<0.05
	SWAT form	7.412	<0.05
	Pilot description	14.574	<0.05
Pilot student 3	NASA-TLX form	12.137	<0.05
	SWAT form	4.214	<0.05
	Pilot description	13.428	<0.05

Table 4. ANOVA analysis results

Index		Sum of squares	Degree of freedom	Mean square	F	P
Fixation frequency	Inter group	30.411	1	30.411	0.075	<0.05
	Within the group	812.977	2	406.488		
	Total	843.388	3			
Scan frequency	Inter group	21.002	1	21.002	0.056	<0.05
	Within the group	753.579	2	376.789		
	Total	774.581	3			
Average fixation duration	Inter group	57035.852	1	57035.852	20.07	<0.05
	Within the group	5683.314	2	2841.657		
	Total	62719.167	3			
Average scan time	Inter group	43.201	1	43.201	45.51	<0.05
	Within the group	1.898	2	0.949		
	Total	45.100	3			

(*continued*)

Table 4. (*continued*)

Index		Sum of squares	Degree of freedom	Mean square	F	P
Average scan amplitude	Inter group	3127.767	1	3127.767	2.43	<0.05
	Within the group	2569.903	2	1284.952		
	Total	5697.670	3			
Average diameter of left pupil (total)	Inter group	0.657	1	0.657	33.24	<0.05
	Within the group	0.040	2	0.020		
	Total	0.697	3			
Average diameter of right pupil (total)	Inter group	0.532	1	0.532	15.07	<0.05
	Within the group	0.071	2	0.035		
	Total	0.603	3			

1. Attention scanning frequency ratio: fixation frequency/video scanning rate;
2. Average scanning time ratio: average fixation time/average scanning time;
3. The average pupil ratio for gaze scanning: the average diameter of the left pupil during fixation/the average diameter of the left pupil during scanning, or the average diameter of the right pupil during fixation/the average diameter of the right pupil during scanning;
4. Smoothness ratio of fixation time: fixation time smoothing/scanning time (fixation time smoothing refers to the average of two fixation times);
5. Average rate of pupil variation: average value of left and right gaze pupils/scanning time.

Due to the rich flight experience and strong data reliability of the instructor, for schemes ④ and ⑤ priority is given to using the instructor's flight eye movement data for indicator correlation analysis, and for other schemes, indicator extraction and processing are carried out to eliminate indexes with insignificant correlation.

4.1 Correlation Analysis of Indexes

Correlation analysis of schemes ① ② and ③. The indexes of the instructor and three students were processed and imported into SPSS for correlation analysis. The analysis results are as follows: after correlation analysis, it was found that the ratio of the average diameter of the left pupil to the average scanning time was highly correlated ($R > 0.980$), with a significance level of 0.05 (bilateral), indicating a significant correlation. The correlation between the average diameter ratio of the right pupil and the average scanning time ratio is extremely high ($R > 0.950$), with a significance level of 0.05, indicating a significant correlation. Although the correlation coefficients between the other pairwise indexes are stable, there is no significant difference.

Correlation analysis of schemes ④ and ⑤. The smoothness ratio of gaze time and six other indexes related to pupil diameter were imported into SPSS for correlation analysis. Non-significant data were excluded to obtain the results, as shown in Table 5.

Table 5. The results of correlation analysis of ④ scheme

Index		Smoothness ratio of fixation time	Observe the diameter of the left pupil	Observe the diameter of the right pupil	Pay attention to the average diameter of the left and right pupils	Scanning left pupil diameter	Scanning right pupil diameter	Scanning the average diameter of left and right pupils
Smoothness ratio of fixation time	Correlation coefficient	1	−0.016	0.012	−0.002	0.145*	0.058	0.111
	Significance		0.818	0.866	0.980	0.037	0.407	0.112
Average rate of pupil variation	Correlation coefficient	0.145*	0.003	−0.031	−0.016	1	0.703	0.925
	Significance	0.037	0.967	0.660	0.823		0.000	0.000

Note: *. At the 0.05 level (double tailed), the correlation is significant

There is a positive correlation between the smoothness ratio of gaze time and the diameter of the left pupil during scanning. Although the correlation is weak (R < 0.3), the significance is at the 0.05 level (bilateral), and the correlation is significant. This indicator should be retained.

The average rate of pupil variation was imported into SPSS for correlation analysis with six other indexes related to pupil diameter. Non significant data were excluded and the results are shown in Table 6.

The average rate of pupil variation is positively correlated with all pupil diameter related indexes in the scanning category. Although the correlation is weak (R < 0.300), the significance is at the 0.05 level (bilateral) or 0.01 level (bilateral), and the correlation is significant. This indicator should be retained.

Table 6. The results of correlation analysis of ⑤ scheme

Index		Observe the diameter of the left pupil	Observe the diameter of the right pupil	Pay attention to the average diameter of the left and right pupils	Scanning left pupil diameter	Scanning right pupil diameter	Scanning the average diameter of left and right pupils	Average rate of pupil variation
Observe the diameter of the left pupil	R	1	0.745**	0.929**	0.003	−0.038	−0.019
	P		0.000	0.000	0.967	0.586	0.789
Observe the diameter of the right pupil	R	0.745**	1	0.939**	−0.031	0.001	−0.016
	P	0.000		0.000	0.660	0.985	0.817
Pay attention to the average diameter of the left and right pupils	R	0.929**	0.939**	1	−0.016	−0.019	−0.019
	P	0.000	0.000		0.823	0.788	0.790
Scanning left pupil diameter	R	0.003	−0.031	−0.016	1	0.703**	0.925**
	P	0.967	0.660	0.823		0.000	0.000
Scanning right pupil diameter	R	−0.038	0.001	−0.019	0.703**	1	0.921**
	P	0.586	0.985	0.788	0.000		0.000
Scanning the average diameter of left and right pupils	R	−0.019	−0.016	−0.019	0.925**	0.921**	1

(*continued*)

Table 6. (*continued*)

Index		Observe the diameter of the left pupil	Observe the diameter of the right pupil	Pay attention to the average diameter of the left and right pupils	Scanning left pupil diameter	Scanning right pupil diameter	Scanning the average diameter of left and right pupils	Average rate of pupil variation
	P	0.789	0.817	0.790	0.000	0.000		
Average rate of pupil variation	R	0.023	0.111	0.073	0.165*	0.176*	0.184**	
	P	0.740	0.113	0.293	0.018	0.011	0.008	
Average rate of pupil variation	R	1	0.745**	0.929**	0.003	−0.038	−0.019	
	P		0.000	0.000	0.967	0.586	0.789	
Observe the diameter of the right pupil	R	0.745**	1	0.939**	−0.031	0.001	−0.016	
	P	0.000		0.000	0.660	0.985	0.817	

Note 1: * * At the 0.01 level (two tailed), the correlation is significant
Note 2: * At the 0.05 level (two tailed), the correlation is significant

4.2 Inspection and Analysis of Indexes

A single factor ANOVA test was conducted on the indexes of schemes ④ and ⑤, and the results are shown in Table 7.

Table 7. Test Results of Homogeneity of Variance

Index		Levin statistics	Degree of freedom 1	Degree of freedom 2	Significance
Smoothness ratio of fixation time	average value	10.813	3	865	0.000
	median	6.197	3	865	0.000

(*continued*)

Table 7. (*continued*)

Index		Levin statistics	Degree of freedom 1	Degree of freedom 2	Significance
	Based on median and with adjusted degrees of freedom	6.197	3	596.368	0.000
	Based on the average value after pruning	7.629	3	865	0.000
Average rate of pupil variation	average value	274.811	3	865	0.000
	median	77.579	3	865	0.000
	Based on median and with adjusted degrees of freedom	77.579	3	705.966	0.000
	Based on the average value after pruning	275.599	3	865	0.000

The results of the homogeneity of variance test analysis indicate that both indexes have statistical significance, with a significance level of 0.01 (on both sides).

The analysis results of the smoothness ratio of fixation time and the average rate of pupil variation using ANOVA are shown in Table 8.

Table 8. ANOVA analysis results

Index		Sum of squares	Degree of freedom	mean square	F	Significance
Smoothness ratio of fixation time	Between groups	14965.883	3	4988.628	8.779	0.000
	Inter group	491541.411	865	568.256		
	Total	506507.294	868			
Average rate of pupil variation	Between groups	1.871	3	0.624	140.756	0.000
	Inter group	3.832	865	0.004		
	Total	5.703	868			

238   N. Chen et al.

The analysis results indicate that there is a significant difference in the smoothness ratio of gaze time under different flight experiences (F = 8.779, P < 0.01). There is a significant difference in the average rate of pupil variation under different flight experiences (F = 140.756, P < 0.01).

4.3 Verification of the Applicability of Indexes

To verify the applicability of the indexes, a flight simulation experiment was conducted with the experimental subjects unchanged. Data from four groups of subjects were analyzed, and the same indexes were extracted. A line chart with observable data fluctuations was used for graphical analysis (in the following figure, 1 is the instructor, 2, 3, and 4 are all students, and 3 and 4 failed the task during the experiment. The horizontal axis represents the task execution time, measured in seconds).

1. As shown in Fig. 2, the line graph of gaze time smoothing ratio

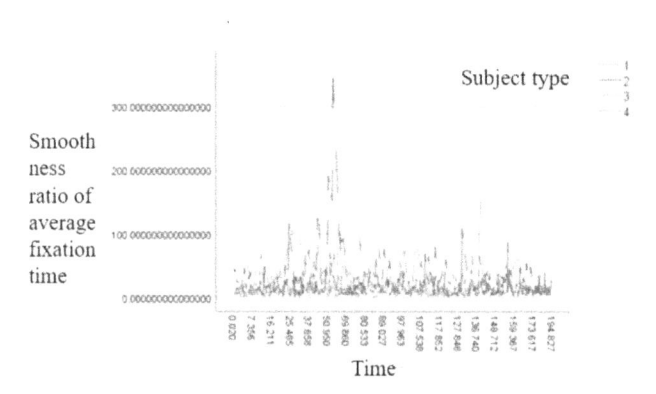

Fig. 2. Fixation time smoothing ratio line chart.

Based on the experimental process and line graph, it can be seen that as the workload increases, the fluctuation amplitude and ratio of gaze time smoothing ratio decrease. Conversely, as the workload decreases, the fluctuation amplitude and ratio of gaze time smoothing ratio increase.

2. The line graph of average pupil variation rate (m/s) is shown in Fig. 3.

Considering that the instructor has rich experience in teaching flight, the fluctuation area of the instructor's indexes is defined as the normal workload area. As the workload increases, the fluctuation area of the average pupil variation rate coincides with the normal workload area, and vice versa. The fluctuation area of the average pupil variation rate coincides with the normal workload area, and the larger the overlap area.

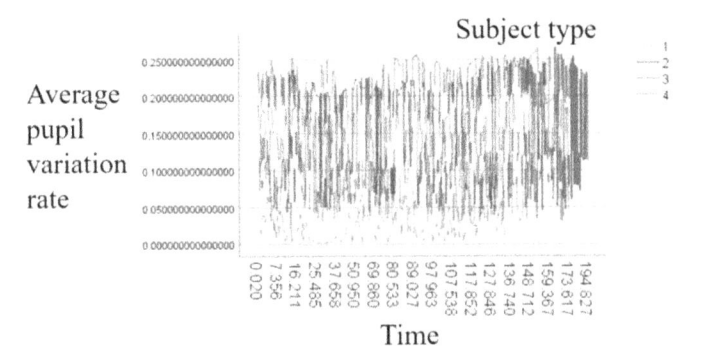

Fig. 3. Mean pupil variation rate line chart.

5 Conclusion

1. Interpret the airworthiness clause CCAR25.1523 for crew workload and analyze the verification method for crew workload compliance. Through eye movement physiological testing experiments, the 10 initial eye movement indexes were processed and analyzed using ANOVA, and significant differences were found in the indexes.
2. By using four arithmetic operations for indicator blending and correlation analysis, the results of homogeneity of variance test showed that the smoothness ratio of gaze time and the average rate of pupil variation were statistically significant.
3. The smoothness ratio of gaze time and the average rate of pupil variation can be used to evaluate the workload among pilots during the approach landing phase. When the workload is higher, the fluctuation amplitude and ratio of gaze time smoothing ratio are smaller. Conversely, when the workload is lower, the fluctuation amplitude and ratio of gaze time smoothing ratio are larger. When the workload is higher, the fluctuation area of the average pupil variation rate coincides with the normal workload area, and vice versa. The fluctuation area of the average pupil variation rate coincides with the normal workload area, and vice versa.

Acknowledgments. This research was funded by the National Natural Science Foundation of China (grant number: U2033202); Key R&D Program of the Sichuan Provincial Department of Science and Technology (2022YFG0213); Safety Capability Fund Project of the Civil Aviation Administration of China (ASSA2022/17).

Disclosure of Interests. The Authors Report There Are no Competing Interest to Declare.

References

1. Cheng, D.L., Yang, L., Yi, C.J.: Human factors analysis of aircraft flight accident causes. J. Civ. Aviat. Univ. China 3–8 (2006)
2. Guo, Y.C., Zhang, X.O.: Flight safety-the eternal theme of aviation-brief introduction of the 15th International Symposium on Cabin Safety. Civil Aviat. Med. **8**(3), 14–179 (1998)

3. Huang, Y.S., Cheng, Y.P., Wang, Y.W., et al.: Evaluating female pilot cadets 'mental workload by National aeronautics and space administration-task load index and heart rate variability index. Chin. J. Aerospace Med. **29**(1), 14–21 (2018)
4. Luximon, A., Goonetilleke, R.: Simplified subjective workload assessment technique. Ergonomics **44**(3), 229–243 (2001)
5. George, C.: Handling qualities and pilot evaluation. J. Guid. Control. Dyn. **9**(5), 515 (1986)
6. Bai, J., Feng, C.Y., Yang, K.: Research progress of physiological measurement of mental workload in Pilots. Space Med. Med. Eng. **29**(2), 150–156 (2016)
7. Zhou, Z.D.: The Research of Control Methods of Virtual Reality Based on Multi-classMotor Imagery Recognition. Hangzhou Dianzi University, Hangzhou (2015)
8. Zhou, L.X., Ding, Y.Q., Dai, Y.M., et al.: Research of driver's workload based on microstates analysis with EEG signals. J. Hangzhou Dianzi Univ. **34**(4), 23–26 (2014)
9. Meng, G., Li, M.G.: Study on the changes of heart rate and heart rate variability in the first solo flight of Navy cadet trainer aircraft. J. Navy Med. **40**(2), 118–119 (2019)
10. Dong, M.Q., Ma, R.S., Cheng, H.W., et al.: Psychophysiological assessment of mental workload of dual tasks. Chin. J. Aerospace Med. **3**, 12–17 (1997)
11. Humphrey, D., Sirevaag, E., Kramer, A.F., et al.: Psychophysiological measures real-time measurement of mental workload using psychophysiological measures (2019)
12. Liu, Z.Q., Yuan, X.G., Liu, W., et al.: Eye movement research and its application in aviation ergonomics. In: The Academic Annual Meeting of the Professional Committee of Human Engineering, Aeronautical Medicine and Lifesaving of China Aeronautical Society (2003)
13. Jin, H.B., Hong, Y., Cai, Y.M.: Research on real-time measurement method of air traffic controller workload based on interaction index. Saf. Environ. Eng. **22**(3), 147–150 (2015)
14. Sun, G.Y.: Research on unit workload evaluation technology. Civ. Aircraft Des. Res. **2**, 43–44, 50 (2010)
15. ICAO. Safety Management Manual (SMM). Doc 9859 AN/474 (2013)
16. Halverson, T., Estepp, J., Christensen, J., et al.: Classifying workload with eye movements in a complex task. In: Proceedings of the Human Factors and Ergonomics Society Annual Meeting, vol. 56, no. 1, pp. 168–172 (2012)
17. Gomer, J., Walker, A., Gilles, F., et al.: Eye-tracking in a dual-task design: investigating eye-movements, mental workload, and performance. In: Human Factors and Ergonomics Society Annual Meeting Proceedings, vol. 52, no. 19, 1589–1593 (2008)
18. Zheng, B., Jiangx, X., Tien, G., et al.: Workload assessment of surgeons: correlation between NASA TLX and blinks. Surgical Endoscopy **26**(10), 2746–2750 (2012)
19. Takahasshi, K., Nakayama, M., Shimizu, Y.: The response of eye- movement and pupil size to audio instruction while viewing a moving target. In: Proceedings of the Eye Tracking Research and Applications Symposium, pp. 131–138. Association for Computing Machinery, Boston (2000)
20. Yan, G.L., Bai, X.J.: Introduction to Psychology of Eye Movement Research: The Magic Science of Uncovering the Mystery of the Window of Mind, pp. 303–304. Science Press, Beijing (2012)
21. Du, J.M., He, X.L., Kang, W.Y.: Pilot Workload, pp. 78–83. Beihang University Press, Beijing (2021)

Wings of Wisdom: Learning from Pilot Decision Data with Interpretable AI Models

Boris Djartov[✉], Anne Papenfuß, and Matthias Wies

German Aerospace Center (DLR), Cologne, Germany
{boris.djartov,anne.papenfuss,matthias.wies}@dlr.de
https://www.dlr.de/de

Abstract. This paper explores how an AI model might aid pilots facing time-sensitive, multi-criteria decision-making challenges, focusing on the dynamic alternate airport selection problem. Traditional decision-making methods from the literature are ill suited in time-constrained, stressful situations. This has prompted an exploration into how incorporating AI models might provide decision-makers, pilots in this case, recommendations in such predicaments. Within the paper we explore how a Learning Classifier Systems (LCS), might be employed to tackle the problem. To train the LCS, an augmented dataset is derived from an online survey study featuring scenarios simulating alternate airport decision-making problems where state variables, reflecting aircraft conditions, and three airport options were presented to pilots. The LCS system showed promising results and appears to be a suitable model for the task.

Keywords: mutli-criteria decision-making · learning classifier system · artificial intelligence

1 Introduction

Making decisions that involve multiple criteria is inherently challenging, and the complexity of such tasks is further exacerbated when the decision needs to be made in a time-sensitive emergency situation. A real world example of this is the dynamic alternate airport selection (DAAS) problem [1]. The DAAS problem aims to represent a situation that pilots may find themselves in, specifically when certain factors necessitate the selection of a new destination airport midflight. In [1] and here, the problem is presented as a multi-criteria decision-making problem in which pilots need to gather information on possible airports, compare their characteristics, and select a new final destination. Although structured schemes such as FORDEC (Facts, Options, Risks, Decision, Execution, Control) or TDODAR (Time, Diagnosis, Options, Decide, Assign Task, Review) are used [2,3], pilots in interviews expressed their desire for additional decision-support in emergency situations [4].

At the DLR (Deutsches Zentrum für Luft- und Raumfahrt e.V., engl. German Aerospace Center), an Intelligent Pilot Advisory System (IPAS) [4] is being developed to explore how an AI-powered decision support system might be integrated into the cockpit. Currently, one of the focuses behind this advisory system is to provide pilots assistance during a DAAS problem situation. The idea is that the system would take in relevant input data and provide the pilots with a suggested course of action. This paper delves into how the AI of such a system might be trained using data gathered from a survey, where pilots were tasked to solve a DAAS problem consisting of three alternate airports. Additionally, given the importance of safety in aviation, emphasis was placed on using a more interpretable model whose recommendation would be easier to check. Thus, the lesser-known Learning Classifier System (LCS) was selected to tackle the pilot dataset.

The structure of this paper is as follows: The following section provides a description of the pilot dataset used to train the model Afterwards, the LCS is described along with the precise implementation used. Then in Sect. 4 the experimental design and results analysis are presented. Finally we have the conclusions drawn and avenues for future research.

2 Dataset

2.1 Data Collection

The pilot dataset used was compiled as part of the master's thesis titled "Are there any factors that make the pilots' decisions predictable? An analysis of the impact of conditions on the choice of alternate airports" [7]. The data was gathered through an anonymous online survey using LimeSurvey. The survey took place between October 28, 2022 and November 12, 2022 and had 46 participants. The recruitment of the participants was carried out by direct mail with contacts who were in the Institute of Flight Guidance's mailing list and were not compensated for their participation. The study consisted of:

- An inclusion criterion: active type approval for the Airbus A320 family (yes or no question).
- Sociodemographic questions: year of birth, gender.
- Experience questions: total flight hours, flight hours last year, flight hours on the A320 type approval, pilot rank.
- Twelve decision-making scenarios.

The scenarios consist of a decision-making problem, in which the participants are asked to rank three airports in terms of what they would choose if they had to select a new destination airport midflight. Within the scenarios the reason to select the new airport is not specified. The aircraft in the scenarios are defined to be fully operational with no technical failures. The following information was provided for the twelve scenarios to provide additional context details to the participants:

Airbus A320 fully loaded with passengers and luggage which weighs 64.5 tons along with the maximum possible landing weight. Cruising altitude FL350.

Normal weather according to ISA conditions without wind until you reach the alternates. Manual landing, A/THR off, auto brake medium, reversers. The information provided was to indicate that the status of the aircraft reflected that of what would be considered average for the aircraft type. Regarding the twelve scenarios themselves, the following characteristics for each airport were provided:

1. Distance alternate to original airport: This factor describes the distance between the originally planned airport and the alternate airport.
2. Related Landing Performance: This code translates runway conditions, such as wet, snowy, icy, etc., into a classification of the expected landing performance of the aircraft.
3. Margin landing distance: This factor is the difference between the length of a runway and the braking distance of the aircraft.
4. Crosswind: the wind blowing across the direction of movement.
5. Tailwind: This factor is calculated from the wind direction and speed using trigonometric functions.
6. Fuel remaining: This factor gives the amount of fuel that is left when the airspace of an airport is reached. The minimum amount can be calculated based on regulatory requirements and the current conditions.
7. Number of runways at the airport.

Additionally, the airports were given generic names with two letters to avoid biasing the pilots' responses. This was done to ensure that the pilots were not influenced by their own personal preferences or experiences. Within the study the twelve scenarios were designed to be difficult in order to challenge the participants. This meant that the scenarios showcased where more extreme scenarios where the true answers is not clear. In fact, in [7] the idea was to use extreme cases so that more insight could be gathered into the trade-offs that pilots would make in terms of airport characteristics. Additionally, the scenarios were divided into difficult and very difficult categories. In this context difficulty refers to the how extreme the values are for the factors in terms of how much they close to breaking the safety guidelines.

2.2 Data Analysis

Figure 1 shows the favored or Rank 1 choice of the pilots for each of the scenarios. It is important to note that although 46 participants took part in the study not all of them evaluated all the scenarios presented, hence there are some discrepancy's in the number of evaluations in Fig. 1. From the figure one can ascertain that many scenarios have more apparent preferences, and it would seem that the participants were of a similar mind in their choices. However, in some scenarios, such as S7 and S9, we see that the margin between the airport ranked first most often and the second-best ranked one is not as big as it is in the other scenarios where we can see a more decisive clear preference. While the participants did not always agree, the dataset was still compiled from experts in a specific field, making it a valuable treasure trove of information that models can learn from.

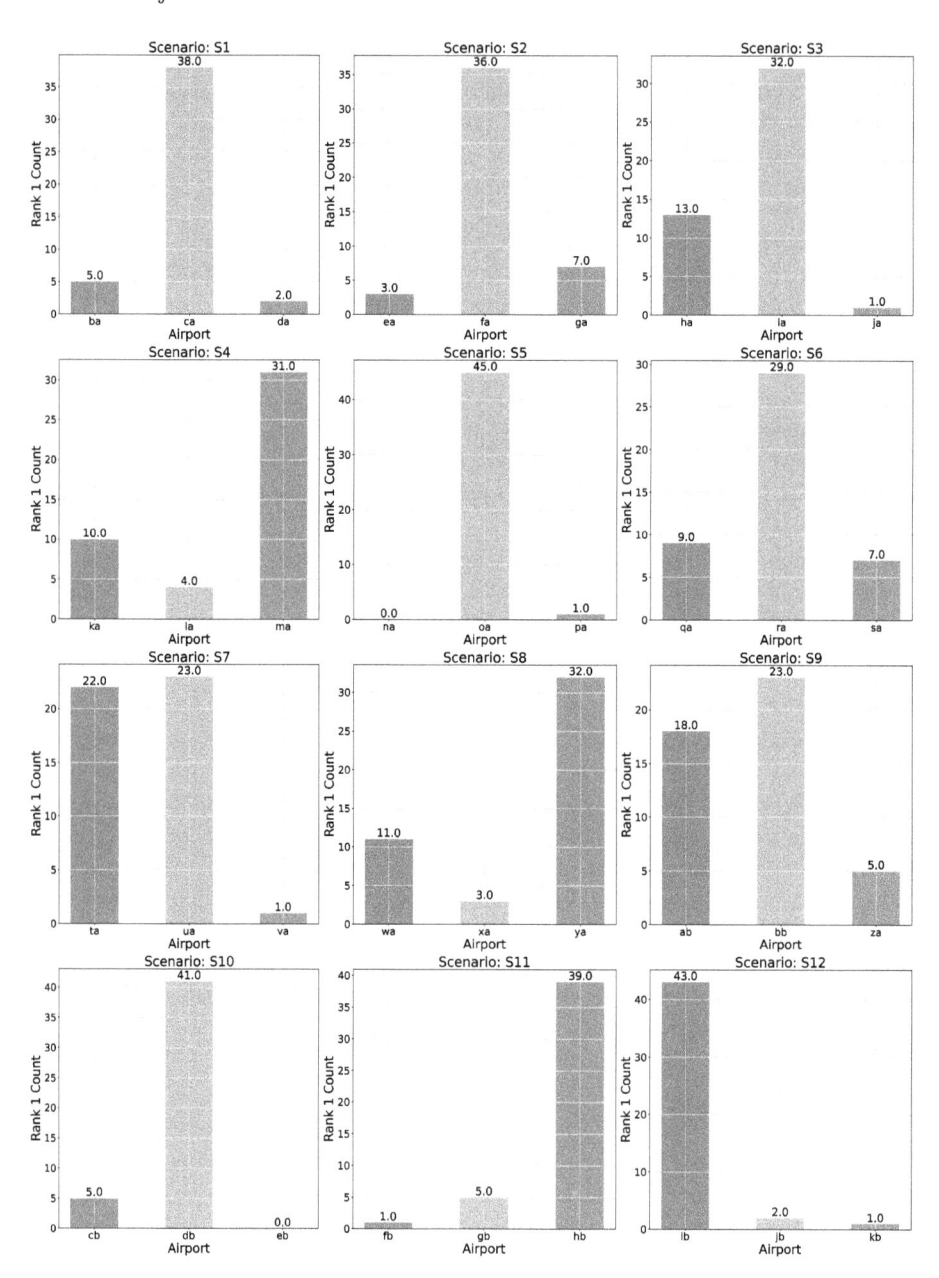

Fig. 1. Analysis of pilot choices

In [7], aside from the wider breath of the investigation analysis the examination of the scenario data was primarily approached by treating all the options/airports as separate instances of a complete dataset. It is worth mentioning that analysis focusing on the scenarios as complete separate units was included but to a limited degree. To better understand the factors influencing participants' decisions, an additional analysis was conducted. In it each scenario was treated as a separate subdataset of the whole dataset. The initial step taken was to simplify the target variable by transforming the answers from the pilot survey to a single variable instead of having three variables for each of the rankings. To accomplish this, a score for each option/airport was calculated based which incorporates all three ranking. The new score was calculated as:

$$SC(a_i) = R1(a) + \frac{R2(a_i)}{2} + \frac{R3(a_i)}{3} \qquad (1)$$

where a refers to the airport selected and Rm refers to the mth ranking from the dataset. This enables the scoring function to take into account the values corresponding to the other rankings and not just focus on the airport which was ranked first. This is needed as Fig. 1 showcased that in certain scenarios the preferred choice is not entirely clear. This score was then used to calculate the Pearson correlation. The correlations for each scenario were calculated and then averaged. Fisher's z-transform was used for this purpose [9], as it stabilizes the variance of correlation coefficients and makes them more suitable for statistical analysis by normalizing their distribution. Using this transformation the influence of the features across all the scenarios can be examined as depicted in Fig. 2. Based on Fig. 2, the Marginal Landing Distance and Related Landing Performance emerge as the most influential factors when making decisions, exhibiting a correlation of nearly 1. This observation aligns with the logical consideration that pilots prioritize information about available landing distance, recognizing its critical role in preventing runway excursions. A runway excursion refers to an incident in aviation where an aircraft departs from the runway during either takeoff or landing. This can occur due to various factors, such as adverse weather conditions, pilot error, technical malfunctions, or a combination of these elements. Runway excursions may involve the aircraft veering off the side of the runway, overshooting the runway end, or, in more severe cases, going off the runway surface entirely. These incidents can pose safety risks and often prompt investigations to determine the causes and implement preventive measures to enhance aviation safety. Similarly, the substantial correlation for Related Landing Performance is justifiable, given that runway conditions significantly impact the aircraft's braking coefficient, thereby influencing the likelihood of a runway excursion.

Interestingly, crosswind and tailwind exhibit a negative correlation, with crosswind exerting a more pronounced influence. It was initially hypothesized that tailwind might be the more influential factor due to the potential dangers associated with strong tailwinds, making landing precarious or even impossible at certain speeds. However, the data suggests a stronger association with crosswind, challenging the initial assumption and emphasizing the need for a

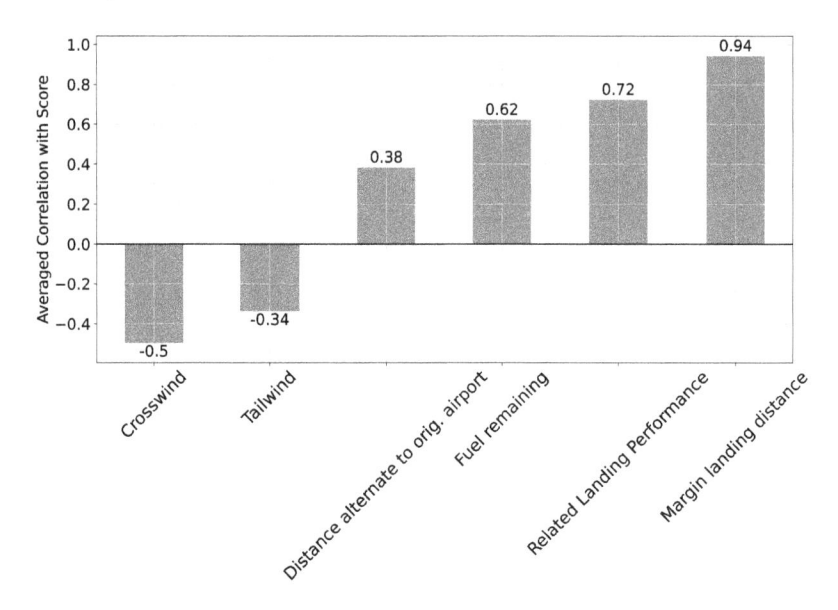

Fig. 2. Feature correlations

nuanced understanding of the interplay between wind conditions and landing performance.

2.3 Traning Dataset Creation

With a better understanding of the dataset, attention can now shift to how it can be utilized for training the model. The scenarios evaluated by participants were designed to reflect a real-world decision-making problem, albeit in a simplified form. Due to time and resource constraints, only this limited subset of scenarios could be assessed. However, training a model on such a small and restricted dataset may not be optimal, as the algorithm would benefit more if it could generalize and handle a broader range of scenarios. Consequently, the model should not only perform well on the smaller pool of evaluated scenarios but also on scenarios that differ from those assessed. To tackle this, a dataset comprising new scenarios was created. These scenarios were generated by sampling airports, including their characteristics, and incorporating them into new scenarios consisting of three airports. The sampling was performed to ensure that no new scenario would contain duplicate airports. Using this method and the fact that $12 * 3 = 36$ airports were available to sample, a total of 988 new scenarios were generated. These new scenarios were combined with the original twelve scenarios to create a dataset of $1,000$ scenarios that could be used to train the LCS. The new dataset, unlike the sampling pool, consists of unlabeled data. "Unlabeled" refers to the fact that the new scenarios have not been evaluated, and there is no established measure of what constitutes a correct response. Hence, the initial idea was to approach this dataset as a reinforcement learning

(RL) problem. In an RL problem, an intelligent agent learns through trial and error by receiving rewards or penalties for its actions [8]. However given that the dataset comprised a single step problem, i.e. only a single action/classification was needed per scenario the dataset was instead converted to a labeled dataset. This was done by making use of a weighted similarity function for each of the airports/options in the new scenarios. The evaluation for an option a from a scenario S is calculated using:

$$EV(a_i, S_n) = \frac{1}{d_{min}(\vec{x}, \vec{b_j})} * SC(a_i) \qquad (2)$$

where n refers to the nth scenario, $d_{min}(\vec{x}, \vec{b_j})$ represent the smallest Euclidean distance between the current input $\vec{S}$ and $\vec{b_j}$ which represents the jth element of the created reference matrix b. The reference matrix comprises the original twelve scenarios, flattened so that each scenario is represented by a single row in the reference matrix. The Eucledian distance between any scenario $\vec{S}$ and a scenario from the reference matrix is calculated as:

$$d(S_n, b_j) = \sqrt{(S_1 - b_{j1})^2 + (S_2 - b_{j2})^2 + ...(S_{nk} - b_{jk})^2} \qquad (3)$$

where k is the number of factors in our dataset, i.e., the number of airport characteristics being considered. Using the evaluation, we measure the similarity between the scenario from the newly created dataset and an evaluated scenario. Subsequently, each of the available actions in the scenario is evaluated based on the scores from the original twelve scenarios. The closer the scenarios resemble each other, the more the ranking of the options ought to resemble each other. Using this new evaluation for the options, the correct class or label is the airport/option that has the highest value. Thus, the unlabeled dataset, using the original twelve scenarios as a reference guide, is transformed into a labeled dataset that can be used to train the model.

3 Model Configuration

An LCS consists of a set of rules known as the population of classifiers. The primary goal is for these classifiers to collectively emulate an intelligent decision maker. This is done through evolution and learning. The genetic algorithm and a problem-specific learning mechanism guide the system toward better rules. Both mechanisms rely on the system's "environment," which, in the context of LCS literature, refers to the source of input data for the algorithm. The information received from the environment depends on the problem being addressed. In this instance, the system will receive decision-making scenarios requiring the selection of one out of three airports. After the interaction with the environment, the LCS will receive feedback in the form of numerical rewards, which then in turn drive the learning process. While various LCS algorithm implementations exist, a basic framework includes a finite population of classifiers representing system knowledge, a performance component regulating interaction with the environment, a reinforcement component distributing rewards to classifiers, and a discovery component improving rules through different genetic operators. These components serve as the foundation for numerous variations in LCS algorithms. Figure 3 illustrates how specific mechanisms of LCS interact within the context of these major components [18,19]. Aside from the interpretability and explainability of the model, LCS has also been extensively used for problems characterized by both epistasis, complex interactions between features of a dataset, and heterogeneity, different features or subset of features are important for different instances of the dataset. The same characteristics are present in popular benchmark problems such as the multiplexer problem [18,20]. Given that these characteristics are also present in the dynamic alternate airport selection problem and that the problem was used as inspiration for the construction of a multi-objective multiplexer benchmark problem [21], using an LCS seems like a suitable model to employ.

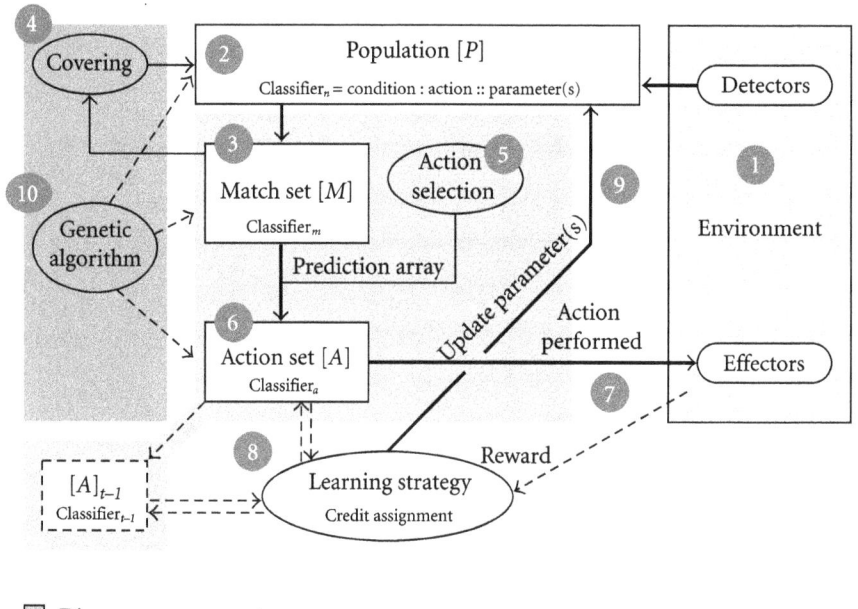

Fig. 3. Visual representation of a LCS, taken from [19]

Due to the large number of LCS variants and the lack of a standardized implementation, here the exact structure of the LCS will be presented. The LCS implemented is loosely based on [24] and is in fact a variation on an enhanced Michigan-style learning classifier, often called XCSF [25,26]. The LCS is comprised of:

1. The condition C which is a hyperellipsoidal condition and is mathematically represented as:

$$C = (\vec{m}, \Sigma) = ((m_1, m_2, ..., m_n)^T, (\sigma_1, \sigma_2, ..., \sigma_n)), \quad (4)$$

   where $\vec{m}$ specifies the center of the ellipsoid, T denotes the transpose of a (column) vector or matrix, and Σ defines the fully weighted Euclidean distance metric of the ellipsoid, also termed Mahalanobis distance [27]. This transformation matrix determines the stretch of the ellipsoid and the rotation in the n-dimensional problem space.
2. The possible action set A, that is, $A \in A$ where $A = \{a1, ..., a_m\}$ represents the set of all possible actions.
3. The linear function prediction R which is specified by the weight vector

$$R = \vec{w} = (w_0, w_1, ..., w_n)^T, \quad (5)$$

   where w_o is the offset weight
4. The prediction error ε which estimates the mean absolute deviation of the reward predictions.
5. F which is the fitness of the classifier.

The values are iteratively modified and evolved. The LCS is initialized with an empty population. Each learning iteration t, the LCS receives a instance x_t along with the function value y_t. LCS then forms a match set $[M]$ of all classifiers whose conditions are active. Classifier activity is determined by

$$\text{cl.ac} = \exp\left(-\frac{(\mathbf{x} - \mathbf{m})^T \Sigma^{-1} (\mathbf{x} - \mathbf{m})}{2}\right),$$

which determines the distance from the current input and then applies the Gaussian kernel on the distance. A classifier is active, that is, it matches if its current activity is above the threshold θ_m. For each step within a learning trial the LCS constructs a match set $[M]$ comprised of active classifiers from the population. Each classifier in $[M]$ has its numerocity increased by 1, $cl.num = cl.num + 1$. Should the match set $[M]$ generate fewer than $\theta_m na$ actions a covering mechanism generates new classifiers and adds them to the population $[P]$. The center of the hyperellipsoid (**m**) fro the newly generated classifiers is set to the current input (**x**). Only the diagonal entries in the transformation matrix (Σ) are initialized to the squared inverse of the uniformly randomly chosen number between zero and the parameter r_0. All other matrix entries are set to zero. In this way, covering creates axis-parallel hyperellipsoidal condition parts. During learning for each possible action a_k in $[M]$ a classifier prediction p_j is calculated as:

$$cl.P(\vec{x}) = cl.w_0 \times x_0 + \sum_{i>0} cl.w_i \times x_i \quad (6)$$

For each action a_k, prediction p_j, and classifier fitness F_j the expected payoff is computed using:
$$P_k = \frac{\sum_j F_j p_j}{\sum_j F_j} \qquad (7)$$

Afterwards a system action is chosen and all of the classifiers in $[M]$ advocating the chosen action are used to create a action set $[A]$. The chosen action is then performed and a scalar reward r is received along with the next input. Upon receiving the reward each classifier in $[A]$ has its weight vector updated according to:
$$cl.w_i \leftarrow cl.w_i + \Delta w_i \qquad (8)$$
where Δw_i is calculated as:
$$\Delta w_i = \frac{\eta}{|\vec{x}|^2}(y - cl.P(\vec{x}))x_i \qquad (9)$$

where $\eta \in [0,1]$ denotes the learning rate and y the target output. The error for each classifier is then calculated as:
$$\varepsilon_j \leftarrow \varepsilon_j + \eta(|y - p_j| - \varepsilon_j) \qquad (10)$$

The fitness is updated next using:
$$F \leftarrow F + \eta(\kappa' - F) \qquad (11)$$

$$\kappa = \begin{cases} 1 & \text{if } \varepsilon_0 \leq \alpha \left|\frac{\varepsilon}{\varepsilon_0} - \nu\right| \\ 0 & \text{otherwise} \end{cases}$$

$$\kappa' = \frac{\kappa \cdot num}{\sum_{cl \in [M]} cl.k \cdot cl.num} \qquad (12)$$

where $cl.k$ refers to the k value for the specific classifier and $cl.num$ refers to the numerocity of the classifier. Finally the set size estimate of each classifier is updated:
$$a_j \leftarrow a_j + \eta(|[M]| - a_j) \qquad (13)$$

The LCS employs a Evolutionary algorithm (EA) for the evolution of classifiers. EAs are a type of algorithm inspired by the natural process of evolution and attempt to solve a problem by evolving and mutating potential solutions to the problem while also applying specific selection pressures. The EA applied to classifiers within $[A]$ it he average time since it's last execution exceeds θ_{EA}. The EA used here employs set-size relative tournament selection [28] based on the fitness estimates of classifiers to choose two parental classifiers from the current match set $[M]$. This means that from the set $[M]$, a random sample is selected to participate in a tournament of varying size. The size of the tournament refers to the number of classifiers that will be compared simultaneously. The classifiers are compared based on their fitness, as this is the mechanism the GA uses to determine how "fit" a classifier is. Subsequently, two offspring are produced through crossover and mutation operations. Uniform crossover is used in which the corresponding values in the two selected classifier are exchanged with a probability of 0.5. Mutation, with a probability of μ, modifies each entry in the condition part by either randomly shifting the center of the hyperellipsoid within its current interval. During mutation, a matrix entry undergoes a maximal increase or decrease of the value by 50%. If the value is initially set to zero, it is initialized to a randomly selected value, using the same method from covering process for diagonal matrix entries, while taking into account the parameter μ_0. The implemented LCS also has a deletion operator in order to maintain the population size. The deletion mechanism initially establishes the average fitness of all classifiers in the population. Next, each classifier is assigned a deletion vote based on its match count and fitness. The deletion vote initially equals the classifier's estimated set size. If the classifier's match count exceeds a threshold θ_{del} and its fitness falls below a fraction δ, its deletion vote is further increased. This ensures that classifiers with many matches and low fitness are more likely to be selected for deletion. A probability distribution where classifiers with higher deletion votes have a higher probability of being selected for deletion is created by normalizing the deletion votes. Using this probability distribution, a classifier is randomly chosen for deletion and removed from the population. This process is repeated until the population size reaches the maximum allowed limit.

4 Experimental Design and Results Analysis

The experiments were carried out in Python version 3.9.6 and made use of the XCSF Python package [30]. LCS is characterized by a large number of hyperparameters, i.e., parameters that need to be given beforehand. Due to this, hyperparameter tuning was done using Bayesian optimization and made use of the Bayesian Optimization: Open-source constrained global optimization tool for Python package [29]. This method employs a Gaussian process to establish a posterior distribution of functions that accurately represents the function being optimized. As the number of observations increases, the posterior distribution becomes more refined, empowering the algorithm to make more informed decisions about which regions of the parameter space are worth exploring and which are not [31]. The Bayesian optimization was carried out using twenty initial points and fifty additional evaluation points. For each combination of parameters, the model was run thirty one times due to its stochastic nature and had 10% of the dataset used as a validation set. The weighted F1 score was used as a measure for hyperparameter tuning, i.e., the parameters were optimized to obtain the highest average (from the thirty one runs per combination of parameters) weighted F1 score. The Weighted F1 Score is calculated using the following formula:

$$\text{Precision} = \frac{\text{TP}}{\text{TP} + \text{FP}} \qquad (14)$$

where TP refers to the number of true positives predictions and FP refers to the number of false positives, additionally FN refers to the number of false negatives and TN refers to the number of true negative predictions.

$$\text{Recall} = \frac{\text{TP}}{\text{TP} + \text{FN}} \tag{15}$$

$$\text{F1 Score} = 2 \times \frac{\text{Precision} \times \text{Recall}}{\text{Precision} + \text{Recall}} \tag{16}$$

The Weighted F1 Score is then computed as the weighted average of the F1 Scores for each class, where the weights are based on the number of true instances for each class:

$$\text{Weighted F1 Score} = \frac{\sum_i (\text{TP}_i + \text{TN}_i) \times \text{F1 Score}_i}{\sum_i (\text{TP}_i + \text{FN}_i)} \tag{17}$$

The Weighted F1 Score is then computed as the weighted average of the F1 Scores for each class, where the weights are based on the number of true instances for each class:

$$\text{Weighted F1 Score} = \frac{\sum_i \text{TP}_i \times \text{F1 Score}_i}{\sum_i \text{TP}_i + \text{FN}_i} \tag{18}$$

The best-found hyperparameters are illustrated in Table 1.

Table 1. Hyperparameter values

Hyperparameter	Lower bound	Upper Bound	Optimal Value
population size	100	200	163
α	0.01	1	0.30
β	0.01	1	0.1
δ	0.01	1	0.4646
error reduc.	0.01	1	0.264
fit reduc.	0.01	1	0.265
max nu. trials	1000	10000	7937
ν	1	10	5.383
crossover probability	0.01	1	0.46
patience	10	10000	4540
perf. trials	1	500	142
θ_{del}	20	200	159.873
θ_{EA}	20	200	155.066

As depicted in Table 1, the population for the LCS was chosen quite conservatively, ranging between 100 and 200 classifiers. This decision was made to exert additional pressure on the LCS to create classifiers that can generalize well. The optimal number found was 163 classifiers, meaning that, on average, one rule would represent $1000/163 = 6.13$ inputs/scenarios from the dataset. However, this is a very rough and simplified estimate, as the classifiers in this configuration of the LCS can overlap. Therefore, it is challenging to determine if solely one classifier from the population represents 6 inputs/scenarios. It is more likely that various subsets of classifiers from the population together are responsible for multiple similar inputs. Another noteworthy hyperparameter is the patience parameter, whose optimal value was estimated to be 4540. This hyperparameter is used as a stopping criterion for the algorithm. If there is no improvement within the last patience number of inputs/scenarios, the algorithm stops training. The chosen number seems quite high compared to the total number of trials. In this context, trials refer to the number of inputs/scenarios given to the algorithm, with a number greater than the size of the dataset indicating multiple passes on the dataset. For the maximum number of trials, it would indicate that the LCS went over the dataset almost 8 times, as the optimal value for this number is 7937.

Using the best-found hyperparameters, an instance of the LCS was run thirty one times, and its precision was measured and compared to that of a random agent. The random agent randomly selects from one of the three available classes for its prediction. The comparison can be seen on Fig. 4. Examining the figure we an observe that the average accuracy of the LCS lies somewhere between 0.55 and 0.6, which would indicate that it gets the answer right around 60% of the time. Although the LCS has a wider distribution for it's accuracy values even

Fig. 4. LCS accuracy versus random agent accuracy

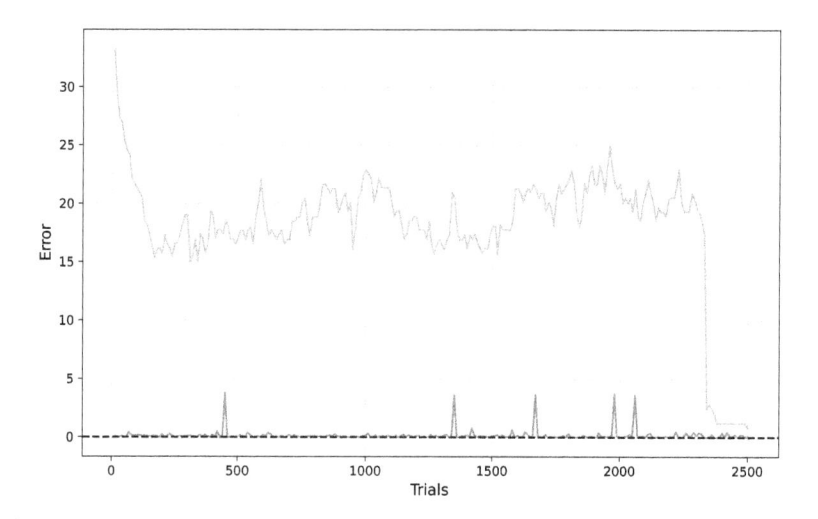

Fig. 5. LCS error across trials

at it's worst it would still outperform the random agent. Although being able to outperform a random agent the LCS still has a mildly impressive accuracy. Additionally, during an exploration into the training of the algorithm it was noticed that in many training sessions of the model there would be a decline of the validation error followed by a plateau or oscillation by the validation error and often, but not always a sudden drop in the validation error. An example of it can be seen in Fig. 5. This behavior could be caused by the more stochastic nature of the algorithm, as the evolution of classifiers may not be sufficient, and at some point, one or a subset of classifiers is created in the population that drastically improves performance. However, it does seem like a problem, as this oscillation can last for many trials, and in some cases, it was never able to reduce. To this end, greater investigation should be given to the stability and consistency of the training of the algorithm, as this undoubtedly influences the overall performance of the algorithm.

5 Conclusion and Future Work

This paper explores the utilization of an AI model to assist pilot decision-making in emergency situations. The model was trained on a dataset from an online survey assessing how pilots would decide in twelve scenarios representing a simplified version of midflight emergency alternate airport selection. The dataset was processed using the Learning Classifier System (LCS), a machine learning approach employing a set of classifiers to simulate intelligent decision-making. LCS was chosen for its enhanced explainability and interpretability compared to more contemporary models like neural networks. The LCS demonstrated promise, achieving an accuracy of approximately 0.6 and outperforming a random agent. However, the algorithm exhibited training instability, leading to a lack of reduction in validation error. Moving forward, efforts focus on enhancing LCS performance and constructing more elaborate datasets for model testing. The ultimate goal is to develop a real-world system that enhances aviation safety and earns pilots' trust.

References

1. Djartov, B., Mostaghim, S., Papenfuß, A., Wies, M.: Description and first evaluation of an approach for a pilot decision support system based on multi-attribute decision making. In: IEEE Symposium Series on Computational Intelligence (SSCI), Singapore, Singapore, pp. 141–147 (2022). https://doi.org/10.1109/SSCI51031.2022.10022076
2. Walters, A.J.: Crew resource management is no accident. Aries (2002)
3. Hörmann, H.J.: FOR-DEC-a prescriptive model for aeronautical decision making (1994)
4. Würfel, J., Djartov, B., Papenfuß, A., Wies, M.: Intelligent pilot advisory system: the journey from ideation to an early system design of an AI-based decision support system for airline flight decks. In: AHFE 2023 (2023)
5. European Union Aviation Safety Agency. EASA-AI-Roadmap 2.0: A human-centric approach to AI in aviation, Cologne (2023)
6. Majumder, M., Majumder, M.: Multi criteria decision making. In: Impact of Urbanization on Water Shortage in Face of Climatic Aberrations, pp. 35–47 (2015)
7. Keul, M.: Are there any factors that make the pilots decision predictable? An analysis about the influence of the conditions on the choice of alternate airports. (Master's thesis). Hochschule Fresenius, Frankfurt am Main (2023)
8. Arulkumaran, K., Deisenroth, M.P., Brundage, M., Bharath, A.A.: Deep reinforcement learning: a brief survey. IEEE Signal Process. Mag. **34**(6), 26–38 (2017). https://doi.org/10.1109/MSP.2017.2743240
9. Howell, D.C.: Statistical Methods for Psychology, 8th edn., pp. 222–224. Wadsworth Publishing Company (2014)
10. Mi, X., Tang, M., Liao, H., Shen, W., Lev, B.: The state-of-the-art survey on integrations and applications of the best worst method in decision making: why, what, what for and what's next? Omega **87**, 205–225 (2019)
11. Lempert, R.J., Groves, D.G., Popper, S.W., Bankes, S.C.: A general, analytic method for generating robust strategies and narrative scenarios. Manage. Sci. **52**(4), 514–528 (2006)
12. Groves, D.G., Lempert, R.J.: A new analytic method for finding policy-relevant scenarios. Glob. Environ. Chang. **17**(1), 73–85 (2007)
13. Kwakkel, J.H., Haasnoot, M., Walker, W.E.: Developing dynamic adaptive policy pathways: a computer-assisted approach for developing adaptive strategies for a deeply uncertain world. Clim. Change **132**, 373–386 (2015)
14. Hamarat, C., Kwakkel, J.H., Pruyt, E., Loonen, E.T.: An exploratory approach for adaptive policymaking by using multi-objective robust optimization. Simul. Model. Pract. Theory **46**, 25–39 (2014)
15. Trindade, B.C., Reed, P.M., Herman, J.D., Zeff, H.B., Characklis, G.W.: Reducing regional drought vulnerabilities and multi-city robustness conflicts using many-objective optimization under deep uncertainty. Adv. Water Resour. **104**, 195–209 (2017)

16. Watson, A.A., Kasprzyk, J.R.: Incorporating deeply uncertain factors into the many objective search process. Environ. Model. Softw. **89**, 159–171 (2017)
17. Bozorg-Haddad, O., Zolghadr-Asli, B., Loaiciga, H.A.: A Handbook on Multi-attribute Decision-Making Methods. Wiley, New York (2021)
18. Urbanowicz, R.J., Browne, W.N.: Introduction to Learning Classifier Systems. Springer, Cham (2017). https://doi.org/10.1007/978-3-662-55007-6
19. Urbanowicz, R.J., Moore, J.H.: Learning classifier systems: a complete introduction, review, and roadmap. J. Artif. Evol. Appl. **2009**(1), 736398 (2009)
20. Alvarez, I.M., Browne, W.N., Zhang, M.: Human-inspired scaling in learning classifier systems: case study on the n-bit multiplexer problem set. In: Proceedings of the Genetic and Evolutionary Computation Conference 2016, pp. 429–436, July 2016
21. Djartov, B., Mostaghim, S.: Multi-objective multiplexer decision making benchmark problem. In: Proceedings of the Companion Conference on Genetic and Evolutionary Computation, pp. 1676–1683, July 2023
22. Olive, X., et al.: OpenSky report 2020: analysing in-flight emergencies using big data. In: 2020 AIAA/IEEE 39th Digital Avionics Systems Conference (DASC), pp. 1–10. IEEE, October 2020
23. Eurocontrol. Aircraft Performance Details: Airbus A320 (2024). https://contentzone.eurocontrol.int/aircraftperformance/details.aspx?ICAO=A320
24. Butz, M.V., Lanzi, P.L., Wilson, S.W.: Hyper-ellipsoidal conditions in XCS: rotation, linear approximation, and solution structure. In: Proceedings of the 8th Annual Conference on Genetic and Evolutionary Computation, pp. 1457–1464, July 2006
25. Wilson, S.W.: Get Real! XCS with continuous-valued inputs. In: Lanzi, P.L., Stolzmann, W., Wilson, S.W. (eds.) IWLCS 1999. LNCS (LNAI), vol. 1813, pp. 209–219. Springer, Heidelberg (2000). https://doi.org/10.1007/3-540-45027-0_11
26. Wilson, S.W.: Classifiers that approximate functions. Nat. Comput. **1**(2–3), 211–234 (2002)
27. Atkeson, C.G., Moore, A.W., Schaal, S.: Locally weighted learning. Lazy learning, pp. 11–73 (1997)
28. Butz, M.V., Goldberg, D.E., Tharakunnel, K.: Analysis and improvement of fitness exploitation in XCS: bounding models, tournament selection, and bilateral accuracy. Evol. Comput. **11**(3), 239–277 (2003)
29. Nogueira, F.: Bayesian Optimization: Open source constrained global optimization tool for Python (2014). https://github.com/fmfn/BayesianOptimization
30. Preen, R.J., Pätzel, D.P.: XCSF. https://doi.org/10.5281/zenodo.10699246, https://github.com/xcsf-dev/xcsf/wiki
31. Snoek, J., Larochelle, H., Adams, R.P.: Practical Bayesian optimization of machine learning algorithms. In: Advances in Neural Information Processing Systems, vol. 25 (2012)

Enhancing Safety in Business and General Aviation Through Real-Time Aircraft Telemetry

Hannes S. Griebel[✉], Simon Hewett, and Juliette O. Littlewood

CGI IT UK Ltd., London, UK
{hannes.griebel,simon.hewett,juliette.littlewood}@cgi.com

Abstract. Commercial air transport has seen a significant decline in accident rates over the past 25 years. Despite steadily growing passenger numbers, cargo tonnage, and miles flown, the absolute number of air accidents in commercial jet operations continues to decrease. At the time of writing, the total number of jet passenger fatalities since 2009 in the United States is fewer than 10.

Over the same period, fatal accident rates in business and general aviation (BGA) have remained relatively constant. While the total miles flown is more difficult to ascertain due to less stringent requirements on flight planning and reporting, the absolute number of accidents saw little to no decline over the same period compared to commercial air transport.

Part of the reason for this discrepancy is the fact that commercial air transport operations are heavily monitored, audited, and in general held to a much higher safety standard than private or business charter operations. Private individuals owning and operating aircraft will also find it harder, if not impossible, to become part of an organisational safety culture. Consequently, the majority of BGA accidents relate to pilot error and maintenance shortcomings. Pilot error related accidents can further be attributed to either one or several of the following root causes: poor decision making, poor airmanship, insufficient proficiency (including lack of qualification), physical impairment, and task saturation in single pilot operations. Moreover, less stringent maintenance regimes in BGA lead to a higher rate of mechanical issues occurring in flight.

A further increase in regulatory oversight is not desirable, as BGA is often seen as an overregulated industry as it is. Furthermore, safety management programmes and technical support functions require the organisational procedures and structures of a larger organisation. Aircraft fleet operators offering commercial charter operations, flight schools, aeroclubs, and large corporations with flight departments might have existing safety management structures, but often lack the resources of larger, commercial air transport operators. Equally, Private individuals operating aircraft without access to organisational safety management systems are currently entirely unable to benefit from such safety programmes.

A subscription service which monitors real-time telemetry could make available to private and small charter operators some, if not most, of the benefits of a safety management culture. To that end, smaller businesses could incorporate a real-time telemetry-based safety support service into their operations, and private individuals could subscribe to a service that provides access to a larger community, replicating the safety management and monitoring functions of larger organisations for individual subscribers. Consequently, voluntary flight recording, and

© The Author(s), under exclusive license to Springer Nature Switzerland AG 2025
D. Harris et al. (Eds.): HCII 2024, LNCS 15381, pp. 257–268, 2025.
https://doi.org/10.1007/978-3-031-76824-8_18

real-time monitoring could offer an alternative way of becoming part of a larger safety culture, not only encouraging safer behaviour, but also offering the opportunity of assisting single pilots struggling with unforeseen circumstances. Through better insurance premiums and similar advantages (e.g., favourable leasing rates), operators could be incentivised to participate in such programmes, negating the need for additional regulations.

This paper explores cost-effective ways of offering a real-time (or at least near-real-time) telemetry and tracking service, how it could be incentivised, and how interventions could be carried out should a situation deteriorate to the point where avoiding an accident likely requires external assistance.

Keywords: Aviation · Real-time telemetry · Accident investigation

1 Introduction

Today, air accidents are rare events. While still a safe mode of transport in absolute terms, business and general aviation (BGA) has not seen the same decline in fatal accident rates as commercial air transport. This is in part due to fewer investigation technologies available to accident investigators (e.g., a lack of flight recorder carriage requirements for light aircraft) leaving the cause of many accidents unresolved, the lower safety standards compared to commercial aviation, a lower level of oversight (airline-type regulations would not be practical in BGA), and the absence of the resources available to major airlines when it comes to the implementation of safety management systems, flight data monitoring (FDM), and flight operations quality assurance (FOQA).

Requiring the carriage of crash protected flight recorders may not be practical for business and general aviation, and neither would be a mandate for sophisticated safety management support services requiring the size and resources of a large company such as an airline. However, current developments in satellite and air-to-ground telecommunication technologies, along with the rapid evolution of artificial intelligence (AI) and machine learning (ML) in big data analysis, may offer alternatives for small companies and private owner-operators to avail themselves of the same safety support functions currently accessible only to large companies and airlines.

With future smartphones expected to have built-in satellite communication terminals, decreasing satcom data volume prices driven by an increase in capacity offered by mega-constellations and air-to-ground networks, it becomes possible to use comparatively inexpensive devices for flight data collection and transmission. Artificial intelligence and machine learning (ML) systems currently under development across various industries offer the potential for automated and inexpensive monitoring, alerting, and de-briefing services. It therefore becomes feasible to provide sophisticated safety functions, currently enjoyed by commercial airlines, through subscription services that reduce the price to the individual subscriber by spreading the relatively high cost of providing a safety service over a large number of subscribers.

To be effective, such services would need to take the human factors element of the pilot in command, and potential ground-based support agents, into account. Improving the performance and effectiveness of human interactions, traditionally trained as part of certain crew resource management regimes, now need to transcend space (e.g., in case of real-time interactions) and time (e.g., in terms of long-term lessons-learnt, flight operations de-brief and review), and may sometimes even require interacting with automated (AI powered) systems. This is not a new concept in itself. For example, air traffic controllers are trained to deal with flight crews in distress.

2 Overview of Real-Time Telemetry and Technical Requirements

There are currently no requirements for light BGA aircraft to carry any means of global tracking or flight recorder data recovery. However, it is prudent to look at standards and recommended practices for commercial air transport. Although not fully applicable to BGA, many of the considerations influencing provisions for commercial air transport can equally inform design choices for similar systems outside of commercial air transport. ICAO (International Civil Aviation Organisation) created a standards and regulatory framework known as the Global Aeronautic Distress and Safety System (GADSS), which is currently being mandated in steps throughout the 2020s by the ICAO member states. For commercial aviation the GADSS ConOps defines requirements and global mandates for all aircraft with Minimum Take-off Weight (MTOW) > 27,000 kg:

1. Global Aircraft Tracking (GAT) with position updates to be sent at least every 15 min.
2. Autonomous Tracking of Aircraft in Distress (ADT) with position updates to be sent at least every 60 s and autonomous detection of a state of distress.
3. Timely Recovery of Flight Data (TRFD) as specified in ICAO Annex 6, and ICAO DOC-10054 [1–3].

Requirements for ADT are elaborated in ARINC-680 and for TRFD in ARINC-681 [4, 5]. The mandatory aircraft parameters (approx. 80) to be recorded by flight data recorders mandated for heavy commercial air transport category aircraft are defined in 14 CFR Appendix B to Part 121, ICAO Annex 6 Part 1 Appendix 8, and ED-112B [2, 6, 7].

ED-112B identifies approaches to satisfying these mandates, either with Automatic Deployable Flight Recorders (ADFR) which release the memory module from the aircraft under certain triggering conditions, or Transmission of Flight Recorder Data (TFRD). The concepts arising from the TFRD based solution for commercial aviation are considered in this paper and their cross-over into private and charter operations in General and Business Aviation [7].

For commercial aviation, the mandatory flight data parameters to be captured by the Flight Data Recorder (FDR) cover primary flight data such as speed, heading, location, attitude, and accelerations, together with aircraft systems status such as engine thrust & power, brakes, pilot inputs, navigation aids and the warnings.

ED-112B identifies the transmission interval for flight data to be at least at once per second when transmission has started. This interval may increase to at least once every 15 s when operating in a non-distress state if the system can detect a distressed state and then transmit at least once per second [7]. Other requirements driving performance of real-time flight data reporting are identified in ARINC-681: the accuracy requirement for detecting the location of end-of-flight is 6 Nautical Miles (NM) for non-survivable accidents and 200 m for survivable accidents [5]. The 6 NM requirement is defined in ICAO Annex 6 Part 1 Sect. 1 and EASA CS.ACNS.E.LAD 410 [2, 8]. The 200-m requirement for end-of-flight location for the purposes of survivor rescue is defined in EASA CS.ACNS.E.LAD.420 [8]. Position reports at a 15 s interval, for a commercial airliner, results in a search radius of approximately 1.5 NM which matches the search field of a Search and Rescue (SAR) aircraft executing a typical search at 1,500 ft.

The availability of Aircraft Interface Devices (AIDs) on commercial aircraft makes it easier to securely integrate with the avionics data buses to access flight record data. AIDs can also be used to maintain the required separation between the three aircraft data domains [Aircraft Control Domain (ACD), Airline Information Services Domain (AISD), and Passenger Information & Entertainment Services Domain (PIESD)] and data routing functions. The continuous streaming of real-time flight-data can be run over any available medium such as Inmarsat's SwiftBroadband or Iridium's Certus for assured cockpit communications, or communication links shared with the Inflight Entertainment (IFE) system. The data is typically encrypted and/or sent over a VPN. As noted before the required data volume is small by comparison with common IP applications but may nevertheless generate significant costs when using exclusively safety-approved radio spectrum and cockpit communication channels. The data stored in a standard, 1024-word FDP data frame amounts to a fraction of common internet traffic and can be always streamed inside of a 9.6kbps data link. The advantages of safety services are their relatively small antenna footprint, resiliency against all kinds of weather, physical separation from other, non-safety related users and global coverage. Their downside, however, is their comparatively high price per megabyte of data.

The goal of routinely transmitting aircraft data, is to gain benefits that exceed the costs of data transmission. A growing number of operators are learning how to leverage this technology for long-term economic, operational, and environmental benefits. Therefore, timely actionable information about flights is becoming increasingly available to large organisations such as aircraft fleet operators and maintenance providers.

Real-time data transmission systems for flight data on commercial air transport aeroplanes come either integrated into the AID, as part of the Electronic Flight Bag (EFB), integrated into the flight recorder (e.g., Honeywell's Black Box in the Sky), integrated into the satellite terminal or even stand-alone (e.g., SatAuth or FLYHT Aerospace Solutions) [9]. While we do not wish to endorse any of the products above over solutions we haven't mentioned, these represent examples of the available technology. Also new Low-Earth Orbit (LEO) satcom providers such as OneWeb and StarLink offer new satcom services being trialled on commercial airlines. This growing competition will lead to ubiquitous low cost satcom downlink capacity for aviation users.

2.1 Considerations for the Business and General Aviation (BGA) Sector

The ARINC-429 data-bus is mainly used on commercial transport aircraft with some use in business aviation. The CSDB (Commercial Standard Digital Bus) is more common in the BGA sector. However, the AIDs produced by the main avionics manufacturers only support the ARINC standards common on large airliners. Consequently, AID based solutions are limited to a subset of the business aviation community.

Solutions relevant to business aviation without integration with the avionics bus are only able to report general characteristics such as: altitude, heading, location, attitude and accelerations which can be determined independently from the avionics system. A range of independent devices with integrated satcom can be fitted to aircraft to provide this capability which satisfy the GADSS mandates, (e.g., SatAuth). For even smaller and lighter aircraft, such as typical single-engine piston aircraft, a modern smartphone or tablet is able to provide basic aircraft movement and acceleration data. Where the tablet, smartphone, or other smart device in question is being used for flight planning and execution purposes, intent weight- and balance, and other flight planning data could be transmitted to support assisting partie. Whilst not providing complete information about the operation of an aircraft, these devices can provide information sufficient to contribute to quality monitoring for business aviation operators and information of potential use to incident investigations and more precise end-of-flight location.

We expect the availability of suitable devices and software solutions will only increase. This is favourable because General aviation aircraft rarely have data connectivity integrated with the aircraft avionics systems. Therefore, data regarding the aircraft state is limited to that which can be provided by methods such as the independent devices described previously. Therefore, while the cost to the general aviation community for installed equipment may be prohibitive, emerging satellite connectivity for conventional smartphones (e.g., such as the Apple iPhone 14 capability to send SOS messages using the Globalstar Inc LEO constellation [10]) offers the potential for data link capability in remote locations even with comparatively affordable hand-held devices. Also, air-to-ground connectivity with terrestrial networks based on 5G technology is available with providers such as SmartSky Network and Gogo [11]. This provides on-board connectivity at more competitive rates than satcom connectivity and routing can be prioritised where available. These connectivity solutions allow for devices such as smart phones with satellite connectivity to act as flight recorder devices (exploiting their built-in GNSS positioning, heading, accelerometers, barometer, voice & video recording features) which can capture some flight data representative of the aircraft state. Where the connected smartphone or tablet is used for flight planning and navigation purposes (e.g., as an electronic flight bag), further information about the progress of the flight and the pilot's intentions can be obtained. That this information is already useful to investigators is evident in the tremendous efforts accident investigation authorities go through to retrieve relevant information from smart devices recovered from crash sites.

Another route to flight data and related downlink connectivity for general aviation is the retrofit of avionics systems with Electronic Flight Instrument Systems (EFIS) (e.g., the Garmin G1000 NXi), which together with a satcom solution (e.g., Iridium GSR 56) can offer global datalink capability that can be used to transmit avionics flight data.

Different connectivity solutions are relevant according to the differing needs of aircraft operations. For remote operations with connectivity out of range of terrestrial communication networks, satcom offers potentially ubiquitous connectivity but at higher cost. While cost-prohibitive to some private owner-operators, communities depending heavily on business and general aviation (such as in Alaska, Northern Canada, in the South Pacific island chains, across South America and many parts of Africa, tracking and flight recorder data recovery over remote areas may significantly reduce the risk associated with these operations, therefore improving the reliability of the aviation infrastructure for many remote communities. For local and regional operations within the vicinity of terrestrial communication networks, connectivity at lower cost is available. Connectivity solutions do not necessarily need to be real-time to provide benefits. Portable electronic devices such as smart phones or EFBs can capture flight parameters during a flight (using the intrinsic sensors of the device) and automatically download the data on the ground using WiFi or standard mobile LTE connectivity at the airfield after the flight. This would be comparable to the processes followed by commercial aviation using Quick Access Records (QARs) for FOQA programmes.

The primary distinguishing feature between business aviation and general aviation is the growing ubiquity of high bandwidth continuous in-flight cabin connectivity for business aviation. For aircraft equipped with broadband passenger connectivity, the additional cost of bandwidth for continuous transmission of flight data can be a marginal cost, due to the relatively low volume of data compared to common internet related data communications such as e-mails and general web browsing. In the case of general aviation aircraft without existing data connectivity, adding a data connectivity solutions will be an additional cost both as a one-time cost to install the equipment, and for operating an aircraft. This cost would need to be traded-off against the benefit gained by operators of small general aviation fleets through access to a comparatively low cost maintenance and FOQA programme across the pilots that use the aircraft fleet. Current systems powered by AI-based big data analytics, such as the ones developed by CGI for monitoring satellite fleets [12], already pave the way for potential future systems capable of integrating assets on a large scale, subscriber basis, allowing small businesses and private individuals to join a larger community for the purpose of collectively improving flight operations performance in a way which is similar to pilots flying for a large operator, such as an airline.

2.2 Data Storage and Access

In their 2023 report on a study commissioned by EASA to investigate acceptable means of compliance with GADSS related mandates, investigators found that the biggest remaining challenge to using transmitted data in accident and incident investigations is the absence of an internationally trusted data storage solution. CGI's Universal Virtual Flight Recorder (UVFDR) service creates such a trustworthy data storage solution through both its system architecture, and its business model: built around the CGI TrustedFabric blockchain solution, the UVFDR service ensures both raw data as well as decoded engineering values are immutably stored, provenance controlled, secured and assured. This provenance control with a demonstrable chain of custody will allow the UVFDR service to satisfy digital-evidence legal-admissibility standards required for any formal use of the data in a legal setting.

Because flight data transmission is not critical to the safe continuation of the flight, satellite or terrestrial data links other than safety certified channels may be used. As described above an increasing number of business aviation aircraft come equipped with low-cost passenger connectivity services, intelligent data routing can allow most flight data to be sent through the least expensive communications link, reverting to more costly, safety certified links only where mandated. Moreover, the UVFDR service can equally accommodate continuous transmission of flight data as well as triggered transmission schemes as per ARINC 681.

To gain benefit from flight monitoring the data does not necessarily need to be downlinked during flight, though this does bring benefits where an aircraft ends its flight away from an aerodrome.

Because BGA operators operate outside of a formal flight recorder data recovery mandate, lower cost equipment without the time and expense of sophisticated aircraft installations of traditional recorders may be used to transmit the data off the aircraft. Equally, the universal nature of the UVFDR lowers the barrier of entry to a professional flight recording, FDM, and FOQA programme. Meanwhile, the non-safety critical nature of the data itself allows it to be sent over low-cost satellite or ground links, and advanced AI data analytics developed for space operations can significantly reduce the cost of FDM and FOQA programmes. Consequently, it becomes easier for BGA operators to avail themselves of such programmes, potentially simply by signing up. While initially designed for commercial aviation, the ease of installation and the growing connectivity options for BGA aircraft means that in the long run, even BGA aircraft can have access to many of the same mechanisms that have helped dramatically reduce the accident rates in commercial air transport.

3 Incentivising Adoption

Though there are clear advantages and technical feasibility of such a system, thought must be given to how uptake is incentivised.

Despite the higher rates of accidents in business and general aviation compared to commercial air transport, there is an agreement within the general aviation industry that BGA is overregulated. The GA Alliance in the UK has claimed that regulations are often far easier for large-scale aircraft operators and airlines to adopt and are significantly more costly for general aviation aircraft to adhere to [13]. In the US, where there is a distinct set of requirements for general aviation, it is still the case that regulations are behind technological advancements, and often policies increase the cost of participation in GA, without having provided equivalent safety benefits [14].

It is therefore apparent that introducing additional regulation would be unfavourable within the industry. In order to encourage uptake, it is necessary to take a look at similar safety approaches within the transport sector, and how rollout has been encouraged.

In the automotive industry, event data recorders (colloquially known as black boxes, named after flight recorders) started being equipped in cars in the 1990s. While these weren't initially mandated, uptake due to improved accident investigations, reduced insurance premiums, and safety gains, have resulted in their use becoming so widespread, that recent US and EU regulations have now begun to mandate they are installed in all new vehicles.

Road telematics were initially implemented to aid in more accurately pinpointing causation in the case of an accident, however in the decades since it has been observed that they also contribute to reduced accident rates. Analysis of some fleets have shown up to a 25% reduction in accident rates when black boxes were knowingly installed in cars [15]. This is largely due to the psychological effects on the driver, the knowledge that they are being observed leads to safer behaviour on the roads.

One of the main benefits to the driver, which encouraged voluntary installation of black boxes, is the promise of lower insurance premiums. For new drivers in particular, car insurance is one of the biggest financial hurdles to driving. Some insurance providers offer a reduction of up to 60% of insurance premiums if a black box is installed.

A similar approach to insurance premiums could aid adoption of real-time telemetry within business and general aviation. Where black boxes on planes are not mandated, and their cost is non-trivial to smaller operators, little to no data about the progress of the flight is available in the case of an accident except for the non-volatile memory that happens to be part of the on-board avionics, air traffic recordings, or smart devices carried on board by the aircraft occupants. By signing up to a third-party service provider that streams data in real-time, data will be available in the case of an accident. The same psychological effect that occurs in drivers could also lead to safer flying behaviour, enabling cheaper insurance premiums for those who have signed up to such a service.

Reviews of safety within general aviation have identified that human error is the most significant cause of accidents [16], so it is inferred that similar safety gains could be made as compared to the automotive industry when using a data streaming service.

In addition to incentivising pilots to avail themselves of connected devices for use on their existing aircraft, aircraft manufacturers could be incentivised to install suitable data collection and transmission equipment on new aircraft as they will benefit from the availability of improved information when incidents occur. These could be technical faults that they can directly address, or safer aircraft operations due to the observation effect which reduces maintenance or repair costs.

Scrutiny of the business and general aviation industry is unlikely to decrease, due to the non-decreasing rates of accidents. Business and general aviation operators could combat this scrutiny by demonstrating commitment to tangible action aimed at improving safety of operations through adoption of a flight recording, flight data monitoring, and flight operations quality assurance service while not having to commit to the cost of a crash-protected flight recorder. Through this the safety culture of commercial aviation becomes accessible to business and general aviation, without significantly increased cost or large resourcing needs.

4 Intervention Mechanisms

While there are currently no regulations available to define how interventions should be carried out using a real-time telemetry service, there are a few avenues of possible intervention mechanisms that could be explored:

4.1 Real-Time Accident Prevention

Real-time data streaming creates potential for remote teams to monitor aircraft and pilot performance from afar, so long as the costs incurred by the provision of a safety system can be kept sufficiently low for individual subscribers. This allows for earlier intervention before an issue can develop into a more serious incident. Data could be analysed real-time to determine any trends before critical situations are reached. These would give support crews more time to reach an aircraft in case of a crash or contact with the pilot could be made to ensure they are well and aware of the situation. Communication with the pilot using information captured in real-time by a UVFDR service would elevate the safety level of the service because of the potential to act on misleading or missing information. This aspect would need to be considered in any capability offered in this respect.

It is worth noting that general aviation may have less crew resource management (CRM) training than commercial aviation. As a result, there may not be available resources on hand from the operator to monitor the data or act in the case of an emergency. In this situation, it may be an option for this real-time monitoring to be performed by a third-party service provider, or by automated alerting or artificial intelligence services. Before any contact is made with the pilot, or before any decisions to dispatch crews are made, any alerts raised by software or AI should be reviewed by a trained operator. This would also help spread the cost of such services across a larger number of subscribers.

4.2 Offline Intervention Mechanisms

Regular performance reports could help operators or pilots identify trends of risk factors or unsafe operating behaviours that could potentially lead to accidents or maintenance issues if continued. This allows for proactive prevention of safety incidents and could feed into training programmes over time.

4.3 Behaviour-Change Mechanisms

Subscribers to a third-party service could be given the opportunity to join a virtual safety community within General Aviation, providing pilots who primarily fly individual flights with valuable insights into their flying performance relative to others.

Virtual communities can become a method of encouraging improved performance and building positive habits. An example of this kind of community is Strava, which connects individual runners and cyclists in a manner that allows for the sharing of activity data and performance analysis. This allows for the creation of a semi-competitive atmosphere for athletes who are otherwise training in isolation, which can promote more focused training and enhanced performance.

Nudge-like interventions, such as notifications about how your metrics are changing over time or how they compare against other users of the service, could be also used to improve behaviour. These analytics are made possible via the common statistical data set across all the members subscribed to the service or community.

These notification types can be used to change behaviour as they enhance self-awareness and use social comparison to encourage change.

Social comparison theory suggests that individuals are more likely to adjust their behaviour when they find out their performance doesn't measure up to their peers and get satisfaction when outperforming others. Through receiving positive or negative notifications or reports, and seeing how their performance compares to others, behavioural conditioning can occur where people become more likely to adopt safer behaviours to achieve that positive feedback loop [17].

5 Establishing a BGA Safety Programme

We identified a number of key elements that need to be in place for a UVFDR-based safety programme for BGA. These are, in no particular order:

- A storage service which can receive and provide access to the flight data together with the data analysis which supports some of the intervention mechanisms suggested above, around which the BGA community can develop behaviours resulting in reduced accident rates.
- A service with the necessary data protection and access control to protect the privacy of the flight data and the identities of the pilots and operating organisations using the service whilst maintaining the integrity and provenance of the data.
- BGA aircraft equipped with either integrated avionics/satcom solutions for reporting real-time transmission of flight profile and avionics data, or independent solutions able to report the flight profile parameters in real-time over terrestrial radio or satcom links, or through on-ground services after landing.
- A frictionless experience for pilots and organisations to participate in the service so that they can easily establish communities of shared best practice and safety culture mirroring the collective safety culture of commercial aviation.
- A critical mass of aircraft operators and pilots to establish a community eager to participate in reducing the BGA accident rate.
- A monitoring mechanism to identify the impact of the BGA UVFDR safety programme on BGA accident rates.
- A market signal from aviation regulators and commercial participants such as insurers which recognises the benefit gained from aircraft, aircraft operators and pilots participating in a BGA UVFDR safety programme.

Some of these are technology based, such as the aircraft equipment and UVFDR storage solutions, others are human based such as the desire to improve BGA safety and to participate in a BGA UVFDR community, and others are market based driving the commercial benefits gained from participation.

6 Conclusion

The decline in accident rates within commercial air transport over the past 25 years can be attributed to the stringent safety standards and monitoring in commercial operations, contrasting with the relatively stagnant rates in business and general aviation. A potential solution to bridge this gap lies in the adoption of a subscription-based real-time telemetry service, offering compliance with ICAO's GADSS mandates through Transmission of Flight Recorder Data provisions set by ED-112B.

Emerging means, including leveraging smartphone capabilities, and retrofitting Electronic Flight Instrument Systems, offer promising avenues for data collection. Existing cabin connectivity infrastructure, non-safety satcom or terrestrial data links could be leveraged for cost-effective data transmission. Ensuring the integrity and reliability of collected data is paramount in case data is ever required for investigative purposes, with the development of assured storage solutions like CGI's UVFDR service offering a crucial piece of the puzzle.

Incentivizing the adoption of such real-time flight recorder services could be achieved through reduced insurance premiums and enhanced safety outcomes. This service would be able to provide smaller operators with access to a safety culture otherwise beyond their resource capabilities and could encourage safety behaviours in BGA that are commonplace in commercial aviation.

Specifically, these services could enable various intervention mechanisms, including post-flight performance analysis and real-time remote monitoring across all pilots who partake in the service. Continuous improvement in safety behaviour could then be encouraged through performance notifications and social comparison, mechanisms resulting in improved safety outcomes.

Just as flight operations quality assurance wasn't considered necessary a few decades ago, yet is now considered best practice, business self-regulation driven by incentives explored in this paper could encourage uptake of a UVFDR-type service without the need for additional regulation in an industry that already deems itself to be overregulated.

With many of the necessary features for a BGA UVFDR programme already available or in development, cohesive integration and market support are essential to realizing this programme's potential in enhancing safety across business and general aviation sectors.

Acknowledgements. For the development and operational demonstration of the UVFDR service, CGI is working together with industry partners SatAuth, Code Magus Ltd, Cranfield University, and Amazon Web Services (AWS), along with other stakeholders. The project is supported by the UK Space Agency and the European Space Agency through the ARTES – Space Systems for Safety and Security (4S) programme.

Disclosure of Interests. The authors have no competing interests to declare that are relevant to the content of this article.

References

1. ICAO: Global Aeronautical Distress & Safety System - Concept of Operations. Version 6.0. https://www.icao.int/safety/globaltracking/Documents/GADSS%20Concept%20of%20Operations%20-%20Version%206.0%20-%2007%20June%202017.pdf. Accessed 08 Mar 2024
2. ICAO: Annex 6 Operator of Part 1 Appendix 8 Flight Recorders
3. ICAO: Doc 10054 - Manual on Location of Aircraft in Distress and Flight Recorder Data Recovery Notice to Users
4. ARINC: ARINC 680 Aircraft Autonomous Distress Tracking (ADT)
5. ARINC: ARINC 681 Timely Recovery of Flight Data (TRFD)
6. FAA: 14 CFR Appendix B to Part 121 - Code of Federal Regulations Title 14 - Aeronautics and Space Chapter I - Federal Aviation Administration, Department of Transportation Subchapter G - Air Carriers and Operators for Compensation or Hire: Certification and Operations Part 121 - Operating Requirements: Domestic, Flag, and Supplemental Operations Appendix B - Airplane Flight Recorder Specification
7. EUROCAE: ED-112B - MOPS for Crash Protected Airborne Recorder Systems
8. EASA: CS-ACNS - EASA Certification Specifications and Acceptable Means of Compliance for Airborne Communications, Navigation and Surveillance

9. ISASI: J. Int. Soc. Air Safety Invest. **50**(3), 16–21 (2022)
10. Android Authority: Android and iPhone satellite connectivity: Here's what you need to know. https://www.androidauthority.com/smartphone-satellite-connectivity-3295162/. Accessed 29 Feb 2024
11. Anne Wainscott-Sargent: Business Jet Market Enjoys a Boon in New In-flight Connectivity Options. https://interactive.aviationtoday.com/avionicsmagazine/september-october-2022/business-jet-market-enjoys-a-boon-in-new-in-flight-connectivity-options/. Accessed 29 Feb 2024
12. CGI: CGI to develop innovative Artificial Intelligence enabled platform for the global satellite communications marketplace. https://www.cgi.com/uk/en-gb/news/space/cgi-develop-innovative-artificial-intelligence-enabled-platform-global-satellite-communications-marketplace. Accessed 08 Mar 2024
13. House of Commons: House of Commons - Transport - Thirteenth Report. https://publications.parliament.uk/pa/cm200506/cmselect/cmtran/809/80910.htm. Accessed 20 Feb 2024
14. Royal Aircraft Services: The FAA's Impact on Small Business in the General Aviation Industry. https://smallbusiness.house.gov/uploadedfiles/2-5-2014_heffernan_testimony.pdf. Accessed 20 Feb 2024
15. Roberts, G.: 'Black box' plays key role in death crash prosecution. Fleet News, https://www.fleetnews.co.uk/fleet-management/-black-box-plays-key-role-in-death-crash-prosecution/38851/#:~:text=A%20Dutch%20study%2C%20examining%20several,boxes%20fitted%20to%20their%20vehicle. Accessed 20 Feb 2024/02/20
16. CAA: UK Approach to Recreational General Aviation Safety: An Independent Review. https://publicapps.caa.co.uk/docs/33/GA%20Safety%20Review.pdf. Accessed 20 Feb 2024
17. Vris, R., Lemke, M., Ludden, G.: Blueprints: systematizing behavior change designs—the case of social comparison theory. Assoc. Comput. Mach. **31**(1), 1–32 (2023)

Which Train Should Be Stopped First? The Impact of Working Memory Capacity and Relative Risk Level on Priority Judgment of High-Speed Railway Dispatchers During Emergency

Yan Jiang[1], Lei Shi[1,2,3], Jun Zhang[4], Jingyu Zhang[5,6(✉)], Zizheng Guo[1,2,3], Zhenqi Chen[1], Qiaofeng Guo[1,2], and Yan Zhang[7]

[1] School of Transportation and Logistics, Southwest Jiaotong University, Chengdu 610031, China
[2] Comprehensive Transportation Key Laboratory of Sichuan Province, Chengdu 610031, China
[3] National Engineering Laboratory of Integrated Transportation Big Data Application Technology, Chengdu 611756, China
[4] Technology Transfer Research Institute, Southwest Jiaotong University, Chengdu 610031, China
[5] CAS Key Laboratory of Behavioral Science, Institute of Psychology, Beijing 100101, China
zhangjingyu@psych.ac.cn
[6] Department of Psychology, University of Chinese Academy of Sciences, Beijing 100049, China
[7] Guoneng Shuohuang Railway Development Co., Ltd, China National Energy Investment, Beijing, China

Abstract. High-speed railway is a highly automated and reliable system, but during natural disasters, it still relies on dispatchers to execute fast andaccurateemergency responses. This study examines the core decision problem faced by dispatchers in emergency management - the issue of priority judgment. Focusing on earthquake scenarios, this study examined how situational factors and individual competence as measured by working memory capacity jointly affect this process. A total of 71 professional high-speed rail dispatchers participated. Their working memory was first assessed using 2-back tasks. They then made priority judgments in a series of scenarios involving two trains with varying distal differences toward earthquake center (ΔD: 0 km, 4 km, 8 km, 12 km, 16 km, 20 km) and directions (toward/away from the earthquake zone). The results show that all factors jointly influenced the dispatchers' priority judgments. Crucially, the distal differences (ΔD) had a decisive impact, with trains closer to the epicenter more likely to be prioritized. Furthermore, only dispatchers with high working memory capacity considered the influence of train movement direction. This study not only introduces a new approach to understanding human decision in complex systems but also provides theoretical support for dispatcher training programs - an important practical step to ensure the safe and efficient operation of high-speed rail networks during emergencies.

Keywords: High-speed railway dispatcher · Priority judgment · Working memory capacity · Related risk factors · multi-level analysis

1 Introduction

The safety of high-speed rail operations is the basic demand of the railway transportation industry. Seismic events occur frequently and cause serious harm. At present, earthquake early warning technology is an effective means of disaster reduction, but it also has its limitations and uncertainties, and cannot completely replace earthquake prediction and earthquake prevention and disaster reduction work. There are forecast blind spots and false positives in earthquake prediction work, which is a global problem, and long-term scientific research is needed to break through this problem. The analysis of the causes behind seismic events has become the focus of academic research. However, compared with the study of physical effects, the study of human factors in the railway system is rarely involved. The automated and intelligent development of the train scheduling system is in full swing, and dispatchers need to complete daily scheduling tasks with the help of CTC system scheduling terminals [1]. High-speed railway dispatchers play a crucial role in ensuring the safety of railway operations, especially in emergencies such as floods, debris flow, earthquakes, etc. In these situations, they must make a rapid judgment to stop the trains that are in or will be in danger. As the time window is short and the execution to stop trains is also time-consuming, it is important that the dispatchers prioritize trains that are under the highest level of risk.

There are few direct studies on the priority decision-making of high-speed railway dispatchers when dealing with emergency events. The study of priority events mainly involves the Strategic Task Overload Management (STOM) Model and the Salience-Expectancy-Effort-Value (SEEV) Model [2]. STOM model is a multi-attribute decision-making model [3], which is used to solve the problem of how to select and switch tasks when multiple tasks are processed at the same time [4]. The model takes into account the influence of factors such as interest, difficulty, significance, and priority on task selection. Priority refers to the operator's subjective evaluation of the importance of each task. In the case of task overload, the operator is more inclined to switch to high-priority tasks rather than low-priority tasks. The SEEV model considers four factors that affect attention, namely prominence, expectation, effort, and value. The priority in the model reflects the importance of an area or event to the goal or task, and it will cost a lot to ignore or miss the area or event [5]. Most of the existing studies assume that the attribute of event priority is known and focus on the impact of priority events on attention allocation. From the perspective of task switching, we will explore the criterion of priority determination in seismic events and study the impact of task priority characteristics on the decision-making of relevant personnel.

According to existing studies and theories, there are two factors that affect the decision-making performance of high-speed railway dispatchers. On the one hand, the characteristics of the task itself are the relative risk in the emergency, and the relevant personnel will prioritize the train with greater relative risk. Generally speaking, when an earthquake affects railway operation, the trains driving into the earthquake center and closer to the center will face greater dangers. When the relative distances between different trains are different, the relative risks faced by the trains are inconsistent.

On the other hand, the ability of dispatchers is an important factor affecting their decision-making performance. Although there are many objective factors affecting event handling, high-speed railway dispatchers need to process the objective factors with their own limited cognitive resources, which will involve the cognitive bottleneck, that is, working memory capacity [6]. Working memory is closely related to cognitive processes such as information processing and decision making [7]. In the actual working environment, dispatchers need to process a large amount of information quickly and accurately, and take on important decision-making responsibilities. Working memory can help them effectively manage and utilize information [8]. Dispatchers with large working memory capacity can accurately process information and make correct decisions.

Research paradigms on working memory mainly include the Recall Paradigm, Change Detection Task and Continuous Reproduction Task [9]. Among them, the recall paradigm means that subjects remember a series of numbers, words or pictures [10, 11], each stimulus is displayed at a consistent time interval, and finally subjects complete the reordering according to the prompt. The change detection task requires the subjects to first memorize the presented items, maintain the memory in the empty screen state, and finally judge whether one or more items appear and the memory items are the same. The continuous reporting task pays more attention to the color and orientation of the memorized items, and tests the accuracy of the memory of the subjects. The more salient the information is, the more it can arouse the working memory level of the subjects. It can be started from training the working memory to expect the subjects to achieve the best performance [12]. The working memory mechanism of the subjects will produce dynamic decision bias [13]. Based on this, this paper sets out to test the working memory of the subjects and study the influence of their working memory level on the characteristics of emergency decision making.

Therefore, the purpose of this study is to comprehensively investigate the impact of objective risk difference and dispatcher working memory ability on the priority decision-making of high-speed railway dispatchers, and propose the following hypotheses to enrich the research on train scheduling.

H1: Compared with the train leaving the earthquake affected area, when the train enters the earthquake affected area, the train is more affected by the earthquake, and all high-speed rail dispatchers give higher priority to the stopping of the incoming train.

H2: Controlling other variables unchanged, when the relative distance between trains is far, train B is far away from the focal center, and the high-speed rail dispatcher will pay more attention to train A, which is closer to the focal center.

H3: In the emergency earthquake decision-making event, this paper believes that dispatchers with high working memory cognition can better deal with earthquake events and accurately stop trains with higher danger degrees, while dispatchers with low working memory need to improve their performance (Fig. 1).

Fig. 1. High-speed rail dispatcher working scene diagram

2 Method

2.1 Subjects

A total of 71 subjects were recruited in the F Railway Bureau of China Railway. These dispatchers in professional high-speed railway were all male, with an average age of 37.24 (SD = 1.939) and their ages ranged from 34 to 40. All subjects were proficient in computer operation. They were from the same railway bureau, in good health and had no bad habits.

2.2 Procedure

The experimental program was hosted on an HTML web page and administered on laptop computers, allowing subjects to complete all the required tests. In the working memory assessment section, the study utilized the standardized 2-back paradigm to measure participants' cognitive capabilities. According to the daily work requirements of high-speed railway dispatchers, the 2-back form was used to design the test process [14], the interface displayed irregular and complex graphics, and the switch of task flow modules was triggered by Spaces to complete the conversion.

The main test protocol involved completing a series of scheduled assessments, including determining the number of tests, test durations, and test locations. The researchers arrived at the experimental site in advance to verify the proper functioning of the computer equipment and ensure successful login to the testing system.

Once the test officially commenced, the facilitator provided instructions, answered participant questions, and allowed subjects to log in and begin the tasks after entering the required information. The experimental scenarios were presented in random order. After completing 32 practice trials, participants could choose to repeat the practice phase or proceed to the formal test. Upon finishing 4 × 32 formal tasks, the working memory assessment portion concluded, and the system prompted subjects to move on to additional tasks. Throughout the test, the researchers closely monitored the participants, addressed any issues that arose, and recorded the overall response patterns.

After completing the working memory test, the subjects completed the earthquake priority test, which has a total of 36 questions, and the test interface is shown in Fig. 2. According to the interface presented, the subjects made four choices: withholding train B before train A, withholding only train B without withholding train A, withholding train A after train B, withholding only train A without withholding train B.

The correct answer rate of the subjects was coded as working memory data. In the decision-making part of the subjects, the code of withholding train A before train B and withholding train B without withholding train A was 0, and the code of withholding train B before train A and withholding train B without withholding train B was 1.

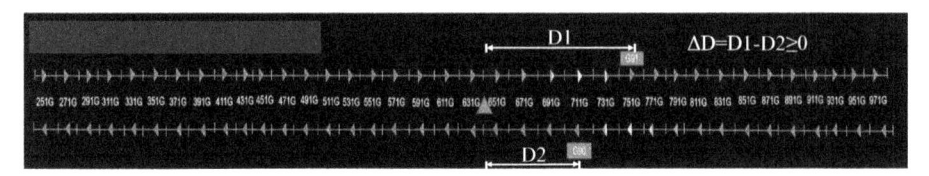

Fig. 2. Task scenarios and variable setting diagram.

3 Results

3.1 Initial Analysis

Table 1 presents the means, standard deviations, and correlations for all variables. Moving direction relative distance and working memory were significantly correlated with priority stopping probability for relatively dangerous trains.

3.2 HLM Analysis

HLM Results Predicting Priority Stopping Probability. To simultaneously examine the effects of scenario parameters and individual differences, while avoiding issues caused by missing data, the researchers adopted a hierarchical linear modeling (HLM) approach using R 4.3.2. The HLM analysis followed a two-level structure: level 1 accounted for task-level variables (i.e., the manipulated scenario parameters), while Level 2 captured individual differences (i.e., working memory capacity). The calculated intraclass correlation coefficient (ICC) was 37.76%, indicating that individual-level variables could explain a substantial proportion of the observed variance.

As shown in Table 2, Model 2 showed that the relationship between moving direction and priority stopping probability was positive and significant ($\beta = 1.338$, $p < 0.001$), which tested Hypothesis 1. Multi-level linear regression revealed that ΔD significantly predicts priority judgment ($\beta = 0.049$, $p < 0.001$). Trains closer to the earthquake center

Table 1. Correlation matrix of all variables.

	Mean	SD	1	2	3	4
Scenario level Predictors(N = 2556)						
1. Moving direction	0.520	0.500	1			
2. Relative distance	10.000	6.833	.000	1		
Individual level Predictors(N = 71)						
3. Working memory	63.410	15.309	-.030	.000	1	
4. Priority stopping probability	0.630	0.483	.183**	.108**	.102**	1

Note: * $p < 0.05$, ** $p < 0.01$, *** $p < 0.001$

are more likely to be stopped earlier. We further found a marginally significant interaction between moving direction and dispatchers' working memory capacity ($\beta = 0.036$, $p < 0.1$).

Table 2. HLM results predicting Priority stopping probability for relatively dangerous trains.

	Model1		Model2	
	β (Std. Error)	P value	β (Std. Error)	P value
Intercept	0.161(0.220)	0.4663	0.166(0.216)	0.4417
Scenario level Predictors				
Moving direction	1.327(0.318)	0.0000***	1.338(0.312) 0.238	0.0000***
Relative distance	0.049(0.009)	0.0000***	0.049(0.009)	0.0000***
Moving direction × Relative distance	-0.020(0.014)	0.1371	-0.020(0.014)	0.1392
Individual level Predictors				
Working memory	0.021(0.010)	0.0422*	0.008(0.013)	0.5211
Cross-level Interactions				
Moving direction × Working memory			0.036(0.021)	0.0883+
Relative distance × Working memory			0.000(0.000)	0.9343

Note: N = 71 subjects

In parentheses, there are robust standard errors.
+ $p < 0.1$, * $p < 0.05$, ** $p < 0.01$, *** $p < 0.001$.

HLM Results Predicting Intervention Decision. To identify the form of the interaction, we plotted the interaction at conditional values of moving direction (1 SD above and below the mean). This relationship is presented in Fig. 3.

For dispatchers who have a relatively lower level of working memory, the Priority given toward/outward was not different. For dispatchers who have relatively higher levels of working memory, they gave far more Priority to trains moving toward the earthquake zone than those moving outward. This finding also suggests that working memory capacity is a critical cognitive factor influencing high-speed railway dispatchers' performance. Dispatchers with higher working memory tend to have a higher rate of stopping trains when necessary and are more sensitive to changes in relevant cues.

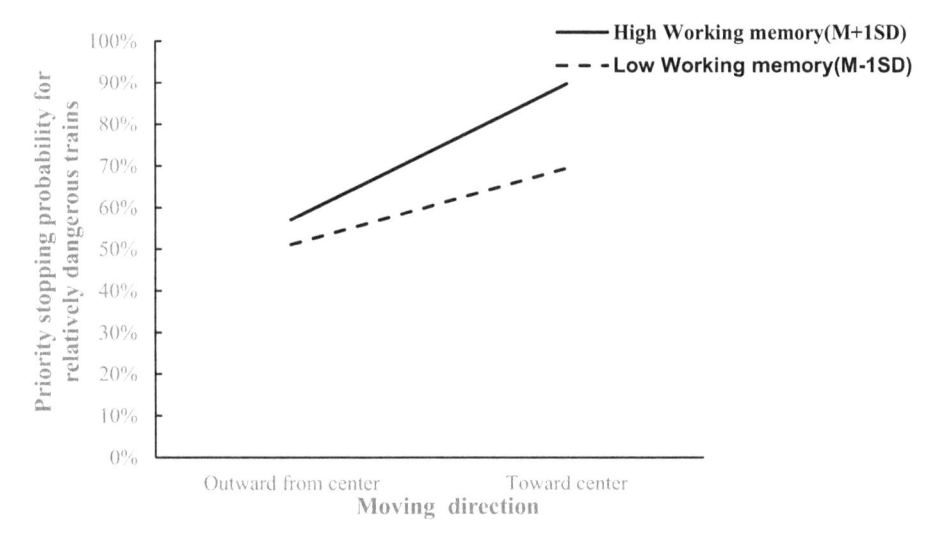

Fig. 3. The joint effect of Moving direction and Working memory on Priority stopping probability for relatively dangerous trains.

4 Discussion

This study pioneered a novel approach to examining the priority judgments made by personnel in specialized roles during emergency events. The findings indicate that both scenario-level and individual-level factors jointly influenced the priority judgments of high-speed rail dispatchers. Crucially, the variable ΔD, representing the distance from the earthquake epicenter, had a decisive impact, with trains closer to the center more likely to be prioritized. This variable appears to be the most significant factor, unaffected by the dispatcher's ability level.

Additionally, the results reveal that only dispatchers with high working memory capacity considered the influence of train movement direction. They can also apply it to seismic decisions, making it more likely that dangerous trains will be stopped first. This may be because it is difficult for dispatchers to directly perceive train speeds on the control interface, especially when processing multiple other information sources simultaneously. As a result, movement direction does not become a salient cue for lower-capacity individuals.

Overall, this study expands decision-making research in train dispatching by elucidating the roles of scenario factors and working memory in priority judgments. The findings offer practical guidance for the selection, training, and performance evaluation of high-speed rail dispatchers. Future research can further explore expanded variables to gain deeper insights into the decision-making processes of these critical personnel.

Funding. This study was supported by the National Natural Science Foundation of China (Grant NO. 52072320), the Science and Technology Research and Development Plan Project of China National Railway Group Co., Ltd (N2022Z016), the key project of Chongqing Technology Innovation and Application Development (grant no. cstc2021jscx-dxwtBX0020) and the Research Project of Shuohuang Railway Company (SHTL-21-18 and GJNY-22–84).

References

1. Chen, Z., Guo, Z., Feng, G., Shi, L., Zhang, J.: A Qualitative Study on the Workload of High-Speed Railway Dispatchers. In: Harris, D., Li, WC. (eds.) Engineering Psychology and Cognitive Ergonomics. HCII 2021. LNCS, vol. 12767. Springer, Cham (2021). https://doi.org/10.1007/978-3-030-77932-0_21
2. Santamaria, A., Wickens, C.D., Gutzwiller, R.S., et al.: Discrete task switching in overload: a meta-analysis and a model. Int. J. Hum. Comput. Stud. **79**. 79–84 (2015). https://doi.org/10.1016/j.ijhcs.2015.01.002
3. Wickens, C.D., Gutzwiller, R.S., Vieane, A., et al.: Time sharing between robotics and process control: validating a model of attention switching. Hum. Fact. J. Hum. Fact. Ergon. Soc. **58**(2), 322–343 (2016)
4. Wickens, C.D., Gutzwiller, R.S.: The status of the strategic task overload model (STOM) for predicting multi-Task management. Proc. Hum. Fact. Ergon. Soc. Ann. Meet. **61**(1), 757–761 (2017)
5. Gutzwiller, R.S., Wickens, C.D., Clegg, B.A.: Workload overload modeling: an experiment with MATB II to inform a computational model of task management. Proc. Hum. Factors Ergon. Soc. Ann. Meet. **58**(1), 849–853 (2014)
6. Baddeley, A.: Working memory or working attention? Attent. Sel. Awaren. Control **51**(S1), S27–S38 (1993)
7. Lamichhane, B., Westbrook, A., Cole, M.W., et al.: Exploring brain-behavior relationships in the N-back task. Neuroimage **212**, 116683 (2020)
8. Zilli, E.A., Hasselmo, M.E.: Modeling the role of working memory and episodic memory in behavioral tasks. Hippocampus **18**, 193–209 (2008).https://doi.org/10.1002/hipo.20382
9. Hannak, Cognitive training based on human-computer interaction and susceptibility to visual illusions. Reduction of the Ponzo effect through working memory training. Int. J. Hum.–Comput. Stud. **184**. 103226 (2024). https://doi.org/10.1016/j.ijhcs
10. Luck, S.J., Vogel, E.K.: The capacity of visual working memory for features and conjunctions. Nature **390**(6657), 279–281 (1997)
11. Jones, A., Ward, E.V.: Rhythmic temporal structure at encoding enhances recognition memory. J. Cogn. Neurosci. **31**(10), 1549–1562 (2019)

12. Bednarek, H., Przedniczek, M., Wujcik, R., et al.: Cognitive training based on human-computer interaction and susceptibility to visual illusions. Reduction of the Ponzo effect through working memory training. Int. J. Hum. Comput. Stud. **184**, 103226 (2024)
13. Zerr, P., Gayet, S., Van Der Stigchel, S.: Memory reports are biased by all relevant contents of working memory. Sci. Rep. **14**(1), 2507 (2024)
14. Jaeggi, S.M., Seewer, R., Nirkko, A.C., et al.: Does excessive memory load attenuate activation in the prefrontal cortex? Load-dependent processing in single and dual tasks: functional magnetic resonance imaging study. Neuroimage **19**(2), 210–225 (2003)

Field Trials of an AI-AR-Based System for Remote Bridge Inspection by Drone

Jean-François Lapointe[1](✉), Mohand Saïd Allili[2], and Nadir Hammouche[1]

[1] National Research Council Canada, Digital Technologies Research Centre, Ottawa, Canada
{jean-francois.lapointe,nadir.hammouche}@nrc-cnrc.gc.ca
[2] Département d'informatique et d'ingénierie, Université du Québec en Outaouais, Gatineau, Canada
mohandsaid.allili@uqo.ca
https://nrc-cnrc.canada.ca

Abstract. Bridge inspections are important to ensure the safety of users of these critical transportation infrastructures and avoid tragedies that could be caused by the collapse of these infrastructures. This paper describes the results of field trials of an advanced system for remotely guided inspection of bridges by a drone, which relies on artificial intelligence and augmented reality to achieve it. Results indicate that a high speed network link is critical to achieve good performance.

Keywords: Bridge inspection · Remote guidance · Concrete bridges · drone · UAV · artificial intelligence (AI) · augmented reality (AR) · field trial

1 Introduction

Regular and proactive inspections of bridges and overpasses (which are structurally equivalent to bridges) are important to ensure the safety of users of these critical transportation infrastructures and avoid tragedies such as the recent collapse of the Morandi bridge in Italy [2]. The use of *unmanned aerial vehicles (UAVs)*, commonly referred to as *drones*, combined with AI to perform bridge inspections is an emerging topic [5,7]. This paper describes the results of field trials of such an advanced system for remotely guided bridge inspection that also combines AR to achieve it. It is a specific case of remote guidance, as described in [9]. It combines the benefits of drones (easy access to hard-to-reach areas and fast visual scanning), Artificial Intelligence (AI) (automated defect detection) and Augmented Reality (AR) (overlaying digital information over real images, thus allowing to combine real and virtual information within the same field-of view). Figure 1 illustrates such a use case. The figure contains the different system components, which are discussed in details in the next section.

This project was supported in part by collaborative research funding from the National Research Council of Canada's Artificial Intelligence for Logistics Program.

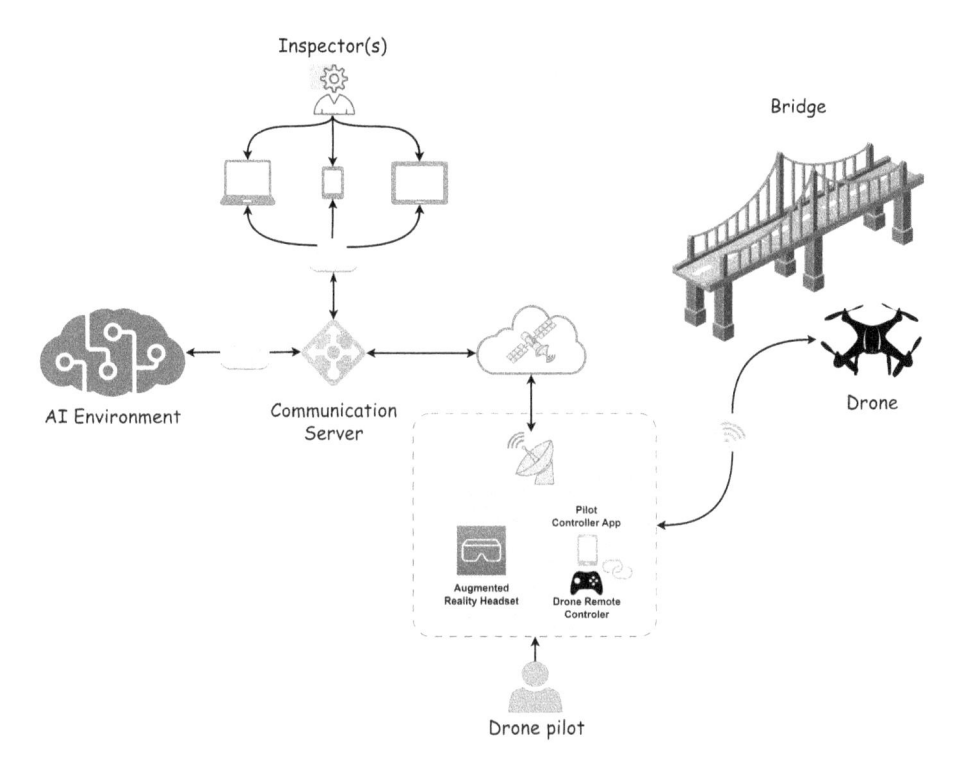

Fig. 1. Illustration of the AI-AR remote inspection system

2 System Overview

The remote bridge inspection system presented in this paper comprises a collection of multiple components working together to achieve an effective, accurate and safe assessment of such infrastructure. As shown in the Fig. 1, the drone is capturing detailed imagery of the bridge. The drone's pilot is equipped with an augmented reality headset that assist him/her during the inspection. An AI environment is set up to process the data collected in real time in order to detect surface defects. Then, the inspectors and drone pilot can visualize the augmented video stream. Communications between the subsystems are handled by a server and satellite link.

2.1 Drone

To capture the video stream of the bridge that will be processed to detect surface defects, the drone (DJI Mini 2) has been used for this task as illustrated in the Fig. 2. This drone has the characteristics of being both lightweight and able to capture high resolution imagery.

Fig. 2. DJI Mini 2 Drone.

2.2 Communication Modules

A Starlink system and a communication server are responsible for the communications between the different parts of the inspection system. The Starlink system links the onsite modules with the communication server as shown in Fig. 1. As illustrated in Fig. 3, the Starlink kit includes an antenna and modem. It provides a high speed connection, especially in rural areas where traditional broadband services might be unavailable or unreliable.

Fig. 3. Illustration of the satellite antenna deployed onsite

In the other side, a communication server is deployed to regulate the communications on the system. As shown in Fig. 1, the communication server handles both raw and augmented stream video at the same time between the different endpoints.

2.3 AI Environment

It includes the Nvidia Triton Inference server, which is an optimized platform that hosts deep learning models for defect detection. The detection model is YOLOX [3] which is already trained on bridge defects. To speed up the inference during the inspection process, these two components are deployed on a laptop equipped with an Nvidia GPU.

2.4 AR Subsystem

It includes a Microsoft HoloLens 2 optical-see-through AR headset for the drone's pilot, as illustrated in the Fig. 4.

Fig. 4. Illustration of gesture control through the AR headset

In addition, an augmented realty application is deployed on this headset to provide an effective control assistance and environment awareness to the pilot during the inspection process. The AR based interface that the pilot can see during the process is shown in Fig. 5.

Fig. 5. Illustration of the drone in operation as seen from the AR headset

2.5 Inspector Web Interface

The web interface that is used by the inspector(s) is illustrated in Fig. 6. We can see that it displays various flight parameters, the drone's Battery level and location on a map. It also allows the inspector to pass from a raw video display to an augmented video display.

Fig. 6. Illustration of the web interface of inspector(s)

3 Flight Plan

In order to safely fly the drone for the field trials, a flight plan has been established. This flight plan defines the conditions under which the drone could be flown.

3.1 Flight Test Procedure

Test Area. The test area is a concrete bridge located in the city of Gatineau. This bridge is illustrated in Fig. 7.

Weather Limits. No rain, No fog. Maximum wind speeds of 20 km/h and a temperature above the water freezing point (0 °C).

Contingencies/Cease Test. When battery level is under 30%, the drone will be landed for recharge.

Fig. 7. Illustration of bridge in the test area

Pre-flight. Ensure all the equipment is available. Ensure that all the devices are properly charged. The equipment list goes as follows:

1. Drone
2. Drone's remote control
3. Smartphone
4. Drone spare batteries
5. Spare propeller blades
6. Drone battery charger and cable
7. Phone charger and cable
8. Electrical power station
9. Anemometer

10. Take-off/landing platform
11. First aid kit
12. Fire blanket
13. Visibility vest
14. Gloves
15. Laptop
16. A paper copy of the flight plan
17. Satellite link antenna and router

In-Flight. No flight above 122 m (400 ft high). Take-off from the side of the bridge. No flying directly above the bridge, people or vehicles. Always flying with a line-of-sight between the pilot and the drone. Ensure a minimum distance of 1.5 m between the drone and the bridge.

Privacy Issues. To avoid privacy issues, video recording will be stopped when vehicles or pedestrians enter the field-of-view of the camera.

4 Field Trials

Two field trials have been conducted to test all the components of the system.

4.1 Flight Conditions

The flights were performed in the afternoon with the following weather conditions:

1. Temperature: 18 °C
2. Wind: 10 km/h
3. Sky: Sunny
4. Humidity: 53% relative humidity (RH)

4.2 Setup

Field Trial 1: The setup of the system went well except for the planned satellite communication link (see Fig. 3) which failed.

Field Trial 2: To avoid the previous problem, we relied on 5G cell phone network link to deploy the system (as shown in Fig. 8).

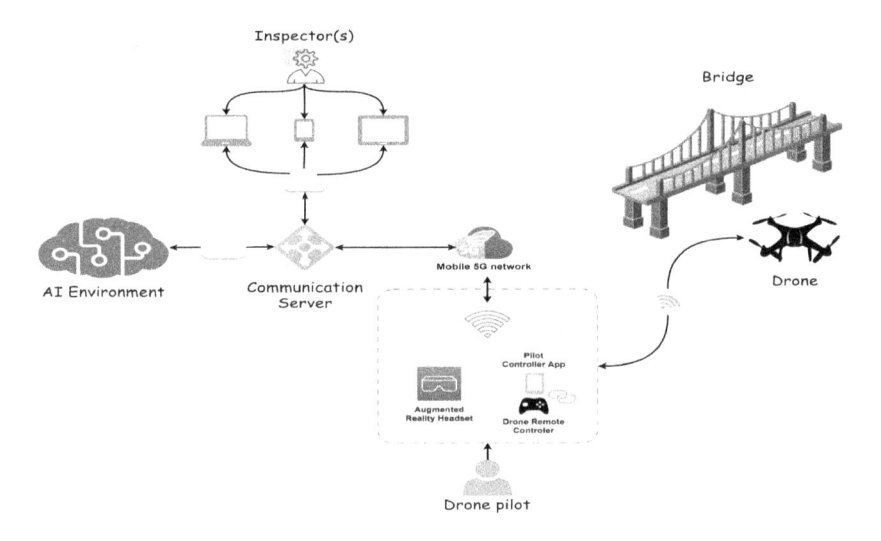

Fig. 8. Illustration of the system with cell phone link

4.3 Results

First Trial: As indicated previously, the satellite connection between the onsite drone setup and the communication server failed to be established during the first trial. This could be explained by the fact that the communication server follows an access control list policy that grants or denies the access to its resources for security concerns. In addition, the onsite drone setup is allocated an IP address that is related to its geolocation and from time-to-time this IP address changes for resilience, as network capacity increases, or when new countries are added to the network. Consequently, the communication server denies access to requests sent via this satellite network.

Second Trial: Figure 5 illustrates the drone in operation as seen from the AR headset. The view from the AR headset includes pilot view point overlaid with an interactive interface. This interface displays the live video stream captured by the drone's camera on either raw or augmented version. The latter one highlights the bridge surface defects detected by the AI module of the system. The switch between both video streams is controlled by a toggle button in the AR headset's view, as illustrated in Fig. 5. This toggle is controlled by the pilot using hand gesture, as illustrated in Fig. 4. The overlaid interface also shows real-time drone's information, such as its battery level and its altitude.

5 Discussion

The drone technology used here is for a remote guidance collaboration scenario involving a remote helper (the inspector) guiding in real time a local worker (the drone's pilot) in performing tasks on physical objects (the bridge) [6,9]. Since inspectors work in teams, the drone's pilot might well be also an inspector too. The scenario envisioned is illustrated in Figs. 8 and 9 and is described in details in [7].

6 Future Work

Setting up a Virtual Private Network on top of this satellite network is an envisioned solution that could fix the previous connection issue. The proposed system is illustrated in Fig. 9. This VPN-based approach will increase the security and privacy level of the system, and it can improve the internet connection speed in some cases by bypassing congestion or network throttling imposed by internet service providers.

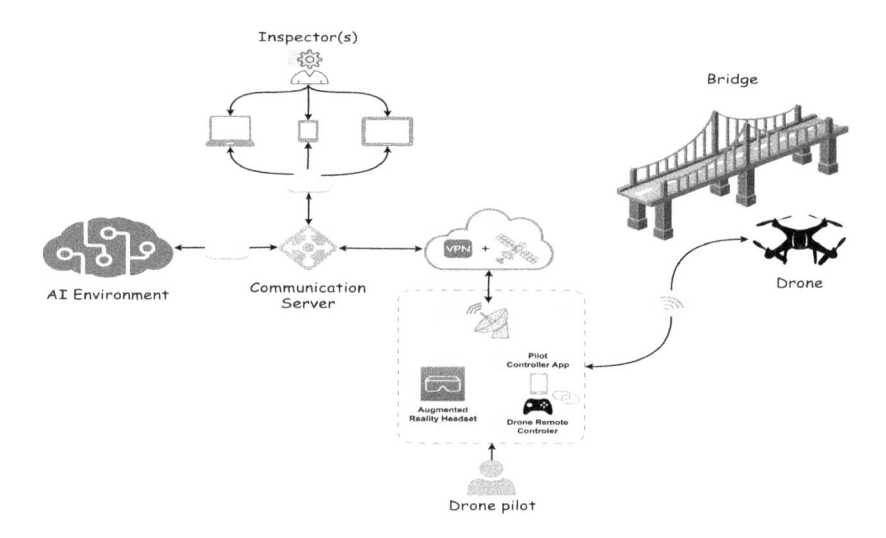

Fig. 9. Illustration of the system with satellite link and the VPN

New field trials will have to be conducted. The flight will initially involve a functional satellite link that will provide a faster network speed. Bidirectional network speed of about 13 Mbps could be reached using this method. The system is illustrated in Fig. 9. In addition to increasing network speed, optimization of the video stream is also envisioned. Later on, subject-matter experts, i.e. real inspectors, will be involved, in order to assess the benefits of the system in assisting their task. This is to validate the potential of this technology for real-world concrete bridge inspection, a task already described in [8]. Some further work could also be done to improve the current AI module that detect bridge surface defect by using models such as SMDD-NET [4]. Also, a recent systematic review of visual defect detection on concrete bridges helped to create a basis to leverage on for the next steps [1].

7 Conclusion

This paper presented the results of field trials conducted on an AI-AR based system for remote visual inspection of concrete bridges. It also presents a plan for future field trials based on the results of this first field trial. Results indicate that a high speed network link is critical to achieve good performance.

References

1. Amirkhani, D., Hebbache, L., Allili, M., Hebbache, L., Hammouche, N., Lapointe, J.F.: Visual concrete bridge defect classification and detection using deep learning: a systematic review. IEEE Trans. Intell. Transp. Syst. **25**(9), 10483–10505 (2024). https://doi.org/10.1109/TITS.2024.3365296
2. Calvi, G.M., et al.: Once upon a time in Italy: the tale of the Morandi bridge. Struct. Eng. Int. **29**, 198–217 (2019). https://doi.org/10.1080/10168664.2018.1558033
3. Ge, Z., Liu, S., Wang, F., Li, Z., Sun, J.: YOLOX: exceeding YOLO series in 2021. CoRR abs/2107.08430 (2021). https://arxiv.org/abs/2107.08430
4. Hebbache, L., Amirkhani, D., Allili, M., Hammouche, N., Lapointe, J.F.: Leveraging saliency in single-stage multi-label concrete defect detection using unmanned aerial vehicle imagery. Remote Sen. **15**, 1218 (2023). https://doi.org/10.3390/rs15051218
5. Hu, D., Yee, T., Goff, D.: Automated crack detection and mapping of bridge decks using deep learning and drones. J. Civil Struct. Health Monit. **14**, 729–743 (2024). https://doi.org/10.1007/s13349-023-00750-0
6. Huang, W., Alem, L., Tecchia, F.: HandsIn3D: supporting remote guidance with immersive virtual environments. In: Kotzé, P., Marsden, G., Lindgaard, G., Wesson, J., Winckler, M. (eds.) Human-Computer Interaction – INTERACT 2013, pp. 70–77. Springer, Heidelberg (2013). https://doi.org/10.1007/978-3-642-40483-2_5
7. Lapointe, J.F., Allili, M.S., Belliveau, L., Hebbache, L., Amirkhani, D., Sekkati, H.: AI-AR for bridge inspection by drone. In: Chen, J.Y.C., Fragomeni, G. (eds.) Virtual, Augmented and Mixed Reality: Applications in Education, Aviation and Industry, pp. 302–313. Springer, Cham (2022). https://doi.org/10.1007/978-3-031-06015-1_21
8. Lapointe, J.F., Kondratova, I.: A bridge inspection task analysis. In: Harris, D., Li, W.C. (eds.) Engineering Psychology and Cognitive Ergonomics, pp. 280–290. Springer, Cham (2023). https://doi.org/10.1007/978-3-031-35389-5_19
9. Lapointe, J.F., Molyneaux, H., Allili, M.S.: A literature review of AR-based remote guidance tasks with user studies. In: Chen, J.Y.C., Fragomeni, G. (eds.) Virtual, Augmented and Mixed Reality. Industrial and Everyday Life Applications, pp. 111–120. Springer, Cham (2020). https://doi.org/10.1007/978-3-030-49698-2_8

Proactive Workload Estimation for Pilots

Miwa Nakanishi[✉] and Riku Adachi

Keio University, Hiyoshi 3-14-1, Kohoku, Yokohama, Japan
miwa_nakanishi@ae.keio.ac.jp

Abstract. Workload management is an important component of Crew Resource Management, which is now a mandatory training and screening requirement for all airline pilots worldwide. A pilot's workload per flight typically varies from time to time, influenced by the flight phase (climb, cruise, descent), weather conditions, and other factors such as mental state and skill level. A competent pilot will strive to manage the workload by conducting tasks such as checklists and communicating with ATC timely during each flight phase to avoid creating situations where the workload is extremely high. However, it is not easy for pilots to understand and predict changes in their own workload. In this study, as a new method to support the pilot's workload management during flight, we construct a model to estimate the pilot's workload at t + Δt from various data at time t in flight. Furthermore, we propose and validate a system in which the workload after Δt output by this model is always displayed in the cockpit at t.

Keywords: Workload · Pilot · Crew Resource Management

1 Introduction

Even today, it is estimated that human factors are responsible for about 70% of all accidents in general aviation (AOPA, 2021) [1]. One of the major frameworks of human factors that contribute to accidents is workload (FAA, 2021) [2], and workload management is an important component of Crew Resource Management, which currently requires training and screening for all airline pilots worldwide. A pilot's workload per flight typically varies from time to time, influenced by the flight phase (climb, cruise, descent), weather conditions, and other factors such as mental state and skill level. A competent pilot will strive to manage the workload by conducting tasks such as checklists and communicating with ATC timely during each flight phase to avoid creating situations where the workload is extremely high. However, it is not easy for pilots to understand and predict changes in their own workload. In fact, in the 2016 Peach Aviation Flight 1028 critical incident at Tokyo International Airport, where an aircraft attempted to land on a closed runway, inadequate workload management was identified as a cause of the incident [3].

Therefore, as a new method to support pilot workload management during flight, this study constructs a model to estimate the pilot workload at t + Δt from various data at time t in flight. Furthermore, this study proposes and verifies a system in which the workload at Δt output by this model is always displayed in the cockpit at t.

2 Data Acquisition Experiment for Model Construction

Experiments were conducted using a flight simulator to acquire the data necessary to construct a model to estimate the workload level after Δt from various in-flight data.

The subjects of the experiment were seven private pilot license holders.

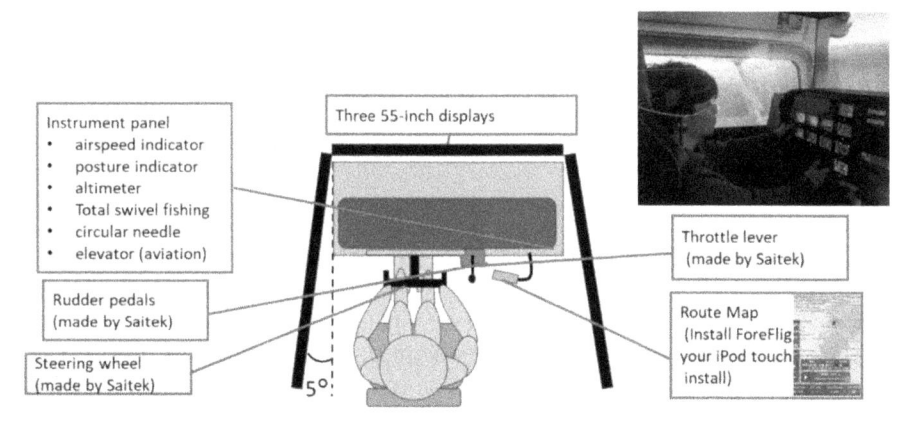

The configuration of the flight simulator is shown in Fig. 1. The flight simulator software was X-Plane11 (manufactured by Laminar Research, certified by the FAA as a training simulator), and the aircraft used was a Cessna 172SP, a small aircraft that is commonly used for training and the most sold aircraft in the world.

Each participant in the experiment flew four patterns from takeoff to landing on a designated flight route. The flight routes took approximately 20 min and were assigned to each participant without bias from the 12 prepared routes. Different weather conditions, including clear, rainy, and stormy weather, were assigned without bias, and the time of day was assigned without bias to the morning, midday, dusk, and nighttime hours. Participants were required to 1) fly the designated route without detours, 2) maintain a speed within the normal operating range and 110 kts during cruise, 3) maintain an altitude of 4,000 ft during cruise and enter the perimeter flight path at 1,000 ft, and 4) start the flight after studying the flight path using airport maps.

Flight data was acquired every 0.1 s from X-Plane 11 (Table 1). In addition, an automatic voice cue was given every 30 s, at which time the participants in the experiment were asked to answer their own workload level on a 5-point scale from 1 to 5 (1 being the lowest and 5 being the highest). In addition, in order to acquire data on visibility conditions, the monitor image of the flight simulator was recorded every second. The data from the monitor images were quantified by processing masking to extract only the external visibility, and nonlinearly complemented to the HSV color space. In addition to the above, physiological data related to workload were obtained as shown in Table 2.

Fig. 1. Configuration of the flight simulator.

Table 1. Flight data acquired every 0.1 s from the fright simulator.

Element	Data Items
Airframe Attitude	Pitch, Roll, Yaw Angle, Nose True Azimuth, Angle of Attack, Angle of Sideslip,
Airframe operation	Airspeed, Ground speed, Throttle power, Altitude, Flight distance,
Input	Elevator input, Aileron input, Rudder input, Throttle input, Flaps, Trim
External Environment	Wind speed, Wind Direction

Table 2. Measurement parameters, evaluation indices, and interpretation [3–10].

Measurement index	Measurement method	Device HP/LP Filter	Evaluation index	Changes when workload rises
ECG	3-point induction II induction	ECG100C (made by BIOPAC) 0.5~35Hz	Pulse rate	+
Breath	Abdominal circumference	RSP100C (made by BIOPAC) 0.05~10Hz	Respiratory frequency	+
Skin temperature	Nasal skin temperature	SKT100C (made by Biopac) ~1.0Hz	Degrees Fahrenheit	−
Pulse wave	Diffuse reflected light	PPG100C (made by Biopac) 0.05~3.0Hz	Amplitude (of vibration)	−
Brain waves	A1, Fz, Cz, Pz for 10-20 method	EEG100C (made by Biopac) 0.5~35Hz	Alpha wave band power	−
			Band power of beta wave	+
			Band power of theta wave	+
Cerebral blood volume change	NIRS	OEG-16 (made by Spectratech)	Oxygenated hemoglobin concentration change	+

3 Construction of Workload Prediction Model

The data obtained from the experiments on the flight simulator were used to construct a model by machine learning: to predict the workload level at time $t + \Delta t$, the workload level subjectively answered at time $t + \Delta t$ was corresponded to the other data at time t, and the former was used as the objective variable and the latter as the explanatory variable. The Δt was set to 30 (s), because in aircraft operations, knowing the future status, even if it is only a few tens of seconds later, is considered useful for workload management.

The structure of the model is shown in Fig. 2. All data obtained were linearly complemented so that the data were sampled every 0.1 s. However, since there was an imbalance in the number of samples that varied significantly by workload level, this imbalance was mitigated by under-sampling. Considering that all workload levels (1–5) were included in equal proportions in the training and test data, both data were prepared by assigning them to training or test data on a task-by-task basis. The number of training data and test data prepared in this way was 18,985 and 7,017, respectively.

In building the models, three different algorithms were applied: Random Forest Classification (RFC), Support Vector Machine (SVM), and Neural Network (NN). In all cases, the optimal model was searched by grid search.

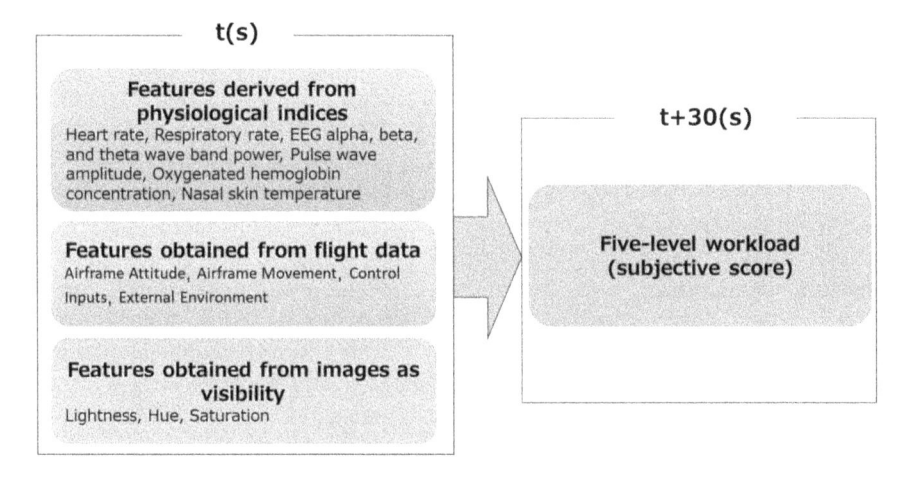

Fig. 2. Structure of the model.

Table 3. Results of predicting five workload levels using SVM, RFC, and NN.

model	hyper parameter	Accuracy(%) ±0	Accuracy(%) ±1
RFC	n_estimator=50,. criterion=entropy, max_feature=sqrt,. max_depth=5	52.0	87.3
SVM	Kernel=rbf,. C=1,. gamma=0.01	43.8	90.0
NN	hidden layer sizes=(100,) activation=relu,. solver=adam,. max_iter=1000,.	42.1	89.9

Model	WL level	Recall ±0	Recall ±1	Precision ±0	Precision ±1
RFC	1	85.8%	100.0%	60.9%	87.7%
RFC	2	63.8%	96.0%	59.1%	76.7%
RFC	3	41.2%	80.9%	37.0%	95.5%
RFC	4	30.2%	86.7%	43.2%	92.4%
RFC	5	30.9%	60.2%	48.9%	98.1%
SVM	1	73.6%	95.2%	48.0%	87.3%
SVM	2	45.3%	99.5%	50.4%	80.7%
SVM	3	45.8%	86.9%	31.1%	95.6%
SVM	4	38.9%	90.1%	43.9%	99.3%
SVM	5	5.1%	65.7%	67.6%	88.2%
NN	1	57.2%	97.7%	53.0%	91.6%
NN	2	52.4%	99.4%	46.4%	81.8%
NN	3	46.1%	86.3%	29.0%	94.4%
NN	4	38.0%	90.1%	43.9%	99.0%
NN	5	0.0%	62.3%	0.0%	15.3%

The results of predicting five workload levels using SVM, RFC, and NN are shown in Table 3. Table 3 (left) shows the accuracy rates in the test data. The accuracy rate for

Table 4. Confusion matrix for workload level prediction.

Confusion matrix for 30-second posterior estimation in RFC

		Predicted value				
Measured value		1	2	3	4	5
	1	1055	175	0	0	0
	2	463	1279	182	81	0
	3	213	206	482	258	11
	4	0	203	581	459	279
	5	0	300	58	264	278

Confusion matrix for 30-second posterior estimation in SVM

		Predicted value				
Measured value		1	2	3	4	5
	1	905	266	59	0	0
	2	742	909	344	10	0
	3	145	279	536	202	8
	4	0	150	766	592	14
	5	94	198	17	545	46

predicting workload levels at ±0 was about 50%, while the accuracy rate for predicting workload levels with a margin of error of ±1 was about 90%. Table 3 (right) also shows the recall and precision rates. The NN had very poor accuracy for workload level 5. Table 4 (left) shows the confusion matrix for workload level prediction in RFC and Table 4 (right) shows the confusion matrix for workload level prediction in SVM. The results show that in a few cases, SVM predicted 1 when the actual level was 5. Thus, it is undesirable to predict much lower than the true workload, even though the true workload is high, because it may have a negative impact on the pilot's decision making. Therefore, a model with an RFC was adopted in this study. This adopted model can predict the workload 30 s later with 87.1% accuracy when an error of ±1 is allowed in 5 levels, based on various data reflecting the external environment, aircraft condition, and pilot's mental state that can be obtained in-flight.

By the way, the above prediction model uses physiological data reflecting the pilot's mental state as input data. Although there are already experimental studies that use physiological data to monitor the pilot's mental state in real time, this is not realistically easy to apply to general aviation, considering the financial cost and the time required for airworthiness tests. Therefore, we again tried to build a model to estimate the workload level after 30 s, using data excluding physiological data as explanatory variables. The accuracy of the prediction is shown in Table 5 (right), and the confusion matrix between the predicted and actual levels is shown in Table 5 (left). Since the workload naturally

Table 5. Confusion matrix between the predicted and actual levels (left) and accuracy, recall, and precision of the prediction (right) using data excluding physiological data as explanatory variables.

		Predicted value				
Measured value		1	2	3	4	5
	1	6587	2012	161	60	0
	2	3343	3638	1595	244	0
	3	879	3265	2400	2274	2
	4	0	691	1612	6069	448
	5	0	1735	2340	1340	3405

	Accuracy		WL level	Recall		Precision	
	±0	±1		±0	±1	±0	±1
Excluding physiological data	50.1%	86.1%	1	74.7%	97.5%	60.9%	91.9%
			2	41.2%	97.2%	32.1%	78.6%
			3	27.2%	90.0%	29.6%	69.2%
			4	68.8%	92.2%	60.8%	97.0%
			5	38.6%	53.8%	88.3%	99.9%
Including physiological data	52.0%	87.3%	1	85.8%	100.0%	60.9%	87.7%
			2	63.8%	96.0%	59.1%	76.7%
			3	41.2%	80.9%	37.0%	95.5%
			4	30.2%	86.7%	43.2%	92.4%
			5	30.9%	60.2%	48.9%	98.1%

involves the pilot's own mental state, the accuracy was slightly lower in the model that excluded the physiological data reflecting it from the explanatory variables. However, the difference was small, and with an error margin of ±1 on a 5-point scale, the model was able to predict 86.1% accurately. Thus, the results suggest that workload level predictions can be used with high accuracy even during general aviation flights.

4 Validation of the Effectiveness of the System Implementing the Workload Prediction Model

4.1 Implementation and Validation of Workload Prediction Model

The model constructed above (an RFC model that predicts the workload level after 30 s by excluding physiological data from the explanatory variables) was implemented on a flight simulator, and a system was constructed to constantly display the workload level predicted after 30(s) on a gauge to the pilot in flight. The workload gauge was installed beside the instruments. The workload gauge was presented in different colors according to the high and low workload levels (Fig. 3).

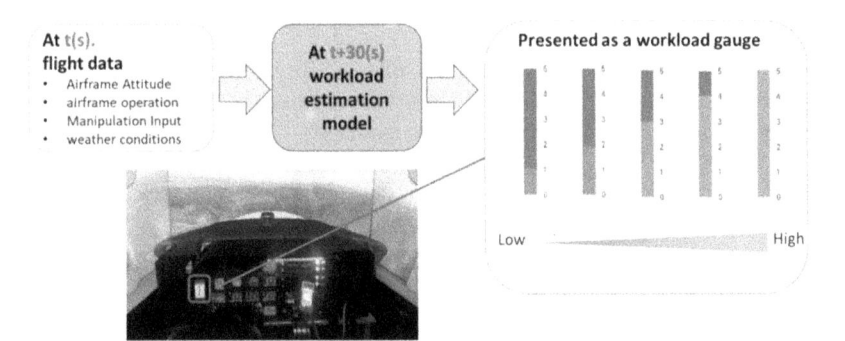

Fig. 3. Workload presentation

To verify the effectiveness of this system, an experiment was conducted using a flight simulator. The participants in the experiment were six private pilot license holders. The flight simulator used in the experiment was the same as in the previous experiment. Of the four designated flight routes, two were flown without the workload gauge, and the other two were flown with the workload gauge. Each flight route lasted approximately 20 min. Three of the six participants flew from with the workload gauge to without the workload gauge, and the remaining three flew from without the workload gauge to with the workload gauge. As in the previous experiment, the participants were asked to follow the same instructions regarding flight route, speed, and altitude. In addition, as in the actual flight, the participants were asked to perform the following tasks during the flight: 1) perform a checklist during the takeoff, climb, cruise, descent, and landing phases; 2) communicate with ATC prior to the traffic pattern; and 3) check the airport map prior to the traffic pattern.

The data acquired during the experiment were as follows. To analyze the timing of viewing the workload gauge, eye tracking data of the participants were recorded with an EMR-10 (made by nac). Flight data, such as aircraft attitude, and data related to the external environment, such as wind speed and direction, were also recorded from the flight simulator. To evaluate the workload of the participants, electrocardiogram and respiration were measured as physiological data that could be obtained without interfering with the eye tracking device. After each flight, participants were interviewed about the extent to which and for what purpose they utilized the workload gauge.

4.2 Experimental Results

Utilization of the Workload Gauge. Figure 4 shows the timing of viewing the workload gauge (timing of gazing) for each participant. The workload gauge tended to be viewed at the timing of moving from climb to cruise and from cruise to descent. This suggests that while the participants concentrated on the maneuvers during the climb and descent phases, they were interested in how their own workload would change afterwards in order to plan for the rest of the flight when they were calm after the climb and when they were preparing for the descent. In post-flight interviews with the participants, they also stated, "When my workload was low, I had more time to spare, so I used that time to check the instruments and think about what I needed to do next." "I decided to do the checklist when the workload was low if possible." "I tried to relax when the workload was high in order to calm my mind." These results indicate that the participants tried to utilize the workload gauge for workload management.

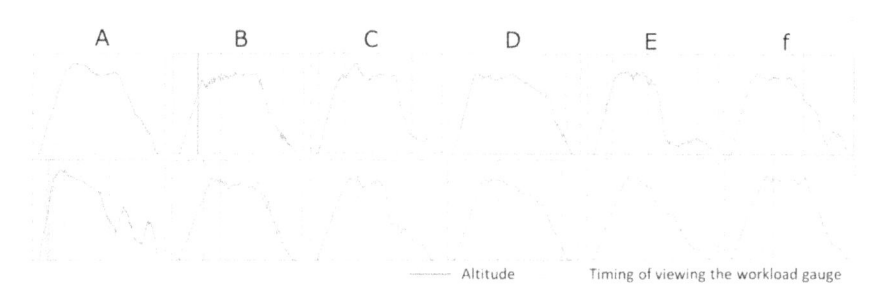

Fig. 4. Timing of viewing the workload gauge for each participant.

Timing of Tasks Performed. The timing of the checklist, ATC communication, and airport map confirmation tasks were compared between the cases in which the workload gauge was installed and those in which it was not. Figure 5 shows the results of the comparison of the timing of ATC communication and airport map confirmation with and without the workload gauge. Since the checklists were to be performed during each flight phase, there was no significant difference in the timing of the checklists between with and without the workload gauge. The results show that all tasks were performed earlier when there was a workload gauge. These results suggest that the use of the workload gauge for workload management may have helped avoid tasks being concentrated at the end of the flight or not being performed properly.

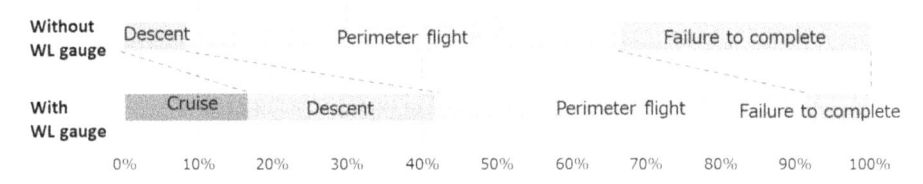

Fig. 5. Comparison of ATC communication timing.

Pilot's Workload During Flight. The workload of the participants during flight was analyzed using physiological data. Figure 6 shows the results of the comparison of heart rate (left) and respiratory rate (right) between with and without the workload gauge. In both cases, the data were standardized using resting state values in order to eliminate the influence of individual differences. Both heart rate and respiratory rate are known to increase with higher workload. The results show that both indicators had smaller values when the workload gauge was provided, meaning that the workload was generally lower.

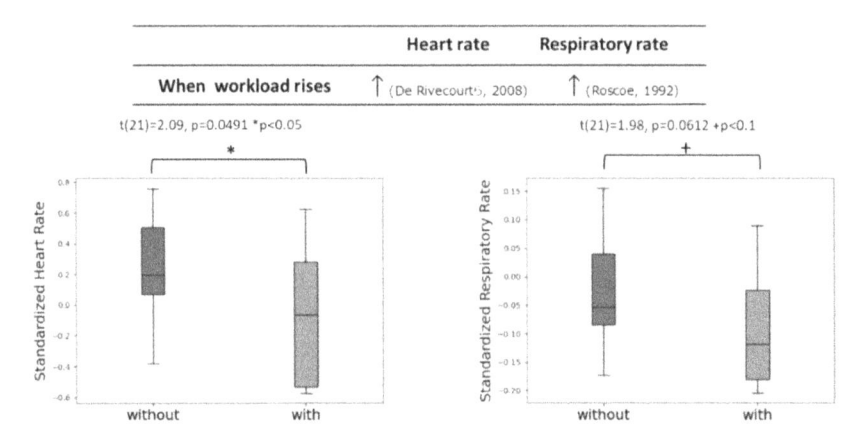

Fig. 6. Comparison of heart rate (left) and respiratory rate (right) between with and with-out the workload gauge.

Flight Stability. We further compared the flight stability in each flight phase with and without the workload gauge using the RMSE ratio, a measure of flight stability developed [10].

$$\text{RMSE} = \sqrt{\frac{\sum_{i=1}^{n}(\text{Measured value} - \text{Target value})^2}{n}}$$

RMSE ratio = (RMSE with the workload gauge − RMSE without the workload gauge)/RMSE without the workload gauge.

Figure 7 shows the RMSE ratio for each flight phase. The smaller this value indicates more stable flight with the workload gauge.

The results show that during the climb and cruise phases, the RMSE ratios for the three indices are smaller, showing that flight stability increased when the workload gage is available. The results particularly suggest that airspeed, which is important in the climb phase, and altitude, which is important in the cruise phase, were properly managed. Also, during the descent phase, stability of velocity and heading, which are particularly important in this phase, were increased, indicating that these were properly managed.

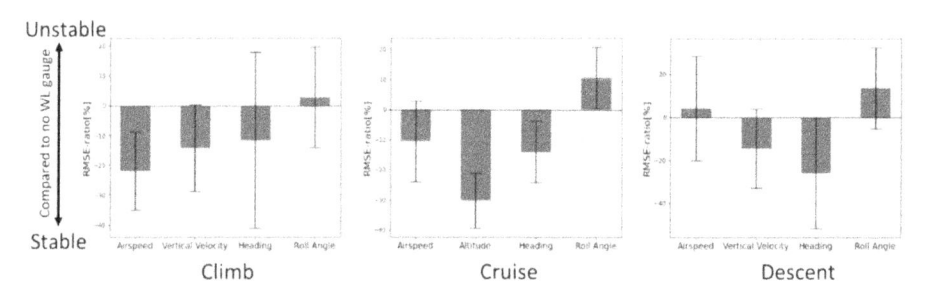

Fig. 7. RMSE ratio for each flight phase.

5 Conclusion

In this study, with the aim of supporting pilots in better managing their workloads in flight, we constructed a model for proactively estimating workloads, and proposed and verified a system that implements this model.

The model achieved an accuracy of about 87%, allowing an error margin of ± 1, in five levels of workload estimation after 30(s) using data that could be acquired in flight. Furthermore, the model was implemented in the system and experimentally demonstrated that visualizing the workload after 30(s) and presenting it to the pilot at all times in flight encourages proper workload management, and that this generally reduces the workload during flight, thereby improving flight stability as a result.

References

1. Aircraft Owners and Pilots Association. 33rd AOPA Air Safety Institute Accident Report (2021)
2. Federal Aviation Administration. FAA-H-8083-30 AMG Handbook, Chapter 14, Human Factors (2005)
3. Japan Transport Safety Board. Aircraft Serious Incident Investigation Report: Peach Aviation Co., LTD. AIRBUS A320-214, JA811P (2018)
4. De Rivecourt, M., Kuperus, M.N., Post, W.J., Mulder, L.J.M.: Cardiovascular and eye activity measures as indices for momentary changes in mental effort during simulated flight. Ergonomics **51**(9), 1295–1319 (2008)
5. Roscoe, A.H.: Assessing pilot workload. Why measure heart rate, HRV and respiration? Biol. Psychol. **34**(2–3), 259–287 (1992)
6. Mizuno, T., Nomura, S., Nozawa, A., Asano, Y., Ide, H.: Evaluation of the effect of intermittent mental work-load on nasal skin temperature. IEICE Trans. Inf. Syst. **93**(4), 535–543 (2010)

7. Veltman, J.A., Gaillard, A.W.K.: Physiological workload reactions to increasing levels of task difficulty. Ergonomics **41**(5), 656–669 (1998)
8. Brookings, J.B., Wilson, G.F., Swain, C.R.: Psychophysiological responses to changes in workload during simulated air traffic control. Biol. Psychol. **42**(3), 361–377 (1996)
9. Fairclough, S.H., Venables, L., Tattersall, A.: The influence of task demand and learning on the psychophysiological response. Int. J. Psychophysiol. **56**(2), 171–184 (2005)
10. Jang, K.E.: Wavelet-MDL detrending for near infrared spectroscopy (NIRS). J. Biomed. Opt. **14**(3), 1–13 (2009)
11. Hebbar, P.A., Pashilkar, A.A.: Pilot performance evaluation of simulated flight approach and landing manoeuvres using quantitative assessment tools. Sādhanā **42**, 405–415 (2017)

CRM for Providing Distress Assistance with Real-Time Aircraft Telemetry – DART

Daniel C. Smith[1(✉)] and Hannes S. Griebel[2]

[1] University of Hawaii West Oahu, Kapolei, HI 96707, USA
smithdan@hawaii.edu
[2] CGI IT UK Ltd., London, UK
hannes.griebel@cgi.com

Abstract. We present a comprehensive discussion on the implementation of a crew resource management (CRM) training regime required for an effective Distress Assistance with Real-Time Aircraft Telemetry (DART) program.

The DART concept aims to enhance aviation safety by providing continuous streaming of aircraft telemetry data, and an open voice communication channel, to ground-based support teams, enabling timely and informed assistance to flight crews in non-nominal situations or a state of emergency. Because this requires the integration of remote parties into CRM, we focus this paper on the CRM protocols essential for the successful integration of DART in general, and the remote aspects in particular. We explore the CRM training frameworks that would support the DART program's operational efficacy and analyze the impact of real-time data streaming on decision-making processes within the flight crew and between the crew and ground support personnel. The paper also discusses the technical and psychological aspects of CRM, emphasizing the importance of stress reduction techniques, structured decision-making models, and effective communication strategies.

Our findings indicate that incorporating comprehensive CRM training tailored to the needs of a DART program can significantly improve response times and decision quality in critical situations. The paper concludes with recommendations for future research and development, suggesting pathways for integrating advanced technologies and refining CRM practices to further enhance aviation safety.

By addressing both the technical implementation and human factors involved in the DART system, this paper provides a holistic view of its potential to improve distress management in aviation, ultimately aiming to reduce the incidence of incidents and accidents and improve the overall decision quality even in non-critical situations.

Keywords: Aircraft · Distress · Telemetry

1 Introduction

We have previously proposed providing Distress Assistance with Real-time Aircraft Telemetry (DART). In this concept transport aircraft data, DFDR data or QAR data or a superset thereof, would be continuously streamed over a satellite link enabling ground personnel to provide timely advice to a flight crew experiencing operational distress. We illustrated how ground support personnel could have used real-time data to help in the cases of several well-known aircraft emergencies such as Air France 447. We also suggested that real-time data collection would be a better data preservation solution than ejectable flight data recorders (Griebel & Smith, 2022).

Obviously, real-time display on the ground of what the crew sees – and more – is not enough for a DART program. Therefore, in this paper we discuss the crew resource management (CRM) requirements and related organizational, manual, communication, protocol and cultural changes required for a DART system. CRM is the effective use of all resources – equipment, protocols, people. DART would be a new resource. The goal is the prevention of disasters and facilitation of better outcomes. Communication resources such as a voice "party line" should also be opened when DART is active in an emergency. This would initially be used to monitor, not intervene. An additional benefit is the ready availability of data to several organizations in the airline for data mining. The technical pre-requisites for the creation of a DART program are already in place and require little if any technical adaptations to enable an aircraft to becoming so enabled. Declining satellite data transmission costs lower the economic barrier to entry. Early discussion of flight data transmission at ICAO was in the context of radio spectrum allocation for transmission of both Digital Flight Data Recorder (DFDR) and Cockpit Voice Recorders (CVR) data (ICAO, 2010). However, with Ka and Ku band mobile satellite services providing broadband connectivity for hundreds of passengers on each flight, spectrum availability is no longer an issue in today's environment.

A DART-enabled airline would have computers in key locations such as dispatch, maintenance control, and flight crew ready-rooms constantly able to display automatically for an in-distress aircraft, what the flight crew sees. Other data the crew can't see might be menu-selectable. For non-critical aircraft situations, just a few keystrokes would reasonably be required to activate the displays.

But the display of telemetry data is the easy part. Creating the protocols, procedures, and training needed for a DART program require substantial preparation.

We suggest that a DART program may be able to detect, and help with tools to correct, issues arising during a flight before the situation deteriorates catastrophically. Such issues may not just be equipment failures, but also human performance related lapses. Particularly if CVR channels were also available. Here is one list of typical human performance related issues that could be observed in the past (Kułakowski, 2019):

- the use of improper procedures.
- loss of spatial orientation by one or more flight crew members (that is, loss of situational awareness of level I).
- improper management of aircraft energy.
- the distraction of one or more flight crew members.
- improper training.

Clues observed in these instances include the apparent use (or improper use or even lack) of QRH checklists, conversations unrelated to the flight during high-workload situations, emotional distress unrelated to the aircraft or its flight, and signs of fatigue, to name but a few.

To address these issues, typical early CRM programs primarily included cockpit and cabin crews. However, the FAA has long considered the concept to be broadening the scope of CRM to include other parties involved in a flight as illustrated by Advisory Circular AC 120-51E – Crew Resource Management Training, stating:

> Other groups routinely working with the cockpit crew, who are involved in decisions required to operate a flight safely, are also essential participants in an effective CRM process. These groups include but are not limited to:

- Aircraft dispatchers.
- Flight attendants.
- Maintenance personnel.
- Air traffic controllers (FAA, 2004, p. 2)

In a potential future DART scenario, where flight recorder data can also be shared live, in whole or in part, we must therefore necessarily consider the parties this data is shared with as belonging to the group of people to be included in the DART CRM scope. Especially parties actively participating in a real-world DART response. This may include aircraft or component manufacturers who may wish to offer a standby support crew. Furthermore, their specialists already at work could be alerted and activated. Offering such a service in addition to any services that mine performance data over time to increase efficiency (and along with it, increase reliability and/or decrease costs), may be a desirable service offering to aircraft operators. It would, however, necessitate the inclusion of these teams in the operators' CRM training programs.

2 Organizational Changes

Following the CRM training guidance of AC 120-51E is part of the FAA's Advanced Qualification Program (AQP):

> Unlike traditional aviation training, AQP provides a multitude of training and safety benefits including data-driven improvement and program flexibility; integration of CRM; crew evaluation; planned hours (i.e., 'trained-to-proficiency'); and scenario-based training and evaluations (FAA, 2024).

We see DART as an addition to existing systematic aircraft data collection programs, such as periodic swapping of data cards and downloading data after each flight by cellular data, in support of wider Flight Data Monitoring (FDM) and Flight Operations Quality Assurance (FOQA) programs. This is not a radical idea considering the substantial routine near real-time data transmission of engine reports and fault messages by ACARS, flight following and ADS-B transmissions. Of course, use of real-time data in distress involves a team or crew of people who must train and practice together. Therefore, their training design with DART must still adhere to the fundamentals of CRM program implementation (FAA, 2004):

a. Assess the Status of the Organization Before Implementation.
b. Get Commitment from All Managers, Starting with Senior Managers.

c. Customize the Training to Reflect the Nature and Needs of the Organization.
d. Define the Scope of the Program and an Implementation Plan.
e. Communicate the Nature and Scope of the Program Before Startup.
f. Institute Quality Control Procedures.

Technical systems supporting DART should be more or less straight forward to implement. Many operators have some, if not all, required components already in place. The hardware and data streaming parts may therefore be considered the relatively easy, if non-trivial components (e.g., think data integrity and preservation). The infrastructure required to support a DART program can therefore be started and tested quickly as an approved company project with a modest budget. Reproduction of cockpit displays is equally available, offered by many commercially available software solutions, even if there may be initial challenges such as showing fault messages as part of MCDU simulations.

Suitable display devices may be adapted from those used by pilots at airlines with established flight data monitoring programs, enabling easy access by pilots to review their specific flights. See, for example, those supplied by CEFA (CEFA, 2024). Those programs represent a relaxation of the pattern of restricting flight data sharing (de Courville, 2019). A DART program would routinely make available, with controls, the equivalent of DFDR data to flight and maintenance personnel. Concurrently, airlines would reaffirm the non-punitive use of flight data in benign circumstances. A cultural shift to more-to-more open use of flight data has many benefits, we assert.

In addition to displays of what the flight crew is seeing, potential ground assisting staff would have the QRH and other manuals identical to those that the flight crew should be using.

A few data usage wins such as cost-saving efficiencies will justify the initial investment while the more detailed, more resource-demanding, multi-disciplinary human factors parts are being planned. We imagine DART in its ultimate implementation to be a real-time complement in support of existing FDM and Safety Management Systems (SMS) systems, including an evaluation of its own effectiveness. It would thus be also a complement to a Flight Operations Quality Assurance (FOQA) that uses aggregated data.

3 Course Content

Having established the context and scope of a DART program and its CRM needs, we can proceed to determine the content of a DART related CRM training. Following again the Advisory Circular guidance, the components of the CRM training for DART introduction are three to be integrated into an existing CRM program:

a. Initial Indoctrination Awareness
b. Recurrent Practice and Feedback
c. Continuing Reinforcement

To discuss the many topics that should be covered in a CRM curriculum or syllabus, the CRM Advisory Circular is a good starting point along with current research and courses. Another well-established source is EASA's list of topics:

- human factors in aviation, general instructions on the CRM principles and objectives, human performance and limitations, threat and error management.
- personality awareness, human error and reliability, attitudes and behaviours, self-assessment and self-critique, stress and stress management, fatigue and vigilance, assertiveness, situation awareness, information acquisition and processing.
- automation and philosophy on the use of automation.
- specific type-related differences.
- monitoring and intervention.
- shared situation awareness, shared information acquisition and processing, workload management, effective communication and coordination inside and outside the flight crew compartment, leadership, cooperation, synergy, delegation, decision-making, actions, Cultural differences.
- resilience development, surprise and startle effect.
- operator's safety culture and company culture, Standard Operating Procedures (SOPs), organisational factors, factors linked to the type of operations.
- effective communication and coordination with other operational personnel and ground services.
- case studies connected with the human factor (Kułakowski, 2019).

To the initial CRM training we would need to add the DART topics. That would likely extend the training time at significant costs. Among the initial commercial CRM training offerings two days was the most common duration we found. ICAO's was three days. Based on our experience, adding about four hours should be reasonable for adding DART related CRM training, including simulator or at least desktop exercise activities. For a list and a thorough discussion of CRM training and competencies see MacLeod's book (MacLeod, 2021).

For DART crews, the training must first and foremost build competences for crises.

4 Reinforcement

Reinforcement opportunities such as well-planned drills on repositioning or maintenance verification flights will be especially valuable alongside ground exercises in aircraft, aircraft simulators, computer simulations and tabletop exercises. Moreover, a working DART program with the necessary data displays could be the ideal monitoring service for verification flights such as those made after flight control maintenance. Another potential benefit is that the DART system should feed AI services to detect trends before alert conditions are reached. A protocol would be needed to determine when DART would be triggered from and by ground monitoring. Think of it as part of proper assertiveness in teamwork and deemphasis of hierarchy, as taught in CRM. Flight crews could also request DART assistance perhaps with a button push and/or ACARS message with non-emergency but significant problems. Even looking into minor problems on long flights would provide practice opportunities at modest cost.

Whether during reinforcement or practice, assessment of both the on-going human performance and preparatory training is essential. Another component of real-time data CRM training, performance reinforcement and on-going assessment is incorporation into the company culture via standard operating procedures (SOPs). SOPs regarding

DART must also be built into documents such as the quick reference handbook (QRH) and personalized to the particular airline. CRM is already part of the Safety Management Systems (SMS) that part 121 operators (airlines) are required to have (Bennett, 2019), and that will soon be required by part 135 (charter) and certain part 91 (private) operators, as per the FAA re-authorization bill of May 2024. Bennett also demonstrated the benefits of surveys of crews on CRM issues. Finally, Line Oriented Flight Training would flesh out the matters found from surveys.

For low threat problems, the QRH works well. For more complex problems with startle and surprise elements, a rehearsed mnemonic procedure was found to be more effective over a range of scenarios created in a full motion simulator compared to a control group (Landman, et al., 2020). The mnemonic was Calm down; Observe; Outline; Lead (COOL). Individual airlines have their own mnemonics to be activated in conjunction with the QRH.

The QRH deals first with the immediate emergency. Then the QRH, when required, will call out planning to land safely. That's particularly needed and to be augmented with the use of DART. CRM principles and teamwork of course apply to completing the flight with a defective aircraft, imposing a high cognitive load. In a series of simulator experimental emergencies, researchers found that the initial responses were all correct but human communication factors significantly affected the performance of crews. Crews performed better when the captain included the copilot in the decision-making process and when captains asked open-ended questions (Hagen & Lei, 2019).

5 Special Considerations for DART

5.1 Integration of Remote Parties into CRM

In addition to the topics already discussed, it is important to recognize that DART requires the effective application of Remote CRM. Remote CRM might consider additional topics pertaining to the nature of some interactions being carried out over remote data links. While generally reliable, the interaction between CRM members may be degraded through several factors:

– The other CRM member is not physically present,
– Voice alone forms only part of the human interaction,
– Degraded link performance can lead to a heightened potential for misunderstandings.

Consequently, the following topics might be considered for a training syllabus for remotely supported CRM:

– Effective communication over voice links,
– Sensibility to detecting distress levels in a CRM members voice,
– Understanding factors influencing remote link performance,
– Effectively cooperating with CRM members without ever having met them.

Support for annual recurrent training concerning DART should have new events, real or constructed for competency evaluation. As with any CRM training, it is essential not to repeat last year's scenarios! That contrasts with demonstrating routine skills such as flying a challenging ILS approach with a "routine" emergency.

None of these topics are, in and of themselves, new areas of research. Tailoring them for incorporation into a DART program will require a reasonable, but manageable amount of additional research including pilot programs (no pun intended).

5.2 Voice Communication

We assert that activation of displays on the ground showing what the flight crew sees is the relatively easy part of a DART program. Voice communication should also be made easy – opening a permanent audio link at the same time as DART activation -- to facilitate teamwork, a key factor in good outcomes following an emergency. There remain, however, important issues to be addressed. For example, whether cockpit voice channels should be automatically activated rather than requiring crews to press a push to talk button. Ground staff could just listen in to monitor if the flight crew was managing the situation well. One option to facilitate this function might be to put the voice channels over an IP link on an otherwise primarily passenger-use internet circuit in the cabin. Another important issue would be to decide whether to enable a big party line with air traffic controllers monitoring, allowing better situational awareness at the expense of ATC workload. As in traditional CRM, ground crews would be trained on when and how (or not) to be assertive in giving advice or asking questions.

5.3 Risk Management – What Could Go Wrong?

At the first level, DART would be just another resource to be used in accordance with CRM practice. It would be analogous to the available off-duty crew on flights like UA232, UA1175 and QF32 who provided essential support to the flight crew at the controls. As noted above, the presence of an assisting party, whether onboard or remote, does not automatically translate into good and effective CRM. Typical CRM errors, such as omissions or commissions, may still happen. An omission would be a failure to assertively give advice based on significant data seen on the ground. The error of commission would be asserting inaccurate technical advice or distraction to the crew when silence would have been the better option. The advantage of remote CRM scenarios, like DART, allow the Ground support crews to have the advantage of being able to debate issues without bothering the flight crew. Prevention of "open mics" from the ground crew debating solutions is a small risk reduction item.

In any case, the only proven way to reduce human error in CRM is a well-stablished training program which is regularly rehearsed, practiced, and audited.

5.4 Stress Management

Effective Crew Resource Management (CRM) training must address the psychological aspects that influence pilot performance, particularly stress management. Because stress is an inevitable component of piloting aircraft, especially in high-workload flight phases, pilots are particularly exposed to risks resulting from unmanaged stress. Unmanaged stress can impair cognitive functions, leading to errors in judgment and decision-making.

CRM training for DART should therefore not only equip pilots with the ability to recognize classic stressors such as adverse weather conditions, mechanical failures, or unexpected air traffic control (ATC) instructions, but must ensure that the DART environment itself will not result additional stressors.

This, in turn, requires the CRM training to provide an understanding of the limitations of remote communications (as outlined previously), and must include techniques for stress identification and reduction. Remote CRM training for DART can incorporate cognitive-behavioral strategies that address the typical challenges for remote connections, whether they are standard (e.g., spatial separation between the parties, voice only, absence of body language) or random (link quality, audio issues, user interface instructions).

A well-established method of addressing stressors such as this in training is the exposure to high-pressure scenarios. Creating such scenarios in simulations involving a remote party through a data and voice link simulator can help both pilots and ground crews to build confidence operating in such scenarios, improving their ability to perform well even in demanding DART scenarios. Realistic simulations that mimic emergency situations with remote connections could, for example, be established using participants placed in different rooms, connected through electronic communication simulation equipment based on a combination of commercially-off-the-shelf communication software (e.g., video conferencing software) and sound effect systems (e.g., to introduce white noise or other interference).

6 Summary and Conclusion

In this paper we explored key aspects of how remote Crew Resource Management (CRM) can enable the implementation of a program for the Distress Assistance with Real-Time Aircraft Telemetry (DART), emphasizing the pivotal role of CRM training. The integration of continuous, near-real-time telemetry data and open voice links with established CRM practices is not only feasible, but also practical, offering powerful additional tools in a proactive approach to managing in-flight anomalies and emergencies.

6.1 Key Findings and Implications

1. Enhanced Situational Awareness: A DART program's ability to afford ground crews the ability to monitor continuous, real-time telemetry data enhances situational awareness for both flight crews and support personnel. This increased awareness allows for more informed decision-making, potentially preventing accidents and improving response times during in-flight anomalies.
2. Criticality of CRM Training: Effective CRM training tailored to the requirements of a DART program is crucial. Such training must cover stress management techniques, structured decision-making models, and advanced communication protocols, while taking into account that some crew members are present while others must communicate over long distances. This necessarily includes dealing with the technical and interpersonal failure modes of telecommunications equipment. Only by equipping pilots and ground staff with these skills can a DART program be utilized effectively and to its full potential, ensuring better coordination and more effective intervention.

6.2 Future Directions

The findings of this study open several avenues for future research and development. Integrating artificial intelligence and machine learning technologies with the systems required to support a DART program could enhance predictive analytics, allowing for even earlier detection of potential issues. Additionally, exploring the use of virtual reality (VR) and augmented reality (AR) in CRM training could provide more immersive and effective learning experiences. Furthermore, ongoing collaboration with technology providers, research institutions, and aviation industry partners will be crucial in driving innovation and refining the DART approach. Continuous feedback from real-world applications should inform iterative improvements, ensuring the approach evolves with the experience gained through its application.

6.3 Conclusion

In summary, robust remote CRM training can unlock the ability to leverage real-time data and enhance human factors to further advance both aviation safety and efficiency. When part of a well-crafted DART program, remote CRM training provides an insurance policy for a major event, but can equally increasing airline operational efficiency by providing useful assistance and practice opportunities with faults that do not threaten the aircraft.

The insights gained from this study highlight the importance of a holistic approach, addressing both technological and human elements to create a resilient and responsive aviation safety framework. The potential to combine gains in operational efficiencies with a potential to save lives and prevent accidents makes the DART approach a key opportunity in the ongoing effort to further enhance global aviation operations.

We'll be looking for airlines eager to start on the path to DART.

References

Bennett, S.A.: Aviation crew resource management - a critical appraisal, in the tradition of reflecttive practice, informed by flight and cabin crew feedback. J. Risk Res. 1357–1373 (2019)

CEFA. Flight safety and pilot training, 20 May 2024. Retrieved from CEFA Corporation Website: https://www.cefa-aviation.com/

de Courville, B.: Breaking Airlines Flight Data Monitoring Barriers: A Pilot's Perspective. IASS, Taipei (2019)

FAA. AC 120-51E - Crew Resource Managemnt Training, 22 January 2004. https://www.faa.gov/regulations_policies/advisory_circulars/index.cfm/go/document.information/documentID/22879

FAA. Advanced Qualification Program (AQP), 15 February 2024. www.faa.gov: https://www.faa.gov/training_testing/training/aqp

Griebel, H.S., Smith, D.C.: DART – distress assistance with real-time aircraft telemetry. J. Int. Soc. Air Saf. Investigators **55**(3), 16–21 (2022)

Hagen, J.U., Lei, Z.S.: What aircraft crews know about managing high-pressure situations. Harvard Bus. Rev. (2019)

ICAO. Aeronautical Communications Panel ACP-WGF23-WP04. Agenda. Cairo, Egypt (2010). https://www.icao.int/safety/acp/ACPWGF/ACP-WG-F-23/ACP-WGF23-WP04-Assembly%20Flight%20Data%20paper%20for%20WG%20F%20rev1.doc

Kułakowski, G.N.: Selected aspects of shaping the competence of civil and military air transport crew using Crew Resource Management (CRM) training. Sci. J. Silesian Univ. Technol. Ser. Transp. **102**, 85–97 (2019)

Landman, A., van Meddelaar, S.H., Groen, E.L., van Paassen, M.M., Bronkhorst, A.W., Mulder, M.: The effectiveness of mnemonic-type startle and surprise management procedure for pilots. Int. J. Aerosp. Psychol. **30**(3–4), 104–118 (2020)

MacLeod, N.: Crew Resource Management Training: A Competence-Based Approach for Airline Pilots. CRC Press, Milton (2021)

The Devil Between the Details: Limitations of Probability-Based Approaches to Human Error

Lauren J. Thomas[✉] [iD] and Kathy H. Abbott [iD]

Federal Aviation Administration, 800 Independence Avenue, Washington D.C., USA
{lauren.j.thomas,kathy.abbott}@faa.gov

Abstract. This paper discusses the limitations of probabilistic approaches to human error within the context of aircraft certification and continued operational safety. These approaches attempt to estimate frequency of human error over time, with a view to calculating a probability. This type of quantification may be familiar to safety engineers experienced in using such methods to estimate equipment failure rates. In engineering, these estimates are used to evaluate equipment safety, to better understand component lifespan, and to inform decisions regarding maintenance or replacement schedules. However, it is not appropriate to analyze human error in the same way that equipment is evaluated. This paper illustrates why probabilistic approaches to human error are limited, using case studies and examples. The issues raised will be relevant to those involved with human factors in initial aircraft certification or in continued operational safety, or to engineers who require an appreciation of the challenges in evaluating operational flightcrew error in making safety decisions.

Keywords: Human error · Human reliability analysis · Human error analysis · Probability based risk assessment · Human factors in aircraft certification · Continued operational safety

1 Introduction

Human error is an important topic in aviation safety. In the interest of predicting the occurrence of human error, there is sometimes an effort to quantify the probability of error. There are many different definitions and classifications of human error. An FAA description of human error states:

"Human error is generally characterized as a deviation from what is considered correct in some context, especially in the hindsight of analysis of accidents, incidents, or other events of interest. Some types of error can be the following: an inappropriate action, a difference from what is expected in a procedure, a mistaken decision, an incorrect keystroke, or an omission of some kind" [1, para. 2–1.a.].

The views expressed within this paper are those of the authors, and do not represent the official policy or position of the Federal Aviation Administration, the Department of Transportation, or the United States Government.

© The Author(s), under exclusive license to Springer Nature Switzerland AG 2025
D. Harris et al. (Eds.): HCII 2024, LNCS 15381, pp. 308–325, 2025.
https://doi.org/10.1007/978-3-031-76824-8_23

This description makes clear that error is often identified as such from the vantage point of hindsight. There are also different classifications of error. For example, James Reason's Generic Error Management System (GEMS) describes mistakes, lapses, slips and violations [2, 3]. The GEMS classification is based on intent. If the action was intended, did it go to plan? What about the outcome – was the outcome of the action as planned? And if the action was intended, and had the desired outcome, was it in accordance with procedures and expectations? Reason provides another classification based on the action itself [4]. Examples would include omissions, where a required action is missed from a sequence, or done at the wrong time, and repetitions, where an action is repeated unnecessarily. Rasmussen's categorization [5] makes a distinction between knowledge-based, rule-based, and skill-based performance; different errors are associated with each type of human performance.

There are many areas in aviation where human error is of interest, including aircraft design and operation, air traffic control, and maintenance. This paper focuses on human error within the context of system safety assessments for aircraft certification, and the continued operational safety processes associated with type certified aircraft. Aircraft certification is the process by which regulatory authorities certify an initial or derivative aircraft type design. Continued operational safety is the process by which aircraft conforming to a specific type design are monitored while in-service, to identify potential and actual safety issues, and address them.

Within US civil aviation, the certification of aircraft under Part 25 requires that applicants show compliance with United States Title 14 Code of Federal Regulations 25.1309, *Equipment, systems, and Installations* [6]. Among other things, this regulation requires that:

(b) The airplane systems and associated components, considered separately and in relation to other systems, must be designed so that –

1. The occurrence of any failure condition which would prevent the continued safe flight and landing of the airplane is extremely improbable, and
2. The occurrence of any other failure conditions which would reduce the capability of the airplane or the ability of the crew to cope with adverse operating condition is improbable.

The Federal Aviation Administration provides guidance on how to demonstrate compliance with this regulation within Advisory Circular 25.1309-1A [7][1]. This guidance is supported by recommended practices that outline industry-accepted practices. For example, SAE aerospace recommended practice (ARP) documents provide guidelines for conducting the safety assessment process on civil aircraft, systems, and equipment [8, 9]. The recommended safety assessment process includes evaluating aircraft and system functions; identifying, and classifying failure conditions; determining the level of rigor applied to development assurance processes; and validating safety requirements for completeness and correctness [8]. The process outlines both quantitative and qualitative analysis methods, including fault tree analysis, functional hazard assessments, failure modes and effects analysis, cascading effects analysis and common mode analysis. Some

---

[1] In Europe, there are equivalent regulatory requirements within EASA's CS 25.1309; associated guidance material is available in AMC 25.1309.

quantitative approaches, such as fault tree analyses, attempt to quantify the frequency of equipment or hardware failures, with the goal of estimating the probability of failure within a specific period.

Errors in requirements, design, or implementation of the design are managed via a documented and repeatable development assurance process [9]. The development assurance process is intended to provide a qualitative degree of confidence that errors (including omissions) within product development have been detected and resolved. Development assurance levels are assigned to functions and items based on the severity of the failure condition classification. The development assurance process aims to reduce the probability that errors in requirements, design and implementation will manifest within the final product in a manner that could impact safety.

However, errors in aircraft manufacture, in operations and maintenance, and within decommissioning are not explicitly considered within these system safety documents. Where human intervention on the flight deck is evoked within a system safety analysis, such as a failure condition that requires flightcrew recognition and response, it is assumed to be correct:

> "The safety assessment process described in this document assumes that flight crews, cabin crews, maintenance crews, and other individuals participating in the operation of the aircraft follow documented procedures in foreseeable operating conditions (normal, malfunction or abnormal, and emergency). Intentional or unintentional deviation from these procedures is not considered in the safety assessment process described herein." [8, p. 22].

The reality is that "even well trained, qualified, healthy, and alert flightcrew members make errors" [1, p. 3][2]. Errors will occur that are above and beyond those related to procedures. Recent events have shown that flightcrew recognition and response may not always align with the assumptions made within safety assessments [10, 11]. Some commentators have suggested that incorporating probabilistic human error analyses into system safety assessments, in the way that fault tree analyses are used to assess equipment failure, would adequately address this omission.

Proponents of this view suggest that this approach to human error would allow crew performance to be modelled and predicted with precision, enhancing the way that flightcrew performance is considered within aircraft certification or continued operational safety [12]. These probabilistic approaches are collectively known as human reliability analyses (HRA), and they focus on estimating and quantifying the probability of operator error. HRA approaches are distinct from Human Error Analyses. Human Error Analyses are intended to analyze the flightcrew interactions associated with using specific systems, equipment, and interfaces. A Human Error Analysis aims to identify plausible flightcrew errors that may occur given the phase of flight, environment, and operational context, and assess the potential consequences and outcomes of those errors to inform error mitigation strategies, such as design, training, and procedures.

---

[2] In Europe, there are equivalent regulatory requirements within EASA's CS 25.1302, with the associated guidance material available in AMC 25.1302.

In contrast, HRA methods were developed to estimate generic human error rates, with the aim of integrating human error frequencies into quantitative system reliability analyses. The overall purpose is to derive a figure that describes, in engineering terms, the "reliability" of a specific plant or system. Many HRA approaches were developed for application within the nuclear industry to assess the overall safety of a nuclear power plant e.g. [13, 14]. In the nuclear industry, human reliability analysis is a regulatory requirement [15].

While such analyses are a regulatory requirement within the nuclear industry, within aviation, such approaches are not considered feasible [1, 7]. In nuclear power, a human reliability analysis focuses on a specific plant, with a single control platform and a uniform set of processes and procedures. Within commercial aviation, there is a wide range of airlines, operating different aircraft types. Aircraft of the same basic type design may be equipped differently, and be used in different operational contexts. Although each operator is required to provide a minimum standard of training, there is considerable diversity in how operators meet the regulatory requirements associated with flightcrew training. Standard operating procedures also vary between organizations. Compared to the nuclear industry, within aviation there are opportunities for a wider range of errors, and the influence of performance shaping factors is also more extensive. Table 1 illustrates some of these differences.

Table 1. Comparison of human error considerations between a nuclear power plant and commercial flight deck (adapted with the permission of Boeing).

Error Consideration	Nuclear Power Plant	Commercial Flight Deck
Diversity of user interfaces	Low	High
Diversity of tasks	Low	High
Diversity of contexts	Low	High
Diversity of users	Low	High
Dynamics	Slow	Very fast to very slow
Error opportunities	Constrained (action slips such as data entry/keying errors)	Unbounded (include action slips and cognitive errors)
Performance shaping factors	Limited	Extensive

Human factors guidance published by the FAA recognizes that "flightcrew errors cannot be entirely prevented, and that no validated methods exist to reliably predict either their probability or all of the sequences of events with which they may be associated" [1, p. 37]. This is also acknowledged in FAA system safety assessment guidance: "quantitative assessments of the probabilities of crew or maintenance errors are not currently considered feasible" [16, p. 15]. There are several reasons why it is not appropriate to analyze human error in the same way that equipment is evaluated. Some of the reasons are discussed within this paper, with illustrative case studies and examples.

2 The Past Does Not Always Predict the Future

In many cases, human reliability analyses derive error probability data from historical information. However, estimates of human error based on historical data do not necessarily reflect future reality. The past does not always predict the future. Historical safety is no guarantee of future safety. Making safety decisions based only on statistics drawn from previous events is analogous to driving while only looking in the rear-view mirror [17, pp. 74–75]. Safety events associated with the rudder system on the Boeing 737–300 illustrate this point.

On 8 September 1994, USAir Flight 427 entered an uncontrolled descent on approach to Pittsburgh International Airport. The Boeing 737-300 crashed near Aliquippa, Pennsylvania, with the loss of two flightcrew, three flight attendants, and 127 passengers on board [18]. Just prior to the loss of control, the aircraft had been maneuvering to land, rolling through seven degrees of bank to complete a turn that would put the aircraft on downwind for the active runway, following a Boeing 727. The airspeed of the airplane then fluctuated, the left bank angle increased to approximately 15 degrees, and the heading rate increased to approximately five degrees per second. The aircraft rolled more rapidly to the left, and the stick shaker activated. The bank angle increased to over 40 degrees, and the aircraft began to lose altitude. Early in the investigation, it was surmised that the flight had encountered wake turbulence from the preceding Boeing 727. However, the National Transportation Safety Board (NTSB) considered that the wake turbulence encounter alone would not have caused the continued heading change.

The NTSB recognized that this accident was similar to a Boeing 737-200 accident in Colorado Springs in 1991. Witnesses reported that shortly after completing its turn onto final approach, United Flight 585 rolled steadily to the right, and pitched nose down into an almost vertical attitude. The aircraft was destroyed, with the loss of all five crew and 20 passengers on board. Flight data indicated that about 10 seconds after beginning descent from 8,000 feet, the heading began to change at a rate of $0.5°$ per second. A few seconds before the crash, the heading change rate had increased to about 5^0 per second. Although rudder anomalies had been identified within the flight data, the NTSB could not identify what would have produced a rudder movement that the pilots were unable to counteract. The Board suggested that the most likely explanations were a malfunction of the aircraft's direction control system, or an encounter with an unusual atmospheric disturbance. The NTSB reopened the investigation into Flight 585 when the US Air Flight 427 accident occurred [19].

On 9 June 1996, an Eastwind Airlines Boeing 737-200 completed a successful test flight from Greensboro, following overnight maintenance for excess rudder trim. The crew then flew the aircraft on scheduled legs. On Flight 517 from Trenton, New Jersey, to Richmond, Virginia, the crew experienced rudder anomalies. The captain had disengaged the autopilot at around 10,000 feet, as was his personal habit. On approach, the captain was hand-flying the aircraft with his feet on the rudder pedals. At around 5,000 feet, the captain felt a "bump" on the right rudder pedal; he checked the first officer's feet and saw that they remained on the floor. He then felt a yaw to the right, and a right roll. The first officer later explained that at this point, he observed the captain "fighting, trying to regain control". The captain did regain control and successfully landed [20]. The NTSB examined the rudder components and flight test data. The Board also performed a computer simulation, completed an analysis of human factors data, and were able to interview the flightcrew [18]. The Eastwind Airlines incident provided further insight into the USAir Flight 427 accident.

The 737-300 has a single rudder panel, actuated by a single power control unit (PCU). Within the PCU, there are two concentric valves, once inside the other, inside a case. The inner valve is the primary slide, and the outer is the secondary slide. The valves operate in tandem to allow hydraulic fluid to deflect the rudder. The NTSB demonstrated that in some circumstances, a jam of the secondary slide could allow the primary slide to overtravel, preventing proper alignment of the hydraulic fluid ports. This could cause a flow of hydraulic fluid in a direction that was not intended, resulting in the rudder deflecting in the opposite direction to that commanded by the flightcrew: a rudder reversal. Data from the Flight 427 cockpit voice recorder, along with human factors analyses and computer simulations, were consistent with this type of rudder malfunction [18].

In assessing the safety of the rudder system, the manufacturer's documentation had stated that "rudder PCUs are not susceptible to jams that cause uncommanded motion" and "service history shows there have been NO events or PCU rate jams in flight" [18, p. 173]. The NTSB amended their United 585 accident report, stating that "The rudder surface most likely deflected in a direction opposite to that commanded by the pilots" [19 p. xv]. In this case, a previously unidentified failure condition, that was not anticipated based on previous service history, produced a rudder movement opposite to that commanded by the pilot. The flightcrew were unable to counteract this. As an investment planner might say: "past performance is no guarantee of future results". Historical data is no guarantee of future safety. Using error estimates based on historical data will likely provide incomplete or misleading answers.

3 Hazards, Heroes and Hindsight

Discussing human error in terms of frequency, rates, reliability, and probability tends to imply that the humans within a system are "hazards", and that human errors are "failures" to be eliminated, managed, or "designed out". The reality is that flightcrews usually do a great deal to proactively identify and appropriately remedy any errors that they do make. On the flightdeck, pilots can, and frequently do, reflect on their actions, evaluate the outcomes, and adapt their behavior accordingly. Error has an upside: making errors is a necessary part of learning, adapting, and improving. Everyone makes errors and learns in different ways, and the upside of making errors is that they create opportunities to learn. One accident is an example of how a flightcrew learned to control a stricken aircraft "on the fly", adapting their inputs and responses in an extraordinary manner to land the aircraft.

On July 19, 1989 a United McDonnell Douglas DC-10 took off from Denver, Colorado, en route to Chicago, Illinois [21]. Just over an hour into the flight, the flightcrew heard an explosive sound; they determined that the tail-mounted engine had failed. Shortly afterwards, the flightcrew observed that the hydraulic pressure and fluid had fallen to zero in all three hydraulic systems, severely limiting their ability to control the aircraft. The flightcrew contacted the airline's maintenance and engineering departments, declaring Mayday; the technicians and engineers were not able to provide any instructions or guidance. On requesting emergency assistance from air traffic control, the crew were given vectors to Sioux City airport. An announcement was made to the passengers that an engine had failed; an off-duty training check airman seated in first class made himself known to a flight attendant and offered to help.

The Captain accepted the check airman's offer of assistance, and advised the check airman to take the throttles so that he and the first officer could focus on manipulating flight controls. The check airman realized that the aircraft tended to turn to the right, so used the thrust levers asymmetrically to counter this. The flight engineer went into the passenger cabin to inspect the tail of the aircraft; he reported to the Captain that there was damage to the right and left horizontal stabilizers. In normal flight, the flightcrew trim the aircraft to control pitch and maintain the balance between airspeed and altitude. The damage to the aircraft meant that flightcrew were unable to control pitch directly, so they were learning how to control an aircraft oscillating in phugoid cycles using real-time experimentation.

Phugoid oscillations occur when aircraft speed drops, and then the nose of the aircraft dips and airspeed increases. The increased speed generates lift, and the aircraft nose rises; the aircraft climbs until it loses speed, and the nose again drops. This oscillation is normally easily damped with elevator control, but in this case the flightcrew were having to anticipate the cycle of these oscillations 20 to 40 seconds in advance. No corrections could be made in the 20 to 40 seconds before the landing. Nevertheless, the crew found a way to control the aircraft, and were able to touchdown on a runway. Although 112 people died and the fuselage was destroyed, 184 people survived the accident. Given the challenges of controlling an aircraft in this configuration, reaching a runway and landing at a pre-determined point and airspeed could be regarded as a "highly random event" [19, p. 72].

In the design of these aircraft systems, the loss of all hydraulic powered flight controls had been considered such a remote possibility that no procedure existed. Flightcrew training and procedures only addressed the actions to be taken when two hydraulic systems were lost. Simulator reenactments with flightcrews after the accident demonstrated that pilots could separately control speed, touchdown point, direction, attitude, and vertical velocity. However, it was all but impossible to control those parameters simultaneously, and simultaneous control of these parameters was required to land the aircraft. The NTSB concluded that the performance of the flightcrew on United 232 Flight was "highly commendable and greatly exceeded reasonable expectations" [21, p. 76].

This accident serves as an illustration that flightcrews can diagnose a situation, reflect on their actions, evaluate the outcomes, and adapt their behavior accordingly. The flightcrew were not following standard operating procedures in this instance: none existed. The actions of this flightcrew could not be replicated by other crews, even though the simulator crews had advance knowledge of the failure condition and were aware that there would be a complete loss of hydraulic fluid. This also demonstrates the high degree of variability between crews; approaches to human reliability analysis rarely capture the levels of variability evident in real-world crews.

The performance of the Flight 232 crew might be regarded as a "deviation", in that the crew performed in an atypical manner when benchmarked against the crews tested in the simulator. However, the outcome of the situation in this instance was an exceptional positive. The same attempts to learn what was happening in real time, to adapt to the responses of the aircraft, and to devise a method to control the aircraft may have been regarded as "errors" had the outcome not been so successful. It is often the context and the outcome of an event that determines whether humans involved are regarded as hazards, or as heroes; and this is only known with hindsight. Focusing on the probability of an "error" occurring does not take account of the "after the fact" narrative that may reframe an error as an act of heroism. The probability figure also masks the fact that in some situations, "human error" may save the day.

Calling a behavior an error means making an attribution of some kind. The traditional view of human error describes it as a failure of some type: someone did not do what they "should" have done. This view characterizes humans as hazards or risks to be mitigated or eliminated [22]. Within the human factors discipline, the modern approach to human error is to see it as a natural variation in human behavior, and to accept that people tend to make the best decisions they can, with the information that they have available at the time. Totting up errors to try to determine their probability tells us nothing about why a decision or action made sense to that person, at that time. Probabilities tell us nothing about the context of the error, or the circumstances the person was dealing with.

Dekker [22, Ch. 2] describes several common reactions to error that can influence the way these behaviors are considered within safety. These are:

- **Retrospective** – when we consider errors within the context of incidents and accidents, we benefit from the ability to look back on a sequence of events. This was not possible for the people involved.
- **Counterfactual** - when we consider errors within an incident or accident, we may focus on what could or should have been done to avoid an outcome that we now know about. That outcome may not have been evident to the people involved.
- **Judgmental** – when we consider errors involved in an incident or accident sequence, we may judge the people involved for not doing what we might believe they "should" have done, or for not noticing information that we know to be important with the benefit of hindsight.
- **Proximal** – when we consider errors involved in incidents and accidents, we may focus on the people closest in space and time to the event itself. We may pay less attention to design decisions, organizational processes, and management practices that may also be regarded as "deviations" from an ideal standard.

These reactions potentially influence the consideration of human error within safety analyses, particularly when estimates are based on previous incidents and accidents. Safety analysts, like all of us, are subject to their own perspectives and experiences. These types of subjective influences mean that estimates of the probability of human error are not on the same footing as engineering data. Failure rates for hardware components can be calculated; tolerance levels can be specified. Failure rates and tolerances for human behavior cannot be generated in the same way. In a paper discussing the way that risk is considered in nuclear safety, Brighton makes the point that:

"It must be a fundamental epistemological flaw to put opinions, however expert, on the same footing as physical data. It also seems entirely contrary to common experience of human psychology. Practical engineering decisions are made in organisations of many individuals all having different knowledge and experience. Two similar professionals will make different probability judgements (if they think in those terms at all) because even if their knowledge of the problem in hand is the same, they will have different experience and they will be influenced by personal and organisational attitudes" [23, p. 12].

4 Errors Are Context Dependent

The context of a flightcrew action is vitally important. It is widely acknowledged within the field of human factors that people tend to behave in ways that make sense to them, given the information that they have available at the time [17, 22]. It is critical to understand the context in which someone was carrying out a task to be able to understand why a specific course of action, or decision, was selected. A good illustration of the importance of context in understanding behavior is a leak that occurred on the International Space Station [24].

Although not immediately catastrophic, the pressure within the International Space Station had dropped from 14.7 lb per square inch to 14.0 lb per square inch over a period of three weeks. Air had slowly been seeping into the vacuum of space at five times the normal rate. NASA had decided that the two astronauts needed to isolate each module of the station, checking every valve, hatch, seal, port, and window, to find the source of the leak, and fix it.

The window in the Destiny space laboratory module was an advanced design, and a departure from previous designs. Previous designs had used nitrogen between the windowpanes, to prevent moisture and condensation, even at very low temperatures. On the window in the Destiny space laboratory module, two vents connected by a U-shaped hose allowed the space between the two windowpanes to vent directly into space – creating "the best optical window ever installed in any human space vehicle" [25].

Unfortunately, there were no handholds at the window in the Destiny space laboratory module. There were handholds on a rack assembly intended for installation, but the delivery of that had been delayed. For the three years that the space station had been occupied, the U-shaped hose had been repeatedly used as a handle by astronauts, holding it to stabilize themselves while taking photographs of their home planet [25].

The actions of the astronauts could perhaps be described as errors, since they contributed to the failure of the hose and the development of the leak. Their actions could also be regarded as instances of "foreseeable misuse". With stunning views from the most optically pure window ever installed in a human space vehicle, it's perhaps not surprising that astronauts decided to enjoy the view, or to capture some incredible images. In a weightless environment, this meant that the astronauts steadied themselves by holding a hose that had never been intended for use as a handle. The way that the leak developed cannot be fully understood without appreciating the context of the astronauts' actions.

Contextual factors also apply to errors on civil flight decks. On a modern civil flight deck, manual tasks are mainly associated with activities such as making inputs to avionics systems. Manual errors could arise when the flightcrew type data into the flight management system, perhaps because a crewmember strikes the incorrect key [26]. However, even such an apparently simple error raises questions. What type of keyboard was being used: was this an A-B-C-D-E keyboard, or a QWERTY keyboard? What key did the crewmember intend to strike – was this a case of "fat-finger" syndrome, where the correct action was known, but the error occurred in executing the key-strike? Or was this an error of knowledge – perhaps the flightcrew member made the input as intended, not knowing that a different action was required to achieve their goal? Input errors become more complex when the interaction involves selection from a series of options on a pull-down menu, or requires using a different input device such as a touch screen or tracking ball. Making accurate inputs at the gate is one matter; trying to make accurate inputs in turbulent conditions at 20,000 feet is a different story. Further, there are questions about whether the crewmember recognized and corrected the error immediately, or whether the mistake was identified later in the flight. Estimates of error, even for an apparently simple action such as making a data entry, may be highly questionable without fully appreciating the context of the action.

The reality is that flying a modern commercial aircraft is primarily a series of cognitive tasks, and cognitive errors are more complex than simple action slips. Flightcrews seek information, use the available information to make diagnoses and decisions, and then assess whether their actions have had the intended effect. There are usually several different options a flightcrew has in flying the aircraft; for example, different flightcrews may elect to fly a specific approach in different, but acceptable, ways, and all pilots have their own styles and preferences. Who is to determine whether one way is more "correct" or less error prone than another? Probability estimates for cognitive errors on a modern commercial aircraft cannot reflect all the factors in play, and will not be able to represent all the nuances of context. As Levenson [27] notes, probability analyses seldom include information on the conditions under which the probabilities were derived, so it is often not possible to assess the extent to which the data may apply to new or updated systems, equipment, or interfaces.

A further limitation of HRA approaches is that when probability estimates are derived, they are seldom validated. In science, claiming that it is possible to "predict" future occurrences or events requires evidence. What follow-up analyses are conducted to demonstrate that the human error probabilities claimed within a Human Reliability Analysis are realistic? What assessments or evaluations are undertaken to ensure that the assumptions made are truly warranted? Sometimes human reliability analyses are applied retrospectively, to support an argument that the method accurately "predicts" an accident that has already happened. Such studies are instances of "retro-fitting" a model to an event where the outcome is already known: this is not the same as predicting the winning lottery numbers in advance, and claiming the jackpot.

5 You Cannot Count What You Do Not Know

Many structured approaches to human reliability analysis include a basic consideration of "Performance Shaping Factors". Performance shaping factors are considerations that may increase or decrease the likelihood of human error. Performance shaping factors could be physical, such as the location of an information display, or the ease of manipulating a control. Others may be environmental, such as heat, humidity, noise, and vibration, which could influence human performance and be related to human error. While it is relatively common to include factors such as noise level, flightcrew experience, stressful conditions, or fatigue within a human reliability analysis, some of the factors associated with, or related to, human error, are not always known. Social, supervisory, and organizational factors also influence the expression of human error. Quantifying the influence of intangible factors such as supervisory practices, organizational priorities and prevailing culture is next to impossible [28].

The space shuttle Columbia disintegrated during re-entry on February 1, 2003, with the loss of all seven crew members. The physical cause of the accident was the separation of a piece of insulation from the leading edge of the left wing. This occurred between 8 and 9 seconds after launch. During re-entry, superheated air penetrated this breach in the shuttle's thermal protection system, melting the left wing and leading to a loss of control [29]. The Columbia Accident Investigation Board's investigation and subsequent report went beyond the physical causes of the accident, examining organizational, historical, and cultural factors within NASA. The Board identified factors detrimental to safety that contributed to the accident, including reliance on past success as a substitute for sound engineering practices, organizational barriers that hindered the sharing of safety critical information and inhibited the sharing of professional differences of opinion, and approaches to decision making that were outside of the organizational hierarchy [29]. The Board argued that "NASA's organizational culture had as much to do with this accident as foam did" [29, p. 12]. None of these factors were tangible, physical causes, and they were not "counted" when the shuttle program risks were considered.

In an article examining the strengths and limitations of probabilistic risk assessment, Mosleh [28] noted that NASA had conducted several probability-based risk assessments of the shuttle program, with median estimates of the probability of the loss of the crew and the vehicle coming in between 1 in 78 and 1 in 245 per flight. The observed rate of loss was 1 in 67, with both Challenger and Columbia lost over 134 missions. The human and organizational factors identified by the Columbia Accident Investigation Board were not included in any of these analyses, although they were critical to gaining a complete understanding of the way that the accident happened.

Mosleh acknowledges that "Identifying risk scenarios in case of highly complex, dynamic, hybrid systems of hardware, software, and human components is very difficult, if not impossible, with the static, largely hardware-oriented classical framework" [28, p. 8]. Analysts cannot count what they do not see, so many of the intangible factors that shape human performance will not appear within probabilistic risk assessments. There is also a risk that such assessments become something of an echo chamber: the system vulnerabilities and failure scenarios included in probabilistic risk assessments tend to be those that have already been identified by the analysts. This means that a probabilistic risk assessment may be a manner of documenting and organizing the analysts' own perspectives, rather than being a way to proactively identify currently unknown and unanticipated failures.

A similar point was made by Downer and Ramana in a paper on nuclear reactor safety [30]. They observed that if a meteorologist is unable to accurately predict the weather in London in two months' time, that will not affect the likelihood of it raining. In contrast, a safety engineer's inability to predict the failure behavior of a nuclear reactor does affect the likelihood of that reactor failing. The engineering knowledge that would have supported the prediction of failure would also have informed improvements to the design of the system. In nuclear safety, engineers "must grapple with a problem of recursion: any cause they have to believe that their reliability assessments are uncertain is also cause to believe that their reactors are unreliable" [30, p. 14].

Latent conditions can be another type of "known unknown" within probability-based assessments. Such conditions are "latent" by definition, so they cannot be identified and included within a human reliability analysis. No-one knows that these conditions are present until they contribute to error, or impact safety. In effect, these are "dormant" conditions within a system: they do not cause an issue until they are implicated in an incident or accident. Examples could be errors within software coding that have not been identified and remedied within quality assurance processes. One of the accidents associated with the V-22 Osprey is an example of a latent software error.

On 11 December 2000, a V-22 had a flight control error and crashed near Jacksonville, North Carolina, killing all four aboard. Chafing induced by vibration caused a leak in the hydraulic line that fed the actuators to the right-side rotor blade controls. The leak caused a Primary Flight Control System (PFCS) alert. The standard operating procedure was for the flightcrew to press the Primary Flight Control System Fail/Reset button, to see if the alert would clear. The flightcrew made eight or nine attempts to reset the software in twenty-two seconds. Unknown to them, a previously undiscovered error in the control software caused the aircraft to accelerate and decelerate violently and unpredictably in response to each of their attempts to reset the software. In this instance, the flightcrew were following standard operating procedures, but a latent failure, in combination with other factors, resulted in the aircraft falling 1,600 feet and crashing in a forest [31, 32]. Safety assessments largely deal in the currency of known issues: not all safety threats are knowable.

6 Even the Best Guess is a Still a Guess

Probability estimates may create an undeserved sense of certainty or confidence in the results of safety analyses. There are many assumptions and unknowns within probability-based safety analyses, and yet these uncertainties tend to be over-ridden when a number is provided, even if that number is not much more than a "scientific wild-ass guess". Downer and Ramana make the point that "decades of epistemology—not to mention common sense—speak to the impossibility of formally calculating, via myriad representations and abstractions, the future failure behavior of a highly 'difficult' socio-technical system, over a decades-long timeframe, to an extreme degree of confidence. The task simply requires too many judgments to be made with too much perfection to be plausible. The truth of this should be self-evident" [30, p. 14].

The safety case of the United Kingdom Royal Air Force Hawker Siddeley Nimrod is an example of misplaced confidence in probability-based analyses. On 2 September 2006, a Nimrod suffered a catastrophic in-flight fire after completing air-to-air refueling. The aircraft subsequently crashed in Kandahar, Afghanistan, killing all fourteen crew members on board. An independent review led by Charles Haddon-Cave investigated the circumstances of the accident [33]. The most likely physical cause of the accident was found to be an overflow during air-to-air refueling, leading to an accumulation of fuel within an insulation muff placed around a duct. The insulation around the duct was degraded, and the likely source of ignition was an exposed element. The addition of the duct was a later modification to the aircraft, and the duct was fitted in close proximity to fuel pipes. There was no fire detection or suppression system within the dry bay, and yet this catastrophic fire risk had been assessed as "Tolerable".

However, some of the most interesting lessons from the Haddon-Cave review related to the non-physical, less tangible, causes of the accident. Haddon-Cave considered that the in-service modifications to the Nimrod represented design flaws, and he carefully considered the way that the Nimrod safety case was compiled. A safety case is a dossier compiled to provide a reasoned argument, substantiated with evidence, that demonstrates a system is safe for a specific application in a particular context. The Nimrod safety case should have identified and analyzed hazards, assessed the risks of those hazards, and provided evidence of how those risks were managed or mitigated [33]. Instead, Haddon-Cave found that the task of compiling the Nimrod safety case was undermined because "the task of drawing up the safety case became essentially a paperwork and 'tick-box' exercise" [33, p. 190].

The Nimrod review demonstrated that the caveats and limitations associated with quantitative data are not always applied appropriately. Numbers generated by engineering judgement may be regarded as fact, when they may be no more than a guess. Cloaking such "guesstimates" in a mathematical guise gives them more credibility than is warranted. As Haddon-Cave cautioned: "Care should be taken when using quantitative probabilities, i.e. numerical probabilities such as 1×10^{-6} equating to "Remote". Such figures and their associated nomenclature give the illusion and comfort of accuracy and a well-honed scientific approach. Outside the world of structures, numbers are far from exact" [33, p. 546].

Haddon-Cave also identified that generic probabilities had been applied inappropriately, and that in some instances, risks were downgraded to a less severe category. More worryingly, Haddon-Cave suggested that engineers sometimes generated the data by indulging in a "a considerable element of making it up as they went along" [33, p. 196]. When reviewing photographs of zonal hazards, one engineer raised a question to the Airworthiness Department and was told: "Ask the question and we will try and help you, otherwise do as we do and GUESS" [33, p. 224]. The probability of a fuel pipe leak had been assessed as 10^{-6} and categorized as "Improbable", when "any line engineer would have known this was unrealistic" [33, p. 228].

In developing a safety case, as with any safety assessment process, the aim is not to "guess better". The aim is to understand the way that a product, system, or item of equipment will likely be used, or misused, in real-world contexts, and to make informed decisions that will reduce both the opportunities for risk, and the severity of the consequences.

7 The Bottom Line Is a Decision, Not a Number

Probability-based assessments are often intended to inform decisions about whether a system is "safe enough". However, decisions based on probability judgements are not necessarily objective, or accurate. Research on human perception and evaluation has provided insight into some of the mechanisms by which people evaluate risks and make decisions. For example, Granger Morgan [34] discusses work undertaken to explore people's perceptions of the risk of fatality from various causes. In one study, researchers asked people about the likelihood of different causes of death; there was a clear tendency for people to underestimate the chance of high-probability causes of death, and to overestimate the chances of low-probability causes of death.

Experimental research has shown that people use a range of heuristics to support evaluations of probability, and there is frequently a gulf between a subjective estimate of risk and a probability calculated using more objective data. Even when experts are consulted, using methods intentionally designed to minimize bias, the consensus reached may not reflect reality:

"There is an extensive literature on how people, especially experts, make probability judgements. This has led to procedures designed to detect and allow for biases and to promote a consensus amongst experts to make best use of available knowledge. The fact remains that even with such safeguards the probability estimate may be an apt expression of the scientific community's view, but there is no guarantee that it is close to 'reality'. It is a statement about the beliefs of a population of experts, rather than about the physical world." [23, pp. 11–12].

Another problem with experimental research on decisions regarding risk is that it lacks ecological validity. People do not make decisions in a vacuum: there is always a real-world context that influences decision-making. Asking people to evaluate risk in an experiment is not the same as asking people to evaluate risk in a real-life situation. In the real world, "safety" may not involve an assessment of probability:

"Many of us have been on flights that have run into turbulence. Sometimes people become quite agitated, looking out the window anxiously. Some grasp their armrests for dear life. Others pray or take pens out of their pockets. At the end of the flight some people applaud... From a probabilistic point of view the passenger fears and reactions make no sense. Although I do not know the number, the probability that a large, commercial aeroplane will crash because of turbulence must be quite small. Modern commercial aircraft are designed so that the wings can flex to an astonishing degree, turbulence is entirely normal... Have our fellow fliers lost their minds? I do not believe that they have. They boarded the flight believing that the probabilities of catastrophic aircraft failure were low; they will board another flight in the future with the same belief. But they also know that if they are 10 km up in the sky and their aircraft gets into serious trouble, "probability" has no meaning." [35, p. 191].

Estimating human error probabilities may not be the most effective use of expert time and effort. Instead, resources may be better directed at addressing the factors that are associated with human error. For example, Leveson [36] gives the example of an analyst examining a control panel and looking specifically at the labelling. Using a probabilistic approach, the analyst could determine that poor labelling on a control panel would increase the probability of operator error, while if the labelling were good, the probability of operator error should be decreased. In the world of probabilistic risk assessment, efforts would be directed towards deriving an accurate estimate of operator error. However, this is an inappropriate goal – if an analysis shows that the available labelling increases the likelihood of human error, the safety action is to improve the labelling, not to try and come up with a more accurate probability.

French et al. [37] argue that in complex situations, there are few truly independent barriers to risk. Those that exist may be overcome by humans, because human behavior itself introduces correlations and dependencies that may invalidate calculations of risk. French et al. note that human reliability analysis methods tend to focus on tasks that are easily describable, relatively simple, and sequential in nature: much like a typing or data entry error. In many high reliability or safety critical contexts, and as discussed above, humans are needed to make judgements and decisions in which information needs to be sought and evaluated. In some instances, relationships between cause and effect are well understood, and the consequences of an action can be predicted with some certainty. In other situations, cause and effect may only be discerned with additional data, or perhaps learned about "after-the-fact". There will also be situations in which people will be operating well beyond their current experience. Decision-making in these situations is more chaotic: people will need to take action, see what happens, and hope to make some sense of the situation. A model of error probability does not capture how humans deal with these situations.

When a model of human reliability is used, engineers often hope that the approach will generate a number that can somehow be deemed "acceptable" or "unacceptable"; they want to know the "bottom line". Human factors specialists can usually only discuss what a flightcrew might or might not do within certain situations and constraints, meaning that when asked what a flightcrew will do, the answer will often be "it depends". This is not an answer that engineers with a strong quantitative inclination will expect, value, or appreciate. However, humans do not operate with the same precision and predictability as manufactured components. If a probability-based analysis method is applied to human error, it does not necessarily follow that the results will be meaningful, accurate, or sufficiently robust to justify critical safety decisions. The "bottom line" in numerical terms is not the end of the story in human factors terms.

8 Concluding Remarks

In this paper, we have highlighted some of the issues associated with using probability-based approaches to human error within the context of aviation safety. We have drawn from a selection of case studies to demonstrate some of these limitations. We have argued that it is not appropriate to apply engineering methods used to evaluate equipment safety to human error. However, because these techniques include a form of quantification, questionable results may be regarded as mathematically accurate and scientifically credible.

Within the field of human factors, it is generally accepted that human "error" can only be defined with hindsight, and with knowledge of the outcome. Focusing on error misrepresents the way that humans perform tasks and achieve goals, and disregards the unique and critical role that humans play in failure identification and recovery.

While observable errors are details that can be "counted", they are not the details that matter most. It is what lies between, behind, and beyond, the numbers that provides the richest insights into flightcrew contributions to aviation safety. From a human factors perspective, the limitations of probability-based approaches to human error have been known for some time. Current research efforts in the field of human error are directed at more productive areas than estimating probabilities. As Dekker recently stated:

"None of the people who know what they are talking about are interested in publishing about something that was dead in the water years ago. The problems are obvious - not even academically interesting to critique" [38].

The Aircraft Certification, Safety and Accountability Act of 2020 brought awareness of human error and human factors issues to a broader engineering audience. It is therefore a timely opportunity to revisit the way that human error is considered within the context of aircraft certification and continued operational safety. We hope that the distinction we have drawn between human reliability analysis and human error analysis is a useful one.

Human error analysis methods, as opposed to probability-based approaches to human reliability, provide robust qualitative insights into the plausible flightcrew errors that may occur given the phase of flight, environment, and operational context. These methods allow assessment of the potential consequences and outcomes of error, and can also inform error mitigation strategies, such as design, training, and procedures. Human error analysis methods also have the advantage of being based on empirical, research, and simulation data, rather than relying on the human factors assumptions so often evident in probability-based approaches to human reliability. Probability-based techniques do not capture the range and real-world context of error in aviation. Aviation safety decisions based on these methods are questionable at best, and at worst, inform decisions that are built on foundations of sand.

Acknowledgements. The authors thank Michael Bartron, Jon Holbrook, Bill Kaliardos, Deborah Shaibe, and Vic Riley for reviewing this paper, and Amber Ann-Marie Cole for her assistance with formatting.

References

1. Federal Aviation Administration: Installed Systems and Equipment for Use by the Flightcrew. Advisory Circular 25.1302-1. US Department of Transportation, Washington, D.C. (2013)
2. Reason, J.: Human Error. 1st Edn. Cambridge University Press, Cambridge, England (1990)
3. Reason, J.: Managing the Risks of Organizational Accidents, 1st edn. Ashgate, Farnham, England (2005)
4. Reason, J.: The Human Contribution: Unsafe Acts, Accidents and Heroic Recoveries, 1st edn. Ashgate, Farnham, England (2008)
5. Rasmussen, J.: Skills, rules, and knowledge; signals, signs, and symbols, and other distinctions in human performance models. IEEE Trans. Syst. Man Cybern. **SMC-13**(3), 257–266 (1983). https://ieeexplore.ieee.org/document/6313160
6. United States: Title 14 Code of Federal Regulations Aeronautics and Space. https://www.ecfr.gov/current/title-14

7. Federal Aviation Administration: System design and analysis. Advisory Circular 25.1309-1A. US Department of Transportation, 21 June 1988
8. SAE: Aerospace Recommended Practice: Guidelines for Conducting the Safety Assessment Process on Civil Aircraft, Systems and Equipment. SAE International, ARP4761™ Revision A, Warrendale, PA (2023)
9. SAE: Aerospace Recommended Practice: Guidelines for Development of Civil Aircraft and Systems. SAE International, ARP4754™ Revision B (2023)
10. KNKT: Final Aircraft Accident Investigation Report, Lion Mentari Airlines, Boeing 737–8 (MAX); PK-LQP, Tanjung Karawang, West Java, Republic of Indonesia. Komite Nasional Keselamatan Transportasi, Republic of Indonesia, October 2019
11. AIB: Aircraft Accident Investigation Bureau Investigation Report on Accident to the B-737MAX8 Reg ET-AVJ. The Federal Democratic Republic of Ethiopia: Ministry of Transport And Logistics, Report no. AI-01/19 (2022)
12. NASEM: Evaluation of the Transport Airplane Risk Assessment Methodology. The National Academies Press, Washington, D.C. (2022)
13. Swain, A.D., Guttmann, H.E.: Handbook of Human Reliability Analysis with Emphasis on Nuclear Power Plant Applications. US Nuclear Regulatory Commission, Report No. NUREG/CR-1278, SAND-80-0200 (1983). https://www.osti.gov/biblio/5752058
14. Xing, J., Change, Y.J., DeJesus Segarra, J.: The General Methodology of an Integrated Human Event Analysis System (IDHEAS-G"). US Nuclear Regulatory Commission. Report NUREG-2198 (2021). https://www.nrc.gov/reading-rm/doc-collections/nuregs/staff/sr2198/index.html
15. ONR: Safety Assessment Principles for Nuclear Facilities. Bootle, Merseyside, UK: Office for Nuclear Regulation, 2014 Edition, Revision 1 (2020). https://www.onr.org.uk/publications/regulatory-guidance/regulatory-assessment-and-permissioning/safety-assessment-principles-saps/
16. Federal Aviation Administration: System design and analysis. Advisory Circular 25.1309, Arsenal Draft. Aviation Rulemaking Advisory Committee, Systems Design and Analysis Harmonization Working Group, Washington, D.C. (2002)
17. Klein, G.: Streetlights and Shadows: Searching for the Keys to Adaptive Decision Making, Cambridge. MIT Press, MA. (2011)
18. NTSB: Uncontrolled Descent and collision with terrain, US Air Flight 427 Boeing 373-300, N513AU, Near Aliquippa, Pennsylvania, 8 September 1994. National Transportation Safety Board, Report no. NTSB/AAR-99/01 (1999)
19. NTSB: Uncontrolled descent and collision with terrain, United Airlines Flight 585 Boeing 737-200, N999UA, 4 miles South of Colorado Springs Municipal Airport, Colorado Springs, Colorado, 3 March 2001. National Transportation Safety Board, Report no. NTSB/AAR-01/01, Washington, D.C. (2001)
20. NTSB: Group Chairman's Factual Report of Investigation Eastwind Airlines Boeing 737-200, Richmond, Virginia. National Transportation Safety Board Human Performance Group, Washington, D.C., Report No DCA-96-1A-061 (1996)
21. NTSB: United Airlines Flight 232 McDonnell Douglas DC-10-10 Sioux Gateway Airport, Sioux City, Iowa, 19 July 1989. National Transportation Safety Board, Report no. NTSB/AAR-90/06 (1990)
22. Dekker, S.: The Field Guide to Understanding Human Error, 3rd edn. Taylor & Francis, Boca Raton, Florida (2014)
23. Brighton, P.W.M.: Risk concepts in UK nuclear decision-making. Paper presented at International Conference on Topical Issues in Nuclear Safety. International Atomic Energy Agency, Vienna (2001). https://www-pub.iaea.org/MTCD/publications/PDF/pub1120/CD/PDF/Issue1/CN-82-18.pdf

24. Casey, S.: The Atomic Chef. Aegean Publishing Company, Santa Barbara, California (2006)
25. Oberg, J.: Space station leak caused by crew; experts say. NBC News, 15 January 2004. https://www.nbcnews.com/id/wbna3969567
26. IATA: FMS Data Entry Error Prevention Best Practices. First Edition. IATA, Montreal, Canada (2015). https://www.iata.org/contentassets/b6eb2adc248c484192101edd1ed36015/fms-data-entry-error-prevention-ed-1-2015.pdf
27. Leveson, N.G.: Engineering a Safer World: Systems Thinking Applied to Safety. The MIT Press, Cambridge, MA (2017)
28. Mosleh, A.: PRA: a perspective on strengths, current limitations, and possible improvements. Nuclear Eng. Technol. **46**(1), 1–10 (2014). https://www.sciencedirect.com/science/article/pii/S1738573315300851
29. CAIB: Columbia Accident Investigation Board Report. NASA and the Government Printing Office (2003). https://sma.nasa.gov/SignificantIncidents/assets/columbia-accident-investigation-board-report-volume-1.pdf
30. Downer, J., Ramana, M.V.: Empires built on sand: on the fundamental implausibility of reactor safety assessments and the implications for nuclear regulation. Regul. Gov. **15**(4), 1–22 (2020). https://research-information.bris.ac.uk/files/220050080/Empires_Built_on_S and_Uncorrected_Proof_.pdf
31. Whittle, R.: The Dream Machine. The Untold History of the Notorious V-22 Osprey. Simon & Schuster, New York (2010)
32. NASA: Critical Software: Good Design Built Right. NASA System Failure Case Studies, Vol. 6, no. 2, pp. 1–5, January 2012. https://sma.nasa.gov/docs/default-source/safety-messages/safetymessage-2012-02-06-criticalsoftware.pdf?sfvrsn=85ae1ef8_4
33. Haddon-Cave, C.: The Nimrod Review: An independent review into the broader issues surrounding the loss of the RAF Nimrod XR2 Aircraft XV230 in Afghanistan in 2006. The Stationary Office, U.K., London, October 2009. https://assets.publishing.service.gov.uk/media/5a7c652640f0b62aff6c1609/1025.pdf
34. Granger Morgan, M.: Probing the question of technology-induced risk. In: Glickman, T.S., & Gough, M. (eds.) Readings in Risk. RFF Press, Washington, D.C. (1990)
35. Clarke, L.: Thinking possibilistically in a probabilistic world. In: Significance, pp. 190–192, December 2007. https://rss.onlinelibrary.wiley.com/doi/full/https://doi.org/10.1111/j.1740-9713.2007.00270.x
36. Leveson, N.G.: Is estimating probabilities the right goal for system safety?" MIT Partnership for Systems Approaches to Safety and Security (PSASS) (2013). http://sunnyday.mit.edu/papers/Making-Safety-Decisions.pdf
37. French, S., Bedford, T., Pollard, S.J.T., Soane, E.: Human reliability analysis: a critique and review for managers. Saf. Sci. **49**(6), 753–763 (2011). https://www.sciencedirect.com/science/article/abs/pii/S0925753511000555
38. Dekker, S.: Personal Communication. 18 March 2024

Detection of Arousal of Pilots in Event-Related Heart Rate Responses

Karl Tschurtschenthaler[✉] and Axel Schulte

University of the Bundeswehr Munich, Neubiberg, Germany
{karl.tschurtschenthaler,axel.schulte}@unibw.de

Abstract. This study investigates whether the electrocardiogram (ECG) signal of pilots shows responsiveness towards unexpected events in highly dynamic environments. These event-related heart rate (HR) responses are manifestations of arousal and might indicate the beginning of a high-workload phase.

For the collection of HR response data, we conducted an experiment in a fast-jet simulator with eleven participants using a three-lead ECG sensor. The participants had a high degree of motivation and prior experience with flight simulators. The experiment consisted of six experiment blocks with varying difficulties. To trigger arousal, we included six types of events.

After the experiment, we computed differences in the HR and heart rate variability (HRV) for the pre- and post-exposure to each event. The results show that the response is highly dependent on the type of event and the individual. It appears that both ΔHR and $\Delta SD1/SD2$ may be indicative of arousal. However, given that the flight missions set in a naturalistic environment, it is not possible to ensure that mental workload did not affect responses. Results also indicate that HR and HRV alone are not reliable precursors to the onset of a workload phase. Someone must take the task context into account. Nevertheless, HR-related responses appear to be valuable features for the capture of coping mechanisms and can be used in an early operating adaptive assistance system.

The underlying objective of this research is the development of an adaptive assistance system in the field of Manned-Unmanned Teaming (MUM-T) missions.

Keywords: Electrocardiography · ECG · heart rate · heart rate variability · arousal · adaptive assistance systems · human autonomy teaming · manned-unmanned teaming · signal processing · biosignals

1 Introduction

Aerial Manned-Unmanned Teaming (MUM-T) describes how unmanned aerial vehicles (UAVs), and humans will work together in future military air operations. This cooperation will be achieved by pilots managing the automated vehicles from their aircraft cockpits. Although this type of operation gives pilots more capabilities, it causes problems in human-machine interactions. To resolve these, human factors research is essential when working with unmanned platforms. One concern of these studies is human error and a commonly reported construct that causes it is mental workload. The aim of human factors engineers is therefore the development of systems that reduce and resolve problems of high mental workload and cognitive saturation [1].

1.1 Mental Workload Determination for Adaptive Assistance

Our approach to solving the human factors-related challenges in MUM-T is an assistance system which adapts to the mental state of the human operator. For instance, if the mental workload is too high, these systems initiate intervention strategies. They shall simplify the task context for the pilot. To do this, they collect and process operator-centric data (e.g., physiological data) in real-time.

One of the challenges in the development of adaptive assistance systems is the design of an intervention strategy. The strategy must take the task context and mental workload of the pilot into account [2]. Furthermore, the intervention must appropriately address the event that caused the increased mental workload. Additionally, when the system detects that the pilot is in a demanding phase, the pilot is already saturated with tasks. As a result, assistance comes too late and it is difficult to apply an intervention appropriately aligned with the current task context [3, 4].

1.2 Early Operating Adaptive Assistance Systems

To circumvent the dilemma of late intervention, systems must operate at an early stage to avoid imminent task saturation [1]. However, they must not only be able to detect mental workload but also to predict it. This dilemma was also reported by Brand et al. [5]. They developed a preventatively operating assistance system that was able to determine the future task context of the pilot based on the current mission plan. The context was then used to compute the future workload caused by the predicted conflict of mental resources.

However, their approach leaves out two characteristics of imminent workload phases. First, workload management is highly dependent on coping mechanisms [6]. This relates to the individual personality, experience, and disposition of the pilot in how to cope with task saturation. However, this aspect is not easily incorporated into a model-based approach. Second, pilots are trained to prevent high workload situations. Problems arise when the mental workload is increased by an unexpected event [7, 8]. Therefore, the second aspect is related to the human emotion of surprise. In such cases, the pilot or a planner-based assistance agent cannot foresee the upcoming task context.

Consequently, an assistance system that operates at an early stage should address coping and surprises.

1.3 Heart Rate Response as an Indicator for Arousal

Arousal is defined as an autonomic physiological response to a stimulus. It is dependent on the individual and, as a state of sensory alertness, it can be triggered by events that lead to surprise [9, 10]. A higher magnitude of arousal indicates that the operator is currently more vigilant due to an imminent, mentally demanding task. We hypothesize that arousal in these cases may serve as a cognitive state that is valuable for an adaptive assistance system.

Heart rate (HR) and heart rate variability (HRV) are reported physiological variables derived from electrocardiograms (ECG), which are strongly influenced by arousal [11, 12]. ECG sensors assess the electrical activity of the heart, which is influenced by the autonomic nervous system that controls arousal levels [13]. Compared to other arousal sensors such as electroencephalograms (EEG), they are more suitable for real-time applications [14]. Studies have demonstrated that ECG-responses can occur within milliseconds in response to external stimuli. Consequently, they are used for studies addressing startle [15] and pilot performance [16]. Their high responsiveness makes ECG sensors particularly interesting for real-time applications. Furthermore, psychophysiological sensors such as ECG sensors can also be found in the field of adaptive assistance systems [17].

Fig. 1. Pilot candidate in the MUM-T research flight simulator. The central touchscreen shows the tactical map and is the primary interface for the delegation of UAVs. Delegated UAV-tasks are scheduled by an on-board mission planner.

1.4 Detection of HR-Responsiveness Triggered by Critical Events

This study investigates whether stimuli by critical events can induce arousal. Furthermore, it aims to determine whether HR is sensitive towards that arousal.

We conducted an experiment in the field of MUM-T including different events using a fast-jet simulator. Subsequently, we collected (ECG-)data, calculated HR and HRV, and evaluated the responsiveness when these events were perceived. In contrast to literature on mental workload and cognitive load, we anticipated that each event would lead to an increase in HR and simultaneous decrease in HRV [18, 19].

In the following we discuss if these responses can be used as indicators for arousal and an early operating adaptive assistance agent.

2 Experiment

2.1 Experimental Setup

One participant in the research simulator is depicted in Fig. 1. The simulator provides hardware and software instruments to perform aviation, mission planning, and UAV delegation tasks in a MUM-T scenario.

Interactions with the UAVs are conducted by task-based guidance [20]: the pilot selects a target (hostile building or hostile surface-to-air missile (SAM) site), a suitable asset and the desired task to delegate (e.g., an engage or investigate task). The UAV then executes the task automatically. The tactical map and the mission planner interface display the current progress of the delegated task.

Interaction with the cockpit is conducted using touchscreens. For the primary flight control, the pilot uses HOTAS (Hands on Throttle and Stick) controls. In case of a critical event (e.g., low fuel or an active enemy track), the cockpit alerts the pilot. Notifications are carried out via auditory means and displayed visually as a dialog window on the central screen.

We used a Biopac® MP160, BioNomadix® 2Ch wireless transmitter and a wired 3-lead electrode (BN-EL45-LEAD3) for the collection of ECG-data. The sample rate was 200 Hz. The Biopac® was connected to an instance of the iMotions® software. We used the latter to send ECG-data via Transmission Control Protocol (TCP) to a custom application. It labeled the data with the simulation time. This assured time-synchronization between the ECG signal and the events. We also used this software to record ECG-data.

For skin preparation, we shaved the electrode area of the participants using a disposable razor, roughened it with a sponge, and cleaned it using wipes. As electrodes we used Ag/AgCl ECG-pads. To avoid contamination of the signal by muscular activity, we found the best electrode configuration in left clavicle (plus), left inferior thoracic aperture (neutral) and right inferior thoracic aperture (minus).

During the experiment we captured the time-labelled ECG signal using our custom application.

Furthermore, we used a 4-camera eye tracker (SmartEye® with a sampling rate of 60 Hz) to determine the timepoints when an operator visually perceived an event. We also recorded each cockpit screen during the experiment blocks for the debriefing. The screencasts included the eye movements of the eye tracker.

2.2 Participants

We recruited eleven participants whose ages ranged from 20 to 34 years (with an average age of 23.6 years and a standard deviation of 3.9 years). Each participant possessed expertise in either video games (averaging 6.9 h per week, with a standard deviation of 7.8 h), flight simulators (with an average total of 42.9 h spent in flight simulations, and a standard deviation of 83.1 h), or actual flight experience (averaging 3.9 h, with a standard deviation of 3.1 h). Notably, all study participants exhibited a high level of motivation (mean motivation score on a scale of 0 to 10: 9.0, with a standard deviation of 0.9). To enhance motivation further, we evaluated pilot performance using a comprehensive score. This score incorporated factors such as resource utilization (such as payload and fuel), asset preservation, and overall mission duration.

The participants did not report any known cardiovascular diseases.

Prior to the experiment, the participants were trained until they appeared to be familiar with all the functions of the fast-jet simulator required for the experiment. Training took approximately three to four hours. After training participants underwent ECG-baseline measurements. For that, they were asked to read a text for 5 min while we recorded ECG-data.

The experiment blocks were followed by a debriefing whether the events initiated a phase of high mental workload. Overall, the participants responded in the affirmative (Table 1).

Table 1. Event types to trigger arousal in the experiment.

Event type	State causing the event
Fighter under fire	The pilot is threatened by a launched missile
Fighter down	Pilot loses control over the aircraft due bombardment
UAV under fire	An UAV is threatened by a launched missile
UAV down	Pilot loses a UAV due to bombardment
Bomb release	Pilot launches missile from own ship
Pop-up SAM	Previously unknown, hostile SAM-site appears

2.3 Experimental Design

The experiment consisted of six experiment blocks, each with durations between 5 and 10 min. The main mission objective of each block was either the neutralization of a hostile building or SAM-site. In half of the blocks, the tasks of the pilot included the guidance of UAVs.

We incorporated six types of events in our experiment which we assumed would lead to detectable arousal. An overview of the events is given in Table 2. Overview of the HR- and HRV measurands that are used in this study. Most events are considered to introduce an upcoming high workload phase for the pilot. The event *Bomb release* represents the end of the main task. Since we tried to keep the experiment design as naturalistic as possible, *UAV/Fighter under fire* or *UAV/Fighter down* events were not triggered by scripting (such as in the event *Pop-up SAM*). These events were caused by human error and are thus consequences of low pilot performance. As a result, they are dependent on the individual pilot and are not guaranteed to occur on every experiment block. Note that the event *Fighter down* means that the participant has failed the mission. Failed missions were not repeated.

The outline of an experiment block can be seen in Fig. 2. Due to the positioning of the SAM-site, a certain loss of assets is inevitable. The loss of an UAV represents an elevated risk for the pilot to reach the mission goal.

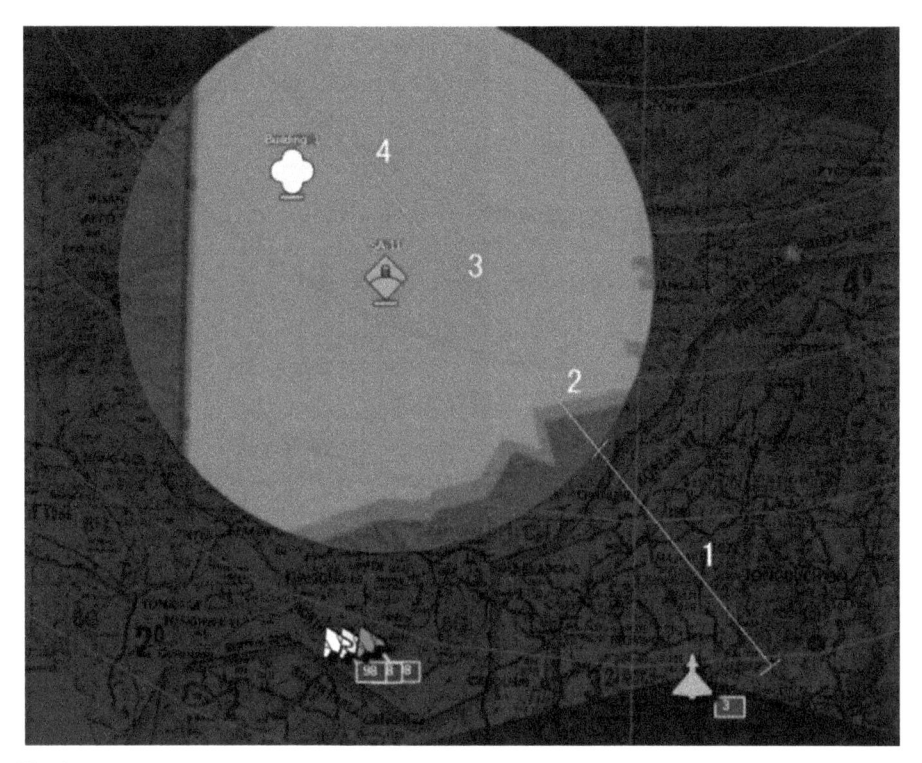

Detection of Arousal of Pilots in Event-Related Heart Rate Responses   331

Fig. 2. An example of the tactical map in one experiment block: The map depicts the fast-jet (grey) and the main target building (Building_1), which is to be engaged. The pilot is supported by three UAVs (white, yellow, and blue). The pilot must surpass the hostile SAM-site (SA-11) in order to reach the building. To complete the main task, pilots must undergo four phases: transition flight to the outer SAM radius (1), probable loss of UAV(s) (2), engagement on SA-11 (3), and engagement on building (4). (Color figure online)

The difficulty of the experiment was defined by time and payload constraints and increased by each experiment block. The difficulty increase was intended to guarantee engagement. To build up a detectable level of arousal we assumed that pilots required a minimum degree of engagement.

Table 2. Overview of the HR- and HRV measurands that are used in this study.

Measurand	Description	HR/HRV
HR	Number of heart beats per minute	HR
SDNN	standard deviation of the time between successive heartbeats	HRV

(*continued*)

Table 2. (*continued*)

Measurand	Description	HR/HRV
SDSD	standard deviation of the differences between successive heartbeats	HRV
RMSSD	RMS (root mean square) of the differences between successive heartbeats	HRV
SD1/SD2	Ratio of short-term and long-term (Poincaré) HRV	HRV

3 Data Analysis

We used screencasts from the experiment blocks that included the participant's eye movements from the eye tracker to deduct the times at which participants first perceived the event. We used these to label the occurrence of events in time.

We preprocessed each ECG signal (baseline signals and signals per block) by applying a bandpass Butterworth filter (lower cutoff: 0.05 Hz, upper cutoff: 50 Hz).

We hypothesized that the response in the ECG signal can be identified by assessing the changes in HR and HRV during the occurrence of the event. We chose to use measurands that are commonly used in studies in the areas of mental workload and arousal.

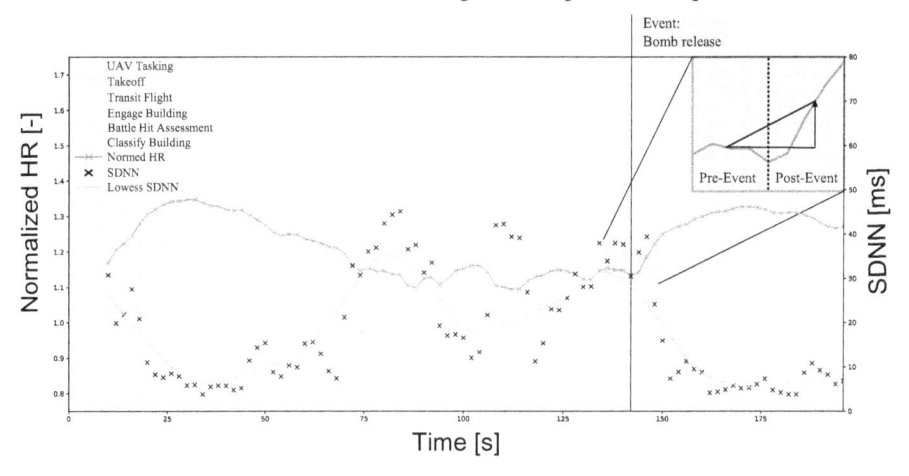

Fig. 3. Progression of HR and SDNN of a participant over the first block. Both were computed using a moving window (window length: 10 s; displacement: 2 s). For the presentation of the SDNN data we used a LOWESS (locally estimated/weighted scatterplot smoothing) regression. During the event Bomb release, there is a measurable HR-increase from the pre- to post-event in the time window. The pilot reported that he was highly focused on the engagement task (pre-event). Then the following flight maneuver (post-event) was very demanding.

An overview is given in Table 2. The measurands can be divided into two types: HR and HRV. The former is based on the frequency of the heartbeat, the latter addresses the arrhythmia of the heart. We also treat *SD1/SD2* as an HRV-measurand since it incorporates the ratio between short-term (*SD1*) and long-term variability (*SD2*).

The behavior of HR and HRV of a single pilot behave during one block can be seen in Fig. 3. Here the response to the event resulted in an increase in the HR signal.

To isolate only the responses to arousal, we extracted a short segment of the signal before (pre-event) and after the event (post-event). We chose a segment length of 7 s. This resulted in a still acceptable number of heartbeats for the calculation of standard-deviation-based measurands such as the *SDNN*. To compute HR and HRV we used the Python library *heartpy* [21]. For each segment analyzed, we made sure that no erroneously detected R-peaks were included in the computation of HR and HRV. Finally, we calculated the responses by subtracting the pre-event measurands from the post-event measurands.

To normalize the measurands, we used the ECG signal from the baseline measurements.

4 Results

Figure 4 gives an overview of all calculated HR- and HRV-responses according to the events. Note that the subplots incorporate all data points from the experiment blocks.

As described, we expected an increase in HR, and decrease in HRV when participants were exposed to an event. As it can be seen in Fig. 4, the majority of the data points indicate that the ΔHR is increased for the Fighter under Fire (1), Bomb release (5) and Pop-up SAM (6) events. For ΔSDNN, ΔSDSD, ΔRMSSD a decrease can only be seen for the Fighter under fire event (see 7, 13, and 19). There is also a negative ΔSD1/SD2 for UAV down and Fighter down (see 25, 26, and 28). The results for the Fighter down event directly oppose the behavior postulated by the hypothesis. The datapoints for the other plots are centered around the zero-response line, indicating we were unable to detect any responses from the participants.

In terms of the event type, *Fighter under fire*, *Bomb release* and *Pop-up SAM* indicate higher responses. Furthermore, all events except *Fighter down* show a high degree of dispersion, suggesting that HR-responses are highly dependent on the individual participant.

In general, the number of samples in Fig. 4 are sufficient for a statistical significance test, except for the event *Fighter down*. Due to the p-values, the null hypothesis that the measurand was not significant in terms of capturing arousal could not be rejected for 2, 12, 18, 23 and 26 confirming that ΔHR and $\Delta SD1/SD2$ show better responsiveness than the other measurands.

5 Discussion

As mentioned, the way in which arousal manifests itself is highly dependent on the individual. This was confirmed by the results, as the responses were highly dispersed and not all participants showed the same tendency in response. Additionally, not all events triggered a detectable magnitude of arousal.

Event-related Heart rate-Responses

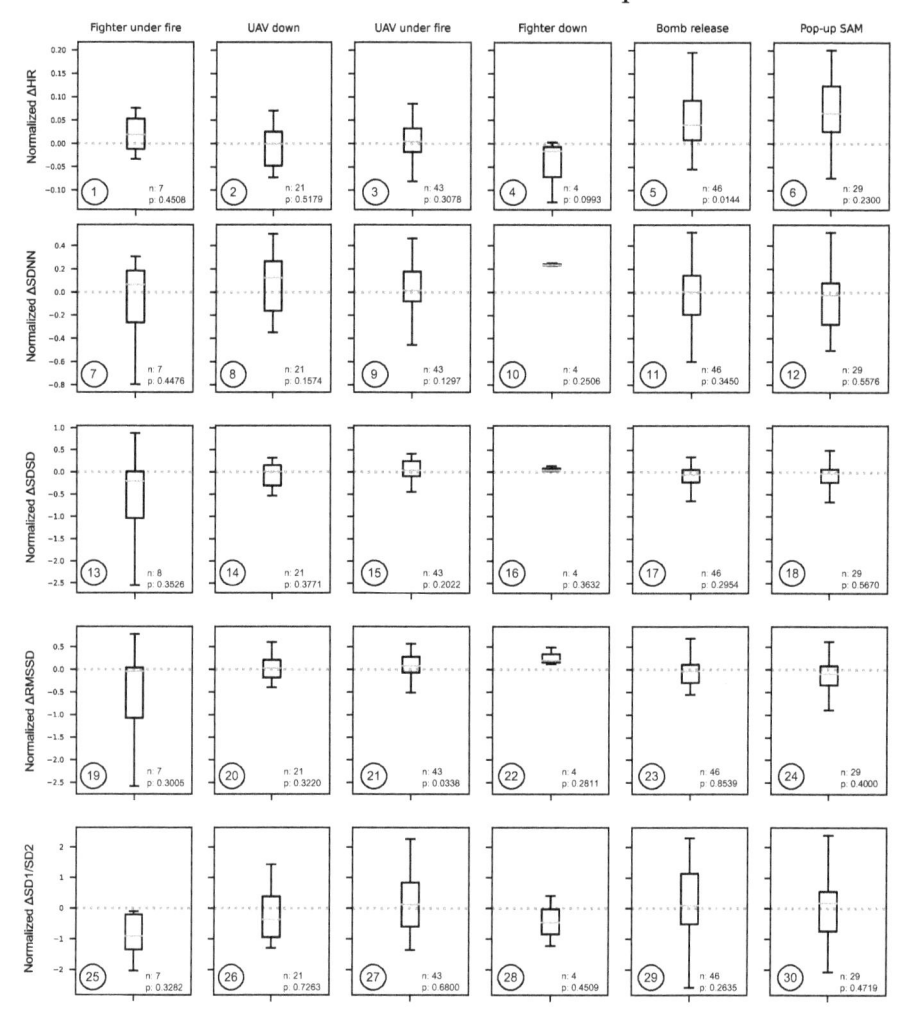

Fig. 4. Overview of the pre-event to post-event differences of HR and HRV as response to arousal. Differences are presented on the vertical, events on the horizontal axis. Datapoints are displayed as box plots and include all participants and experiment blocks. All datapoints are normalized. The textbox in the plot shows the sample number and the p-value of each individual plot.

The measurands $\Delta SDNN$, $\Delta SDSD$ and $\Delta RMSSD$ show no significant response to arousal. However, we see ΔHR and $\Delta SD1/SD2$ as valuable indicators of arousal if the assistance function is based on the threat of the own ship. They showed very low response during UAV-related events. We argue that the higher response in the short segment is mainly caused by the high sensitivity towards arousal of HR and the short-term variability $SD1$.

We hypothesize that the experiment is useful to explore the potential of some measurands to detect arousal for assistance system purposes. However, the experiment had low value of controllability. This is due to the naturalistic environment and the freedom the participants had during the experiment blocks. Therefore, not every participant was operating in the same situation and task context when the events occurred. Furthermore, we cannot guarantee that the ECG signal after the event was influenced by task load rather than arousal (e.g. by an unexpected event). As a result, the segment length may already be too long which makes it impossible to derive HRV. Additionally, we cannot state that participants were not already saturated with tasks during the pre-event segment. As some events were triggered by low performance (e.g. *Fighter under fire*), participants who performed better were less likely to be exposed to threat-related events. Consequently, a successfully triggered arousal was not always evident. In general, we are not able to confirm the actual presence of arousal during our experiment.

6 Conclusion

This study shows that HR and HRV alone is not a reliable indicator for arousal. Reliability in terms of software agents that make decisions based on sensory data. Event-related heart rate responses are too dependent on the individual operator. However, we think that a number of different HR and HRV measurands can serve as valuable features for the detection of arousal for an early operating assistance system. To do so, someone requires training and test data for a machine learning model to detect arousal at an early stage.

Event-related HR-responses may be able to capture the coping capabilities of a pilot. However, an early-operating assistance system cannot operate solely on the basis of these responses. Therefore, responses are not clear indicators for a demand for pilot assistance. To do so, an assistance system needs to operate based on additional variables such as the task context of the pilot in order to identify what task is connected to the arousal.

Acknowledgments. The author would like to express sincere gratitude to Axel Schulte for his invaluable support in the experimental design of this study. Additionally, the author is immensely thankful to Emilia Fischer for her exceptional master thesis, which significantly contributed to this publication.

References

1. Gaydos, S.J., Curry, I.P.: Manned-unmanned teaming: expanding the envelope of UAS operational employment. Aviat. Space Environ. Med. **85**(12), 1231–1232 (2014). https://doi.org/10.3357/ASEM.4164.2014
2. Tschurtschenthaler, K., Schulte, A.: Clustering to determine interconnected activities in supervisory control tasks of pilots, vol. XX, pp. 1–10 (2023). https://doi.org/10.54941/ahfeXXXX
3. Honecker, F., Brand, Y., Schulte, A.: A task-centered approach for workload-adaptive pilot associate systems. In: The 32nd Conference of the European Association for Aviation Psychology (EAAP) (2016)

4. Brand, Y., Schulte, A.: Model-based prediction of workload for adaptive associate systems. In: 2017 IEEE International Conference on Systems, Man, and Cybernetics, SMC 2017, pp. 1722–1727 (2017). https://doi.org/10.1109/SMC.2017.8122864
5. Brand, Y., Schulte, A.: Workload-adaptive and task-specific support for cockpit crews: design and evaluation of an adaptive associate system. Hum. Intell. Syst. Integr. 3(2), 187–199 (2021). https://doi.org/10.1007/s42454-020-00018-8
6. Hidalgo-Muñoz, A.R., et al.: Cognitive workload and personality style in pilots heart rate study to cite this version: HAL Id: hal-02122186 (2019)
7. Landman, A., Groen, E.L., (René) van Paassen, M.M., Bronkhorst, A.W., Mulder, M.: Dealing with unexpected events on the flight deck: a conceptual model of startle and surprise. Hum. Fact. 59(8), 1161–1172 (2017). https://doi.org/10.1177/0018720817723428
8. Sarter, N.B., et al.: Pilots' decision-making under high workload : recognition-primed or not – an engineering point of view. Proc. Hum. Fact. Ergon. Soc. Ann. Meet. 55, 1–10 (2014)
9. Martin, W.L., Murray, P.S., Bates, P.R., Lee, P.S.Y.: Fear-potentiated startle: a review from an aviation perspective. Int. J. Aviat. Psychol. 25(2), 97–107 (2015). https://doi.org/10.1080/10508414.2015.1128293
10. Diarra, M., Marchitto, M., Bressolle, M.-C., Baccino, T., Drai-Zerbib, V.: A narrative review of the interconnection between pilot acute stress, startle, and surprise effects in the aviation context: contribution of physiological measurements. Front. Neuroergonomics 4 (2023). https://doi.org/10.3389/fnrgo.2023.1059476
11. Mohammadpoor Faskhodi, M., Fernández-Chimeno, M., García-González, M.A.: Arousal detection by using ultra-short-term heart rate variability (HRV) analysis. Front. Med. Eng. 1, 1–12 (2023). https://doi.org/10.3389/fmede.2023.1209252
12. Wascher, C.A.F.: Heart rate as a measure of emotional arousal in evolutionary biology. Philos. Trans. Roy. Soc. B Biol. Sci. 376, 2021 (1831). https://doi.org/10.1098/rstb.2020.0479
13. Olsen, M., et al.: Automatic, electrocardiographic-based detection of autonomic arousals and their association with cortical arousals, leg movements, and respiratory events in sleep. Sleep 41(3), 1 (2018). https://doi.org/10.1093/sleep/zsy006
14. Rinella, S., et al.: Emotion recognition: photoplethysmography and electrocardiography in comparison. Biosensors (Basel) 12(10) (2022). https://doi.org/10.3390/bios12100811
15. Vossel, G., Zimmer, H.: Stimulus rise time, intensity and the elicitation of unconditioned cardiac and electrodermal responses. Int. J. Psychophysiol. 12(1), 41–51 (1992). https://doi.org/10.1016/0167-8760(92)90041-9
16. Jorna, P.: Pilot performance in automated cockpits: event related heart rate responses to datalink applications NLR-TP-97639 U Pilot performance in automated cockpits: event related heart rate responses to datalink applications, May 2020
17. Loewe, N., Nadj, M.: Physio-adaptive systems - a state-of-the-art review and future research directions. In: ECIS 2020 Proceedings - Twenty-Eighth European Conference on Information Systems, Marrakesh, Marokko, 15–17 June 2020, p. 19 (2020)
18. Alaimo, A., Esposito, A., Orlando, C., Simoncini, A.: Aircraft pilots workload analysis: heart rate variability objective measures and NASA-Task Load Index subjective evaluation. Aerospace 7(9), 1–17 (2020). https://doi.org/10.3390/AEROSPACE7090137
19. Prell, R., Opatz, O., Merati, G., Gesche, B., Gunga, H.C., Maggioni, M.A.: Heart rate variability, risk-taking behavior and resilience in firefighters during a simulated extinguish-fire task. Front. Physiol. 11, 1–11 (2020). https://doi.org/10.3389/fphys.2020.00482
20. Strenzke, R., Schulte, A.: The MMP: a mixed-initiative mission planning system for the multi-aircraft domain, May 2014
21. van Gent, P., Farah, H., van Nes, N., van Arem, B.: HeartPy: a novel heart rate algorithm for the analysis of noisy signals. Transp. Res. Part F Traffic Psychol. Behav. 66, 368–378 (2019). https://doi.org/10.1016/j.trf.2019.09.015

Emerging Technologies in Aviation Competency-Based Training and Assessment Framework: The Simulated Air Traffic Control Environment (SATCE) Influence on Communication Competency

Dimitrios Ziakkas[1](✉), Neil Waterman[2], and Konstantinos Pechlivanis[3]

[1] School of Aviation and Transportation Technology, Purdue University, West Lafayette, IN 47907, USA
dziakkas@purdue.edu
[2] 500A Huntmar Park Drive, Herndon, VA 20170, USA
[3] HF Horizons, Blvd. Dacia 101, Sector 2, 010730 Bucharest, Romania

Abstract. The Simulated Air Traffic Control Environment (SATCE) is an emerging technology training environment designed to replicate Air Traffic Control (ATC) scenarios, intending to enhance communication competency. The adoption of SATCE in aviation training offers a training environment that is more realistic and immersive. This is achieved by the use of artificial intelligence (AI) in communication, which accommodates the training needs by simulating regulated traffic volume and events. SATCE also incorporates characteristics of Competency-Based Training & Assessment (CBTA), namely in the areas of phraseology and procedures. The presented research was conducted by Purdue University School of Aviation and Transportation Technology (SATT) and Advanced Simulation Technology inc.'s (ASTi) - Simulated Environment for Realistic ATC (SERA) technology in the A320 MPS Flight Simulation Training Device (FSTD). The ongoing research focuses on the implementation of the SATCE to facilitate the improvement of knowledge and skill development for aviation subject matter experts (SMEs). ASTi-SERA technology provides a realistic and immersive environment for SMEs to strengthen their understanding and practical abilities - a cognitive approach focusing on communication competency. The studies undertaken by the Purdue team seek to investigate the behavior and performance of various training scenarios within the context of SATCE. The presented case study involves the design, testing, and certification of the implementation of different flight devices in the existing airspace categorization environment.

The Purdue-SATT strategy for SATCE places emphasis on enhancing the efficacy and efficiency of aviation training programs on a worldwide scale, specifically in the context of the Communication Competency-Based Training and Assessment (CBTA).

Keywords: Competency-Based Training and Assessment (CBTA) · Aviation Intelligence (AI) Human Systems · Certification · Aviation training · Advanced Air Mobility

1 Introduction

Simulated Air Traffic Control Environments encompass a range of systems and software that replicate real-time air traffic. These environments are equipped with flight simulation, ATC (Air Traffic Control) simulation, and various interactive modules to provide a comprehensive and immersive experience. SATCE simulations integrate live, virtual, and constructive (LVC) components, enabling a realistic and dynamic training atmosphere. The real-time simulation of weather, aircraft performance, and ATC communications ensures that the trainees face scenarios closely resembling actual situations (ICAO, 2019). The primary benefit is the risk-free, cost-effective training environment, allowing for repetition and practice of emergency procedures. However, limitations include the high initial setup cost and the challenge of accurately simulating the unpredictability of real-life scenarios.

Advanced Simulation Technology inc's Simulated Environment for Realistic ATC (SERA) is a leading solution in the SATCE domain, known for its realistic simulation of ATC environments. It's designed to enhance pilot training by providing a lifelike, interactive training environment. SERA offers features such as dynamic weather simulation, realistic ATC communication, and the ability to simulate numerous flight scenarios. This advanced simulation contributes to a comprehensive training regimen, preparing pilots for various situations. Integrating SERA into training programs has improved pilot reaction times, decision-making skills, and overall readiness. Its implementation bridges the gap between theoretical knowledge and practical skills, which is crucial in high-stakes aviation scenarios (ASTi, 2023).

SERA incorporates geospatial data to render accurate terrain. Weather systems are dynamically simulated, affecting flight conditions realistically. Aircraft within SERA behave according to highly detailed flight dynamics models, ensuring that the pilots' inputs yield responses that closely mirror actual aircraft. Focusing on communication competency, SERA uses sophisticated voice recognition and response systems, allowing pilots to interact with ATC in real time and improve their communication skills (ASTi, 2023). One of SERA's technological strengths is its ability to integrate seamlessly with existing training infrastructure and its scalability. This architecture allows for scalability, accommodating the expansion of training modules as per institutional needs without compromising performance (Fig. 1).

Integrating AI could significantly enhance the realism of ATC-communication competency in aviation training. AI can simulate a wide range of ATC scenarios, including emergencies, providing trainees with a comprehensive and realistic communication experience. SERA can generate responsive, unpredictable ATC communications, improving pilots' adaptability and decision-making skills by developing customized scenarios. AI can analyze a pilot's performance and adapt scenarios in real-time to address specific training needs. Data analytics can assess a pilot's performance in various scenarios, identifying strengths and areas for improvement. Training programs can then be tailored to address these specific needs. Predictive models can help design training modules that proactively develop skills in areas where a pilot may face challenges. Early identification of potential performance issues allows for timely intervention, reducing risks during actual flight operations (Ziakkas et al., 2023a).

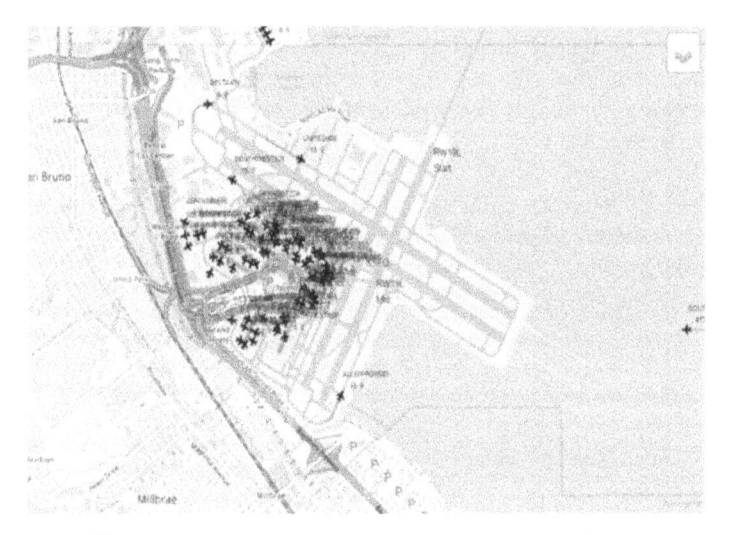

Fig. 1. Purdue SATCE map presentation. (Ziakkas, 2024).

2 Methodology

The Purdue team research methodology is intricately designed to explore the influence of the Simulated Air Traffic Control Environment (SATCE) on communication competency within the aviation Competency-Based Training and Assessment framework (IATA, 2024). This exploration is methodically structured through the lens of the International Civil Aviation Organization (ICAO) Analyze, Design, Develop, Implement, and Evaluate (ADDIE) model, complemented by the systematic approach of the Research Onion method, ensuring a robust and comprehensive research process (ICAO, 2019).

The Purdue SATCE research methodology consists of the following steps (Saunders, 2019):

1. Analysis (Research Onion: Research Philosophy and Approach)
– Research Philosophy and Approach:
- This study adopts a positivist philosophy to ensure an objective analysis of the impact of SATCE on communication competency.
- A mixed-methods approach is employed, combining quantitative data from competency assessments and qualitative insights from structured interviews and observations / SATCE data with aviation training experts and simulator sessions (Saunders, 2019).
– Need Analysis:
- A thorough analysis of current training frameworks and the integration of SATCE is conducted to identify the gaps and potential for enhancement in communication competency.
- Literature Review: A comprehensive literature review on CBTA, SATCE, and communication competency in aviation is performed to ground the research in a solid theoretical framework.
2. Design (Research Onion: Research Strategies and Choices)

- Research Strategies and Choices:
  - Case Study Strategy: The research is designed as a case study, examining the implementation of SATCE in a leading flight training center (Purdue SATT MPS A320-ASTi - SERA).
  - Cross-sectional Study: Data is collected at a specific point in time {simulating Line Oriented Flight Training (LOFT) scenarios} to analyze the immediate effects of SATCE on communication competency (Table 1).
- Framework Design:
  - The research framework is designed to assess the impact of SATCE on the nine core pilot competencies (Fig. 3), with a specific focus on communication competency (Table 1).
  - A comparative analysis is set up between traditional training methods and SATCE-integrated training to evaluate the enhancements in communication competency.

3. Development (Research Onion: Time Horizons)
- Time Horizons:
  - The development phase is conducted over six months, allowing for an in-depth collection and analysis of data.
  - Training Program Development: Customized SATCE training modules are developed, focusing on enhancing communication competency (Table 1).
- Instrument Development:
  - Development of Assessment Tools: Competency assessment tools are developed, including rubrics and simulation performance metrics (Table 1).
  - Development of Interview Guides: Structured interview guides are formulated for gathering qualitative data from instructors and trainees.

4. Implementation (Research Onion: Data Collection Methods)
- Data Collection Methods:
  - Quantitative Data: Pre and post-training assessments are conducted to measure the enhancement in communication competency quantitatively.
  - Qualitative Data: Structured interviews are conducted with trainees and instructors to gather insights into the qualitative aspects of SATCE training. Purdue - SERA debriefing options were used as Observation Behaviors markers (Table 1).
- Training Implementation:
  - The SATCE-based training modules will be implemented in the Purdue SATT flight training center, with a batch of trainees undergoing the newly developed training program.

5. Evaluation (Research Onion: Data Analysis and Interpretation)
- Data Analysis and Interpretation:
  - Statistical Analysis: Quantitative data is analyzed using statistical methods to determine the significance of improvements in communication competency. Machine learning and deep learning applications will be implemented (EASA, 2023a).
  - Thematic Analysis: Qualitative data from interviews is analyzed to identify common themes and perceptions regarding the effectiveness of SATCE in enhancing communication competency (Saunders, 2019).
- Results and Feedback:
  - The results are evaluated against the set competency standards and the objectives of the study.

- Feedback from trainees and instructors is collected and analyzed to provide a comprehensive understanding of the effectiveness of the SATCE-integrated training program.

The described research methodology outlines a structured approach to investigating the influence of SATCE on communication competency in aviation training, employing a rigorous mix of quantitative and qualitative research methods. It ensures the research is grounded in a solid theoretical framework while providing practical, data-driven insights. Figure 2 presents the Purdue research methodology.

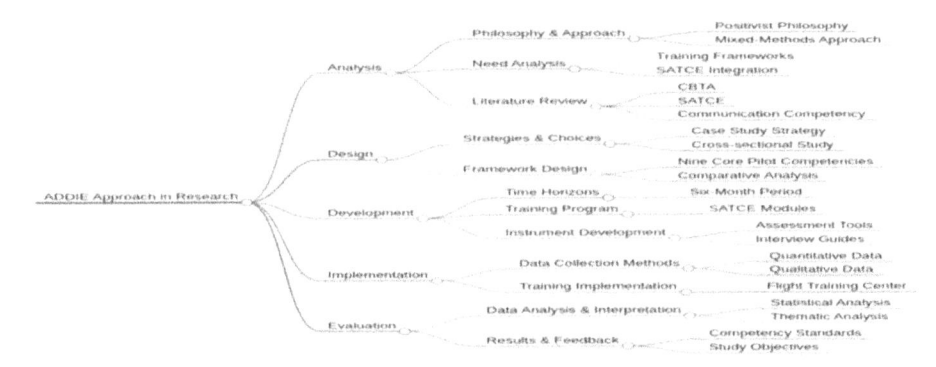

Fig. 2. Purdue SATCE research methodology. (Ziakkas, 2024).

3 Analysis

The Purdue research team thoroughly analyzed current training frameworks and the integration of SATCE to identify the gaps and potential for enhancement in aviation communication competency. A comprehensive literature review on CBTA, SATCE, and communication competency in aviation is performed to ground the research in a solid theoretical framework. CBTA is a holistic approach that emphasizes attaining and demonstrating specific competencies required for a particular role. Unlike traditional training, which is often time-based and prescriptive, CBTA is performance-oriented, ensuring that trainees achieve a certain level of proficiency in key areas - pilot competencies (Fig. 2). In aviation, this approach aligns with the goals of ICAO and other regulatory bodies, aiming to enhance safety and operational efficiency (ICAO, 2019).

Communication is a critical competency in aviation, pivotal to the safety and efficiency of flight operations. It involves not just the clarity and accuracy of information exchange but also the ability to understand and be understood under various, often stressful, conditions. Effective communication is crucial for coordination among crew members, as well as between the cockpit and air traffic control. Moreover, the results of the ongoing research aim to provide feedback for the certification and training process of the Advanced Air Mobility ecosystem, including electric vertical take-off and landing aircrafts, eVTOLs (EASA, 2023b).

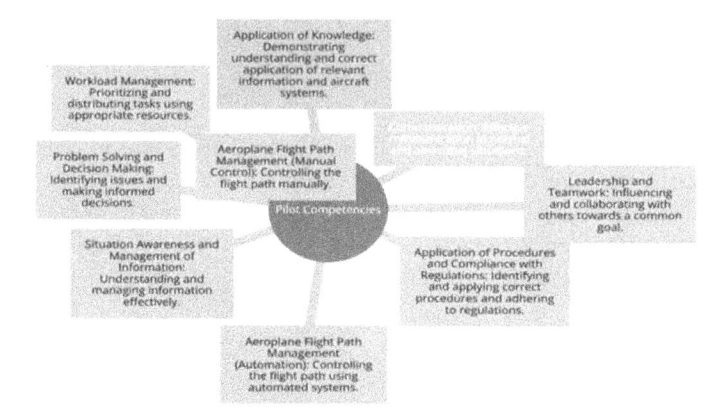

Fig. 3. Pilots' competencies (ICAO, 2024).

- Communication Competency in CBTA

CBTA focuses on specific competencies an individual must possess to perform job functions effectively. It's a personalized approach that allows training to be more flexible and relevant to the actual demands of the workplace. Communication competency in aviation is defined as the ability to convey, receive, and interpret messages accurately, clearly, concisely, and timely, ensuring operational effectiveness and safety. It's crucial in aviation as it directly impacts the coordination, situational awareness, and decision-making processes within a multi-cultural, high-stakes environment (IATA, 2024).

3.1 Key Components of Communication Competency in CBTA:

1. Technical Skills (Hard Skills):
   - Understanding of aviation phraseology and terminology.
   - Proficiency in using communication equipment and technologies.
2. Behavioral Skills (Soft Skills):
   - Assertiveness and clarity in verbal communication.
   - Active listening skills.
   - Cultural awareness and the ability to communicate effectively across diverse cultures.
   - Non-verbal communication skills.
   - Ability to manage stress and maintain clear communication under pressure.

3.2 Integrating OB Principles in CBTA for Enhancing Communication

Observable Behavior (OB) studies how individuals, groups, and systems influence behavior in companies. By incorporating Observable Behaviors (OB) principles into the CBTA framework, aviation training programs can comprehensively address the multifaceted nature of communication competency (Table 1).

This holistic approach not only enhances the technical proficiency of aviation professionals but also ensures they are equipped with the necessary soft skills to navigate the aviation industry's complex interpersonal and organizational dynamics.

Integrating OB principles into CBTA involves:

Table 1. Communication competency Observable Behaviors (OB), (IATA, 2024).

Communication	OB 2.1	Determines that the recipient is ready and able to receive information
	OB 2.2	Selects appropriately what, when, how and with whom to communicate
	OB 2.3	Conveys messages clearly, accurately and concisely
	OB 2.4	Confirms that the recipient demonstrates understanding of important information
	OB 2.5	Listens actively and demonstrates understanding when receiving information
	OB 2.6	Asks relevant and effective questions
	OB 2.7	Uses appropriate escalation in communication to resolve identified deviations
	OB 2.8	Uses and interprets non-verbal communication in a manner appropriate to the organizational and social culture
	OB 2.9	Adheres to standard radiotelephone phraseology and procedures
	OB 2.10	Accurately reads, interprets, constructs, and responds to datalink messages in English

1. Team Dynamics and Communication:
   - Understanding team roles and dynamics can enhance collaborative communication.
   - Training programs can focus on scenarios that require teamwork and coordination, emphasizing the importance of clear, assertive communication.
2. Leadership and Communication:
   - Effective leadership requires excellent communication skills. Training can be oriented towards developing leadership competencies, focusing on motivational communication, conflict resolution, and the ability to give and receive constructive feedback.
3. Stress Management and Emotional Intelligence:
   - High-pressure situations are common in aviation. Training on emotional intelligence and stress management can improve communication under stress, preventing miscommunication and errors.
   - Emotional intelligence skills help in recognizing one's own emotions and those of others, improving empathy, and enhancing interpersonal communication.
4. Cultural Competence:
   - Understanding and respecting cultural differences are crucial in a global industry like aviation.
   - Training can include modules on cultural awareness and sensitivity, ensuring that communication remains effective and respectful across different cultures.
5. Feedback and Continuous Improvement:
   - Regular feedback is a core principle of OB and is essential for continuous improvement in communication skills.
   - CBTA programs should incorporate continuous feedback mechanisms, allowing trainees to reflect on their communication skills, identify areas for improvement, and track their progress over time.

The Purdue team analysis focused on the following training needs analysis elements:

- **SATCE Scenario-Based Learning:** The Purdue research team creates through the Purdue-SERA environment multiple evidence-based scenarios utilizing the scenarios/flights building capability (Fig. 3). These scenarios under a structured training syllabus (CBTA) encourage trainees to enact different roles within fostering an understanding of various perspectives and communication requirements.

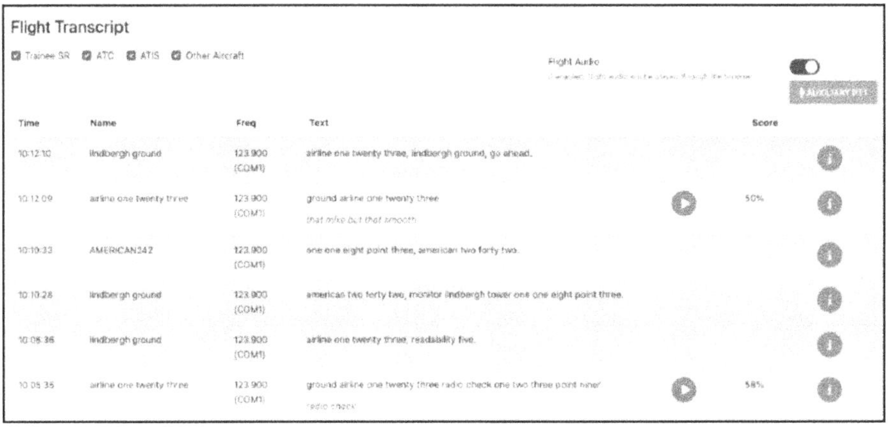

Fig. 4. Flight Transcript – scenarios (ASTi-SERA, 2023).

- **Debriefing Sessions:** Post-simulation debriefings where trainees receive feedback on their communication effectiveness and areas for improvement. The Purdue team assesses the communication competency during simulated scenarios, focusing on clarity, correctness, and appropriateness of the communication in various situations. Communication is monitored and recorded, retrieved, and stored in a cloud environment.
- **English Language Proficiency Test:** Regularly conducted to ensure compliance with ICAO language proficiency requirements.
- **Skill-Based Assessments:** Tailored to evaluate specific communication skills, such as radio communication, crew resource management, and emergency response communication.
- **Case Study on Emergency Communication:** The study highlights how CBTA-trained professionals were better equipped to handle the situation, showcasing the efficacy of competency-based training.
- **Linguistic Diversity:** The global nature of aviation requires professionals to communicate effectively with colleagues from various linguistic backgrounds.
- **Technological Adaptation:** Keeping up with rapidly advancing communication technologies and integrating them into training programs can be challenging.
- **Customized Language Programs:** Tailoring language training to address the specific needs of non-native speakers, ensuring clear and effective communication across diverse linguistic backgrounds.

- **Continuous Curriculum Update:** Regularly updating training programs to include the latest communication technologies and best practices, ensuring that the training remains relevant and effective.

By focusing on these areas, the CBTA approach ensures that aviation professionals are not only skilled in theoretical knowledge but are also proficient in practical, real-world communication scenarios, significantly enhancing the safety and efficiency of aviation operations (Ziakkas et al., 2023b).

4 Findings

The research aimed to investigate the impact of Simulated Air Traffic Control Environment (SATCE) systems, on the communication competency of aviation trainees. The findings are categorized into distinct aspects of communication competency (Table 1) and the role of SERA in enhancing the following identified areas:

1. Enhancement of Communication Clarity
   - **Improved Phraseology:** Trainees exhibited a significant improvement in using standard aviation phraseology. The immersive experience provided by SERA, with its high-fidelity, real-world communication scenarios, reinforced the correct usage of technical language, which is crucial for clear, concise, and unambiguous communication in high-stakes aviation environments.
   - **Reduction in Communication Errors:** A notable decrease in communication errors was observed among participants using Purdue-SERA. The real-time interaction with the simulated ATC environment enabled trainees to receive immediate feedback, allowing for quicker rectification of mistakes and a deeper understanding of the consequences of communication errors.
2. Situational Awareness and Decision Making
   - **Enhanced Situational Awareness:** Purdue - SERA's dynamic and adaptive scenarios facilitated a substantial improvement in trainees' situational awareness. Participants were better able to interpret and anticipate operational situations, leading to more informed and timely decision-making.
   - **Stress Management:** The simulated high-pressure scenarios in Purdue SERA were instrumental in training participants to maintain effective communication under stress, a skill that is vital for ensuring safety and efficiency in real-life air traffic scenarios.
3. Feedback and Continuous Learning
   - **Constructive Feedback:** Purdue - SERA's comprehensive debriefing modules provided detailed feedback to trainees, highlighting areas of strength and those requiring improvement. This feature of SERA was particularly beneficial in fostering a continuous learning environment, encouraging trainees to reflect on their performance and pursue mastery in communication.
   - **Skill Progression Tracking:** The study noted Purdue - SERA's capability to track the progression of a trainee's communication skills over time. This longitudinal approach to skill assessment was pivotal in understanding the learning curve and ensuring that the trainees reached and maintained the competency levels required for aviation professionals.

4. Realism and Engagement
- **High-fidelity Environment:** Participants reported a high level of engagement with the training, attributing this to the realistic, immersive nature of Purdue - SERA's simulations. The authenticity of the scenarios contributed to a deeper understanding of the operational environment and a more genuine communication experience.
- **Adaptability to Individual Learning Needs:** The ability of Purdue-SERA to adapt to the individual learning pace and style of each trainee was highlighted as a key factor in the success of the training program. Personalized learning paths ensured that each participant could maximize their learning outcomes, catering to their unique needs and areas for improvement.

5 Conclusions

The integration of the Simulated Air Traffic Control Environment (SATCE), particularly through Purdue University's collaboration with Advanced Simulation Technology inc.'s Simulated Environment for Realistic ATC (SERA), has demonstrated significant strides in enhancing communication competency within aviation training. This research proposes a pivotal shift from traditional training methodologies to a more immersive, AI-driven, and competency-based framework. The adoption of SATCE, grounded in the Competency-Based Training & Assessment (CBTA) approach, not only aligns with the increasing complexity and demands of modern aviation but also addresses the nuanced facets of communication skills essential for aviation professionals.

The findings from the Purdue University study underscore the multifaceted impact of SATCE on aviation training. The notable enhancements in communication clarity, situational awareness, decision-making, and the ability to maintain composure under stress are not just incremental improvements but represent a paradigm shift in aviation training. The meticulous integration of AI to simulate diverse and unpredictable ATC scenarios, coupled with the structured and personalized feedback mechanisms, ensures that the training is not just comprehensive but also cognizant of individual learning trajectories. As the aviation industry continues to evolve, the role of technologies like SATCE in shaping the future of aviation training becomes increasingly paramount.

The Purdue-SATT and ASTi-SERA collaboration, therefore, sets a precedent, highlighting the synergy between advanced technology and educational methodologies in creating a resilient, competent, and future-ready aviation workforce. Purdue future research plans aim to:

1. Investigate the long-term impact of SATCE training on operational efficiency and safety in real-world aviation scenarios including CBTA airliners training case studies.
2. Explore the potential of integrating emerging technologies (e.g., VR/AR, machine learning) with SATCE to further enhance the training experience.
3. Assess the scalability and adaptability of SATCE systems like SERA in diverse cultural and linguistic aviation landscapes worldwide.

Acknowledgment. The authors thank faculty members of Purdue University, and Human Factors analysts from ASTi and HFHorizons, for their invaluable feedback contributing to this work.

References

Competency assessment and evaluation for pilots, instructors and ... - IATA (2024). https://www.iata.org/contentassets/c0f61fc821dc4f62bb6441d7abedb076/competency-assessment-and-evaluation-for-pilots-instructors-and-evaluators-gm.pdf

EASA: Artificial Intelligence Roadmap 2.0: Human-centric approach to AI in aviation (2023a)

EASA: EASA Concept Paper: guidance for Level 1 & 2 machine learning applications Proposed Issue 02 (2023b)

ICAO: ICAO addresses the shortage of skilled aviation professionals. ICAO (2019). https://www.icao.int/Newsroom/Pages/ICAO-Addresses-Shortage-of-Skilled-Aviation-Professionals.aspx

A. S. T. inc.: ASTI awarded enterprise-level contract to deliver AI training capabilities to the Naval Aviation Training Command (2023)

https://asti-usa.com/news/2023/0915.html

Saunders, M., Lewis, P., Thornhill, A.: Research Methods for Business Students Eighth Edition. In Research Methods for Business Students. Pearson Education Limited (2019)

Shackelford, S.J.: The Internet of Things: What Everyone Needs to Know®. Oxford University Press (2020)

Ziakkas, D., Pechlivanis, K., Keller, J.: The implementation of Artificial Intelligence (AI) in Aviation Collegiate education: a simple to complex approach. In: Proceedings of the 6th International Conference on Intelligent Human Systems Integration (IHSI 2023) Integrating People and Intelligent Systems, February 22–24, 2023, Venice, Italy (2023a). https://doi.org/10.54941/ahfe1002863

Ziakkas, D., Vink, L.-S., Pechlivanis, K., Flores, A.: Implementation Guide for Artificial Intelligence In Aviation: A Human-Centric Guide for Practitioners and Organizations (2023b)

Author Index

A
Abbott, Kathy H. 308
Adachi, Riku 288
Adams, Felix 191
Allili, Mohand Saïd 278

B
Balakrishna, Arun 3
Barbosa, Luís 92
Barroso, João 13, 92
Benesch, Danielle 207
Bengler, Klaus 103

C
Cesarano, Salvatore 78
Chang, Chia-Ming 61
Chen, Kai 225
Chen, Na 156
Chen, Nongtian 225
Chen, Zhenqi 269
Chiesa, Silvia 144
Chilro, Gabriel 13

D
Denti, Paolo 144
Ding, Zhengming 172
Djartov, Boris 241
Duan, Yujia 51
Duffy, Vincent G. 172

G
Giannini, Stefano 144
Gong, Zaiyan 23, 36
Griebel, Hannes S. 257, 298
Gross, Tom 3
Gu, Yaoqin 51
Gui, Xinyue 61
Guo, Qiaofeng 269
Guo, Zizheng 269

H
Hagl, Maria 191
Hammouche, Nadir 278
Han, Yiyang 225
Hewett, Simon 257
Huang, Bofei 61

J
Jiang, Yan 269
Jin, Quanxin 156

K
Kratzig, Gregory P. 207

L
Lapointe, Jean-François 278
Lehto, Mark R. 172
Littlewood, Juliette O. 257

M
Ma, Ting 225
Marchetti, Marco 144
Marois, Alexandre 207
Mengoni, Maura 144
Mosaferchi, Saeedeh 78

N
Naddeo, Alessandro 78
Nakanishi, Miwa 288
Nunes, Ricardo 13

O
Oliveira, Pedro 13

P
Pagot, Edoardo 144
Papenfuß, Anne 241
Paré, Simon 207
Paul, Tanya S. 207
Pechlivanis, Konstantinos 337

Penelas, Gonçalo 92
Pinto, Tiago 92
Pongratz, Verena 103

R
Reis, Arsénio 92
Rocha, Tânia 13

S
Schulte, Axel 326
Sheng, Youyu 51
Shi, Jintian 122
Shi, Lei 269
Smith, Daniel C. 298
Steckhan, Lorenz 103

T
Tezçi, Buse 144
Thomas, Lauren J. 308
Tian, Renran 172

Tramarin, Luca 144
Tschurtschenthaler, Karl 326

W
Waterman, Neil 337
Wies, Matthias 241

X
Xie, Haoran 61

Y
Yang, Hao 156

Z
Zennaro, Giuliana 144
Zhang, Jingyu 51, 269
Zhang, Jun 269
Zhang, Yan 269
Zhang, Zhengming 172
Zhao, Ying 156
Ziakkas, Dimitrios 337